RECOGNISING ACHIEVEMENT

Business Studies

FOR OCR GCSE

Peter Kennerdell, Alan Williams and Mike Schofield

Hodder & Stoughton

A MEMBER OF THE HODDER HEADLINE GROUP

Acknowledgements:
The authors and publishers are grateful to the following for permission to reproduce illustrative material:

amazon.com, page 190; Andrew Lambert, page 180; B&Q page 28; BSI, page 200; British Energy, page 59; CGNU, page 61; Chartwell Illustrators, pages 44, 64, 77, 117, 153, 191, 263; Corbis, page 29, 248; Friends of the Earth, page 24; Greenpeace, page 24; Halfords, page 28; lastminute.com, page 190; Life File, pages 13, 14, 29, 45, 63, 133, 147, 161, 174, 214, 241, 243, 250; Manchester United plc, pages 82, 89; Meadowhall Shopping Centre, page 239, Next plc, page 31; Photodisk, pages 91, 105, 142, 143; Severn Trent Energy, page 56; The Daily Telegraph, page 61; Top Shop, page 28; Virgin, page 3; Virgin Energy, page 57; Ian West, pages 6, 7, 12, 14, 16, 18, 19, 32, 33, 36, 37, 38, 47, 64, 65, 68, 76, 78, 99, 100, 109, 113, 120, 123, 132, 148, 150, 154, 160, 164, 168, 170, 175, 178, 184, 192, 194, 196, 199, 203, 255, 264, 265, 270, 271, 278.

Orders: please contact Bookpoint Ltd, 130 Milton Park, Abingdon, Oxon OX14 4SB. Telephone: (44) 01235 827720, Fax: (44) 01235 400454. Lines are open from 9.00 – 6.00, Monday to Saturday, with a 24 hour message answering service. Email address: orders@bookpoint.co.uk

British Library Cataloguing in Publication Data
A catalogue record for this title is available from The British Library

ISBN 0 340 790520

First published 2001
Impression number 10 9 8 7 6 5 4 3 2 1
Year 2005 2004 2003 2002 2001

Typeset by Dorchester Typesetting Group Ltd.
Printed in Italy for Hodder & Stoughton Educational, a division of Hodder Headline Ltd, 338 Euston Road, London NW1 3BH.

LIST OF CONTENTS

Preface

About this book

This book has been prepared specifically for the new Specifications in GCSE Business Studies for first teaching in September 2001. Whilst it is not intended to be a scheme of work, the book will clearly provide the necessary teacher support to deliver the specification. Students will find the book a valuable resource in preparing for GCSE Business Studies.

The effectiveness with which this resource is used will depend on the skill and professionalism of the teacher. In writing the book we have endeavoured to include materials which cater for the full range of ability from A* to G. Some of the material is specifically aimed at the upper end of the ability range and hence may prove difficult for less able candidates. Where this is the case, we have included visual material in the form of charts, pictures, diagrams, etc to help teachers make the material more accessible to less able candidates. All the materials have been trialled with mixed ability classes in the schools in which we teach and we are confident that the resource will work with all levels of ability.

Whilst the material in the book has been written to support the OCR Full and Short Course Linear GCSE Business Studies Specifications, large amounts of the material in the book will be relevant to Specifications offered by other Awarding Bodies. All GCSE Business Studies Specifications in England, Wales and Northern Ireland are written to the same criteria specified by QCA, ACCAC and CCEA.

The contents have been designed to provide a knowledge base appropriate to GCSE Business Studies. Activities and exercises have been included to help students practise and develop the skills of application analysis and evaluation within similar contents to those they will experience in the GCSE examinations.

It must also be remembered that GCSE question papers writers are extremely skilled and inventive in seeking new ways to test the ability of candidates. For this reason, it is vital that teachers prepare their candidates to apply the information they have available in providing an answer to the question which has been set.

Teacher's Book

A complementary Teacher's Book with additional student activities and advice is available. It contains a series of tests and work sheets linked to the sections of the book to help monitor the progress of their students.

How to use this book

The **Introductory Activity** to each Section is designed to give students an overview of the content of the Units in that Section. The student activity is designed to get students involved in an investigatory or active series of tasks which will help broaden understanding and prepare them for the detailed content of the Units.

Each Unit follows the same basic pattern. The subject content in each Unit is supported by a series of student **Activities**. Where this symbol appears the Activity is capable of providing a range of opportunities for candidates to acquire evidence which can be included in the Key Skills Portfolio. Further guidance on what candidates need to do to meet the Key Skills requirements at various Levels is provided in a section at the end of each Unit.

Adapted **Examination Questions**, which have appeared in previous examination papers, are also provided in most Units. Where the Specification content is new and has not been examined previously, practice questions similar in style to those used in examinations have been included. These questions should help to reinforce and support learning as well as providing an opportunity for candidates to become accustomed to the type and style of questioning which they can expect to experience on certain topics. Our interpretation of what the examiner was looking for, **Advice on How to Answer the Question**, gives guidance on how candidates will need to respond in order to answer the question successfully. The **command word** used in a question is perhaps one of the most important pointers with regard to what candidates have to do in order to answer a question successfully. Candidates will need to be trained to recognise **command words** and respond accordingly.

For candidates to be successful they will also need to have a sound understanding of basic business knowledge and terminology upon which they can build and develop their skills. This basic information can be found in the **Key Terms** section of each Unit. It is essential that candidates are familiar with all the Key Terms and able to both provide a definition and apply this information to unfamiliar situations.

Finally, each Unit contains an **Examination Summary Tips** section giving further guidance on the key features of each Unit which candidates will need to be able to do if they are to improve their chances of success.

Full course options

For the full course, each candidate is required to study **one** of two options. The Specification content of each option should be seen as an extension of the core content of the Specification. The options should not be taught in a 'bolt-on' manner but as part of an integrated whole. This is particularly important as the Option examination papers may seek to test elements of the core content.

Where a topic is particularly relevant to the Business and Change option, this symbol appears. Where a topic is particularly relevant to the Business Communications and Marketing option, this symbol appears. However, the use of one of these symbols does not necessarily mean that the topic can be ignored because a candidate is entered for the other option – the content may be questioned in the core paper if the topic is part of the core specification. Teachers will need to use their judgement in deciding how much detail to include when seeking to integrate the material for the Core and Option.

The short course

The short course has a subject content which equates to approximately half the content of the full course. The content of the book more than covers the GCSE Specification content and teachers will need to exercise care when using the book as the resource to deliver this course. Careful reference will need to be made to the specification content.

The case study

A written examination paper with a pre-seen case study scenario is available as an alternative to course work for both the full and short courses. The short course version will be a reduced version of that used for the full course, making co-teachability of the two courses possible.

The subject material and questions for the full course version of the case study will be drawn from the Core content of the Specification and **not** the Option content of the Specification.

The examination paper for the case study will assess the same skills as those assessed by the coursework. Therefore, **no** marks will be available for pure recall of basic business knowledge. Candidates will be assessed on their ability to demonstrate skills of Application, Analysis and Evaluation.

Acknowledgements

We are grateful to a number of people in helping us to prepare this book, in particular our families, who have been patient with us while the preparation of the material was being carried out. The OCR Business and Commerce Subject Team, especially Jane Wykes, were very supportive and helpful throughout. Finally, without the drive and determination of Llinos Edwards from Hodder & Stoughton this publication would not have been possible.

Key Skills 2000

From **September 2000**, students under the age of 16 can aim for the Key Skills of Communication, Application of Number and Information Technology, as they are now included in the Section 400 list which sets out the qualifications that are approved for delivery in schools.

Each Key Skills Unit can be achieved at Levels 1 to 4. It is expected that **most** students under the age of 16 will be working at **Level 1** or **Level 2**. However, students can work at a higher level if this is deemed appropriate.

In order to achieve the Key Skills Units of Communication, Application of Number and IT the student must produce a portfolio of evidence which meets the specifications, and also pass the relevant external assessment test.

A student can submit evidence for their Key Skills Portfolio that has been produced while undertaking other qualifications such as GCSEs, or as part of an enrichment programme. Key Skills evidence does not have to be filed separately from evidence for other qualifications; if the Key Skills evidence is embedded within another qualification then it should be clearly cross-referenced to the Key Skills evidence requirements so that it is easily located for the purpose of moderation.

The **specifications** for all of the Key Skills Units have been produced by QCA, CCEA and ACCAC and are awarded by Oxford Cambridge and RSA Examinations. Copies of the Specifications are available from QCA or can be purchased from OCR Publications in the Key Skills Scheme Book.

Business Studies lends itself to the development of all Key Skills **Units**. Activities that involve the application of Key Skills have been included in each Unit. These have been **signposted** with the following symbol: . The **suggested** activities can be used in two ways:

- they may provide an opportunity for students to improve their Key Skills through practice
- alternatively, they may be used to generate evidence that can be assessed and, if satisfactory, can be included in the portfolio of evidence submitted for assessment.

A commentary has been added at the end of the Unit, advising the student about the Key Skill. This indicates what is required in terms of evidence and for work at different levels. Some Activities are appropriate to both Level 1 and Level 2. The level achieved will depend upon the complexity of the work produced and the degree of autonomy with which the task was completed.

If the Activities are used to generate evidence it is critical that the work is produced in such a way that it meets the **evidence** requirements of the **Specifications**. For example, for evidence of discussions related to the Key Skill of Communication it is not enough for an assessor to provide a witness statement asserting that the requirements have been met. The portfolio should contain a record, written or visual, of the contribution of the individual and how he or she listened and responded to the contribution of others **and how in doing so they have met the Specifications**.

OCR has produced **Recording Documents** for recording Key Skills evidence. These are available in the **Key Skills Centre Support Pack**; this can be purchased from OCR Publications.

OCR has produced a number of documents that are designed to assist Centres with the implementation of Key Skills 2000. A full publications listing can be obtained from OCR Publications on telephone 0870 870 6622.

The External Environment of Business

SECTION 1

- Introductory Activity
- Unit 1.1 The economic problem facing businesses
- Unit 1.2 The different sectors of business activity
- Unit 1.3 Business objectives and the role of stakeholders
- Unit 1.4 The community, government and business

Learning Objectives: To develop:

- an understanding of the economic problem of scarce resources that faces all businesses
- knowledge and understanding of opportunity cost
- an understanding of how business activity is divided into different sectors
- an understanding of the changing role and importance that stakeholders have in a business
- an understanding of the different objectives a business may develop
- an understanding of the private and public sectors of business activity
- an appreciation of the changing roles and responsibilities that businesses face in the community
- skills of numeracy, selection, analysis and evaluation.

Introductory Activity

Following the sudden sinking of their ship in the Pacific Ocean, Chris and Holly, the only survivors, found themselves on a remote island where little had changed for centuries. The inhabitants on the island made them welcome; they did not have many visitors. Chris and Holly soon recovered from the sinking of their ship and began to explore the island. Chris had been in business making fruit drinks in America; Holly had been employed in selling hand-made craft items. Both Chris and Holly soon saw the opportunity of turning the island into a money-making business. The island had the following resources that would help any business development:

- **good natural resources:** the correct climate and soil for fruit growing (fruits were already growing naturally)
- **labour:** native people in the village were available to pick fruit
- **skills:** there were many fine craft items being made by the village people.

There were some resources that would need to be provided:

- a larger harbour for ships to take products to sell in America
- a factory for making the fruit products
- supervisors and managers for the business
- capital (money) to build the factory; some new roads and the harbour.

Chris and Holly thought this was really good news for the island and the people who lived there. Some of the local people were in favour of the idea, though many were against. What was clear was that there had to be a choice: either the island changed to a 21st-century business development or it remained unchanged.

Your tasks:

1. Imagine that you have to write out a plan for the development of the businesses on the island, to help Chris and Holly. You will have to think of the problems that need to be solved and the benefits that may come to the island and its people. Use the chart on page 2 to help you write your plan. Draw your own chart, using ITC if available.
2. In pairs or small groups, discuss whether or not the development should go ahead. In your discussions think of:
   - the difficulty in providing all the necessary **resources** (the capital needed, the different workers, the land for the factory etc)

Problem to solve	Solution to problem
Capital to build factory, road and harbour	
Labour (workers) needed for the businesses	
Land for fruit growing	
How the local environment might be changed	
How to persuade the local people who are against the idea	

- the costs and benefits to the environment and community living on the island
- the importance of the islanders; they have a real interest in their island and their own future. They will not all agree with each other!
- how a choice has to be made; the island cannot stay unchanged **and** develop the new businesses.

3. Summarise the outcome of your discussions.

Unit 1.1 The economic problem facing businesses

As you discovered in the Introductory Activity, people face a problem of having many needs and wants, with no real chance of **everyone** being able to fulfil all their wishes. There will always be some disagreement about development and so tough choices have to be made. Businesses too face the same problems. They too cannot do everything they want, otherwise everyone in the world would have their own business, making their own fortunes!

The **economic problem** is the **scarcity** of the resources that go into making products. We would all like to buy lots of things when we go shopping; the problem is usually a lack of money. In other words, there is a **scarcity** of money. A business once again has the same problem. It might **want** to buy some new machinery but a lack of money, or capital, prevents this from happening. To understand the economic problem fully we need to understand the **factors of production**.

The four factors of production are:

- land
- labour
- capital
- enterprise.

Land

All businesses must have land to build on, though 'land' in this context also means all the other resources and raw materials in the world such as oil, gas, trees, plants etc. Businesses need a supply of these materials to manufacture products. The world does **not** have an unlimited supply of these resources, which results in scarcity.

Labour

This refers to the workers who are needed by a business to make a product or provide a service. It may be the case that a number of workers are needed who can be found easily by a business. Another business may also require workers, but with a high level of skill. These workers may be less easy to find and so the problem of scarcity arises once again. There simply isn't the correct number of workers to do **every** job required in the world.

Capital

The factors of production, 'capital' means the money that is required to start and maintain a business. We would all like to have more money, and a business is much the same. Once again there is the problem of **scarcity**, with a business never really having the amount of money it would like. Just like all of us!

Enterprise

Enterprise is a rather different factor of production. Enterprise is all about the sort of people who would make a business successful. These people need to have:

- an idea to start the business, possibly something that no one else has thought of
- the ability to take risks. All business activity is a risk to some extent, and a lot of people are simply not prepared to take a risk and run their own business
- the ability to persuade others to join the business, possibly lending the business some money
- the energy to keep the business going, especially when faced with competition.

Such people are called **entrepreneurs**, and are themselves scarce. Not everyone has all the above qualities to operate a successful business.

Richard Branson is a very successful entrepreneur.

ACTIVITY 1

Imagine that you are about to start your own business (make sure you have a good idea!). Study the four factors of production, and for **each** factor explain any difficulties you may have in starting the business. Present the work using writing, diagrams and any illustrations you feel will be suitable. ITC should be used if available.

- What land and resources might you need? Where will they come from?
- What labour will you need? Will you be able to find suitable workers easily? If so, where from?
- What capital will you need? Can you provide it all and, if not, where will it come from?
- Do **you** have the qualities to be an entrepreneur? Be honest and explain any difficulties you think you might have.

Opportunity Cost

Because of the scarcity of the factors of production, we all have to make choices in our lives. As we have a limited supply of money, we have to make decisions as to what items we buy, as we can't buy **everything** we would like. These decisions can be quite small, for instance not having enough money to buy a Kit-Kat **and** a Mars Bar. On a larger scale, a family may have to choose between having a new kitchen or a new car. They cannot afford both.

Businesses will face similar choices, as they too don't have all the capital to buy everything they want. For example a business may have to choose between buying some new machinery and building a new office. Even the Government faces the same problem. It may **want** to build lots of new hospitals, schools and roads but, as it too has a limited supply of capital, it has to make a choice.

When a choice has to be made in this way it is called **opportunity cost** (see Unit 3.1, page 64). When a choice is made, the opportunity cost is the next choice you would have made. In the examples given, if the family chose the car, the opportunity cost is the kitchen, as this would be the next choice they would have made. If the business chose the machinery, the opportunity cost is the new office. Where there is more than one alternative choice, as in the example of the Government, the opportunity cost is the next choice it would have made. If the Government chose the building of hospitals first, schools as second choice and roads as third choice, the opportunity cost would be the schools, as this is the next alternative to the hospitals.

EXAM Practice Questions

Hannah Stuart has recently opened a new business, designing and making fashion clothing. She works alone at home, with her orders coming from friends who like to wear something a little different. She now wants to expand and open her own shop, but cannot afford to buy the shop and a new sewing machine she would like.

1. Use the example above to explain the meaning of 'opportunity cost'. (3 marks)
2. Advise Hannah on the skills that she might need to develop in her business if she is to be a successful entrepreneur. (4 marks)
3. Other than the cost of the shop and the new sewing machine, suggest three other items that Hannah might need to buy if she had the capital available. (3 marks)

ADVICE ON HOW TO ANSWER THE QUESTIONS

1. In this question you **must** use the example you have been given to explain 'opportunity cost'. Using any other example will simply lose marks.
2. You have been asked to advise Hannah. This means that you need to think of the skills Hannah needs to develop in **her** business, not any other. You need to look at the skills a successful entrepreneur needs, and then **apply** them to Hannah in her business.
3. This question asks you to suggest items that Hannah will need to buy. There is no need to explain why they are needed, because you have not been instructed to do this. Think of what the business is trying to do and suggest three items that Hannah might need to find the capital to buy.

KEY TERMS

The **economic problem** *is the problem of limited resources in the world, which cannot meet the unlimited needs of the population. This leads to scarcity.*

Factors of production *are the four resources that are needed to produce goods or services in a business. They are land, labour, capital and enterprise.*

Entrepreneur *A person who has the necessary skills to start and maintain a business successfully.*

Opportunity cost *The cost of making a choice. The opportunity cost is the next alternative that would have been chosen.*

EXAMINATION SUMMARY TIPS

- Make sure you learn the four factors of production and a definition of 'opportunity cost'.
- Understand how the factors of production work together. You cannot have a successful business simply with a lot of capital. The other factors are very important.
- Remember that you are often required to **apply** ideas to a business situation. Be prepared to explain how the factors of production and opportunity cost are important to different businesses.

Key Skills

The Introductory Activity provides opportunity for Communication Level 1 (C1.1 and C1.3) and Information Technology Level 1 (IT1.2).

For C1.1 you must show that you have the information needed for the discussion, speak clearly and take notice of what others in your group say.

For C1.3 you must present the information in chart/diagram form clearly, and in a way which suits the purpose of the exercise.

Unit 1.2 The different sectors of business activity

Business activity can be divided into three sectors or parts:

1. primary sector
2. secondary sector
3. tertiary sector.

Primary sector

The word 'primary' means 'first' (like a primary school). In business activity the primary sector is the first stage or first part of production. Businesses in the primary sector include:

- fishing
- mining and quarrying
- farming
- mineral extraction, such as oil drilling
- forestry.

All these businesses are at the first stage of production, producing **raw materials** for other businesses to use.

Some businesses in the primary sector.

Secondary sector

Secondary, as the name suggests, is the second stage of production. Businesses in the secondary sector will use the raw materials from the primary sector and **manufacture** products from them. The number of different secondary businesses is huge, as it includes **anything** that is manufactured. Some of the larger secondary businesses include:

- car manufacturers
- furniture manufacturers
- electrical appliance manufacturers.

And lots, lots more!

Example of a business in the secondary sector.

Tertiary sector

The word 'tertiary' means 'third', though thinking of the tertiary sector as the third stage of production can be a little misleading. The tertiary sector is really concerned with providing a **service** for its customers and includes businesses such as:

- retailing
- banking
- insurance
- travel

- entertainment
- transport
- hotels
- customer service.

Although not really thought of as businesses, the tertiary sector also includes education, health, police, tax offices, local and national Government and the armed forces.

In all of these examples, the people who work for these organisations are there to provide a **service** for others. At the end of their day's work they will not be able to see something they have made, as will workers who work in the secondary sector.

Examples of businesses in the tertiary sector.

How the three sectors of business activity depend on each other

No matter what sector a business is in, it will depend on businesses in the **other** sectors.

For example, diamonds are mined (primary sector), which then need a business to use them in making a diamond ring (secondary sector). A jeweller's shop is then needed to sell the ring (tertiary sector). This is called **interdependence**. The process by which a product starts as raw materials, goes through secondary production, and is then sold in the tertiary sector is often

All sectors of business activity depend on each other.

referred to as **the chain of production** as each part is connected to the other like the links in a chain.

Specialisation

When a business is in one particular sector, it will often specialise in that area, and leave other sectors of business activity to their work. For example a toy maker will concentrate on **making** toys, leaving the **selling** of the toys to another specialist firm. By concentrating on, or specialising in, one activity the business can save money by looking at ways of reducing costs in that one area, and so producing cheaper goods.

Added value

As raw materials (primary sector) are then made into finished goods (secondary sector) the secondary business is adding value to the original raw material. When the product is sold, possibly with a guarantee, the tertiary sector is adding more value to the product. The idea of added value is the basis for value added tax (VAT).

ACTIVITY 1

1. State whether the following businesses primary, secondary or tertiary.
   Football club, camera shop, telephone call centre, farm, car factory, computer repair centre, double glazing manufacturer, garden centre, cinema, bank, diamond mine, washing machine manufacturer.
2. Research your local area to find different businesses in each of the three sectors.
   Fill in a chart like the one shown below. You should aim to find at least 20 different businesses.

Local Business Survey

Name of business	What the business does	Primary/Secondary/ Tertiary

3. Draw a bar graph to show the results of your survey.
4. Draw a series of diagrams, to show how the three sectors of business activity depend on each other (interdependence) in the following products:
   (a) a wooden chair
   (b) a pair of jeans.

Changes in the three sectors of business activity

Over the years, the importance of the three sectors that make up business activity in Britain has changed. What must be understood is **what** has changed and **why** the changes have taken place.

Changes in the primary sector

The primary sector in Britain has fallen in importance over recent years, employing far fewer people. This is because of a number of factors.

- Raw materials have been used up, resulting, for example, in the closure of many coal mines and the loss of many thousands of jobs.
- The use of machinery to replace jobs. Workers are expensive, and a business will reduce the number of workers it uses wherever it can. This has resulted, for example, in the loss of many farming jobs over the years.
- Foreign competition has meant that businesses in Britain cannot produce goods as cheaply as other countries. This has further affected industries such as coal, where the mines that remain in Britain are under threat because of cheaper fuels coming from overseas.

Changes in the secondary sector

As with the primary sector, the secondary sector has declined in importance in recent years, with

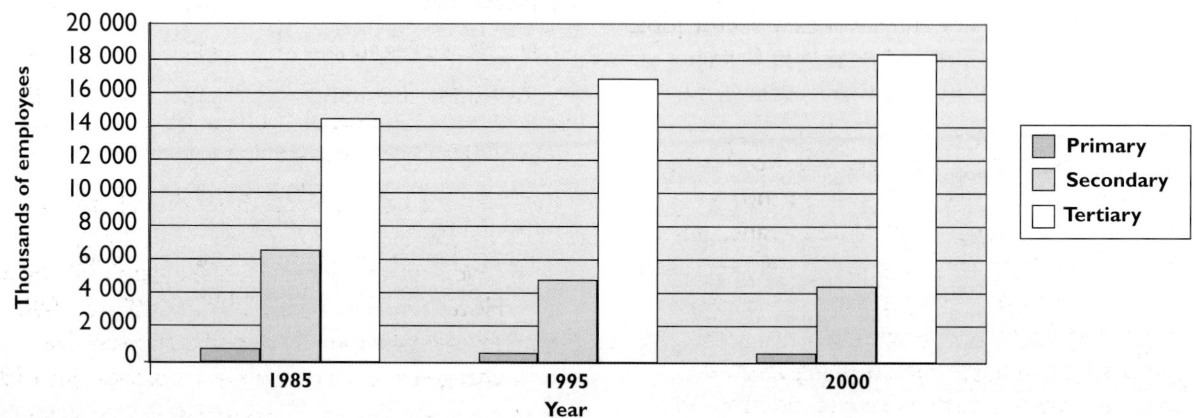

Source: Office for National Statistics

many thousands of jobs being lost. The whole process of secondary sector decline is called **de-industrialisation**, and involves the closure of much of the manufacturing sector in a country. This has happened because:

- Foreign competition has meant that many goods, which were once 'Made in Britain', are now from overseas. This may be because the goods are cheaper, or because consumers in Britain feel that the quality of products from overseas is better than that of those made in Britain. This has especially affected the clothing industry, with many of the items we now wear being made in other countries. The car and motorcycle industry has also been affected in the same way, with large numbers of vehicles bought in Britain being made abroad.
- The use of machinery has meant that many jobs have been lost, with workers being replaced by machines, which are less expensive. The increasing use of robotics and computer control systems has affected many businesses, for example car assembly.

Changes in the tertiary sector

Unlike the primary and secondary sectors, the tertiary sector has seen a large **rise** in importance in recent years, with many new jobs being created. This is because:

- Many tertiary sector jobs are connected to the rise in population, eg health and education. As the population rises, so will the numbers of teachers and nurses. These jobs have not been affected by the introduction of machinery in the same way as primary and secondary sector jobs.
- The increase in wealth of people in Britain means that there is more money that can be spent in shops. This in turn will mean more retail workers being required. Add to this the growth of out-of-town shopping centres and the longer opening hours of shops, and there is a clear rise in the number of workers required.
- The population of Britain also now enjoys more leisure time than ever before. This means that more money is being spent on leisure activities such as sports, cinema and travel, which in turn require more workers.
- Businesses are putting more importance on customer service as a way of keeping existing customers and gaining new ones. This had led to the large increase in telephone call centres, which themselves need large numbers of workers.

ACTIVITY 2

1. At home, research where different items are made. Try to find a range of products, such as clothing, electrical, cosmetics, furniture etc. Construct a chart similar to the one started below. Try to find at least 20 items.

Item	Country of origin

2. Draw a bar graph of your results.
3. Using the figures from your bar graph, calculate the percentage of items in your survey that are made in Britain.
4. Why do you think that only some of the items in your survey are made in Britain?
5. The following table of figures shows the number of employees in different industries for 1985 and 2000. The totals are in thousands.

Industry	1985	2000
Mining and quarrying	228	67
Textiles	278	154
Motor cars	268	211
Hotels and restaurants	940	1 412
Recreation and sport	472	605

Source: Office for National Statistics

(a) Draw a bar graph to show the differences in the five industries for 1985 and 2000.
(b) Calculate the percentage change in Mining and Hotels and restaurants from 1985 to 2000.
(c) Explain why the number of employees has changed in each of the five industries since 1985.

EXAM Practice Questions

1. Study the table of figures below and answer the questions that follow.

% Employment by sector of industry

Sector	% Employment 1989	% Employment 1999
Secondary	33	27
Tertiary	65	71

   (a) Use the figures in the table above to explain the term 'de-industrialisation'. (3 marks)

   (b) Explain one possible reason for the changes in employment in the tertiary sector. (3 marks)

   (Adapted from OCR Business Studies, Business and Change, Higher Paper, June 2000.)

2. Using an example, explain the term 'value added'. (2 marks)
3. Carlton Press Ltd is a publishing company that specialises in educational books. The diagram shows the typical stages of the production of one of its books.

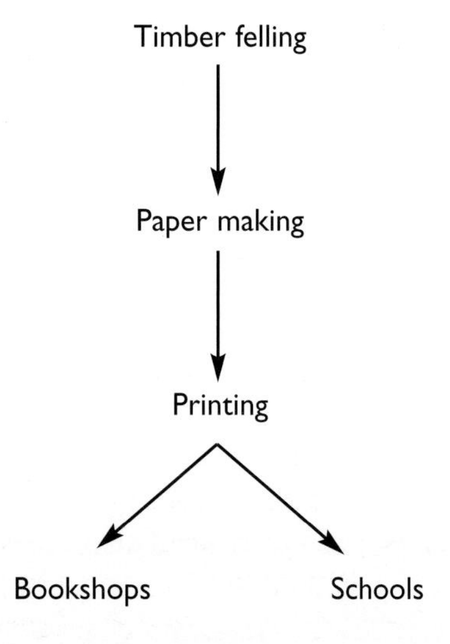

Using examples from the diagram, explain how primary, secondary and tertiary sector businesses rely on each other. (6 marks)

(Adapted from OCR Business Studies, Common Core, Higher Paper, June 1998.)

ADVICE ON HOW TO ANSWER THE QUESTIONS

1. (a) There are two parts to the question: you must explain what 'de-industrialisation' means, **and** use the figures from the table to help your answer.

   (b) The command word is 'explain'. Here you need to explain only **one** reason why the employment in the tertiary sector has changed. Choose a reason you understand clearly.
2. In this type of question you must use an example to help your answer. Keep it short, as the question is only worth 2 marks.
3. Once again, the command word is 'explain'. Here you are also instructed to use the diagram in your answer. Explaining without using the diagram will lose marks. There are 6 marks available for this question, so make sure you write a longer answer, taking each stage in turn from the diagram, and explain clearly how the different stages rely on each other.

KEY TERMS

Primary sector *The first stage of production involving the extraction of the raw materials and natural resources.*

Secondary sector *The second stage of production, where the raw materials are manufactured into finished products.*

Tertiary sector *The third stage of production, where a service is provided for consumers*

De-industrialisation *The reduction of importance of the secondary sector of business activity in a country.*

Interdependence *The way in which business in different sectors of business activity depend on each other. The primary sector depends on the secondary sector to make products from the raw materials it produces. It in turn depends on the tertiary sector to provide the necessary services for the businesses.*

Specialisation *Where a business concentrates on one particular activity.*

Added value *When a business increases the value of a product, eg making a car from pieces of metal or making a meal from various ingredients.*

Chain of production *The process of a product starting as raw materials, manufactured in secondary production and then serviced in some way in tertiary production.*

EXAMINATION SUMMARY TIPS

- Make sure you learn the difference between the three sectors of business activity.
- Understand how the different stages of business activity are linked to each other and how they depend on each other.
- There are many reasons for the fall of primary and secondary sectors, and the rise of tertiary. Try to understand them all.
- Learn to use figures from graphs, and percentages, to add detail and accuracy to your written answers.

Key Skills

Activity 2 provides an opportunity for Application of Number Level 1 (N1.1, N1.2 and N1.3). You need to use the correct information and make accurate calculations as instructed.

Using ICT to present the results from research would help meet IT Level 1 (IT1.1 and IT1.2). Information should be presented in an appropriate format, which meets the requirements of the question. Any information should be saved so that it can be found easily.

In order to evidence IT1.2 you must use IT for the chart and choose a suitable layout for the exercise. Present the information in an accurate, clear way which suits the purpose of the task. The information must be saved so that it can be found easily.

Unit 1.3 Business objectives and the role of stakeholders

Business objectives

All businesses have one or more objectives. The objectives themselves will vary according to the size and situation of the business. Normally speaking, a large multinational plc such as Vodafone will have rather different business objectives from those of a local corner shop. It has become common in recent years for a business to summarise its objectives in a **mission statement**, which is a short declaration of what the business is aiming to achieve.

Clear objectives are needed to succeed in business.

Examples of business objectives

- Profit
- Growth
- Survival
- Providing a service.

Profit

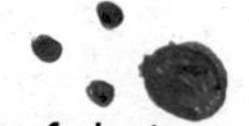

Most businesses will have profit as one of their objectives. For many businesses it will be **the** objective. A business may want to **maximise** profits, which means it will try to make as much profit as possible. This may, however, mean that consumers feel they are not being treated well if a business is seen to make **too much** profit. Sales may fall as a result. In another example a business may aim to make just enough profit to pay for its future plans. This is called **satisficing**.

Growth

Growth is important to a number of businesses as it is seen as a way to raise profits. This is especially important to larger businesses such as plcs, which need the growth to pay increased dividends to their shareholders.

Growth itself can take different forms, including:

- ***Sales growth***. A business may simply want to see sales grow, which may **not** necessarily mean an increase in profit, as prices may have to be lowered in order to attract more customers. Sales growth is often achieved by a business opening more outlets, for example opening shops in different towns.
- ***Increased market share***. A business may wish to see its **market share** grow. This means that the business has a greater percentage share of a market. For example if 1 000 tables were sold in a country, and a business sold 100 of those tables, it would have 10% of the market. If the total number of tables sold rose from 1 000 to 2 000, the business would have to sell more than 200 tables (10% of 2 000) if it were to increase its market share. Car manufacturers are often compared on how much market share they have.
- ***Elimination of competition***. This is another method of increasing market share, where a business takes over its competitors or the competitors themselves close. In these ways a business can achieve 'instant' growth.

Survival

A rather more basic objective in a business is survival. This may be important to a new business for the first few important months. Just to keep going after first opening a business may be something of an achievement! Other more established businesses may see survival as an important objective when they are faced with problems such as falling sales, reduced market share etc. In most cases survival should normally be seen as a temporary, but also vital, objective.

Providing a service

Providing a service may be closely linked to making a profit – the better the service, the more customers will be attracted and so profits will grow. For some businesses, however, providing a service may be **the** objective, even if it means making **less** profit. This may be important in businesses that see customer satisfaction as being a high priority. With good service, the business gets a good reputation, possibly winning awards, which may well be enough to satisfy the owners of the business. Such a business might not even think of growth, being content to continue in its present form, providing a service to customers. This is often found in smaller businesses, which serve the local community.

ACTIVITY 1

1. What might be suitable objectives for the following businesses? Give reasons for your answer.
   - An 18-year-old school leaver just setting up a new business in repairing computers.
   - A plc in the mobile phone business.
   - A local fruit and vegetable shop which discovers that a new hypermarket is to open 100 metres away.
2. Imagine you were to go into business. Make a list of **your** business objectives in order of importance to you, adding a symbol to illustrate each objective. Explain why your objectives are in that particular order.
3. In pairs or small groups, compare and discuss your individual lists of business objectives from question 2. Investigate why there are differences in people's objectives.

Business objectives in the private and public sectors

The private sector

The **private sector** includes all the businesses that are owned by private individuals. All sole traders, partnerships, private and public limited companies are in the private sector, as they are owned by individuals rather than the Government. The private sector is by far the largest part of business activity in Britain, growing in importance over the last 20 years mainly because of privatisation.

Objectives in the private sector are centred on profit and growth. A person starting a business requires some reward for taking the risk of starting the business. That reward will come from the profits of the business. Larger businesses will have to make a profit to maintain and possibly expand. Limited companies are under rather more pressure to make a profit to satisfy shareholders who will be paid a dividend as their reward for buying shares in the company.

Private sector businesses come in all sizes.

The public sector

The public sector includes all the businesses and other organisations that are controlled by central or local Government. The public sector includes health, education, police, fire services and local council services. It also includes the **public corporations** such as the Post Office.

For most organisations in the public sector, providing a good service is seen as the most important objective. It would be difficult to imagine the fire service, for example, having profit as its main objective! Money is provided by local and national Government to operate the public sector services such as health and education, with no shareholders demanding dividends to be paid as in the private sector. In this way the public sector can concentrate on providing the service people need.

Examples of different organisations and business in the public sector.

Conflicts in business objectives

Though some business objectives may work well together, such as providing a service to attract customers in order to make more profit, some of the objectives may well cause conflict in a business.

Growth versus profit

The managers of a business may see expansion as its main aim, which in turn might mean that profits are reduced for a short period of time before they rise. The owners, however, may want to see profits kept at a high level.

ACTIVITY 2

1. Explain the difference between the private and public sectors.
2. What are the differences between the objectives of businesses in the public and private sectors? Give reasons for the differences.
3. Why might it be difficult for a business to have profit, growth and improved service as three objectives at the same time?

Business objectives are often in conflict with each other.

Growth versus service

A business may be able to offer very good service because it is small and knows its customers well. With growth, the business might lose touch with its customers and so the level of service may fall.

Survival versus profit

When a business has survival as its main objective, it is unlikely to have profit (or expansion!) as an objective. It may well, though, see providing a good service as a way of surviving.

Stakeholders in business

What are stakeholders?

Stakeholders are any people or groups of people who have an interest in a business. There are many different stakeholders in a business, and they often go beyond the business itself.

The main stakeholders in business are:

- workers
- managers
- owners
- customers
- suppliers
- Government
- local community.

Workers

Workers have a clear interest in the business where they work. They rely on work for their pay, which they will use to live on. Workers will also look upon work to provide them with some security for the future, and possibly a place to meet and work with other people. A worker has every interest in keeping the business going!

Managers

Managers have a slightly different view of the business they work in. They too will need the business to provide them with the money to live on, but they also have to organise the business and plan for the future, which might mean making some workers redundant if the business is not performing very well. This will put their interests in conflict with those of the workers.

Owners

The owners of a business are not always workers or managers in a business. In a limited company the shareholders are the owners of the business and their interest in the business may be only for the dividend they receive from the company profits. How the business makes that profit might be of little interest to them. One way of making more profit may be to reduce the number of managers in the business. Once again, there is a conflict of interest between two groups of stakeholders.

Customers

Customers want to see low prices and receive good service from a business. They may be pleased if a large hypermarket opens in the area because it will give them a choice of shops and possibly lower prices. Customers of the local corner shop which later closes because of the hypermarket will not be as pleased!

Suppliers

A business which supplies goods and services to another business will clearly want that business to continue and to grow. If a business fails for any reason, other businesses are often affected in some way. A business which feels that one of its business customers is about to fail may stop supplying that business in order to reduce the risk of losses.

Government

The Government has an interest in all businesses succeeding as this means that more people are in work and paying taxes, which gives the Government more money to spend on areas such as health and education. With more people in work, the Government also has to pay less unemployment pay, once again saving money.

Local community

The local community as a whole has an interest in business development. This may **not** mean that **every** business is welcome in an area. A business dealing in toxic waste processing may well provide jobs for some people, but the local community as a whole may be against such a development. Successful business will also bring general prosperity to a local community, which could help reduce crime and contribute to local projects by donations and other support.

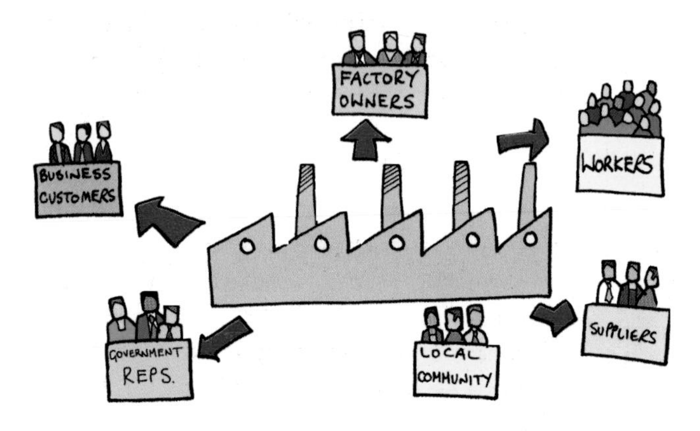

There are many different stakeholders in a business.

ACTIVITY 3

Using your school or college as a business resource, complete the following chart on stakeholders and their interest in the school/college. Think of as many different stakeholders as you can.

Stakeholder	Interest in school/college

EXAM Practice Question

1. Jason Lee works for Colliers plc, which makes and sells chocolate. His friend, Alison Stone, works in the Education Department of Marston Borough Council.
   (a) Which person works in the public sector and which in the private sector? Write your answers in the box below. (2 marks)

Economic sector	Name of worker
Public Sector	
Private Sector	

   (b) State two possible objectives for Colliers plc and two possible objectives for Marston Education Department. (4 marks)
   (c) Explain how and why the objectives of a business might change over time. (6 marks)
   (Adapted from OCR Business Studies Core Paper, Foundation Tier, June 2000.)

2. (a) Explain what is meant by a 'stakeholder'. (2 marks)
   (b) Suggest three possible stakeholders in Colliers plc. (3 marks)

ADVICE ON HOW TO ANSWER THE QUESTIONS

1. (a) In this question you need to think which sectors of the economy employ Alison and Colin.
   (b) Remember that in this question there are a total of four objectives. Make sure you are clear on which objectives are appropriate for which organisation, two in the public sector and two in the private sector.
   (c) This is a longer question (6 marks) in which you must explain how the objectives of a business change **and** why they change. The question says 'over time'.

You can, for instance, begin your answer with a business starting and explain how it then develops. With 6 marks available, try to include three different objectives and explain how and why they change in a business.

2. (a) You need to give a definition of 'stakeholder'.
   (b) Here you must apply the idea of a stakeholder to a plc. The question tells you to 'suggest', so there is no need to explain why your three examples are suitable stakeholders.

Business objectives *Business objectives are what the business is trying to achieve. They may be over a short or long period of time, and include making a profit and providing a service.*

Mission statement *A mission statement is a brief summary of the main objectives a business or organisation has.*

Satisficing *This means that a business will make enough profit to enable it to meet its needs, and not make as much profit as possible.*

Market share *This is the amount of a market a business controls. It is measured as a percentage.*

Public sector *The part of business activity controlled by local and central Government. Includes health, education, fire service, police, and the Post Office.*

Private sector *The part of business activity owned by private individuals. This is the greater part of business activity and includes sole traders, partnerships and plcs.*

Stakeholders *An individual or group of people who have an interest in a business. Includes workers, customers, owners and the local community.*

EXAMINATION SUMMARY TIPS

- Learn the difference between the private and public sectors of business activity.
- There are important differences between the objectives of the private and public sectors. Make sure you learn and understand them.
- Business objectives will vary according to the business and the situation it finds itself in. Make sure any recommendations you make on objectives fit the situation you are given in a question.
- There are many stakeholders in a business. Learn them and understand that they have different interests that may be in conflict.

Key Skills

Activity 1 provides an opportunity for Communications Level 1 (C1.1, C1.2, C1.3).

For C1.1 you must complete question 3, discussion on the reasons for your business objectives.

For C1.2 you must identify clearly your main ideas behind the objectives you suggest, using a suitable image or symbol to illustrate each objective.

For C1.3 you must present the information in a clear way, especially the objectives in question 2, in order that you can use the information for the discussion in question 3.

Unit 1.4 The community, government and business

Business in the community

In recent years, businesses have taken a greater interest in the communities in which they operate. In the wider world, business has shown more concern for the global environment. In part, communities have forced these changes on businesses themselves, with people wanting to see a clean, safe environment, free of pollution and offering a better way of life. The days of businesses operating as they want in countries such as Britain, taking profits without any other care, have long gone.

There are still cases in less developed countries where businesses are not as caring as they might be. This is often due to a lack of action from the Government, with no real control over pollution and other environmental safeguards.

In Britain, the Government is becoming more active in passing laws to protect the environment and safeguard local communities. This itself may be to gain support and therefore mean that a political party is voted into power!

Business, the environment and communities

There are many ways in which businesses might affect the community and environment in which they operate.

When these effects are seen to harm the local environment and community they are known as **social costs**.

Examples of social costs

Pollution

Where businesses are shown to pollute the environment, action can be taken either to fine the business or even to close it down. Pollution itself can take many different forms, for example:

- discharging of materials into rivers or the atmosphere
- spraying of crops where spray may be blown onto other areas
- noise pollution, for example airports
- visual pollution, such as a large power station, which may spoil a view
- workings that create dirty living conditions, for example dust, smoke, mud on roads
- global warming from the increased burning of fossil fuels in business activity
- acid rain caused by fossil fuel use
- smells from certain business activity
- the possible danger of business activity, such as nuclear power
- the need to dispose of an increasing amount of waste.

Pollution is a major example of social costs.

Business closure

When a business closes down there is clearly a negative effect on the local community. Workers will lose their jobs and so the money they would have been paid and then spent in local shops etc will not be there. This in turn may mean that other workers in the community lose their jobs. A closed factory may add to the visual pollution of a community, making it more run down and more difficult to attract new businesses.

As many large businesses are now operating in a global market, it is becoming increasingly common for a business to close down one particular factory in order to move production to another country. In other examples **downsizing** takes place, where a business looks to reduce the numbers of workers it employs.

Business opening

Even when a business opens in an area, there may be some social costs involved.

In addition to the possible pollution problems listed, a new business may have been built on a **greenfield site**, taking away farmland or other community land, for example parkland. A business may like such a site as it offers a clean environment, possibly with good views in a pleasant setting. However, the community will possibly lose a valuable amenity. In other examples, the opening of a business may mean the demolition of other buildings which the local community used.

ACTIVITY 1

1. Explain how the following businesses might bring social costs to a local area:
   (a) a chemical works
   (b) a large car assembly plant
   (c) a night club
   (d) a fish and chip shop
   (e) a hypermarket.
2. Why do businesses like to use greenfield sites?
3. Why are people in a local community often against businesses using greenfield sites?
4. How does a business bring social costs to an area when it closes down?

When a new business is opened, it may force the closure of other businesses. When large hypermarkets are opened, local corner shops nearby may close because they cannot compete, depriving the local community of a service.

Social benefits

Social benefits occur when a business has a positive effect on a community and the environment.

Examples of social benefits

The creation of jobs

When a business opens in an area, more jobs will be created. The pay the new workers receive will often be spent in the local community, which will in turn mean that more workers will be needed in local shops, services etc.

In some cases, the opening of one business will often attract others. If a large airport is opened, other support activities such as catering, cleaning and maintenance will follow. This will increase the number of new jobs created.

In less developed countries the opening of a large multinational business can bring great wealth to a community compared to what was previously

A new business in an area can bring both social costs and benefits.

available. One possible problem in this case is the level of pay sometimes given to workers in these factories. Though it is often much more than they earned before, it is much lower than what would be paid in developed countries such as Britain. This has led to accusations of '**sweat shop**' labour, with young children being worked for long hours and little pay.

The regeneration of an area

When new businesses open on a **brownfield site**, they use land which was previously used for other business purposes. In this way the old, run-down areas are given a new, attractive look, with modern business units, transport and even landscape improvements. This style of regeneration has benefited former coalfield and steel communities, where there was a lot of pollution left by the older closed industries. Meadowhall shopping centre outside Sheffield was built on the site of an old steelworks site, improving the environment as a whole and providing many new jobs in retail and entertainment. However, such developments may mean that other businesses are forced to close because of the increased competition.

Community projects

A new business in an area might offer to improve the sports and other community facilities in order to gain permission to build a new factory. In the past, some businesses, such as Rowntree (now Nestlé), built houses for their workers, though this is not felt necessary in Britain in the 21st century.

Businesses' reactions to environmental and community concerns

Why businesses react to environmental concerns

Consumers are becoming increasingly informed and concerned about 'green issues'.

Businesses are worried about any publicity that might affect their operations as this might mean:

- consumers will stop buying their goods
- sales will fall
- profits will be reduced
- if the business is seen as environmentally friendly then sales and profits might rise.

How businesses react to environmental and community concerns

In order to present an environmentally and community friendly approach (and make sure sales and profits don't fall!), businesses might do the following:

- Use an ethical approach to their business. **Ethical behaviour** by a business means that the business is operating in a morally correct way. This might mean paying workers in less developed countries higher wages, or making sure that their business activities **don't** pollute the environment, even if profits are lower as a result. This can often create conflict in a business between the morally correct decision and the decision that brings the greater profit.
- A business might buy only from other businesses that operate in an ethical way. Some large retailers in Britain which themselves are concerned about the community and the environment have been affected by accusations of buying goods from suppliers in developing countries who use **child labour**. The Co-op Bank will only invest money in companies that operate in an ethical manner, a move which has attracted many customers.
- By making donations to charities, a business might try to gain some good publicity to balance any poor publicity it may receive if it creates problems for the environment and local community.
- Community involvement by a business can also create some good publicity and give the business a good reputation in the local area. Projects might include tree planting and other landscape improvements, local education and hospital support, sports facilities and sponsorship support for local sports teams and prizes for local events.

ACTIVITY 2

Traidcraft: An example of ethical behaviour in business activity

TRAIDCRAFT

the heart of Christianity expressed through practical action.

JUSTICE

responsible relationships remove the causes of poverty.

TRADE

carried out with love and justice benefits both rich and poor nations.

Trading for a fairer world

Some of Traidcraft's product range.

In 2000, Traidcraft celebrated 21 years in business. Its aim is to help people in poorer countries by:

- buying goods at a fair price, at times paying more in order to help development
- making long-term agreements with producers in poor countries
- making payments in advance if necessary.

Traidcraft also has standards of ethical behaviour. These include:

- no use of child labour
- living wages to be paid to all workers
- working hours are not too long
- regular employment is given
- no harsh treatment of workers
- no discrimination against any worker
- working conditions are safe and hygienic.

QUESTIONS

1. Give two examples of how Traidcraft operates in a fair manner.
2. Describe how Traidcraft's ethical behaviour helps workers in poorer countries.
3. Working in small groups, try to find information on other businesses that operate in an ethical way. Aim for at least two businesses from each group member.
4. Look into business activity in your local area. Try to find examples of businesses that do not behave in a totally ethical way. Try to explain why certain businesses might behave in an unethical way.

ACTIVITY 3

Read the following information, study the photographs over the page and answer the questions that follow.

The redevelopment of Manvers, Rotherham

Since 1981, over 6 000 jobs have been lost in the former mining area in the Dearne Valley in South Yorkshire. One part of this area, Manvers, saw the closure of two coal mines and a plant where coke was made from the coal. The closure had a devastating effect on the local community which relied on mining for most of its employment.

The land left when the mines were removed was at the time the largest single area of derelict land in Europe. It needed a massive effort from a number of authorities in order to regenerate the area.

The plan for regeneration includes:

- 400 acres of land for new industrial units
- a 40-acre lake and nature reserve
- an 18-hole golf course
- a community park and sports pitches.

Who is involved in the regeneration plan?

- Rotherham Council
- Department of the Environment
- English Partnerships (supporting coalfield redevelopment)
- Yorkshire Forward (supporting coalfield redevelopment)
- Department of Transport
- Barnsley Council.

The amount of support:

- central Government (derelict land grant, city challenge, industrial development): £60 million
- European Regional Development Fund: £2 800 000
- Rotherham Council: £530 000.

New businesses attracted to the area include:

- One 2 One
- The Post Office
- Ventura (customer services, part of Next group of companies)
- Powergen
- Lifetime Careers
- Danish Bacon Company
- Euro Telecom (security and communication systems)
- Delfa Technologies (refrigeration components)
- Eurocap (Manufacturer of baseball caps).

Number of jobs created by the redevelopment:

- total jobs at October 2000: 2 879
- projected number of jobs if 40% of development occupied: 5 110.

QUESTIONS

1. How many mining and other jobs were lost in the Dearne Valley?
2. Use the information provided and the photographs to describe why this particular area needed a lot of help.
3. Draw a bar graph to show the different amounts of support given for redevelopment.
4. How does the information in your graph show the need for central Government help in this size of project?
5. The redevelopment included new road systems. Explain why this was an important part of the plan.
6. Using all the information available, explain how the regeneration at Manvers is an example of social benefits

The Redevelopment of Manvers

*Manvers, Rotherham **after** regeneration.*

*Manvers, Rotherham **before** regeneration.*

Aerial photos courtesy Richard Bird Photography, Sheffield

Organisations which affect business behaviour in the community

There are a number of different organisations that affect the way businesses operate in the community. They can be divided into three groups:

- local government
- national government
- pressure groups.

Local government

Local government affects the way business operates in the community by using the following methods:

- Granting planning permission for business development where the environment and community will benefit. Where a business will possibly harm the environment the planning permission may be refused.
- Helping businesses find a suitable site on which to build, and where to find the financial support they may need to develop the business.
- Placing rules and regulations on businesses as to how they operate. This often relates to the possible pollution a business might cause. It can include a business having to provide wheel washers for lorries if they are making roads muddy and dangerous.

National government

By passing laws that affect the whole country, rather than on a local level, the Government can influence the way in which businesses affect the environment. These include:

- support for the location of business in Development Areas and Enterprise Zones to assist regeneration (see pages 260–261)
- laws on pollution and the use of chemicals
- the introduction of measures to reduce the amount of pollution in the atmosphere; these include cars having to be fitted with catalytic converters to reduce harmful gases, and the increase in petrol prices to encourage people to use their cars less.

Pressure groups

A pressure group is an organised group of people who try to persuade others to share their views. There are a number of pressure groups who are concerned about the environment and how business activity might affect local communities.

Two well-known pressure groups are Friends of the Earth and Greenpeace. Both are now world-wide organisations and will bring the attention of the public to any business activity that they feel is harmful. Businesses are aware of the influence that such organisations might have, and the bad publicity that might come if a pressure group takes action against it.

Possible action a pressure group might take includes:

- writing letters to the business, to local and national government and to newspapers
- organising marches and other protests
- gaining public support.

All of the above are aimed at highlighting possible conflicts between business, communities and the environment. In this way it is hoped that the business will operate in a way which does not harm the environment or communities.

Friends of the Earth and Greenpeace are two well-known pressure groups.

EXAM Practice Questions

1. Nicole and Colin own a café business, which brings both social costs and social benefits to the local community.
   (a) State whether the following are a social cost or a social benefit:
   - litter
   - increased jobs
   - noise. (3 marks)

   (b) Explain why Nicole and Colin should take into account social costs when locating their café. (4 marks)

   (Adapted from OCR Business and Change, Foundation Tier Paper, June 2000.)
2. Nicole and Colin are concerned that they buy coffee and tea for the café from companies that show ethical behaviour.
   (a) Explain what is meant by 'ethical behaviour'. (2 marks)
   (b) Give two examples of ethical behaviour in business activity. (2 marks)
3. Explain how pressure groups try to bring change to business activity. (4 marks)

A ADVICE ON HOW TO ANSWER THE QUESTIONS

1. (a) In this question you need to think of a café opening and the possible advantages (social benefits) and disadvantages (social costs) that it might bring to an area.
   (b) In this question you must explain your ideas. Social costs are disadvantages for the local community. You must think why the café owners should consider the problems of social costs when they are choosing a place to locate their business. Might one location have fewer social costs than another?
2. (a) Here you need to give a definition of 'ethical behaviour'.
   (b) The command word is 'give'. This means that no explanation is necessary. Make sure the examples you give are clear.
3. You now have to explain ideas on pressure group activity. Don't simply give examples: explain how the actions pressure groups take are designed to change business activity. Examples will make your answer clearer.

Downsizing *A term used to describe the reduction in the number of employees in a business.*

Greenfield site *A site for a business which has not previously been used for building.*

Brownfield site *A site for a business that has previously been used for building purposes.*

Regeneration *The changes to an old industrial area to attract new businesses. This might include new transport and other community facilities as well as the new businesses.*

Social costs *The costs to the environment and community that arise when business activities take place.*

Social benefits *The benefits that business activity brings to a local community and the environment.*

Sweat shop *A term used to describe the payment of very low wages to some workers in developing countries.*

Ethical behaviour *Business behaviour which places moral values above maximising profits.*

Child labour *The use of very young children in business in order to reduce wage costs.*

Pressure groups *Organised groups of people who aim to bring attention to particular issues and problems.*

EXAMINATION SUMMARY TIPS

- Make sure you understand social costs and social benefits.
- There are a number of ways in which business can react to environmental and community concerns.
- The use of greenfield sites is an important consideration in business location.
- Ethical behaviour is becoming more of an issue in business activity.
- Pressure groups are becoming more organised in action against business activity.
- You must be prepared to take a view on the possible advantages and disadvantages (costs and benefits) that business activity brings to an area.
- Business operations in this country may be affected by unethical behaviour of suppliers in other countries.

Key Skills

Activity 2 provides an opportunity for Communication Level 1 and Working with Others Level 1.

For Communication Level 1 (C1.2), you need to use a variety of information available. For Working with Others Level 1 (WO1.1, WO1.2, WO1.3), you need to understand the different responsibilities of the group members, carry out the task you have been set and show that you have succeeded. The evidence needs to show who was responsible for what task, and you should write out (or print) the results of your own contribution and the group's work. You must also write a section on how the work of the group could have been improved.

Business Structure and Organisation

- Introductory Activity
- Unit 2.1 Types of business
- Unit 2.2 Sole traders and partnerships
- Unit 2.3 Private and public limited companies
- Unit 2.4 Franchises, holding and multinational companies, management buyouts
- Unit 2.5 Public corporations

Learning Objectives:
To develop:

- knowledge and understanding of the different types of business organisation which exist and their appropriateness to business situations
- understanding of why businesses may need to change the way in which they are structured and organised
- the skills of selection, interpretation and analysis of information
- the ability of students to apply their understanding of business structure and organisations to given situations
- the skill of making reasoned judgement as it applies to differing business situations.

Introductory Activity

On the right is a copy of map which was used in a recent GCSE Business Studies examination as the stimulus material for a number of different questions. The map shows some of the businesses trading in the imaginary town of Bowton.

Your task is to:

1. Draw a map, similar in style to the one for Bowton, of a shopping centre, town centre or area where there are a number of businesses and shops you are familiar with.
2. Mark on the map the trading names of the different businesses.
3. Find out, perhaps by visiting or telephoning, the name of the business or person who actually owns the business.
4. Draw up a table, similar to the one in Table 2.1 over the page, which compares the trading name of the business with the name of the person or firm that actually owns the business.
5. Insert information in the third column of the table showing the type of activity which each business is involved in.
6. Complete the table by showing which sector of the economy the business is trading in. Leave the last column blank for use in a later Activity.

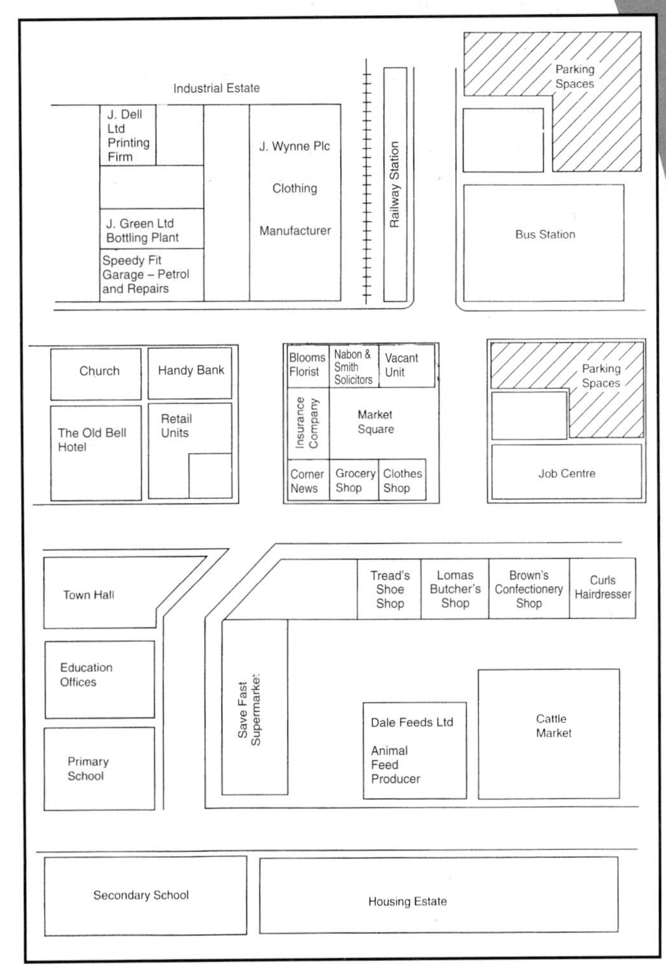

Map of Town Centre of Bowton

(Adapted from OCR GCSE Business Studies, Foundation Tier Core Examination Paper 1, June 1999.)

Trading name of business	Name of person or business owning the business	Trading activity	Sector of the economy	

Table 2.1 Businesses in (insert the name of the area you have chosen)

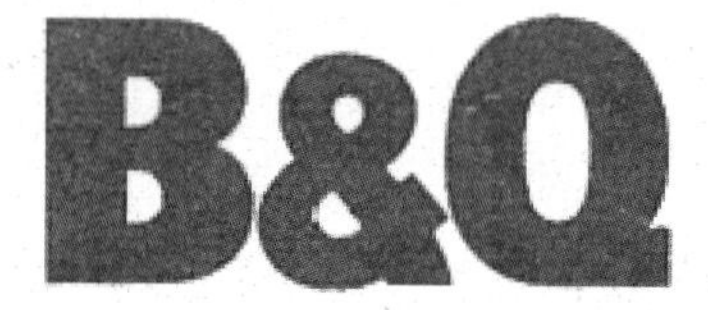

B &Q owned by Kingfisher plc – trading activities gardening and DIY.

TOPSHOP

TopShop owned by The Arcadia Group plc – trading activities clothing and fashion accessories.

Halfords owned by The Boots Company plc – trading activities car and cycle parts and accessories.

Unit 2.1 Types of business

Classifying different types of business

Business activity can be classified in a number of different ways:

1. According to the **sector of the economy** it is involved in. Unit 1.2 provides more information on how business can be classified by this method.

A farm is a Primary activity.

A production line is a secondary activity.

A restaurant is a Tertiary activity.

2. According to whether the activity takes place in the **public sector** or **private sector**. Unit 1.3 provides more information on how business activity can be classified by this method.

A supermarket is a private sector activity.

A hospital is a public sector activity.

3. According to the **type of business organisation and ownership**:
   - There are four basic forms of business ownership in the private sector of the economy. These forms of ownership will be either **incorporated** or **unincorporated** businesses.
   - Those businesses which trade in the public sector of the economy will usually be controlled and financed by central or local government. See Units 1.3 and 2.5 for more information.
   - **Producer co-operatives** are those business which are owned and operated by the people who work in the business. For instance, many farmers are part of a producer co-operative where a number of independent farmers get together so that they can share equipment. Combine harvesters are very expensive and a single

farmer may not be able to afford to buy one or indeed have sufficient work for it. A producer co-operative formed by a number of farmers may buy the equipment and arrange for it to be shared between farms.

Unincorporated businesses

There are two basic types of unincorporated business – **sole traders** and **partnerships**. Further information on these forms of business is in Unit 2.2.

These types of businesses have the following features:

Feature	**Explanation**
Unlimited liability	The owners of the business are personally liable for any debts which the business may have. Personal possessions – TV, video, car – may have to be sold to raise finance, or private wealth used to pay off the debts of the business even though the items have nothing to do with the running of the business.
Tax on profits	Income Tax is paid on the profits which the business may make.
Continuity	The business, in its present form, ceases on the death of one of the owners.
Financial information	Remains private to the owners of the business.
Bankruptcy	This situation occurs when the business is unable to pay its debts.

Incorporated businesses

There are two basic types of incorporated business – **private limited companies** and **public limited companies**. Further information on these forms of business is shown in Unit 2.3.

These types of businesses have the following features:

Feature	**Explanation**
Limited liability	The liability of the owners of the business, the shareholders, to pay off its debts is limited to the amount of money which they have invested in the business when buying the shares.

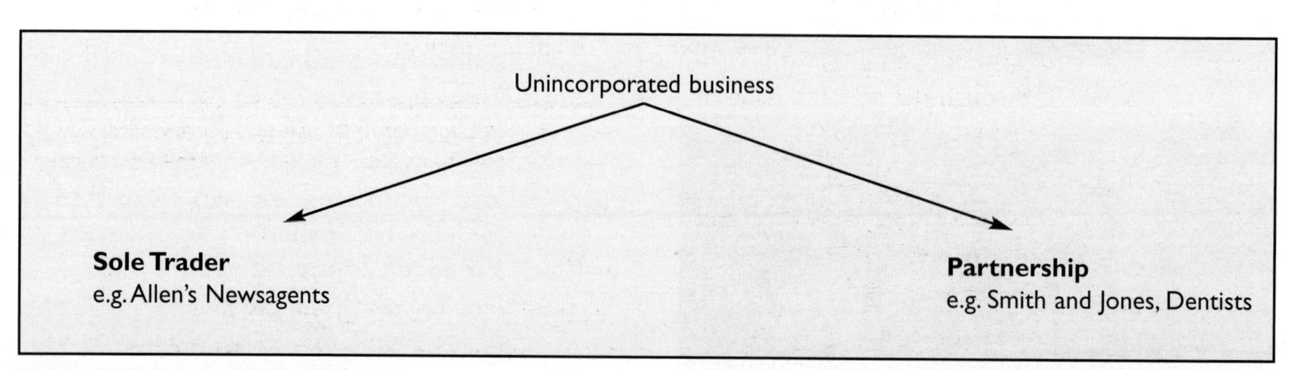

Types of Unincorporated Business

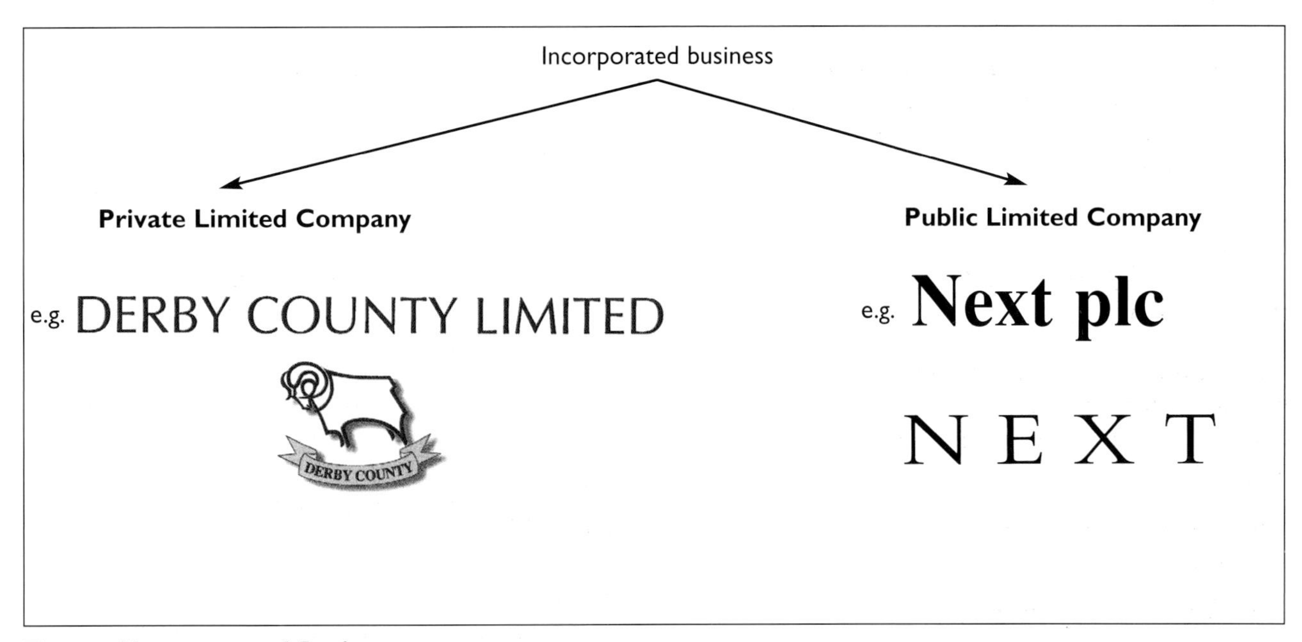

Types of Incorporated Business

Separate legal entity	The business has a separate legal identity from its owners. It can start legal action against another business or individual in order to protect itself. Other businesses and individuals have the right to take legal action against the business.
Tax on profits	Corporation tax is paid on any profits which the business may make.
Finance	Finance can be raised through the sale and issue of shares.
Financial information	Some financial information is available to shareholders and the general public if they request to see it.
Insolvency	This situation occurs when the business is unable to pay its debts.

ACTIVITY

1. Using the information in Table 2.1 that you created in the Introductory Activity task from pages 27 and 28, use the 'blank' column in the table to identify whether you think the business is an incorporated or unincorporated business.
2. Using a memo form similar to the one in the outline below, word-process a memo to your teacher explaining the advantages and disadvantages of incorporation and unincorporation.

INTEROFFICE MEMORANDUM

TO:

FROM:

SUBJECT: BUSINESS ORGANISATION – INCORPORATION versus UNINCORPORATION

DATE:

Are all businesses successful?

Successful business and business that has failed.

What do entrepreneurs do?

An entrepreneur is someone who recognises a business opportunity and who is prepared to take a risk in setting up a business to make the most of the opportunity. Not all business opportunities turn out to be successful. There is always a risk involved. One of the best-known entrepreneurs in the United Kingdom is Richard Branson.

The 'Virgin' name is well known in the United Kingdom and abroad. However, when new Virgin businesses start, there is no guarantee that they are going to be successful.

Reasons why some businesses fail

Running a business can be a challenging and time-consuming activity. It can also be a very profitable experience for the owner or owners. However, not all businesses are successful and they can fail for a variety of reasons. Some of the possible reasons are shown below:

- poor management

Managers need to spend some time at work.

- no demand for product or service

Businesses must recognise the needs of customers.

- business is located in the wrong place

Few people will think of buying paint from a theme park.

- poor cash flow

Little money will be received from sales of fireworks in February.

- costs of running the business are too high

A second-hand van will be much cheaper to run.

- too much competition

Too many businesses selling the same product.

- poor quality goods or services

Shoes must be fit for the job.

- insufficient profit made on goods or services sold

Prices charged must cover the cost of buying the goods.

- unfavourable exchange rate between the pound and other currencies

Holiday companies may find it difficult to sell holidays.

EXAM Practice Question

(a) What do the letters 'plc' stand for? (1 mark)

(b) The following are features of plcs and sole traders. Place them under the correct heading.

- able to sell shares to raise finance
- owned by one person
- the owner has unlimited liability
- the business has separate legal identity from its owners. (4 marks)

Features of a plc	Features of a sole trader

(Adapted from question 3, OCR Business Studies, Foundation Tier Common core question paper, June 2000.)

(c) Some retail businesses are small independent sole traders. Other retailers are large public limited companies. Suggest why both forms of business organisation exist in the retail trade. (7 marks)

(Adapted from question 3, OCR Business Studies. Higher Tier Common core question paper, June 2000.)

ADVICE ON HOW TO ANSWER THE QUESTIONS

(a) This is a simple definition question which requires you to write out what the three letters stand for.

(b) This question requires you to select two features which are appropriate to a plc and two which are appropriate to a sole trader. Each feature can be used only once.

(c) A more detailed response is required in order to answer this question. You will need to provide an answer which relates information to the retail trade and gives reasons why both forms of business organisation exist in the retail trade. Any examples which you can provide will help with your explanation.

KEY TERMS

Limited liability *The owner of a business does not risk losing personal possessions in order to pay off the debts of the business.*

Unlimited liability *Owners of the business are liable for its debts.*

Incorporated *A form of business organisation which is a separate legal entity. It has limited liability and is owned by shareholders.*

Unincorporated *A type of business organisation which has unlimited liability.*

Sole trader *Sometimes known as a sole proprietor. One person owns the business.*

Partnership *A form of unincorporated business organisation which is owned by more than one person.*

Private limited company *A business owned by shareholders. It is normally identified by the word 'Limited' or 'Ltd' somewhere in the name of the business.*

Public limited company *A business owned by shareholders. Shares in the business can be bought and sold without restriction. The business must use the words 'public limited company' or 'plc' somewhere in the name of the business.*

Bankruptcy *A legal process which happens to individuals and unincorporated businesses when liabilities are greater than assets.*

Insolvency *A limited liability company is said to be insolvent when liabilities are greater than assets.*

Entrepreneur *A person who sees a business opportunity and who accepts the risks involved in running a business.*

EXAMINATION SUMMARY TIPS

- Learn the different ways in which business activity can be classified.
- Learn the differences between and key features of unincorporated and incorporated organisations.
- Consider why some businesses are prepared to operate with unlimited liability.
- Think carefully about the appropriateness of a form of business to the size and type of activity.
- Consider why a business might want to change the way in which it is organised as it grows in size.

Key Skills

The Activity provides an opportunity to produce a document at Level 1 (C 1.3) or Level 2 (C 2.3) using IT at Level 1 (IT 1.2).

The completed memo should contain information relevant to the task which has been given. The inclusion of an image may not be relevant to the task.

For the requirements of C2.3 to be satisfied, an extended piece of writing will be required. This should be based on a memo template which may be available in most word-processing applications. The memo must have an appropriate layout which is used in a consistent way if it is to satisfy the requirements of IT1.2.

Unit 2.2 Sole traders and partnerships

Sole traders

There are a very large number of sole trader businesses in the United Kingdom. Sole traders are also known as sole proprietors because there is just one person who owns the business. However, although the business is owned by one person, it does not stop it from employing other people to work in the business.

Sole traders can be found in many different types of business activity.

Advantages of the sole trader form of business organisation

There would not be so many sole trader businesses in the UK if there were not some important advantages of this form of business organisation.

The main reasons for this large number of sole traders are:

- it is a form of business organisation which is suited to a wide variety of different types of business
- many new and small businesses find it a suitable form of business organisation
- it is extremely easy and cheap to set up, with very few forms to be completed
- some sole trader businesses can be set up with very little start-up capital
- the owner is in complete control of the business and does not need to obtain the agreement of other people when making business decisions
- all the financial information about the business is private. No information has to be provided to the general public or other businesses
- the owner is able to keep all the profit which the business makes.

Promotional 'flyer' advertising the services of a sole trader.

Disadvantages of sole trader business organisation

As with most things, there can be some disadvantages. Operating as a sole trader business does have some problems. The main problems which sole trader businesses face are:

Unlimited liability This can be a real problem if the business is not doing well. The owner of the business runs the risk of losing his or her personal possessions to pay off the debts of the business if it fails. Any losses which the business makes will have to be met by the owner of the business. There is no one else to share the losses with.

Shortage of capital Some sole traders may find it difficult to operate or grow in size because they are short of capital. Some small businesses can find it difficult to obtain bank loans because they represent a significant risk to the lender.

Illness If the owner of the business is ill, there may be no one else who can run the business.

Hours of work Some sole traders work long hours in order to make the business successful.

Continuity If the owner of the business wishes to sell it, there is no guarantee that a buyer will be found. Equally, if the owner dies, the business effectively also ceases to exist.

Shortage of skills It is often not possible for the owner of the business to be skilled in all areas of the business's operation. As a result, specialist workers may have to be employed but there may not be enough work for them.

Economies of scale Because sole trader businesses tend to be small, there is limited opportunity for the business to gain financial advantages from large-scale production.

One person cannot do all the jobs.

Partnerships

This form of business organisation is very common in certain sections of the economy. The doctor and dentist you attend are probably in business as partnerships.

BROWN
and Associates
Dental Surgeons

Nameplates like this are very common.

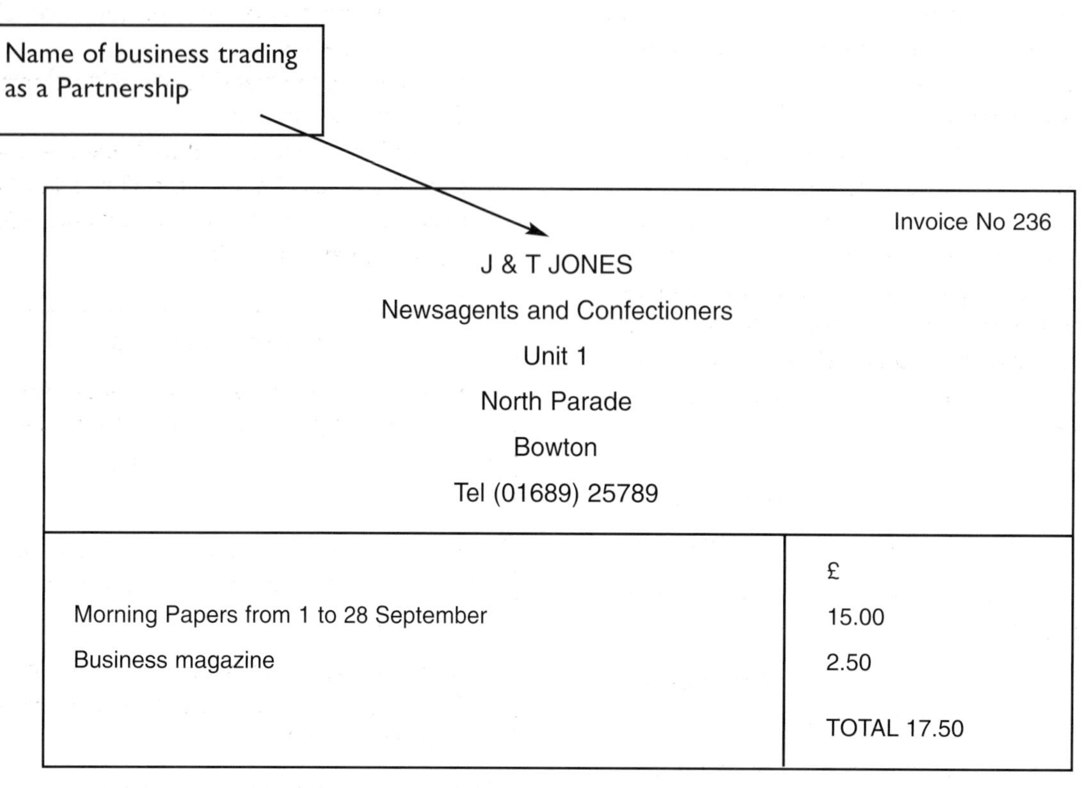

Name of business trading as a Partnership

Invoice No 236

J & T JONES
Newsagents and Confectioners
Unit 1
North Parade
Bowton
Tel (01689) 25789

	£
Morning Papers from 1 to 28 September	15.00
Business magazine	2.50
	TOTAL 17.50

Another example of a business trading as a partnership

Partnerships are often the preferred type of business organisation for veterinary surgeons, solicitors and accountants etc, although many other businesses can be set up as partnerships.

There are very strict rules which control the creation of partnerships. There can be a minimum of two and a maximum of 20 partners although not all the partners need to have an equal share of the business. This form of business organisation has many of the advantages of the sole trader form of organisation and operating as a partnership overcomes many of the disadvantages of operating as a sole trader.

Advantages of the partnership form of business organisation

- Because there are more people who own the business, more capital can be introduced into the business to help it operate or grow in size.
- Each partner may have a different specialist skill which can be used by the business, eg a small building business may be owned by three partners. One partner may be skilled in electrical work, another in bricklaying and another in plumbing.

Each partner in the business is a specialist.

- The work of the business can be shared and in the event of illness of one of the partners the business should not experience a particular problem.
- Easy and cheap to set up.
- Financial information about the business remains private to the partners.
- If extra skills or capital should be needed in the business it is quite easy to admit another partner. Some partners may not wish to take an active part in the running of the business but are happy just to contribute capital to it. These partners are known as **sleeping partners**.

Disadvantages of the partnership form of business organisation

As with sole traders, partnerships do have some disadvantages. The main problems are:

Profit	This has to be shared between the partners.
Unlimited liability	Partnerships with unlimited liability put the personal possessions of the partners at risk in the event of the failure of the business.
Disagreements	The partners may not always agree on how the business should be operated.
Shortage of capital	The ability of the partnership to raise finance is generally restricted to the existing partners introducing more capital into the business; admitting new partners or obtaining bank loans.

Deed of partnership

Because a partnership is a more complicated form of business ownership than a sole trader, most partnerships draw up a **deed of partnership**. If there is no deed of partnership, the law states that each partner's standing is equal regardless of the amount of capital which they have contributed. It is a legally binding agreement which:

- provides information on the way in which the business operates
- states how profits and losses will be shared amongst the partners
- details how much capital each partner has contributed to the business. This is important because partners do not need to provide equal amounts of capital.

Deed of Partnership

between Anthony Brown of 12 Corden Street, James Taft of 52 Porter Drive and John Davey of 16 Copley Road all of the town of Midchester.

Trading name of the business: JPJ Computer Services. The business will sell and repair computer equipment.

Each partner agrees to provide the sum of £10 000 and will share the profits or losses of the business equally.

The responsibilities of each partner are as follows:

A Brown – Repairs to equipment. Technical support to customers.

J Taft – Sales of new computer equipment.

J Davey – Maintaining financial records and accounts.

Signed A Brown

J. Taft. J. Davey

Date 11th July 2001

Extract from a deed of partnership

Limited partnerships

A recent change in the law makes it now possible, under certain circumstances, to set up a business as a partnership, where the partners have limited liability.

ACTIVITY

(a) Study the Deed of Partnership on page 39. Write down any other information which you think should be included in the deed of partnership.
(b) Think of a business activity which you might eventually like to own and operate.
(c) Working with a group of two or three other people, draw up a Deed of Partnership similar in outline to the one on page 39, detailing the responsibilities of each partner and how the business is to operate. You will need to think carefully about what you want to include in your deed of partnership in case you have a disagreement with your partners. Such things as working hours, partners' responsibilities and wages may need to be included. Consider carefully what else you would want to include if you were going into business.

EXAM Practice Questions

(a) Explain how a sole trader might finance the purchase of a shop and its fittings. (4 marks)
(Adapted from OCR Business Studies, Q3 Foundation Tier Common Core paper, June 2000.)

Feature	Answer
Number of owners	
Who provides the capital?	
Who controls the business?	
Who receives the profits?	

(4 marks)

(b) (i) Dave Smith is a sole trader. Complete the table below by providing answers to the questions in the Feature column.
(ii) Explain what 'unlimited liability' means. (2 marks)
(Adapted from OCR Business Studies, Q1 Foundation Tier Combined Course paper, June 2000.)

(c) Using the following headings, explain how a sole trader business might be organised:
- control and management
- distribution of profits. (6 marks)

(Adapted from OCR Business Studies, Q1 Higher Tier Combined Course paper, June 2000.)

d) Many small businesses fail very quickly. Explain three possible reasons for a small business failing. (6 marks)
(Adapted from OCR Business Studies, Q1 Foundation Tier Combined Course paper, June 1999.)

ADVICE ON HOW TO ANSWER THE QUESTIONS

(a) This question requires you to think carefully about the types of finance which are available to sole traders. Not all types of finance will be available. You will then need to think about which of the types of finance are appropriate for the purchase of shop fittings such as shelves and display cabinets. You will need to explain why these types of finance are appropriate.
(b) (i) To answer this question you to need to provide a range of basic facts about the key features of the sole trader form of business organisation.
(ii) A clear and detailed explanation of what the term 'unlimited liability' means is needed to answer this question successfully. The use of examples will help improve your explanation.
(c) Specific information about 'Control and Management' and 'Distribution of Profits' in sole trader organisations needs to be provided in order to answer this question.

(d) You will need to think carefully about the reasons why some businesses fail and eventually go out of business. There are many reasons. You need to think about whether the reasons are particularly relevant to small businesses. Remember to give a detailed explanation for each reason.

KEY TERMS

Sole proprietor *Unincorporated business owned by one person. Also known as a sole trader.*

Capital *Money invested in the business by its owners.*

Economies of scale *These occur when the scale of business activity increases, resulting in a reduction of the average costs of production.*

Sleeping partner *A person who has invested capital in a business but who does not take an active part in the running of it.*

Deed of Partnership *A legal agreement drawn up between the partners of the business stating responsibilities of partners and how the business is to operate.*

EXAMINATION SUMMARY TIPS

- Learn the key features of both forms of unincorporated business organisation.
- Make sure you know the advantages and disadvantages of each form of business organisation and how each is likely to affect the way in which the business operates.
- Consider why both forms of business organisation exist and why they are particularly appropriate to certain types of business.
- Be prepared to apply what you know about both forms of business organisation to different business scenarios.

Key Skills

The Activity provides an opportunity to take part in a one-to-one discussion at Level 1 (C1.1) in preparation for producing a document (C1.3).

For the group discussion, you will need to provide evidence in the form of written notes detailing the discussion you took part in.

- The completed Deed of Partnership will provide evidence for C1.3. You should include an image, perhaps in the form of a logo, in your document.

If you choose to produce deed of partnership using IT, evidence may be available which meets the IT Level One (IT 1.2) Key Skill requirements.

Part (c) of the task provides an opportunity to produce evidence for Working With Others at Level 1 (WO 1.2).

- To meet the evidence requirements, you will need to keep a record of your discussions and indicate who was responsible for which part of the completed task.
- Deadlines for the completion of the task will need to be kept to.

Unit 2.3 Private and public limited companies

There are a large number of private and public limited companies in the United Kingdom and you will have done business with a large number of them. The bus company which brought you to school; the cinema you visited recently; the fast food restaurant where you bought a burger; or the supermarket where your family does its shopping are probably private or public limited companies.

Public limited companies	15 181
Private limited companies	1 619 500

Table 2.2 Number of Private and Public Limited Companies registered in the UK

Source: Companies House CD-ROM Directory, August 2000

Finding out the type of business organisation

All private and public limited companies must let customers know what type of business organisation they are trading as. This information is sometimes written on receipts, company headed paper or other documentation.

Private limited companies must have the word 'Limited' or 'Ltd' somewhere in their title.

BOOTS THE CHEMIISTS LTD
ALLESTREE
Tel. No: (01332) 550855

DISP SALES	2.87
X	
TOTAL	2.87
CASH	3.00
CHANGE	.13
DATE: 7/10/00	TIME: 13:54

THANK YOU FOR SHOPPING
AT BOOTS

Public limited companies must have the letters 'PLC' or words 'Public limited company' in their title.

Marks & Spencer p.l.c.
1 Albert Street
Nottingham
NG1 7DB.
Tel. No: 0115 9580571
VAT No: 232 1288 92

	£
09327368T38 L/S VISCOSE CARDI	35.00
09606302S02 £25 Gift Voucher	25.00
Balance to pay 1 item	60.00

This type of information tells customers and suppliers that they are trading with:

- an incorporated organisation
- owned by shareholders
- which has limited liability. In other words, the owners of the business (shareholders) will not be personally responsible for any debts which the business might have.

There are many reasons why both of these forms of business organisation exist in the United Kingdom. There are, though, important differences between them.

ACTIVITY 1

1. Collect samples of receipts, headed paper and other company documentation which show the name of the company and the words 'Ltd' or 'plc' somewhere in the title of the business.
2. Explain why this information is made so clear.
3. Keep a record of this material which may be useful for your coursework.

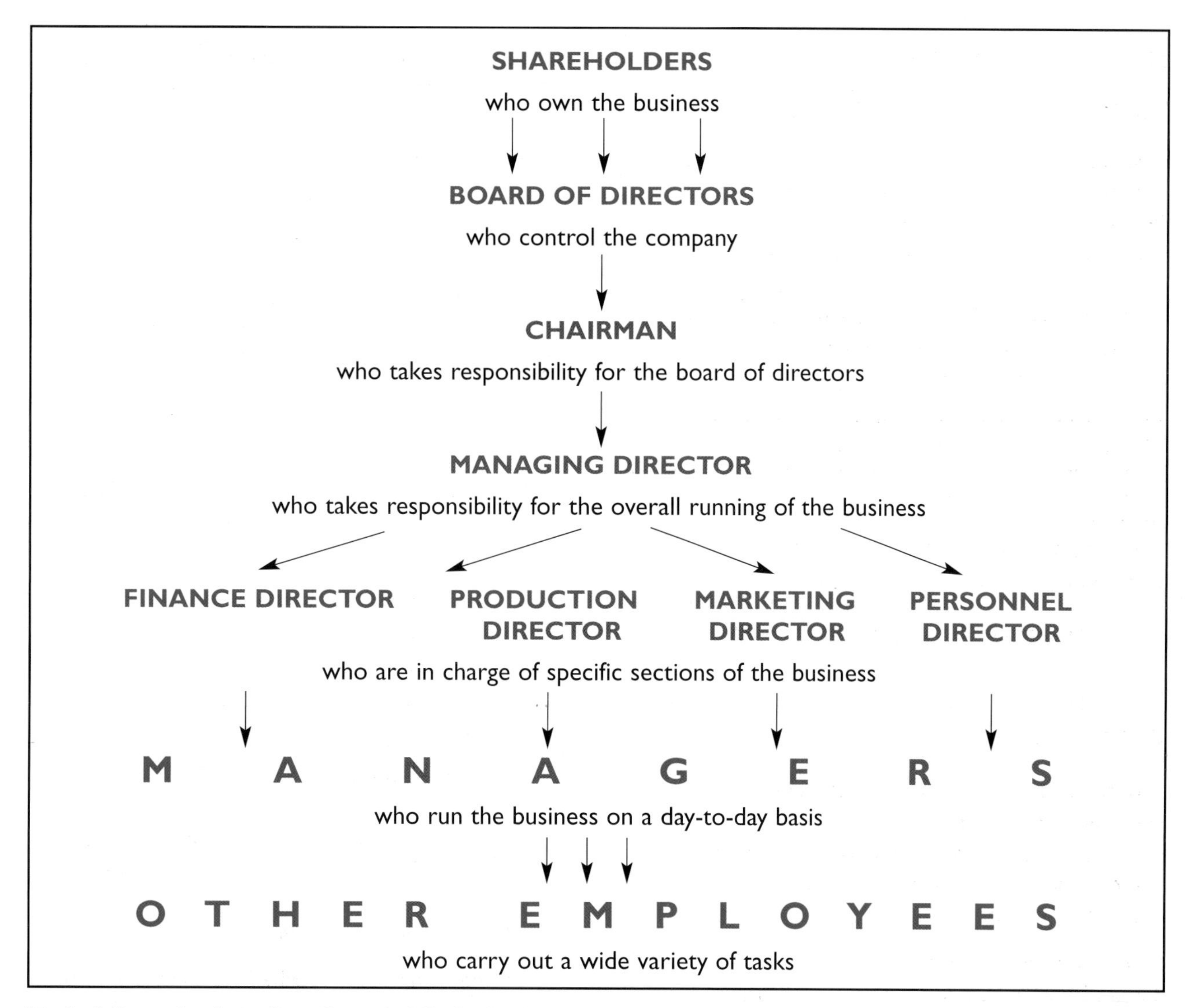

Typical Organisation chart for a public limited company

Incorporation

This is a complicated and sometimes costly legal process which private and public limited companies must go through before they can begin to trade. Once all the requirements of the process have been met, the Registrar of Companies will issue a **certificate of incorporation**.

Board of directors

Both private and public limited companies must have a **board of directors**. Directors are people who are elected by shareholders at the company's **annual general meeting**, to make important decisions and run the company on their behalf. Some directors may hold a specific responsibility for one part of the work of the company. One of the directors is responsible for the way in which the board of directors operates and will have been elected as the **chair(man)**. Another director may take on responsibility for the overall running of the company and act as **Managing Director**.

A typical organisation chart for a large public limited company is shown in the diagram above. The diagram also shows the roles and responsibilities of each of the key groups involved in the running of a public limited company.

See Unit 4.1 for more about Organisational Charts.

In a small business there may be very few directors and it is not uncommon in a family business to find a husband and wife as the only two directors. This means that they may have to do a number of different jobs.

Private limited companies

Features and advantages of the private limited company form of business organisation

We have already discovered that one of the main advantages of this form of business organisation is limited liability and that the business must have the word 'Limited' or 'Ltd' somewhere in its title. This is why there are so many private limited companies registered in the United Kingdom.

There are other advantages as shown in the table below.

Shares	These can be issued as a means of raising capital.
Legal identity	The business is separate from its owners. It can take legal action against other persons or companies and be the subject of legal action against it.
Continuity	Subject to agreement by the shareholders, the business can be sold. Equally, individual shareholders are free to sell the shares they own to other people. In the event of the death of a shareholder, the business will be unaffected and will continue to trade normally.
Directors	There is usually a minimum of two directors. In certain circumstances it may be possible to have just one director. There is no upper limit on the number of directors. Much depends on the size of the business. Too many directors may make it difficult to run the business efficiently.
Finance	Limited companies usually find it easier to borrow money from banks.

Disadvantages of the private limited company form of business organisation

Availability of financial information

Financial information is not private.

Because a private limited company has gone through the process of incorporation, it has to make some of its financial information available for inspection to the general public. This can be a disadvantage in that competitors will then have access to this information.

Availability and sale of shares

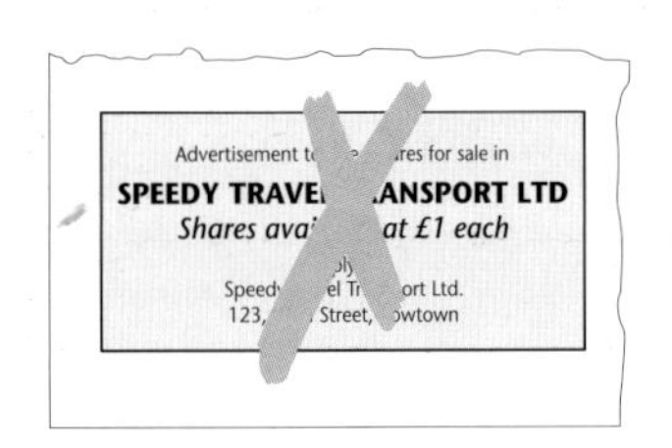

Shares cannot be offered for general sale.

While this can be used as a means of raising finance, there are some restrictions. Private limited companies cannot offer them for sale to the general public.

Lack of capital	If the business wishes to expand it may find that the existing shareholders are unable to provide more capital. Because shares cannot be sold to the general public, it may also be difficult to find new shareholders who are willing to invest money in the business.
Dividends	Shareholders will probably expect a share of the profits in the form of dividends. This can be a drain on the company's assets if the directors decide to pay a dividend. If no dividend is paid, shareholders may become unhappy with the way in which the company is being run.

ACTIVITY 2

Each of the following phrases below relates to either shares or dividends. Copy the outline table below and write each phrase in the appropriate column.

- gives the owner voting rights
- issued as a way of raising finance for the business
- a payment made to shareholders
- the amount paid can vary from year to year depending on the success of the business
- the value can go up or down over time
- allows the owner to attend the AGM of the company
- gives the owner part ownership of the business
- is usually paid twice a year

Dividend	Share

The London Stock Exchange.

Public limited companies

Features and advantages of the public limited company form of business organisation

There are a large number of public limited companies registered in the UK. A look at the share pages of most newspapers will give the names of just a few of the public limited companies which trade their shares on the London Stock Market.

Shares

This is one of the most important features of the this type of company organisation – the ability to trade shares freely on the Stock Exchange. The sale of shares is an extremely important method of raising finance and one of the most important advantages of this form of business organisation.

There are other important features of this form of business organisation:

- for a company to become a public limited company, it must have an issued share capital in excess of £50 000
- it may pay part of its profits to shareholders in the form of dividends.

The value of the shares of a public limited company can change for a number of reasons.

Usually they will increase in value if the Stock Market thinks:

- that the prospects of the company are good
- there is the possibility of a takeover bid
- the economy is doing well
- the asset value of the business is increasing.

They can fall in value for the opposite reasons.

Advantages of the public limited company form of business organisation

We have already seen that one of the main advantages of this form of business organisation is limited liability where shareholders can invest money in the business without running the risk of personal bankruptcy.

There are other advantages:

- Public limited companies can raise large sums of finance by offering shares for sale. The vast majority of capital raised by public limited companies is by this method.
- A public limited company will usually find it relatively easy to borrow money to help finance expansion plans.

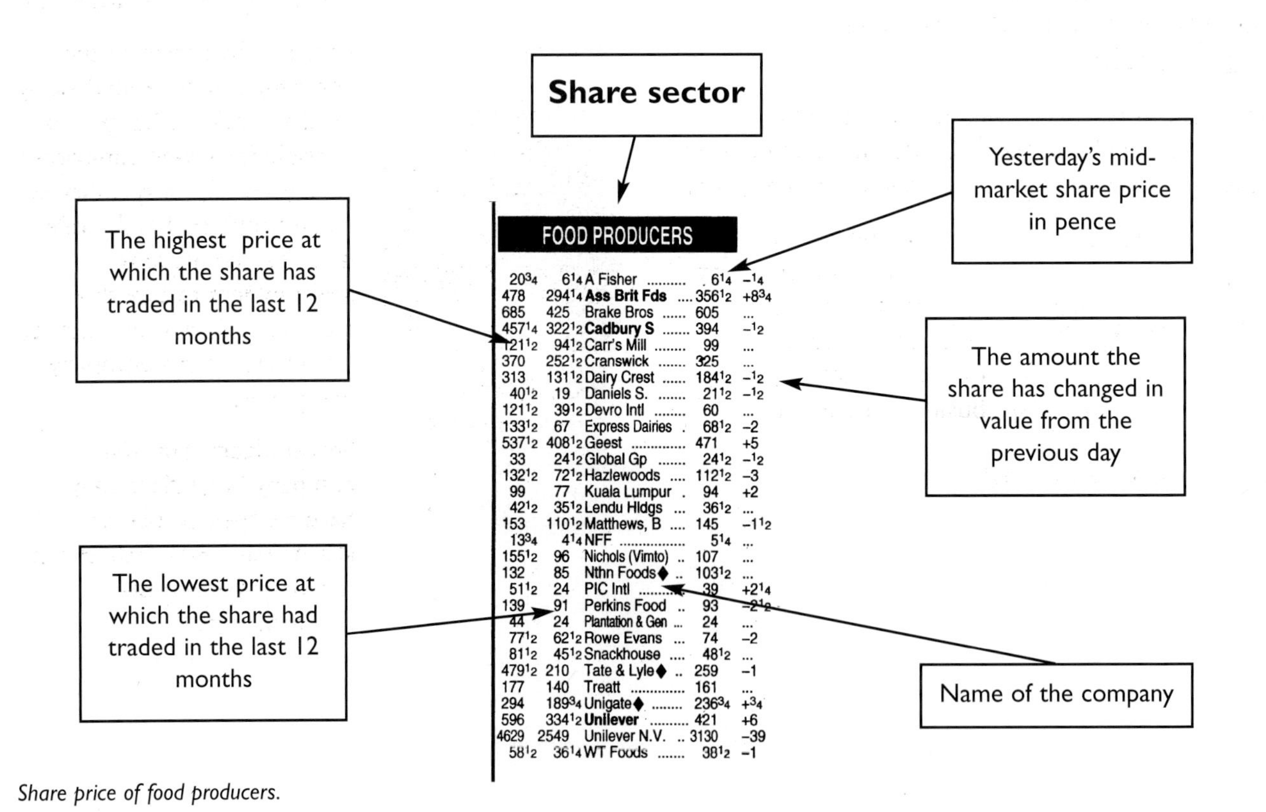

FOOD PRODUCERS				
20¾	6¼	A Fisher	6¼	–¼
478	294¼	**Ass Brit Fds**	356½	+8¾
685	425	Brake Bros	605	...
457¼	322½	**Cadbury S**	394	–½
121½	94½	Carr's Mill	99	...
370	252½	Cranswick	325	...
313	131½	Dairy Crest	184½	–½
40½	19	Daniels S.	21½	–½
121½	39½	Devro Intl	60	...
133½	67	Express Dairies	68½	–2
537½	408½	Geest	471	+5
33	24½	Global Gp	24½	–½
132½	72½	Hazlewoods	112½	–3
99	77	Kuala Lumpur	94	+2
42½	35½	Lendu Hldgs	36½	...
153	110½	Matthews, B	145	–1½
13¾	4¼	NFF	5¼	...
155½	96	Nichols (Vimto)	107	...
132	85	Nthn Foods♦	103½	...
51½	24	PIC Intl	39	+2¼
139	91	Perkins Food	93	–2½
44	24	Plantation & Gen	24	...
77½	62½	Rowe Evans	74	–2
81½	45½	Snackhouse	48½	...
479½	210	Tate & Lyle♦	259	–1
177	140	Treatt	161	...
294	189¾	Unigate♦	236¾	+¾
596	334½	**Unilever**	421	+6
4629	2549	Unilever N.V.	3130	–39
58½	36¼	WT Foods	38½	–1

Share price of food producers.

ACTIVITY 3 

1. Find a newspaper which has the share prices of a range of public limited companies.
2. Choose six companies which you are interested in or are familiar with and follow the way in which the share prices of the companies change over a period of time. Present the information in the form of a table.
3. Look for possible reasons why the price of the shares might have gone up or down on a particular day and present a summary of the information you find.

Disadvantages of the public limited company form of business organisation

Although there are a large number of public limited companies in the UK there are a number of disadvantages of this form of business organisation.

Cost off setting up

It is a complicated and expensive process to set up a public limited company or convert from one of the other forms of business organisation.

The cost of becoming a plc is high.

Financial information

The general public is allowed to request a copy of the company's accounts. This is usually made available in the form of an annual report which is sent to all shareholders automatically.

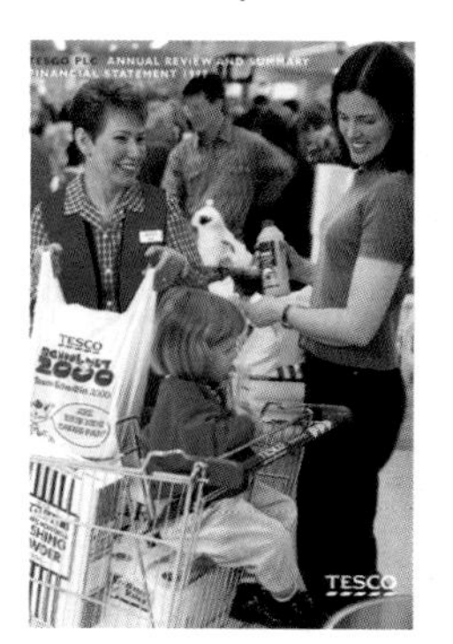

Financial information is sent out to all shareholders and is available for inspection by the general public.

Dividends

Shareholders will expect the company to perform well. They will usually expect a share of the profits to be paid in the form of dividends.

Take-over

Because the shares in the company can be traded easily on the Stock Exchange it is possible for other companies to buy up a large quantity of a company's shares. An offer may then be made to shareholders to buy their shares and, if sufficient agree, ownership of the company will change.

Shares in another company are easy to buy.

Shareholders own the company but, unless they have a large number of shares, have very little say in the way in which the company is run.

Ownership of shares

Public limited companies like BAA plc, the company which owns and operates London's Airports, have a large number of shares in circulation which are owned by other companies, individuals and banks. The pie chart below shows the how the ownership of BAA plc is made up.

BAA plc had the following shareholder analysis on 22 May 2000. There were 1 069 508 440 shares in circulation.

Ownership and division of shares

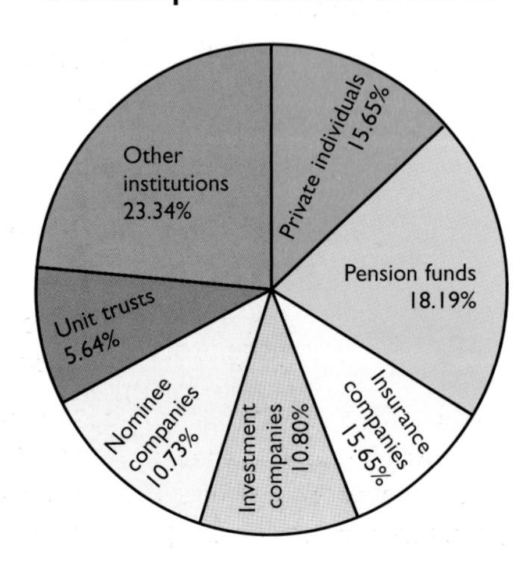

Size of share holding

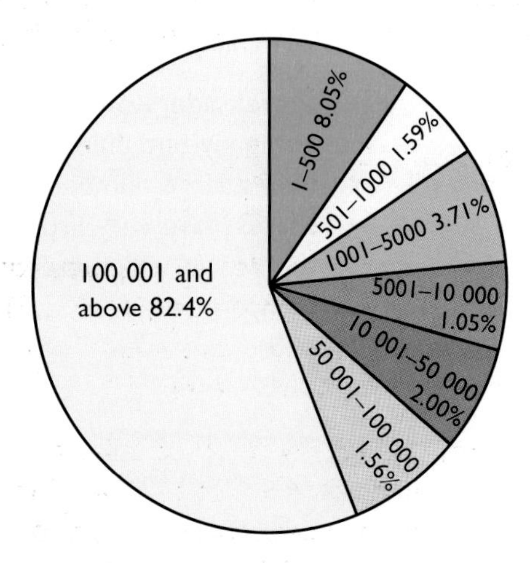

Shareholder profile of BAA plc

Source: BAA plc Annual Report to shareholders, 1999–2000

Major and minority shareholders

Private individuals usually own only a small percentage of most public limited companies. This is because they cannot afford to buy large numbers of shares – they are known as **minority shareholders**.

Major shareholders like banks and investment companies will own a large number of shares – they are known as **institutional investors** or **major shareholders** and will have much greater influence on the way in which the company is operated.

EXAM Practice Questions

1. Gerald Marsh and his wife are concerned about their farm's future as a partnership and are thinking of forming a private limited company.
   (a) Explain why Gerald and his wife may wish to change the business from a partnership to a private limited company. (4 marks)
   (b) Explain how the owners of the partnership would be affected if a private limited company were formed. (4 marks)

   (Adapted from OCR Business Studies, Q1 Higher Tier Case Study paper, June 2000.)

2. Many retailers of chocolates are small independent sole traders whilst the companies which manufacture chocolates are large public limited companies. Are these appropriate forms of ownership for these different businesses? Give reasons for your answers. (7 marks)

   (Adapted from OCR Business Studies, Q3 Higher Tier Common Core paper, June 2000.)

ADVICE ON HOW TO ANSWER THE QUESTIONS

1. (a) You will need to provide reasons explaining the advantages of changing the business to a private limited company. Your answer will be improved if you explain why and how the change to private limited company overcomes some of the disadvantages of the partnership form of business organisation.
   (b) This question requires you to provide an answer which concentrates on who owns the business and the way in which these owners will be affected by the change of company organisation.
2. To answer this question successfully you will need to consider and explain why there are so many sole trader-type businesses which are reasonably small in size. You should also consider the advantages of this particular form of business organisation. An explanation of why the plc form of business organisation is particularly suited to very large businesses will also be required.

EXAMINATION SUMMARY TIPS

- Learn the key features, advantages and disadvantages of both types of Incorporated business organisation.
- Make sure you are able to apply the advantages and disadvantages of each form of business organisation to the scenario given in the exam paper.
- Consider why businesses may decide to change the way in which they are organised.
- Recognise why both forms of business organisation will be appropriate for different business situations and sizes or types of business.

KEY TERMS

AGM *A yearly meeting of shareholders which, amongst other things, will elect directors to the board and confirm the amount of dividend to be paid.*

Board of directors *People usually elected by shareholders to represent their interests and make important decisions on how the company is to be operated.*

Chair(man) *The person who takes responsibility for the board of directors.*

Managing Director *The person responsible for putting into action the decisions made by the board of directors.*

Minority shareholders *Private individuals who may only own a small percentage of the shares of a company.*

Major shareholders *These are shareholders who own a large percentage of the shares of a company.*

Institutional investors *Banks and investment companies which may invest money on behalf of themselves or private individuals. They will own a large percentage of the shares of a company.*

Certificate of incorporation *Legal document issued by the Registrar of Companies allowing a business to trade as a limited liability organisation.*

Key Skills

Activity 3 provides an opportunity to read documents at Level 1 (C1.2) or Level 2 (C2.2), depending on the complexity of the material.

For the activity to be completed:
- material will need to be obtained from newspapers or periodicals and the information summarised and presented in a revised format
- an explanation of why the change in share price has occurred will need to be provided.

Unit 2.4 Franchises, holding and multinational companies, management buyouts

In the previous Units we have seen how businesses in the private sector are organised into four basic business forms.

The way in which these businesses structure the method by which they operate can vary significantly, depending on a wide range of factors. This Unit looks at some of the different ways in which businesses can operate.

Franchises

A franchise is **not** a form of business organisation but a type of marketing arrangement. A business which is trading as a franchise can be organised into any one of the four main forms of business organisation. Franchises have become extremely popular in the UK in recent years and are available in most sectors of business activity.

One of the most well-known businesses in the UK, McDonalds, operates restaurants which are either owned by the company or trade as franchises

There are many other well-known business names which are operated as franchises. An example is shown below.

ESSO – BUSINESS TO BUILD ON

A Leading Player in a tough market place

This is one of today's most exciting and challenging business opportunities. Working with one of Britain's largest retail operations, it's your chance to build on this opportunity now and into the future.

Esso moves with the times, developing its marketing in line with the increasing expectations of consumers. As a result, customers expect Esso to provide wider ranging retail outlets with the blend of services and products they want, wherever they want.

We provide the framework and setting within which you can manage a thriving retail business; you provide the drive and enthusiasm.

A business to build on

As a self-employed business person and agent for Esso, you are responsible for the day-to-day running of a substantial retail outlet.

- It will be a high turnover business, operating 365 days a year.
- Effective advertising helps you to sell fuel on behalf of Esso.
- You trade in the shop and sell goods on your own account.
- You employ, tzrain, manage and motivate your own staff.

A job for enthusiasts

Are you someone with good communication skills who positively wants to be a retailer? A numerate, literate, techno-fearless person who's not afraid of computers?

You need to be a committed businessman or woman with good organisational skills.

You will also need between £10 000 and £20 000 capital dependent upon the size and turnover of the service station shop to which you might be appointed.

An example of a franchise being offered for sale.

What is a franchise?

Franchise opportunities exist where an already established business (the **franchisor**) offers for sale to other businesses or individuals (the **franchisee**) the right to use its products, services and logos, usually in a defined area. Franchises are not cheap to buy. Usually, a considerable initial payment is required (as in the Esso example) and a percentage of the sales turnover of the business, known as a **royalty**, has to be paid on an annual basis in addition to the initial fee.

Advantages of franchises	**Disadvantages of franchises**
A designated area of operation with no competition from other franchises made available from the same company.	All supplies must usually be purchased from the franchisor at the price that they determine.
A tried and tested business idea.	A large amount of initial capital may be required.
Logos and products which are usually already established in the market.	Annual royalty payment based on profit or sales turnover may be required.
National advertising and promotion campaigns may be paid for by the franchisor.	The owner of the business might not have total control over the way in which the business operates.
Training and advice on how to run the business.	The business may not make enough profit to help cover the cost of the initial payment.
Reduced risk of business failure.	Losses have to be paid for by the franchisee.

Holding companies

This is a form of business which will trade as a private or public limited company. It will normally own all or the majority of shares in other businesses which will probably trade under different names. The table on page 52 shows how part of The Boots Company plc is organised.

There are a large number of other subsidiary companies owned by The Boots Company plc. Two of these are mentioned in the article below which explains about the purchase of the 'Clearasil' brand.

34 • • •

Business News

Boots pays £230m for Clearasil

By Adam Jay

BOOTS, the high street healthcare and chemists company, is to buy the acne treatment brand Clearasil from Procter & Gamble in a bid to expand its global coverage.

Boots Healthcare USA and Hermal Kurt Herrman GmbH — both wholly owned subsidiaries of Boots Healthcare International (BHI) — are to pay $340m (£230m) cash for the world's best-selling pimple-fighting medication.

The sum is payable on completion of the deal, which requires regulatory approval in the US, Germany and Japan.

BHI is the division of Boots that develops and markets medicines for over-the-counter sale, with brands including Nurofen painkillers and Strepsils throat lozenges. It is Europe's fastest-growing OTC medicines company, with skincare products accounting for 36pc of last year's £327m turnover.

Clearasil, sold in more than 50 countries and market leader in eight — including the US, UK and Germany — had sales last year amounting to $137m (£94m).

A newspaper headline announcing the purchase of another business.

Until relatively recently, another well-known company owned by The Boots Company plc was 'Do It All' which traded as a retailer providing do-it-yourself tools, and equipment and home furnishings. This business has now been sold to another company and now trades as Focus Do It All.

There are numerous businesses which choose to operate as **holding companies** and there are a number of reasons why this happens:

- A wide range of different business activities can trade under separate names.
- Economies of scale may be obtained by having one head office for all the companies owned by the holding company.
- The company may be able to trade in a number of different markets more easily.
- The overall management of the business may be improved.
- It is relatively easy to sell sections of the business.
- New businesses which have been bought can be integrated quickly into the overall structure.

ACTIVITY 1

The World Wide Web has a lot of pages of information about franchises. Using Internet access:

1. Use a **search engine** to find some web pages providing information about franchises. www.franchisebusiness.co.uk may be a good starting point.
2. Find out some information about a franchise which interests you.
3. Using a memo format similar to the one below, write a report to your teacher, giving your reasons why you think the franchise you have chosen would be a good or bad idea if it were to operate in the area where you live.

To:	Date:
From:	
Subject: Franchise recommendation	

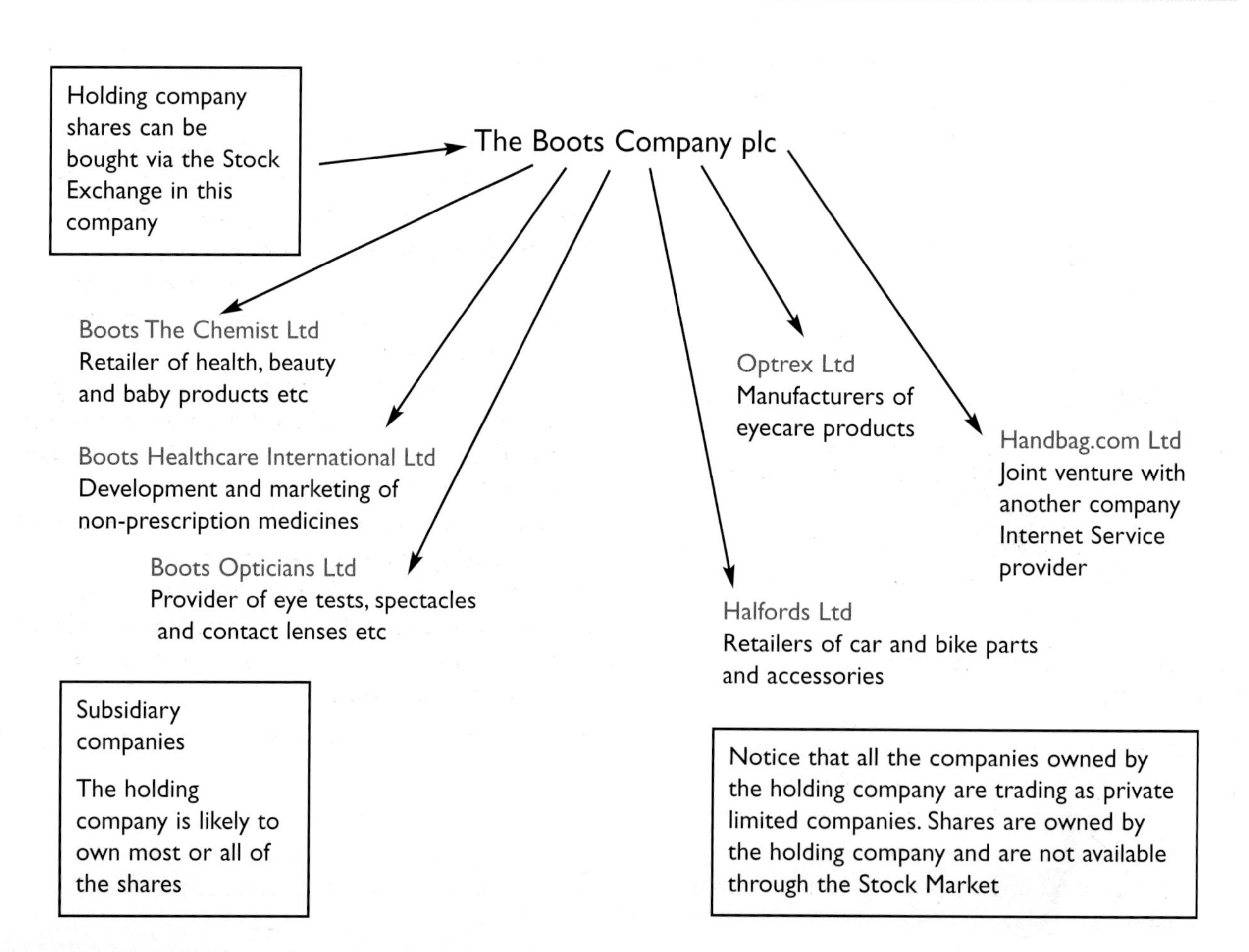

Simplified organisation chart of the Boots Company plc

Multinational companies

These are usually very large companies which may have a head office based in one country but manufacturing or service facilities in other countries. The number of **multinational companies** is increasing every year. This is happening on a world-wide basis but particularly in Europe as business activity in European countries becomes more and more closely integrated.

The Nestlé Group

The Swiss company Nestlé Group is a very large and well-known Multinational company with over 400 factories located in over 60 countries in all five continents. The product range of well-known branded goods produced by the company is enormous.

Advantages for multinational companies

There are a number of reasons why multinational companies exist.

- Manufacturing bases can be spread around the world nearer to the markets they serve.
- Economies of large-scale production can be obtained.
- Production may be located in countries where production costs are lower.

Disadvantages of multinational companies

Operating as a multinational company is not without its problems. The main problems are:

- Communication difficulties caused by being located in different countries.
- The high cost of transporting goods between countries.
- Coping with the differing legal requirements of different countries.
- Fluctuating exchange rates for different currencies.

ACTIVITY 2

1. Name four other multinational companies and list their types of products and services.
2. Explain why so many large public limited companies choose to operate as holding companies.
3. Outline the advantages of allowing companies owned by a holding company to continue to trade under different names.

ACTIVITY 3

The Dixons Group plc is a very large and well-known holding company. The company's website (www.dixons-group-plc.co.uk/) has a lot of information about the company.

1. Visit the website and obtain information about the subsidiary companies controlled by the Dixons Group plc.
2. Draw an organisation chart for the company showing the names of the subsidiary companies and the types of products or services provided by each company.
3. Find out the number of branches which each of the subsidiary companies operates.
4. Find the website of The Arcadia Group plc and find out which well-known High Street or brand names this company owns and operates as subsidiary companies.

Management buyouts

This is not a form of company organisation but a process where the existing management of a business buys the business from the owners. A management buyout is sometimes called an MBO.

Each year, a number of companies will sell all or parts of an existing business to the management team which look after the day-to-day running of the business. The managers will then become shareholders owning the new business.

Why do management buyouts happen?

Businesses change owners for many reasons. Management buyouts usually happen because:

- the owners want to sell the business, perhaps because it does not fit in with the overall objectives of the business or because it is not making much profit
- the managers make an offer to the existing owners to buy the business. This may happen because they feel they can run the business better
- the business has become insolvent and the managers buy the business from the liquidators. This means that managers will also keep their jobs.

One of the main problems of a management buyout is obtaining sufficient capital to buy the business in the first place. It cannot normally be financed through an issue of shares and therefore large sums of money will need to be borrowed to buy the business from the owners. The main problem is finding someone prepared to lend sufficient finance.

Capital is sometimes obtained from a merchant bank or venture capital organisation or both. These organisations specialise in providing finance to industry and commerce.

EXAM Practice Questions

(a) State four features of a franchise. (4 marks)

(b) Jason Lee has worked for Colliers plc for several years. Colliers plc both manufactures and sells chocolates. Jason is thinking of opening a new shop selling sweets and chocolates. Should he open the shop as a franchise or as an independent shop? Discuss the advantages of each option and give reasons for your answers. (8 marks)

(Adapted from OCR Business Studies, Q3 Higher Tier Common Core paper, June 2000.)

(a) This question requires four simple facts about franchises. No explanations are needed.

(b) To answer this question successfully, you will need to make a recommendation based on the evidence you provide. This evidence will need to consider the advantages and disadvantages of both operating as an independent shop and as a franchise selling the products of an already established chocolate business.

KEY TERMS

Franchise *A marketing arrangement which allows another business to trade in the same style as an existing business.*

Franchisor *The name given to the person or business who offers to franchise to other businesses its trading methods, products and business logos.*

Franchisee *The name given to a business or person buying a franchise.*

Royalty *A payment made to the franchisor based on the sales turnover of the franchise.*

Holding company *A company which owns a number of other companies.*

Subsidiary company *A company in which most or all of the shares are owned by a holding company.*

Joint venture *An arrangement where two or more companies set up and own another business which will trade under its own name.*

Multinational company *A company with manufacturing facilities in more than one country.*

Management buyout *A process of transferring the ownership of a company from the existing owners of the business to its managers.*

Venture capital *Finance provided for business activities which may have a high risk.*

Merchant bank *A bank which specialises in providing finance to business and commerce.*

EXAMINATION SUMMARY TIPS

- Learn the features, advantages and disadvantages of franchises and be prepared to write in detail about them with reference to a specific business situation.
- When answering examination questions which require you to explain something, always try to provide examples to illustrate the points you are making.
- Learn the difference between holding companies and multinational companies and consider why some businesses may wish to organise themselves in this way.
- Be prepared to explain why businesses choose to organise themselves in a particular way.

Key Skills

Activity 1 provides an opportunity to find and explore information at Level 1 using the Internet (IT 1.1) and present it (IT 1.2). To access Level 2 (IT 2.1 and IT 2.2), additional relevant websites will need to be searched and a more detailed report produced.

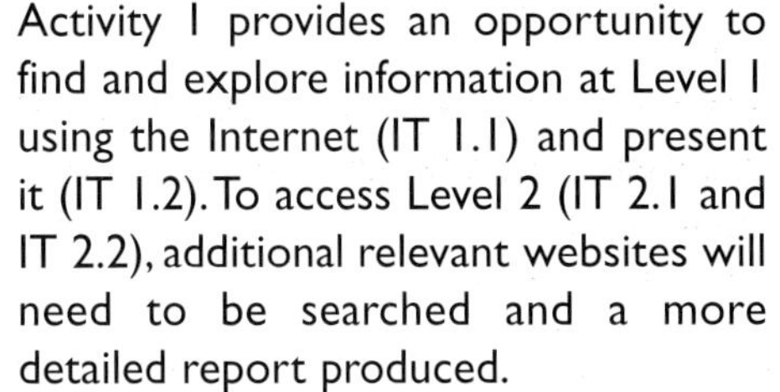

- The third part of the activity provides the opportunity to produce the evidence which will be needed for the Key Skills portfolio.
- This task will require you to write a report in the form of a memo using the information you have obtained.
- Images and data from the website could be included in the report.

Evidence may also be produced which meets the Communication Key Skill requirements at Level 1 (C1.3). A detailed and extended piece of work may satisfy the requirements for Level 2 (C2.3).

Unit 2.5 Public corporations

Public corporations are limited liability business activities in the public sector of the economy which provide a range of goods and services. They are owned and controlled by central government. Unit 1.3 gives more information on the public sector.

The number of public corporations in the United Kingdom has decreased significantly over the last 10 years. Today there are very few public corporations remaining. The BBC (the British Broadcasting Corporation) is one example. It is funded through the TV licence fee.

Another is the Post Office – recently renamed Consignia. Its future as a public corporation has been the subject of debate in Parliament and consideration has been given to transferring it to the private sector. It obtains its finance through the charges it makes for the services provided. Any surplus money goes to the Government.

Privatisation

Since 1979, a large number of public corporations have been privatised. This is a process of selling public corporations to shareholders in the private sector of the economy.

Why did privatisation occur?

There are many reasons why governments decide to sell and transfer business activity from the public to the private sector.

Some of these reasons might include:

- a desire or need by Government to raise money to be used in other projects. Money is raised by selling off the assets of the public corporation to the private sector
- the need to get the private sector to invest money and improve the provision of services for consumers
- some public corporations were too **bureaucratic**. The working relationship between employer and employee was poor, with over-staffing resulting in high costs.
- a wish to improve efficiency and increase the amount of competition. British Gas was once a public corporation and the only supplier of gas in the UK. British Gas now trades in the private sector and faces competition from other gas suppliers. The price of gas has fallen since this has happened.

How much can you save with Severn Trent Energy?

Price list for domestic gas and electricity supply in the Powergen area

Severn Trent Energy, owned by a company previously selling just water, is now able to sell gas and electricity.

Virgin Energy, a new company, is now providing competition for the supply of gas to homes.

Nationalisation

In the United Kingdom, many public corporations came into existence following the end of the Second World War. Today, nationalisation, or the process of transferring the ownership of firms from the private sector to the public sector, is rarely considered by governments.

There are, though, some clear reasons why nationalisation of many of the United Kingdom's industries and firms did occur. These reasons include:

- a decision by a Government that nationalisation is a policy which it wishes to follow
- an attempt to rescue a failing company or industry and therefore protect jobs
- a lack of willingness by private industry to invest money in new business opportunities

ACTIVITY

Investigate the market for domestic electricity supply to your home by:

- find out the name of the business which supplies electricity to your home or school
- find out the name of other suppliers of electricity in the area in which you live
- compare the prices and tariffs charged by each business
- collect together some advertising material provided by domestic electricity suppliers and compare the ways in which they try to market their services
- explain why many of these businesses have information available on the Internet and allow applications for the provision of electricity to be made electronically.

EXAM Practice Questions

Explain one way in which the aims of a public sector enterprise such as the BBC are different from those of a private sector organisation such as Next plc. (2 marks)

(Adapted from OCR Business Studies, Q1 Foundation Tier Combined Course paper, 1 June 1999.)

ADVICE ON HOW TO ANSWER THE QUESTION

This question requires you to consider how the aims of public and private sector organisations differ. You are then required to answer, by providing a detailed explanation of one factor, within the context given, why these two organisations will have differing aims.

KEY TERMS

Public corporation *An organisation which is owned by central government.*

Privatisation *The process of selling a public corporation to the private sector.*

Nationalisation *A process where the Government buys the assets of a firm and transfers it to the public sector.*

Bureaucracy *Too many official procedures. Sometimes referred to as too much 'red tape'.*

Over-staffing *Too many people employed to do a job.*

EXAMINATION SUMMARY TIPS

- Learn the difference between public and private sector organisations.
- Understand and be able to explain why there are now not very many public corporations.
- Recognise why there is a need for both sectors in a modern-day economy.
- Be prepared to give examples from both sectors of the UK economy and say why the changes have occurred.
- Learn the advantages and disadvantages which are associated with the privatisation of public corporations.

Key Skills

The Activity provides an opportunity to read and obtain information from documents at Level 1 (C1.2) and Level 2 (C2.2), depending on the complexity of the material used.

The evidence to be included in the Key Skills portfolio will be a summary of information obtained. The source of the material should also be shown.

Finance

SECTION 3

- Introductory Activity
- Unit 3.1 Profit
- Unit 3.2 Sources of finance
- Unit 3.3 Cash flow forecasts and statements
- Unit 3.4 Trading, profit and loss accounts
- Unit 3.5 Balance sheets

Learning Objectives: To develop:

- knowledge and understanding of the role which finance plays in the operation and development of a business
- understanding of, and the ability to use, techniques used by business in the management of finance
- the skills of selection, interpretation and analysis of financial data
- the ability to apply understanding of finance to given situations
- the skill of making reasoned judgement as it applies to financial decisions.

Introductory Activity

Most public limited companies like J Sainsbury plc and Tesco plc make financial information available to the general public. This can be in the form of:

- information printed in newspapers.
- Annual Reports made available to shareholders and possible new investors.
- newspaper stories detailing the latest financial information about a company.

Newspaper advert by CGNU plc providing information about the company's financial permance.

Group Profit and Loss Account (unaudited)

Loss before tax of £56m due to lower UK electricity prices and nuclear output.

Interim dividend of 2.7p per ordinary share in line with rebased dividend policy.

Further accounting life extensions announced.

Like-for-like output-adjusted operating costs down £32m.

Further progress with North American investments.

Sale of Swalec for £210m and major new offtake contract agreed.

	Business Performance (excluding exceptionals) 6 months ended 30 September 00 £ million	6 months ended 30 September 99 £ million
Turnover	1,084	913
Operating profit	57	148
Share of joint venture	24	–
Loss on disposal of discontinued activities	–	–
Net financing charges	(137)	(93)
(Loss)/profit on ordinary activities before tax	(56)	55
Taxation	5	(18)
(Loss)/profit on ordinary activities after tax	(51)	37

Extract from newspaper advert providing information about the financial performance of British Energy plc.

financial highlights

Group sales	up 10.7%
UK sales	up 7.5%
International sales	up 42.0%
Group profit before tax†	up 10.2%
Earnings per share†‡	up 10.1%
Dividend per share	up 10.4%

	24 weeks 2000	24 weeks 1999
Group sales (including value added tax) (£m)	10,084	9,112
Group profit before tax† (£m)	422	383
Profit on ordinary activities before tax (£m)	415	381
Earnings per share†‡ (p)	4.48	4.07
Dividend per share (p)	1.48	1.34

Front cover and extracts from Tesco plc interim report to Shareholders.

Profits rise for slim Unilever

ANGLO-DUTCH giant Unilever's slimming programme is working a treat.

Yesterday the Magnum ice-cream, Dove soap and Flora margarine group reported fine third-quarter profits and City admirers told each other how well the old biddy was looking.

Late last year Unilever announced a Path To Growth strategy, which involved dumping about 1,200 of its 1,600 brands.

The rest, ranging from Ben & Jerry's to Close-Up toothpaste and the Slim-Fast range, account for more than three-quarters of Unilever's sales. Profits in the third quarter, said UK chairman Niall Fitzgerald, rose 7 per cent to 1,403million euros (£842million).

Unilever shares shot up 21p to 494p, only a touch below their year's high of 497p.

ROGER NUTTALL

Restructuring the business has helped to improve profits.

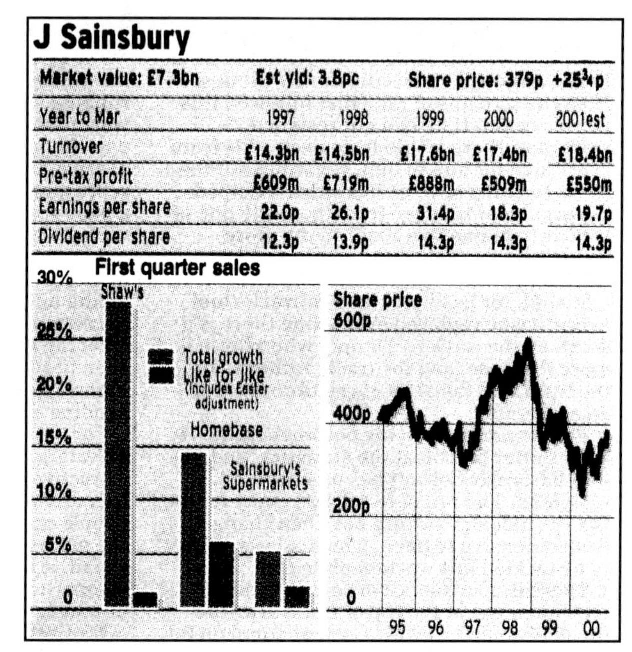
J Sainsbury

Market value: £7.3bn | Est yld: 3.8pc | Share price: 379p +25¾p

Year to Mar	1997	1998	1999	2000	2001est
Turnover	£14.3bn	£14.5bn	£17.6bn	£17.4bn	£18.4bn
Pre-tax profit	£609m	£719m	£888m	£509m	£550m
Earnings per share	22.0p	26.1p	31.4p	18.3p	19.7p
Dividend per share	12.3p	13.9p	14.3p	14.3p	14.3p

Statistical information on the financial performance of J Sainsbury plc.

Arcadia Group

Market value: £81m	Est yld: -		Share price: 42p +2p		
Year to Mar	1997	1998	1999	2000	2001est
Turnover	£1.35bn	£1.45bn	£1.50bn	£1.96bn	£1.75bn
Pre-tax profit	£57.6m	£81.1m	£47.8m	-£153m	£25m
Earnings per share	23.8p	31.2p	16.2p	-83.8p	11p
Dividend per share	10.0p	11.7p	11.7p	-	-

Sales last three years

£1.5bn
Womenswear
£1.2bn
£900m
£600m
Menswear
£300m
0
98 99 00 98 99 00

Share price

600p
500p
400p
300p
200p
100p
0
95 96 97 98 99 00

Source: Daily Telegraph *20 Oct 2000 p.36.*

Arcadia plunges £153m into the red

BY KATE RANKINE
DEPUTY CITY EDITOR

ARCADIA, the country's second biggest clothing retailer after Marks & Spencer, yesterday plunged into a £153m pre-tax loss for the year, axed its final dividend and unveiled plans to close a further 55 shops.

Only six months ago Arcadia, which includes Dorothy Perkins, Top Shop, Wallis and Miss Selfridge, said it would close 400 stores with the loss of 3,500 jobs. Yesterday chief executive John Hoerner vowed to stay at the company until he had succeeded in turning it round.

"When I took on the Arcadia job, I made a commitment to see it through as a success and I intend to see it through. I don't know how long it will take. It's not something that's going to happen in the next three months."

The £153m pre-tax loss, on sales of almost £2 billion, for the year ending August 26 was struck after a £144m exceptional charge. Some £107m covered the costs of closing 455 stores, a quarter of its trading sites, while most of the remainder is for integrating last year's acquisition of the Sears womenswear brands.

Arcadia shares yesterday edged 2 higher to 42p on hopes of more positive current trading. However, Mr Hoerner said: "There's been a relatively robust start to winter. But I've had my head kicked in at Christmas in the past and I'm now a very cautious man."

Mr Hoerner also admitted that Dial, its home shopping venture with Littlewoods, had been very disappointing. Sales fell because of problems fulfilling orders.

Questor: Page 36

Arcadia Group plc reports of disappointing financial performance.

Debenhams buoyed by sales lift

BY ROSIE MURRAY-WEST

DEBENHAMS shares jumped 10pc yesterday as the department store chain posted a better-than-expected 7½pc rise in like-for-like sales for the past seven weeks.

Belinda Earl, chief executive making her City debut, said sales had picked up across the board and the group was well prepared for pre-Christmas sales. "I can't say whether the troubles on the high street are over, but we have seen prices stabilise in the last few months."

Ms Earl said full-year pre-tax profit fell from £139m to £130m, while sales increased 1·4pc to £1·4 billion. This was in line with analysts' expectations.

Rowan Morgan, retail analyst at Teather & Greenwood, said although the sales figures were excellent, the like-for-like figure for the seven weeks to October 14 were distorted by a weak period last year.

He said: "This probably won't continue although the evidence is that the company is doing very well. However, it is difficult to see the shares racing away because of the sector they are in."

Debenhams has invested heavily in its online and catalogue shopping arm. Ms Earl said: "It is very important for our customers to be able to access us through a number of channels."

Debenhams has been working on its brand image, refurbishing the stores and adding clothes by designers such as Jasper Conran. "It is a point of difference for us," Ms Earl said. "We are aiming to challenge the perception of a fuddy-duddy department store. If we can just get people across the threshold, they will find something that is for them."

The group has introduced the designer John Rocha to its range, she said. "The clothes are doing fabulously well, across men's, women's and childrenswear."

The company plans to open three new stores in the next year, in Carlisle, Oxford and Uxbridge. Refurbishments are planned in Torquay, Staines and Crawley.

Debenhams shares closed up 17 at 194½p.

Newspaper report of improved financial performance by Debenhams.

ACTIVITY

Obtain similar examples of the types of information shown above about companies in the news.

Produce a 'scrap book' book of approximately five or six pages showing some of the financial information which has been made available by companies or written about them in the newspapers. Explain briefly what this information tells you about the company.

Unit 3.1 Profit

What is profit?

In its simplest form, **profit** is the amount of money left over from an activity once the costs of that activity have been paid for. Profit is sometimes used as a measure of how successful a business activity has been.

There are several different types of profit figures which can be calculated by businesses.

- **Gross profit** is the amount of profit made by a business as a result of buying and selling goods or services but without paying for any of the day-to-day or other expenses of running the business. It can be calculated using the following formula:

> *Gross profit* = *sales revenue* less the cost of buying the goods which have been sold

- **Net profit** takes into account the profit made as a result of buying and selling goods or services but also makes an allowance for the costs involved in running the business, eg wages and telephone calls. It can be calculated using the following formula:

> *Net profit* = gross profit less the costs of running the business

Table 3.1 below shows how the gross and net profit of a business might be calculated:

	£
Sales	100 000
less Cost of goods sold	40 000
GROSS PROFIT	60 000
less Expenses	40 000
NET PROFIT	20 000

Table 3.1 Gross and Net Profit calculation

There are other definitions of profit which are dealt with in Unit 3.4.

Profit and sales revenue

Instead of calculating profit as an amount of money, some businesses also calculate profit as a percentage of the value of the goods sold. This is called the profit to sales ratio. It can be calculated using one or both of the following formulae:

$$\frac{\text{Gross profit}}{\text{Sales revenue}} \times 100 \quad \text{OR} \quad \frac{\text{Net profit}}{\text{Sales revenue}} \times 100$$

Using the information in Table 3.1, the following profit to sales ratio figures would be obtained:

$$\frac{£60\ 000}{£100\ 000} \times 100 = 60\% \qquad \frac{£20\ 000}{£100\ 000} \times 100 = 20\%$$

These are important measures of profit as they can be used to:

- see if a business activity is worth doing
- make comparisons with profit which has been made in the past
- compare the profitability of different businesses.

Comparing Profit over time

All of these ways of calculating profit can be used as a means of comparing the financial performance of a company over a period of time.

This type of information can be presented in the form of a table:

	1999	2000	2001
Sales revenue (£m)	100	120	140
Gross profit (£m)	20	30	17.5
Profit to sales ratio (%)	20	25	12.5

Table 3.2 Sales revenue and gross profit from 1999 to 2001

	1999	2000	2001
Sales revenue (£m)	100	120	140
Net profit (£m)	5	12	7
Net profit to sales ratio (%)	5	10	5

Table 3.3 Sales revenue and net profit from 1999 to 2001

This information can also be presented in the form of a graph. The line graph below shows the gross and net profit to sales ratios based on the information in Tables 3.2 and 3.3.

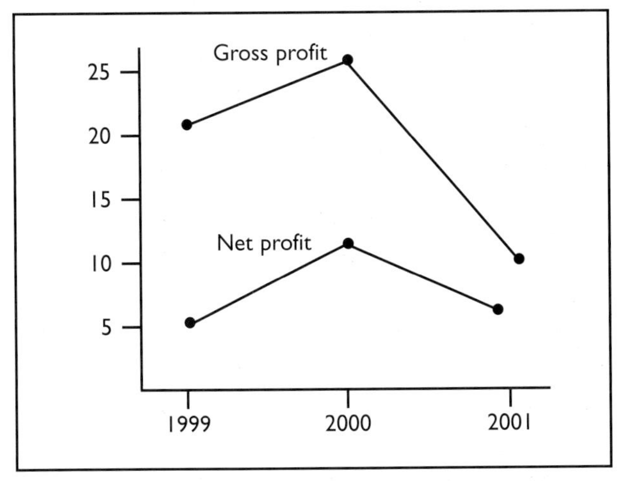

Table 3.4 Gross and net profit to sales ratio from 1999 to 2001

ACTIVITY 1

A firm has annual sales of £100 000 on goods which it has bought for £40 000. Wages and other costs are £20 000.

1. Using the above information calculate:
   - the gross profit
   - the net profit
   - the gross profit to sales ratio
   - the net profit to sales ratio.
2. Give three examples of expenses which a business might have to pay.

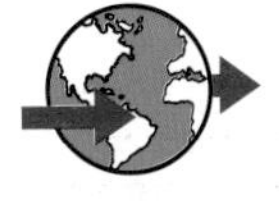

What affects the amount of profit or loss?

The amount of profit or loss which a business makes can depend on a large number of things. These might include:

- the type and size of business. A window cleaner may not have a large value of sales; a public limited company such as Tesco plc which has many branches and sells a large quantity of goods each day will make much more profit than the window cleaner.

A window cleaner.

A supermarket.

- the objectives of the business. A profit-making business such as McDonald's wants to make money selling burgers and other products. A non-profit making activity, such as a charity like Oxfam, may want to concentrate on raising money rather than making a profit.

Businesses may have different objectives.

- the demand for the product. Some products may be popular and sell in large quantities, eg aerosol deodorants. Other products may no longer be in demand due to changing tastes and fashions, eg typewriters.

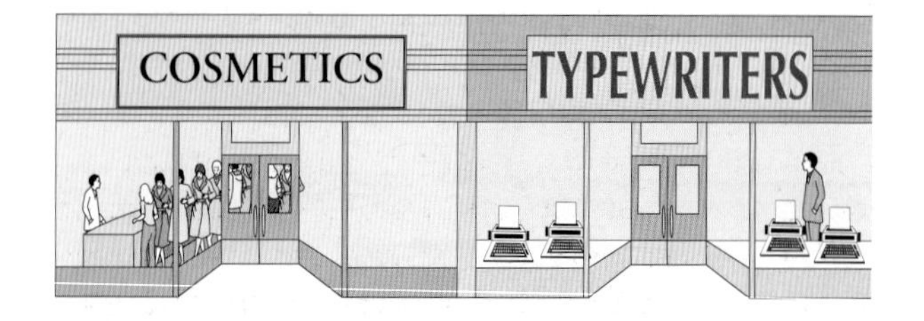

Demand for different products will not be the same.

- the price consumers are willing to pay. Designer jeans and perfume are often sold at prices much higher than the costs of making them. Ballpoint pens are sold at relatively low prices.

Prices of products can vary significantly.

- the way in which the business controls its costs. Paying workers a low hourly wage rate and using a source of cheaper raw materials helps to keep the cost down.
- the **profit margin** or **mark-up** the business is able to use. This is the difference between the price paid for an item and the price at which it is sold. Groceries generally have a low profit margin because they sell in large volumes, whilst other products which do not sell in large numbers may have a high profit

Wage rates are being kept to a minimum.

margin, eg high-class jewellery. The size of the profit margin or mark-up on a product is very important to a business because of the need to pay for the running costs of the business.

These products will not produce much profit per can.

- the amount of competition. Where a business has a lot of competitors and is selling an identical product to its competitors, it is not able to sell the product at a price it would like to charge. The business has to accept the price which consumers are willing to pay. This situation is known as **perfect competition.** In this situation a new business will find it easy to enter the market.

Too much competition affects profits.

- the cost of setting up a business. Starting up a new business can be expensive. Some new businesses may find it hard to break into a market and make a profit.

Loss-making Egg expands

Jill Treanor

More than £400m of deposits were removed from telephone-cum-internet bank Egg over the past three months as investors chased higher savings rates at rival banks.

The defectors had high average balances of up to £100,000 in their accounts.

But the bank, in which Prudential has a majority stake, tried to put a positive gloss on the news by insisting that the lost customers were being replaced by a larger number of younger, potentially more profitable ones.

Egg admitted that its losses had widened by 7% in the nine-months to the end of September to £115m. But, Mike Harris, the chief executive, said the business remained on track to break into profit in the fourth quarter of 2001.

Not all businesses are successful straight away.

Source: Guardian

Why is profit important to most businesses?

Profit can also be considered as 'a return on an investment' where the owners of a business expect something back in return for investing their money in the business. Profit is also 'a reward for taking a risk'.

Profit is usually paid to the owners of the business in the form of:

- **dividends** to shareholders of incorporated businesses (public limited companies and private limited companies)
- **drawings** to the owners of unincorporated businesses (sole traders and partnerships).

Profit also has another important function. It can be used to help finance and develop business activity or buy new equipment and buildings. The profit that is kept by the business is called **retained profit** and it has two real advantages over borrowing money to finance business development:

- it does not have to be paid back, unlike a bank loan or mortgage
- no interest has to be paid, unlike a bank loan or mortgage.

There may, though, be a cost of using profit in this way. This is called **opportunity cost** (see Unit 1.1 page 4). This is the cost associated with not using the profit for some other activity, eg paying out profit in the form of dividends to shareholders. Whenever a business or an individual has to decide between alternatives, an opportunity cost is involved in that there is a 'price' to be paid for not having something.

For example, if you have £1 to spend and cannot decide between a drink and something to eat but cannot afford both, choosing the drink means that you have had to give up the chance of having something to eat. Therefore there is a lost opportunity – the cost of which is not having something to eat.

Profit and financial records

Maintaining financial records and calculating profit is important for a business. It needs to know whether an activity is worthwhile and whether it should continue with it. The process of keeping financial records, calculating, checking and comparing profit along with other financial information is called accounting. The document created by accountants and used to help calculate profit is called a trading, profit and loss account. More information on this is in Unit 3.4.

Profit and break-even analysis

The amount of net profit that a business might make at a given level of output, when goods or services are sold at a particular price, can be calculated using a technique called break-even analysis. This technique is dealt with in more detail in Unit 4.3.

EXAM Practice Questions

Read the information below and answer the questions which follow.

	2000 £ 000	2001 £ 000
Sales revenue	£200	£240
Gross profit	£40	£30
Net profit	£15	£20

Bowton Garage Ltd Summary of Performance 2000–2001

(a) Explain the factors which might have caused an increase in sales revenue between 2000 and 2001. (6 marks)

(b) Calculate the percentage change in:
Gross profit (3 marks)
Net profit (3 marks)
Net profit to sales (7 marks)
between 2000 and 2001.

(c) Based on the financial information in the table above, evaluate the performance of the company in 2001 compared to 2000. (4 marks)

(Adapted from OCR Business Studies, Q2 Higher Tier Common Core paper, June 2000.)

ADVICE ON HOW TO ANSWER THE QUESTIONS

(a) The 'command ' word in the question is 'explain'. Therefore you are required to write a detailed response to the question, not just 'Sales revenue has increased'. Rather than listing the things which might affect sales revenue, make sure that you provide detailed information on **why** the sales revenue of the business has gone up. Your answers should relate to a garage.

(b) This question is designed to test your numerical abilities. When answering questions like this, start off by writing down the formula and then substitute the figures you are working with into the formula. Do not miss out any steps of the calculation as marks will be available for each step.

(c) The command word in the question is 'evaluate'. This means that you have to provide a very detailed answer which considers all possible factors. You may need to look at the information from the point of view of both business and shareholders. Try to determine which of the two sets of financial information is the best, giving reasons for your decision.

KEY TERMS

Profit *Money left over from sales after all costs have been paid.*

Sales revenue *Quantity of goods sold multiplied by the selling price.*

Gross profit *Sales revenue minus cost of sales.*

Net profit *Gross profit minus expenses.*

Profit margin *The difference between sales revenue and the cost of the item. This is sometimes expressed as a percentage.*

Mark-up *The amount added to the purchase price of a product to give the selling price. This is sometimes expressed as a percentage.*

Perfect competition *A situation where a market has a large number of buyers and sellers which are selling an identical product. Firms can enter and leave the market easily. All consumers know the price being paid for the product.*

Dividends *That part of a company's profit paid out to shareholders.*

Drawings *Business profits paid to the owners of a sole trader or partnership.*

Retained profit *Profit which is kept by the business for its own use.*

Opportunity cost *The cost of having to miss out on the next best alternative.*

EXAMINATION SUMMARY TIPS

- Learn the difference between the various types of profit.
- Learn how to calculate profit in different ways.
- Be prepared to comment on how profit can be used as a way of measuring the success of a business over a period of time.
- Consider the factors which can influence the amount of profit which a business makes.
- Recognise why profit is important for the future of a business.

Key Skills

The Activity provides an opportunity for you to achieve Application of Number Key Skills at Level 1 (N 1.2).

- You will need to present your information clearly, including the formula you are using to do the calculations.
- Make sure that you show each step of the calculation.

Unit 3.2 Sources of finance

Why do businesses need finance?

In the previous unit we saw how important profit is to most businesses. All businesses will need finance at some stage in order for them start up, grow in size, perhaps buy new machinery or help with the day-to-day running of the business.

There are many reasons why a business will need finance. Sometimes finance is needed for just a short period of time to help overcome a temporary shortage of funds, for example when waiting for a customer to pay a large bill. On other occasions, finance may be needed for a much longer period of time, for example when buying a new building.

Some other reasons why businesses need finance are given below:

Types of finance

Finance can come from a number of different sources within the business, or from outside the business. Finance that comes from within the business is known as **internal finance** and Finance that comes from outside the business is known as **external finance**.

Not all sources of finance are available to every business. Some of the reasons why not all sources of finance are available are given below:

- sole traders and partnerships (unincorporated businesses) are not able to raise finance by selling shares
- limited companies (incorporated businesses) cannot take extra partners in the hope of raising more finance
- businesses with a poor financial record are unlikely to find many banks willing to lend money
- business activities which are considered to be very risky or have a poor future will also find it difficult raise finance.

Reason	Example
Starting up a new business	A person setting up a new business installing and maintaining burglar alarms.
Internal growth	Buying new manufacturing equipment as a result of increased demand for products.
Take-over or acquisition of another company	The Royal Bank of Scotland plc which has taken over the National Westminster Bank plc
Replacing old machinery and equipment	Buying new computer equipment to replace computers which have been in use for several years.
Moving to new premises	The business may have outgrown its existing premises or may want to move to a more suitable location.

Finance and time

The length of time for which a business needs finance is known as a **time period**. Business may require finance for different lengths of time. These time periods are usually called the short, medium and long term. An indication of the different amounts of time which each time period covers is shown in Tables 3.5 and 3.6 below. Different sources of finance may be used for different time periods. In some cases, the same source of finance may be used to finance an activity over different time periods.

Internal finance

This is money that comes from within the business. There is normally no cost to the business associated with internal finance because the business is using its own money. However, there is an opportunity cost involved because once the business has used the money, it cannot use it for another purpose. Table 3.5 below shows some of the sources of internal finance.

Time period	Short term (Up to 12 months)	Medium term (1–3 years)	Long term (3 years or more)
Internal source of finance	Cash in bank	Retained profit Sale of assets	Retained profit Owners' investment

Table 3.5 Sources of internal finance

External finance

In the case of external finance, there is usually some form of cost involved in obtaining the money. This may be in the form of **interest** which has to be paid or giving up some of the ownership of the business to the person or institution providing the money.

In some cases, **security** in the form of an asset owned by the business, of a similar or greater value, has to be offered to the lender of the money. Providing security for a loan means that in the event of the business being unable to pay back the loan, ownership of the asset transfers to the lender; who may then sell it. For example, when buying a property with the help of a mortgage loan, the document detailing the ownership of the property has to be given to the lender of the money. In the event of the borrowed money not being re-paid, the lender has the right to sell the property in order to get back the money which was lent. Table 3.6 below shows some of the sources of finance available to most businesses and the time periods for which these sources are usually used.

Time period	Short term (Up to 12 months)	Medium term (1–3 years)	Long term (3 years or more)
External source of finance	Overdraft Trade credit Factoring	Bank loan Lease Hire purchase Grants	Bank loan Mortgage Taking a new partner Share issue Lease Hire purchase Debenture

Table 3.6 Sources of external finance

Table 3.7 over the page gives more information on the type, use and costs of finance.

Type of finance	Use of finance	Cost of finance
Overdraft – this is an arrangement with a bank where a business will be able to withdraw more money from its bank account than it actually has. The amount of the overdraft may vary on a daily basis as money is paid into and taken out of the account.	Usually used to help the business overcome a short-term shortage of funds.	Interest is charged on the daily amount of money which the business owes to the bank.
Trade credit – when a business sells goods it sometimes allows its customer to take the goods away without paying for them immediately. The goods will have to be paid for within an agreed period of time.	This source of finance allows a business to sell the goods before payment for them is due. It helps businesses which have a temporary shortage of funds.	The period of credit is usually interest-free.
Factoring – a system of selling off debts to another company.	This source of finance is used mainly to help business manage its cash flow.	The debts may have to be sold at slightly less than their current value.
Retained profit – profit which is made by the business but which is kept back for its own use.	Retained profit may be used to help finance the purchase of many things which could include equipment, premises and even a research and development programme into new products.	There is no cost involved as the business is using its own money. However there is a an opportunity cost involved as once the profit has been used it cannot be used for something else, eg payment of increased dividends to shareholders.
Sale of assets – selling off and turning into cash something which the business owns. The assets which are sold may not be needed any longer by the business.	This source may be used to help finance the purchase of equipment.	No cost involved other than the opportunity cost of not being able to use the asset again.
Bank loan – an amount of money borrowed from a bank, usually for a stated purpose. In some cases, the bank may want to take a security over an asset in case the money is not repaid. The loan is usually for a fixed period of time.	This source may be used to help finance some form of business development or the purchase of new equipment. It may also be used to help a new business start up.	The money which has been borrowed has to be repaid together with interest.
Lease – a method of obtaining items for a stated period of time. At the end of the lease the items return to the owner. This source is ideally suited for items which have a relatively short life because of the amount of use or developments in technology or where the items are very expensive.	Company cars, lorries, computer equipment and buildings such as factories are examples of items obtained through operating leases. Many shops operate from leased premises. Leased goods are not owned by the user.	Monthly or annual payments have to be made for the right to use the equipment.
Hire purchase – a system of obtaining items in return for a monthly payment over a given period of time. The items do not become the property of the user until the final payment has been made.	Company cars, lorries and computer equipment are examples of items obtained through hire purchase.	A deposit has to be paid followed by monthly payments which may include an interest payment.
Grants – an amount of money usually made available for a specific purpose by the Government and/or local councils.	Factories, costs of training of employees in new skills or the purchase of new equipment can sometimes be financed by grants.	Grants do not usually need repaying. The finance obtained from a grant usually has to be used for a specific purpose.
Owners' investment – the existing owners of the business may invest more money.	This source may be used to help pay for a major business development such as a take-over of another business or pay off some long-term debts.	There is no cost involved to the business. The ownership structure of the business may change.
Mortgage – a very long-term method of borrowing money which requires some form of security.	The finance is used to help fund the purchase of property.	The money which has been borrowed has to be repaid together with interest.
Taking a new partner – partnerships can obtain additional finance by selling off part of the business to a new partner.	A new partner may bring new skills to the business. The finance that the partner brings may be used to buy new equipment, premises or buy another business.	The new partner will have a say in the running of the business and will be entitled to a share of any profits.
Share issue – a source of finance used by limited companies to raise finance in return for a 'share' in the business.	Finance raised from a share issue may be used to fund a major business development such as a take-over or extension to a factory.	Dividends may have to be paid on the shares and each share represents part ownership of the business. Shareholders are entitled to have a say in the running of the company.
Debenture – a long-term loan which is usually secured against an asset. The loan is normally for a fixed period of time.	This source of finance may be used to finance the purchase of some new equipment.	The money which has been borrowed has to be repaid together with interest.

Table 3.7 Type, use and costs of finance

Costs and uses of finance

Businesses will need to use finance for a wide variety of reasons. Some of these reasons, together with the costs of the finance, are shown in the table on page 70. In some cases, the provider of the finance may be taking a risk, in which case the cost of the finance may be much higher or some form of security to protect the investment may be required.

ACTIVITY 1

Use each of the different sources of finance in the list below as definitions for the sentences which follow.

HIRE PURCHASE MORTGAGE

LEASING OVERDRAFT LOAN

(a) is when a business uses equipment but does not own it until it has made the final payment
(b) is when a business borrows a large sum of money to purchase or improve a building
(c) is when a bank allows a business to spend more money than there is in its current account
(d) is when a business uses equipment but does not own it.
(e) is an amount of money which is given to the business to buy something. The money has to be paid back in full. (5 marks)

(Adapted from OCR Business Studies, Q4 Higher Tier Combined Course paper, June 2000.)

ACTIVITY 2

The sources of finance and their definitions in the table on page 72 have been mixed up.

(1) Draw up a table outline similar to the one over the page.
(2) Match the source of finance to its correct definition.
(3) Give an example of an advantage and disadvantage for each source of finance.
(4) State an example of what the source of finance may be used for.

Finance for public organisations

Public corporations obtain their finance from different sources. For instance, the BBC receives its money from the sale of television licences and the sale of TV programmes to other countries. See Unit 2.5 for more information.

Hospitals and schools, for example, receive most of their finance direct from the Government. The money will have come from the taxes which have been collected, e.g.

- workers' wages in the form of income tax
- a bag of crisps in the form of value added tax (VAT)
- a bottle of beer in the form of excise duty and VAT.

Source of finance	Definition	Advantage	Disadvantage	Use of finance
1. Overdraft	A. Finance obtained to help with the purchase of property.			
2. Share issue	B. Finance obtained from within the business following successful trading.			
3. Retained profit	C. The right to use goods, in return for a monthly payment. The goods are not owned by the business.			
4. Trade credit	D. Finance obtained usually for a fixed period of time which has to be paid back.			
5. Hire purchase	E. Finance obtained for a specific purpose usually at no cost to the business. The money does not have to be paid back.			
6. Grants	F. A sum of money which has been borrowed. The amount may vary on a daily basis.			
7. Loan	G. A long-term secured loan.			
8. Mortgage	H. Goods obtained from a supplier which do not have to be paid for immediately.			
9. Lease	I. The sale of a part of the business in return for an amount of money.			
10. Debenture	J. A method of obtaining an asset in return for a series of monthly payments. Ownership of the asset does not transfer until the final payment has been made.			

ACTIVITY 3

Recommend, with reasons, suitable sources of finance for the following business situations. More than one source of finance may be suitable for each of the situations given.

1. A small sole trader building business wishing to buy a second-hand lorry.
2. A large plc wishing to finance the take-over of another plc.
3. A family textile business, trading as a private limited company, wishing to invest in some new manufacturing equipment.
4. The Curzon Veterinary Partnership which needs to raise finance to help it buy some new premises.
5. A new business wishing to sell tapes and CDs via the Internet.

EXAM Practice Questions

1. (a) The following are some of the sources of finance that firms use:
   Shares Bank loans Retained profit
   Trade credit Hire purchase
   Which two of these sources would you recommend to a private limited company to use to pay for new equipment costing £800 000? Give reasons for your choice. (6 marks)
   (b) Why do Governments give grants to firms to help to finance this kind of investment? (3 marks)

   (Adapted from OCR Business Studies, Q4 Higher Tier Common Core paper, June 1999.)

2. Pleasurewear plc's board of directors has considered the following methods of financing the building of a new clothing factory:
   Bank overdraft Bank Loan Retained Profit
   (a) Which method of financing the new factory would you recommend to the board of directors? Give two reasons for your choice. (4 marks)
   (b) Explain why you have rejected the other two methods of finance. In each case give one reason for its rejection. (4 marks)
   (c) Why is it important to consider the following before choosing a method of finance?
   (i) the length of time
   (ii) the risk involved (4 marks)
   (d) The opportunity cost of building the new factory is replacement of old machinery in Pleasurewear plc's other two factories in the UK. Explain what is meant by the term 'opportunity cost'. (2 marks)

   (Adapted from OCR Business Studies, Q2 Higher Tier combined Course paper, June 1999.)

ADVICE ON HOW TO ANSWER THE QUESTIONS

1. (a) You will need to choose two sources of finance which are appropriate for a limited company and for the purchase of new equipment. Having made two choices, it is then necessary to provide a detailed explanation saying why that source of finance is appropriate.
   (b) This question requires you to consider why Governments, in effect, give money away. In order to answer the question it will be necessary for you to explain what a Government might expect to get back in return for giving money in the form of a grant.
2. (a) Choose an appropriate method of finance for building the new factory and say why you think it is appropriate.
   (b) Say why you did not consider the other two methods of finance to be appropriate for the building of the new factory.

(c) Explain, in detail, why and how these two factors are important when considering obtaining additional finance.
(d) Explain the meaning of the term 'opportunity cost'. You should make reference to Pleasurewear plc in your answer.

KEY TERMS

Internal finance *Finance obtained from within the business.*

External finance *Finance obtained from outside the business.*

Time period *The length of time for which the finance is required.*

Security *Something of value which is offered to a lender as a form of guarantee of payment.*

Interest *An amount of money which has to be paid on borrowed money.*

EXAMINATION SUMMARY TIPS

- All businesses will require finance at some stage. Recognise why some types of finance are more appropriate to certain situations than other types of finance.
- Finance may be needed to support the business for different lengths of time.
- Not all sources of finance are available to all forms of business.
- The costs of obtaining the finance can vary, depending on the type of finance.
- Be prepared to explain why and how different types of finance are appropriate to certain situations.

Key Skills

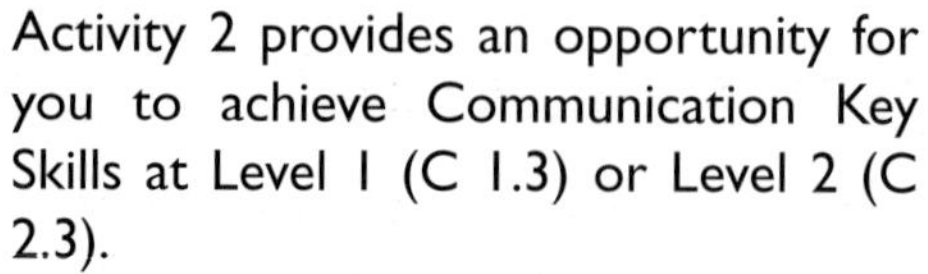

Activity 2 provides an opportunity for you to achieve Communication Key Skills at Level 1 (C 1.3) or Level 2 (C 2.3).

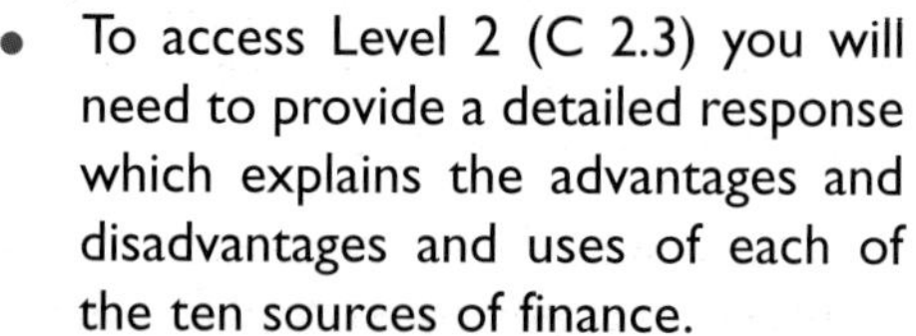

- To access Level 2 (C 2.3) you will need to provide a detailed response which explains the advantages and disadvantages and uses of each of the ten sources of finance.

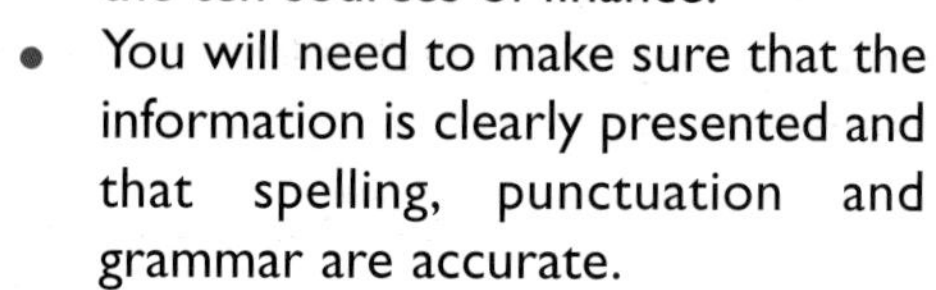

- You will need to make sure that the information is clearly presented and that spelling, punctuation and grammar are accurate.

Unit 3.3 Cash flow forecasts and statements

What is a forecast?

A forecast is an attempt to predict what might happen in the future, just as the weather forecast attempts to predict what the weather might be like tomorrow or in a few days.

Most businesses will try to forecast future events using previous experiences or data which they have collected. This process will help the business plan for the future.

One of the most important forecasts that a business makes concerns the amount of money which it expects to have flowing into (**income**) and out of (**expenditure**) the business in the future. This is called a **cash flow** forecast.

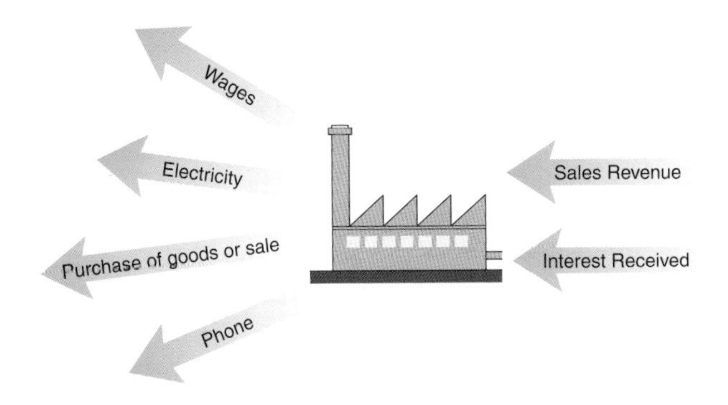

Flow of money into and out of a business.

Knowing when a business might have too much or too little money is important so that plans can be made for the future of the business.

	Jan £	Feb £	Mar £	April £
Balance brought forward	25 000	60 000	15 000	(10 000)
INCOME:				
Sales of goods	100 000	80 000	60 000	70 000
Rental income	10 000	10 000	10 000	10 000
TOTAL INCOME	135 000	150 000	85 000	70 000
EXPENDITURE:				
Materials	50 000	80 000	60 000	40 000
Energy costs	5 000	20 000	5 000	5 000
Wages	10 000	20 000	20 000	10 000
Transport	10 000	15 000	10 000	5 000
TOTAL EXPENDITURE	75 000	135 000	95 000	60 000
Balance carried forward	60 000	15 000	(10 000)	10 000

Table 3.8 Cash flow forecast for Bowton Garage Ltd

In Table 3.8 above, the figure shown in the **Balance carried forward** column is the difference between the Total income and Total expenditure which the business is forecasting.

- For the month of January:
  Total income = £135 000
  Total expenditure = £75 000
  Balance carried forward = Total income – Total expenditure
  Balance carried forward = £135 000 – £75 000 = £60 000
  Any **surplus** money which is left over at the end of one month is carried forward to the start of the next month and is shown in the **Balance brought forward** row. £60 000 has been entered for the month of February. The business has a **positive** cash flow.

- If total expenditure is greater than Total income, the Balance to be carried forward is a minus figure. There is a cash **deficit** in the cash flow of the business for that month. **Minus figures are shown in cash flow forecasts in brackets.** Any figure written in brackets in any financial information about a business will usually be negative. This has happened in the month of March and the negative figure has been carried forward to the beginning of April. The business has a **negative** cash flow.
- For the month of March:
  Total income = £85 000
  Total expenditure = £95 000
  Balance carried forward = Total income − Total Expenditure
  Balance carried forward = £85 000 − £95 000 = (£10 000)
- The balance brought forward is added to the figure for Total income for that month if it is a positive figure (January to March). If the Balance brought forward is a negative figure (April) it is subtracted from the Total income figure.

What is a cash flow statement?

A **cash flow statement** differs from a cash flow forecast in that it details something which has happened to the business. A forecast looks into the future as to what might happen to the business.

A cash flow statement provides information on where the cash in the business has come from – source – and where and how it has been used – uses of cash. It provides a useful summary of the flow of cash into and out over the business which has taken place over a given period of time.

Source of cash	**£ 000**
Sale of goods	500
Interest received	25
Total receipts	525
Use of cash	
Purchase of goods	300
Business expenses	140
Tax	20
Dividends	10
Total payments	470
Surplus of cash	**30**

Table 3.9 Cash flow statement for Bowton Garage Ltd January to June 2001

Budgets

When thinking of buying Christmas presents for members of your family, you will probably have in mind an amount of money which you are prepared to spend in buying a present for each person. In other words, you have set yourself a **budget** for each person for whom you are buying a present. If you spend more than the amount you have budgeted for then you have the problem of trying to find the extra money. If you spend less than the amount you had budgeted for then you will have some spare cash. The budget you set for your Christmas presents acts as a target.

A budget is a target which might help to limit spending.

Budgets are used by businesses for a wide variety of reasons. For instance, individual sales staff may be set a budget of perhaps £10 000 worth of sales which they must achieve in a particular month. If the budget sales figure is achieved, the employee may then receive a bonus. The budget in this case, acts as a means of encouraging sales staff to sell as much as possible which will probably help the business to increase its profits.

Budgets are also used as a means of helping to control costs. For example, a budget of £2 000 may be set to cover the costs of buying materials for a particular project. If the material costs are less than the budgeted amount, the business will have saved money. If the materials cost more, then the business has the problem of finding the extra money.

ACTIVITY 1

Prepare a personal cash flow information chart similar to the one below, either on a piece of paper or using a spreadsheet. Use the chart to record the income and expenditure you:

- have had over the last four weeks. Use the columns headed Weeks 1–4.
- expect to have over the next four weeks. Use the columns headed Weeks 5–8

What problems can you see as a result of completing your forecast?

	Week 1	Week 2	Week 3	Week 4	Week 5	Week 6	Week 7	Week 8
Balance brought forward								
INCOME:								
TOTAL INCOME								
EXPENDITURE:								
TOTAL EXPENDITURE								
Balance carried forward								

Personal cash flow information chart

For the month of March the balance carried forward was (£10 000).

Is a negative cash flow balance a problem?

A negative cash flow balance may:

- be only temporary and may not necessarily cause a problem for the business.

For the month of March in the information above, the balance carried forward was (£10 000). This may

- require the business to obtain additional finance in the form of an overdraft to help it overcome shortage of cash
- mean that the business has to delay payment of money owed until finance is available
- result in the business being unable to buy some equipment until its cash position improves.

By the end of the following month, the balance carried forward had become positive because income for the month was greater than expenditure.

The business will be in serious trouble if it forecasts a negative balance at the end of several consecutive months. Unless things start to improve, the possibility exists that it may go out of business, not because it is unprofitable, but because it has run out of money. A business will always need money to pay for the day-to-day running costs.

Cash flow and profit

A profit and a cash flow surplus are not the same; nor are a loss and a cash flow deficit.

A business with a negative cash flow at the end of a month need not be making a loss. It might just happen that the flow of money out of the business for that month is greater than the flow of money into it. Equally, a business with a positive cash flow at the end of a month is not necessarily profitable. The flow of money into the business for that month is greater than the flow of money out of the business in that month.

Unit 3.1 gave details on different types profit and Unit 3.4 shows how profit is calculated by using a trading, profit and loss account.

Why forecast cash flow?

Most businesses will attempt to forecast the flow of cash into and out of the business for some or all of the following reasons:

- to identify when the business is likely to have a shortage or surplus of cash, and what it might do about the situation
- to help the business plan for the future
- to provide targets for employees of the business to achieve. The cash flow forecast may have been devised on the assumption that the sales staff will achieve a given level of sales in one month. If this figure is not achieved, the business may run into cash flow problems.

Problems and limitations of cash flow

- Cash flow forecasts in the short term covering the next few months are likely to be more accurate than those for more than one year ahead for a variety of reasons. For example, the prices of goods sold and/or the cost of materials may be different from those forecast; the possibility exists that a new competitor enters the market.

- The figures included in the cash flow forecast are only estimates.
- The business may not have much control over some of the figures it has included in its forecast.
- The forecast will need updating at regular intervals.

ACTIVITY 2

1. Complete the cash flow forecast below by calculating the figures which are missing.

	March £	**April £**	**May £**	**June £**
Balance brought forward	20 000			
INCOME:				
Sales Revenue	100 000	125 000	130 000	80 000
Rental income	10 000	10 000	10 000	10 000
TOTAL INCOME				
EXPENDITURE:				
Wages	20 000	25 000	20 000	30 000
Goods for resale	100 000	120 000	70 000	80 000
Electricity	0	10 000	0	0
Phone	5 000	0	0	5 000
TOTAL EXPENDITURE				
Balance carried forward				

Table 3.10 Cash flow forecast for Bowton Electrical Ltd

2. In which month might the next phone and electricity bills be due?
3. Explain why the business in the example above might still be profitable despite the fact that it has a negative cash flow during one month?
4. What problems might there be for this business when attempting to forecast income and expenditure over the next few months?
5. Think of two businesses that will probably have a fairly even flow of income from sales throughout the year and another two businesses which might only receive income from sales during two or three months of the year.

EXAM Practice Questions

Read the following information.

A few months ago Tom and Sue prepared a cash flow forecast for June to September, predicting a surplus of £8 000 at the end of September.

	June	July	August	Sept
	£	£	£	£
OPENING BALANCE brought forward	2 000	(200)		
Sales	500			
TOTAL INCOME	2 500			
EXPENSES:				
Contribution to farm expenses	500	500	500	500
Wages	500			
Insurance	400	–	–	–
Advertising	100	200	100	–
Maintenance	200	200	200	500
Miscellaneous	300	100	200	100
Sue's wages	700	1 000	1 000	1 000
TOTAL EXPENSES	2 700			
BALANCE carried forward	(200)			

Tom and Sue's cash flow forecast June–September

They have now found that some of their figures are inaccurate and will need changing for the following reasons:

- Sales for June are likely to be disappointing – £400 because of bad weather
- Sales estimates for July to September are now: July: £4 000 August: £4 000 September: £2 500
- The insurance premium due in June was £500.
- Workers wage costs are: July: £700 August: £700 September: £500

a) Using the information and the cash flow forecast above, re-work and complete the cash flow forecast for July to September to show how these changes will affect the business and what the surplus will now be at the end of September. (11 marks)

b) Identify three problems shown by the new cash flow forecast and explain how you might solve them. (6 marks)
(Adapted from OCR Business Studies, Q3 Higher Tier Case Study paper, June 2000.)

ADVICE ON HOW TO ANSWER THE QUESTIONS

a) You will need to read the information in the text and the cash flow forecast very carefully. Working systematically through the information about the changes to the forecasts, write in the revised figures on the cash flow forecast. When this has been done you can start to work out the totals and the balance to carry forward at the end of each month to the start of the next month.

b) Having worked out the new cash flow forecast, you will need to look for three problems. These might be at times when the business is spending too much or when its income is insufficient. An explanation of ways in which these problems may be solved will then need to be provided for each problem you have identified.

KEY TERMS

Cash flow forecast *The expected flow of money into and out of a business over a period of time.*

Cash flow statement *A document which shows where cash used by the business has come from and how it has been used.*

Income *Money which the business receives.*

Expenditure *Money which the business pays out.*

Balance carried forward *The amount of cash left at the end of the month. This amount is used at the beginning of the next month.*

Balance brought forward *The amount of cash available at the beginning of the month which was left over at the end of the previous month.*

(Cash flow) Surplus *The amount of cash left when income is greater than expenditure.*

Cash deficit *The amount of cash which a business is short of when expenditure is greater than income.*

Negative cash flow *More cash is flowing out of the business than is flowing into it.*

Positive cash flow *More cash is flowing into the business than is flowing out of it.*

Budget *This is something determined by the business as a way of helping to control what it does. It is also used as a means of setting a target.*

EXAMINATION SUMMARY TIPS

- Recognise how cash flow needs to be managed so that the business does not run out of cash. Good cash flow management is vital for the future of the business.
- Consider how temporary shortages of cash identified by the cash flow forecast may be overcome by short-term borrowing.
- Learn to recognise situations where shortages of cash, which are forecast to go on for several months, may mean that the operation is in danger of going out of business.
- Understand why the business may need to make changes to the way in which it is running its business to help it overcome possible shortages of cash.

Key Skills

Activity 1 provides an opportunity for Application of Number Key Skills at Level 1 (N 1.2) or Level 2 (N2.2) to be achieved, depending on the complexity of the information you include.

If you decide to prepare the chart using a spreadsheet, evidence will be available for IT Key Skills at Level 1 (IT 1.1) or Level 2 (IT 2.2).

- To access IT Level 2 you will need to make sure that you have entered the correct formulae which will do the calculations automatically for you. Your spreadsheet should be capable of transferring the cash balance at the end of the month to the beginning of the next month.

Unit 3.4 Trading, profit and loss accounts

All businesses keep detailed financial records of the business activity which has taken place. This is done by recording the value of the goods sold and the expenses of running the business. It is an important activity.

Users of financial Information

The business which has prepared the financial information is not the only user of the information. Other people and organisations will be interested. In the main, the people and organisations which will have an interest in the financial affairs of the business will be:

- Investors – both current investors and those who are thinking of investing in the business. The financial information will help them to decide whether they have made a good investment or are about to make one.
- Inland Revenue – this organisation is responsible for collecting money due to the Government. Money is collected from such things as taxes on profits, VAT on the value of goods sold and income tax deducted from employees' wages and salaries.
- Workers – this group will want to keep a check on how successful the business has been. Will jobs be safe? Can the firm afford to pay a larger pay increase?
- Competitors – they may want to check on how successful rival businesses have been.
- Lenders of money – before lending money, organisations will want to see how financially secure the borrower of the money is.

These people and organisations are sometimes known as stakeholders. See Unit 1.3.

What does the trading, profit and loss account show?

One of the most important financial documents which businesses prepare is a **trading, profit and loss and appropriation account.** This document is usually prepared at least once a year and sometimes more frequently. The document is made up of three parts. Each part shows different things and the document as a whole shows what has happened to the finances of the business for a given period of time. Comparisons with the financial performance of the company in the previous year can also be made as in the examples below in Tables 3.11 to 3.13. All limited companies must make their profit and loss accounts available to the public.

CONSOLIDATED PROFIT AND LOSS ACCOUNT

For the year ended 31 July 1998

	Notes	1998 £'000	1997 £'000
Turnover	2	87,875	87,939
Cost of sales		(21,637)	(25,052)
Gross profit		66,238	62,887
Operating expenses	3	(39,242)	(36,686)
Operating profit		26,996	26,201
Net interest receivable	4	2,619	1,083
Profit before transfer fees		29,615	27,284
Net transfer fees	5	(15,511)	293
Profit on ordinary activities before taxation		14,104	27,577
Taxation	7	(4,090)	(8,549)
Profit for the year		10,014	19,028
Dividends	9	(4,416)	(4,026)
Retained profit for the year	25	5,598	15,002
Earnings per ordinary share (pence)	10	3.9	7.4

Manchester United plc Profit and Loss Account for the year ended 31 July 1998.

Source: Document taken from 1998 Annual Report

The trading account

This is used to calculate the amount of **gross profit** which the business makes. The amount of sales revenue which the business has received, how much it has paid for goods and how much stock the business has at the beginning and end of the trading period are needed for this calculation to be done. A trading account is shown overleaf in Table 3.11.

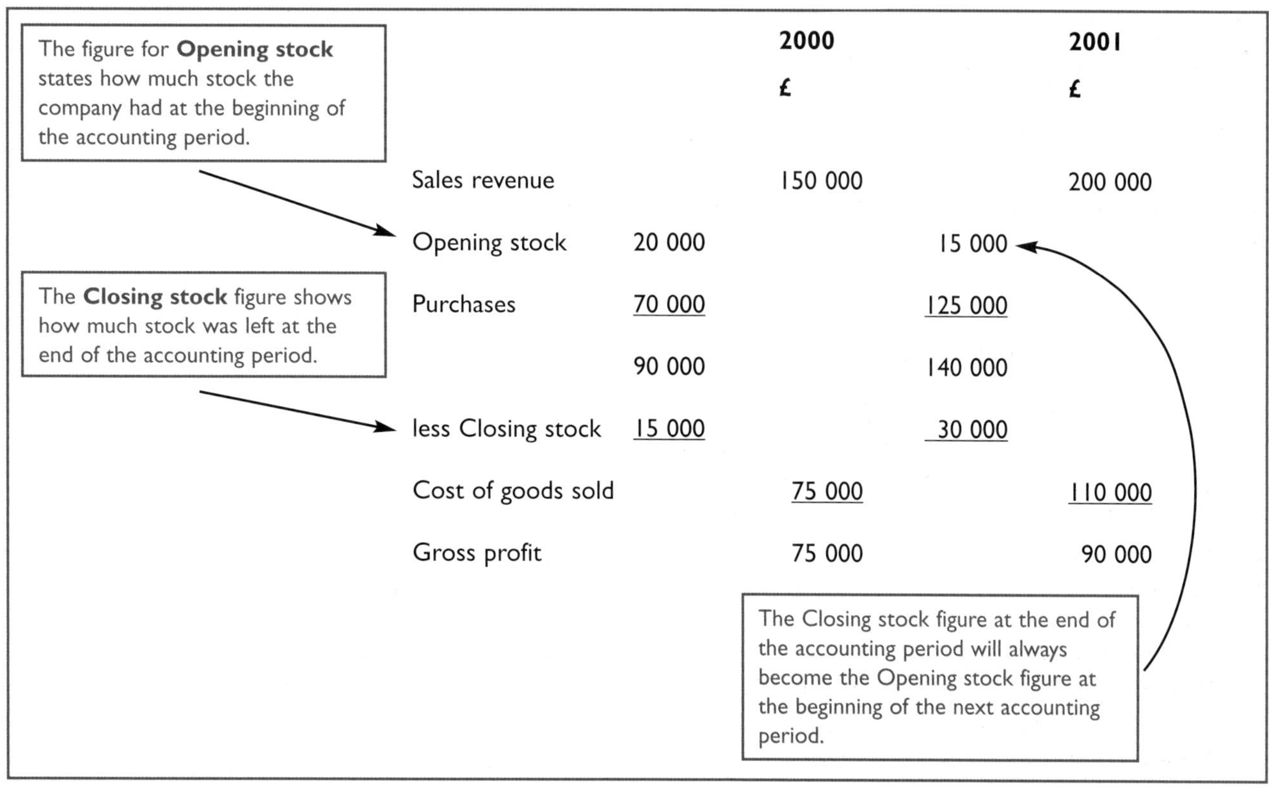

		2000 £		2001 £
Sales revenue		150 000		200 000
Opening stock	20 000		15 000	
Purchases	70 000		125 000	
	90 000		140 000	
less Closing stock	15 000		30 000	
Cost of goods sold		75 000		110 000
Gross profit		75 000		90 000

Table 3.11 Trading account for Bowton Electrical Ltd for the periods ending 31 March 2000 and 2001

The profit and loss account

This is used to calculate the amount of **net profit** which the business has made. This is done by subtracting the expenses of running the business from the gross profit which has been calculated by the trading account.

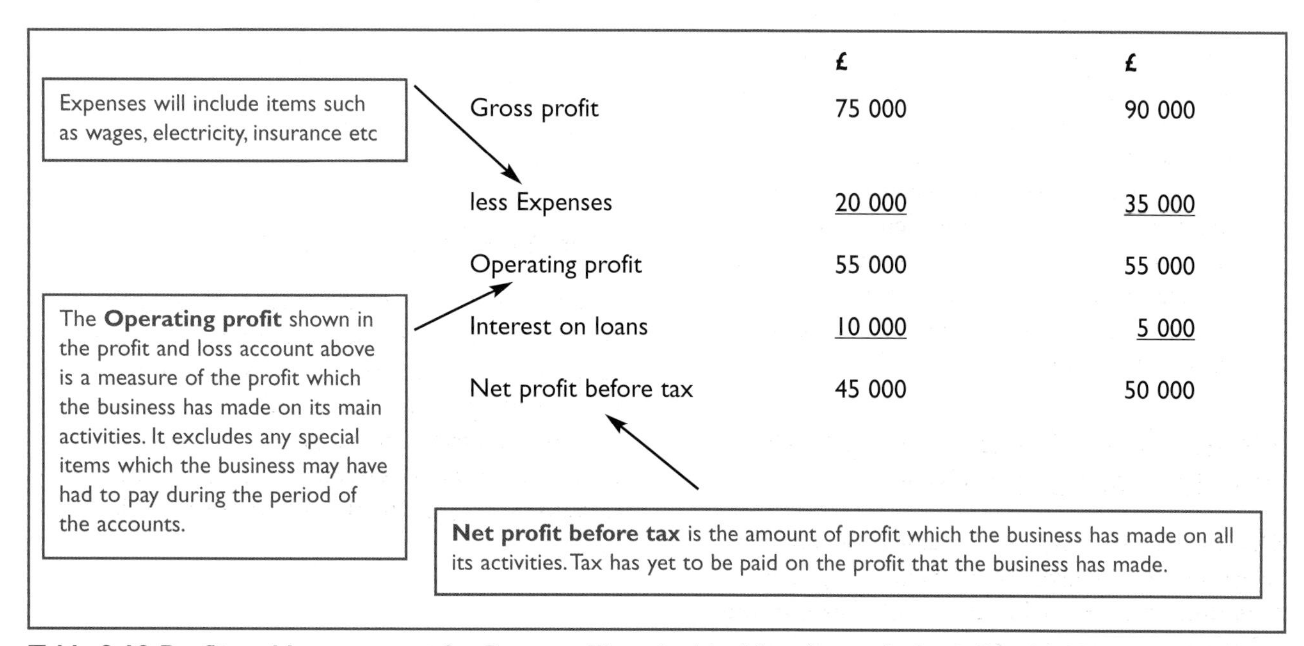

	£	£
Gross profit	75 000	90 000
less Expenses	20 000	35 000
Operating profit	55 000	55 000
Interest on loans	10 000	5 000
Net profit before tax	45 000	50 000

Table 3.12 Profit and loss account for Bowton Electrical Ltd for the periods ending 31 March 2000 and 2001

The appropriation account

This shows what has happened to the net profit made by the business. The profit left over after all expenses have been paid is then used to pay any tax which the business owes. Corporation tax is paid by incorporated businesses and income tax is paid by unincorporated business.

Any money left over after tax has been paid is then either kept by the business in the form of **retained profit**, or paid out to the owners of the business or both.

An unincorporated business does not have an appropriation account. Income tax is paid on any profits which the business makes.

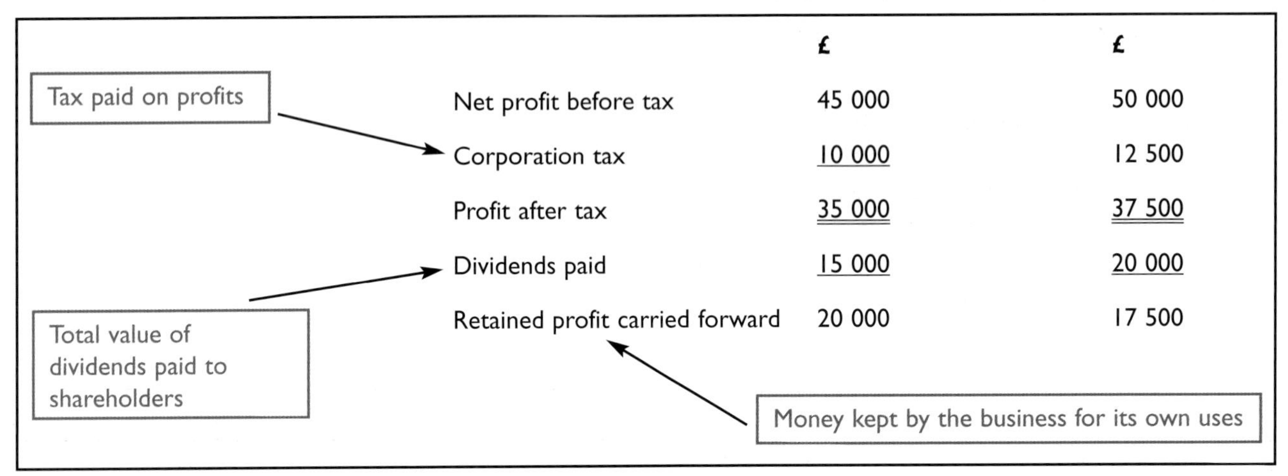

	£	£
Net profit before tax	45 000	50 000
Corporation tax	10 000	12 500
Profit after tax	35 000	37 500
Dividends paid	15 000	20 000
Retained profit carried forward	20 000	17 500

Table 3.13 Appropriation account for Bowton Electrical Ltd for the periods ending 31 March 2000 and 2001

		2000		2001
		£		£
Sales revenue		150 000		200 000
Opening stock	20 000		15 000	
Purchases	70 000		125 000	
	90 000		140 000	
less Closing stock	15 000		30 000	
Cost of goods sold		75 000		110 000
Gross profit		75 000		90 000
less expenses		20 000		35 000
Operating profit		55 000		55 000
Interest on loans		10 000		5 000
Net profit before tax		45 000		50 000
Corporation tax		10 000		12 500
Profit after tax		35 000		37 500
Dividends paid		15 000		20 000
Retained profit carried forward		20 000		17 500

Table 3.14 Trading, profit and loss and appropriation account for Bowton Electrical Ltd for the periods ending March 2000 and 2001

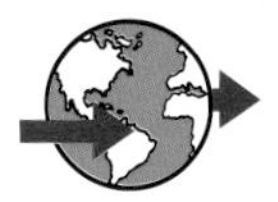

Using ratios to analyse financial performance

Ratios are used widely when analysing the financial performance of a business. A ratio is a means of expressing, through a single figure, a relationship between two related or unrelated variables. It is possible to calculate several different ratios from the information contained in a trading, profit and loss account.

Unit 3.1 introduced the idea of comparing profit with sales. For ratios to be of any use it is necessary to compare the ratio of one set of accounts with those of the following or previous accounting periods. This allows the progress which the business has made to be assessed.

The information below shows how this is done based on the information in Table 3.14 on page 84. This table combines all the information presented in Tables 3.11 to 3.13.

Ratio	Explanation	Formula	2000	2001
Gross profit to sales	This ratio calculates the amount of gross profit made on the sales of goods. It expresses the figure as a percentage by using the formula shown in the next column.	$\frac{\text{Gross profit}}{\text{Sales}} \times 100$	$\frac{75\ 000}{150\ 000} \times 100$ = 50%	$\frac{90\ 000}{200\ 000} \times 100$ = 45%
Operating profit to sales	This ratio calculates the amount of operating profit made on the sales of goods. It expresses the figure as a percentage using the formula shown in the next column.	$\frac{\text{Operating profit}}{\text{Sales}} \times 100$	$\frac{55\ 000}{150\ 000} \times 100$ = 33.67%	$\frac{55\ 000}{200\ 000} \times 100$ = 27.5%
Net profit to sales	This ratio calculates the amount of net profit made on the sales of goods. It expresses the figure as a percentage using the formula shown in the next column.	$\frac{\text{Net profit}}{\text{Sales}} \times 100$	$\frac{45\ 000}{150\ 000} \times 100$ = 30%	$\frac{50\ 000}{200\ 000} \times 100$ = 25%

Trading, Profit and Loss Account ratios

ACTIVITY 

1. Complete the trading, profit and loss account below by calculating the missing figures. The trading, profit and loss account can be completed by writing it out or by entering the data into a spreadsheet.

		2000		2001
		£		£
Sales income		300 000		260 000
Opening stock	50 000		15 000	
Purchases	150 000		95 000	
less Closing stock	15 000		30 000	
Cost of goods sold				
Gross profit				
less Expenses		25 000		35 000
Operating profit				
Interest on loans		10 000		5 000
Net profit before tax				
Corporation tax		20 000		35 000
Profit after tax				
Dividends paid to Shareholders		30 000		40 000
Retained profit carried forward				

Table 3.15 Trading, profit and loss account and appropriation account for Morton Enterprises Ltd for the periods ending 31 March 2000 and 2001

2. Using the information in the completed trading, profit and loss account, compare the financial performance of Morton Enterprises Ltd by calculating the following ratios for 2000 and 2001. Express your answers to two decimal places.
   (a) Gross profit to sales.
   (b) Operating profit to sales.
   (c) Net profit to sales.
3. What does the ratio information tell you about the progress which the business has made between 2000 and 2001?
4. Calculate the percentage of corporation tax paid by the business on its profits in 2000 and 2001.

EXAM Practice Questions

Consolidated trading profit and loss accounts for the years 2000 and 2001 are given below.

Carlton Press Ltd – Trading profit and loss accounts for the years ending 30 June 2000 and 2001

	2000 (£)	2001 (£)
Sales	330 000	580 000
Cost of sales	200 000	300 000
Gross profit	130 000	280 000
Interest payable	0	1 000
Administration expenses	100 000	240 000
Net profit before taxation	30 000	39 000
Taxation	8 000	12 000
Profit after tax	22 000	27 000
Dividends paid	2 000	3 000
Retained profit	20 000	24 000

(a) What is the name of the tax that Carlton Press Ltd will pay on its profits? (1 mark)
(b) Explain the term 'dividend payments'. (2 marks)
(c) Explain why dividend payments are important for a business. (4 marks)
(d) What are the arguments for and against Carlton Press Ltd using retained profits to finance buying new machinery rather than borrowing from a bank? (4 marks)
(e) Would the shareholders of Carlton Press Ltd be pleased with the performance of the company in 2001 compared with the performance in 2000? Give reasons for your answer. (7 marks)
(Adapted from OCR Business Studies, Q4 Higher Tier Common Core Paper, June 1998.)

ADVICE ON HOW TO ANSWER THE QUESTIONS

(a) This question requires a simple fact which relates to a Limited Company. Look carefully at the name of the business to help you provide the correct information.
(b) A short statement is required, explaining what dividend payments are and who receives them.
(c) You will need to consider carefully, from different viewpoints, the effect which dividend payments may have on the future of a business.
(d) This question requires you to consider carefully the costs of different types of finance and the advantages and disadvantages involved.
(e) To answer this question you will need to work out some ratios and pass comment on what the ratios tell you about how the business is progressing over time.

KEY TERMS

Opening stock *The value of the stock which the business has at the beginning of the accounting period. The value is always the same as the closing stock from the* ***previous*** *accounting period.*

Closing stock *The value of the stock which the business has at the end of the accounting period. The value of the closing stock is carried forward to the beginning of the next accounting period.*

Operating profit *The amount of profit which the business has made on its main activities.*

Net profit before tax *The amount of profit which the business has made on all its activities after expenses have been paid and before paying tax.*

Corporation tax *The tax which private and public limited companies must pay on their profits.*

Retained profit *The amount of profit kept by the business for its own use.*

EXAMINATION SUMMARY TIPS

- A trading, profit and loss and appropriation account is made up of three parts. Each part does a different job. Make sure you know what each part is used for.
- Information in the trading, profit and loss account for one accounting period is usually compared with information from previous years.
- Comparisons of how well the business is doing can be made using ratio analysis.
- The are several different ratios which can be calculated from information in the trading, profit and loss account. Learn which ratios can be used.
- All limited companies and public limited companies must produce a trading, profit and loss and appropriation account.

Key Skills

The Activity provides an opportunity to achieve Application of Number Key Skills at Level 1 (N 1.2) and Level 2 (N 2.2).

If you choose to complete the trading, profit and loss account using a spreadsheet, IT Key Skills at Level 1 (IT 1.2) may be achieved.

- When completing calculations, write out the formula you are using and substitute figures into the formula.
- Show all your working. Do not miss out any steps of the calculation.
- Include in your Key Skills portfolio the source document (trading, profit and loss account) for the calculations you have done.

Unit 3.5 Balance sheets

The previous Unit provided information on how businesses can calculate how successful they have been in terms of how much profit they make. Another important financial document prepared by most businesses is called a **balance sheet**. This document shows exactly how much a business is worth on a stated day.

Manchester United PLC

COMPANY BALANCE SHEET

AT 31 JULY 2000

	2000 £'000	1999 £'000
Fixed assets		
Tangible assets	27,480	26,104
Investments	25,738	23,904
	53,218	50,008
Current assets		
Stocks	4,007	3,305
Debtors	33,734	5,685
Marketable securities	–	35,615
Cash at bank and in hand	8,929	2,980
	46,670	47,585
Creditors – amounts falling due within one year	18,650	22,230
Net current assets	28,020	25,355
Total assets less current liabilities	81,238	75,363
Accruals and deferred income		
Other deferred income	5,200	8,176
Net assets	76,038	67,187
Capital and reserves		
Share capital	25,977	25,977
Profit and loss account	50,061	41,210
Shareholders' funds	76,038	67,187

Manchester United plc Company Balance Sheet as at 31 July 2000.

Source: Document taken from Annual Report 2000.

After having worked through this Unit you should be able to understand what the information contained in a balance sheet is telling you about the company.

The balance sheet provides information on what the business **owns** and how it has spent its money – this is shown in the form of **assets**. It also shows where the money has come from and how much it **owes** – this is shown in the form of **liabilities**. Assets must always equal liabilities, hence the name 'balance sheet'.

ASSETS	=	LIABILITIES
e.g. Cars		e.g. Share capital
Machinery		Bank loans
Stock		

Who uses the information in a balance sheet?

- The owners of the business, to make sure that their investment is performing well.
- People who may be thinking of investing in the business.
- Other businesses which may be owed money by that business.

Types of balance sheet

Traditional style of balance sheet

There are two basic styles of balance sheet. One is called the 'traditional style' and lists the assets of the business on one side and the liabilities of the business on the other side. The value of the assets and liabilities must always equal each other, hence the name 'balance sheet'. This style of balance sheet is shown on page 90.

As at 31 March 2001, the business had £250 000 of assets but had liabilities of £250 000.

The balance sheet is only accurate for the day shown in its title. The next day, the values shown in the balance sheet will change as the business goes about its normal trading activities.

Liquidity

The items in a Balance sheet are listed in a particular order according to their liquidity. The assets listed at the bottom of the balance sheet can be turned into cash more quickly than those at the top. Cash is the most liquid of all assets.

	£	£		£	£
FIXED ASSETS			SHAREHOLDERS FUNDS		
Premises	70 000		Share capital	137 500	
Equipment	110 000		Reserves	32 500	170 000
Vehicles	25 000	205 000	LONG-TERM LIABILITIES		
CURRENT ASSETS			Bank loan	50 000	50 000
Stock	15 000		CURRENT LIABILITES		
Debtors	4 000				
Cash at bank	25 000		Creditors	30 000	30 000
Cash in hand	1 000	45 000			
NET ASSETS EMPLOYED		250 000	CAPITAL EMPLOYED		250 000

Liquidity of assets increases

Table 3.16 Balance sheet of Bowton Garage Ltd as at 31 March 2001

Vertical style of balance sheet

A more modern style of balance sheet which presents the same information – the 'vertical style', – is shown in Table 3.17. This style of balance sheet is used much more frequently than the traditional style. It is the style which is more likely to be used in examination papers.

Table 3.17 contains exactly the same information as the traditional style of balance sheet in Table 3.16 but the value of assets and liabilities is £30 000 less. This is because of the way in which the vertical style of presentation subtracts current liabilities from current assets in order to calculate the working capital of the business.

	£	£	£
FIXED ASSETS			
Premises	70 000		
Equipment	110 000		
Vehicles	25 000		205 000
CURRENT ASSETS			
Stock	15 000		
Debtors	4 000		
Cash at bank	25 000		
Cash in hand	1 000	45 000	
CURRENT LIABILITIES			
Creditors	30 000	30 000	
NET WORKING CAPITAL			15 000
NET ASSETS EMPLOYED			220 000
SHAREHOLDERS' FUNDS			
Share capital	137 500		
Reserves	32 500		170 000
LONG-TERM LIABILITIES			
Bank loan	50 000		50 000
CAPITAL EMPLOYED			220 000

Table 3.17 Balance sheet of Bowton Garage Ltd as at 31 March 2001

Fixed assets

Current assets

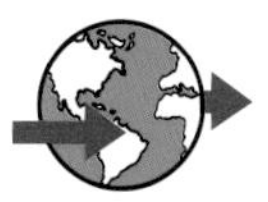

The information in the balance sheet

A lot of information is contained in a balance sheet.

1. There are different types of asset:
   - **Fixed assets** are those items which are owned by the business which tend not to change in value on a day-to-day basis as the business trades. There will, though, be some change in value over a much longer period of time.

     Fixed assets need to be revalued periodically. This is done by a process called **depreciation** which reduces the value of the asset shown in the balance sheet. The cost of the depreciation is an expense to the business and it is charged against the gross profit.
   - **Current assets** are those items owned by the business which tend to change in value (almost on a daily basis) as a result of the activities of the business.

ACTIVITY 1

1. Copy out the following table. Some of the items which can be found in a balance sheet have had their letters jumbled up. Identify each term by writing it in the appropriate column. The first one has been done for you
2. Identify, by placing a tick in the appropriate column, the type of asset or liability.

	Balance sheet term	Fixed asset	Current asset	Shareholders' funds	Long-term liability	Current liability
TOSBRDE	Debtors		✓			
LPTNA NDA PTEENQMIU						
MIESRESP						
XTSEURIF DAN TTSIIGFN						
ARYROIND SSAERH						
NBAK OLNA						
HASC TA KABN						
YEIEDLVR ILVEECH						
DNREETIA FRTPOI						
GGMTOERA						

- The total value of all the assets that the business owns is shown as:

NET ASSETS EMPLOYED

2. There are different types of liability:
   - **Shareholders' funds.** This is the money invested in the business by its owners and will also include any profit which the business has made and which has not been paid to the owners. This is called **reserves** and is owed to the shareholders.
   - **Long-term liabilities** will include any money which the business might have borrowed for a period of more than one year, eg bank loan.
   - **Current liabilities** will include anything which is owed by the business and likely to be paid within the next 12 months, eg trade creditors.
   - The Liabilities section of the balance sheet shows the values of money owed to various people and businesses. This figure is shown as:

     CAPITAL EMPLOYED and consists of all the long-term finance provided to the business.

Types of capital

Capital is another name for money invested in the business. There are several different types of capital:

- **Loan capital** – money lent to a business, usually for a specific purpose. This may consist of bank loans or debentures.
- **Share capital** – money invested in the business by shareholders who are the owners of the business.

Using ratio analysis to analyse financial performance

In Unit 3.4 we saw how ratios can be used to analyse financial performance. It is possible to do the same with the information in a balance sheet by using different ratios. Two of the most important ratios are called the **current ratio** and the **acid test ratio**. Both of these ratios are used to assess the ability of the business to pay off its debts – they are sometimes called 'liquidity ratios'. All the figures in the following examples have been taken from Table 3.16 or Table 3.17.

- The current ratio is calculated using the following formula:

$$\frac{\text{Current assets}}{\text{Current liabilities}} \quad \text{eg} \quad \frac{£45\ 000}{£30\ 000} = 1.5$$

  An answer of :
  - more than 2 using this formula would suggest that the business is not using its assets in the most efficient way.
  - less than 1 shows that the business is in danger of not being able to pay off its debts should it have to do so at short notice. The business needs to aim for a figure of between 1.5 and 2.
- The acid test ratio is calculated using the following formula:

$$\frac{\text{Current assets less stock}}{\text{Current liabilities}}$$

$$\text{eg} \quad \frac{£45\ 000 - 15\ 000}{£30\ 000} = 1.0$$

This ratio assesses the ease with which the business could pay off its debts without having to rely on selling off its stock as a way of raising money. An answer of 1 is thought to be ideal. In the case of Bowton Garage Ltd, it is in as strong position to pay off the money it owes.

An answer of:
- less than 1 would indicate that the business has insufficient liquid funds to pay off its debts.
- more than 1 suggests that the business is not making best use of its liquid funds.

Working capital

This is also a measure of how easily the business is able to meet its short-term debts. It is worked out by using the following formula:

Current Assets – Current Liabilities

£15 000 = £45 000 – £30 000

Sometimes net working capital is referred to as **net current assets**. It is calculated using the same formula as shown above.

A business will need enough cash or working capital to pay for its day-to-day activities. Many businesses fail because they run out of working capital either because they do not have sufficient liquid funds or because the working capital of the business has been badly managed.

One of the advantages of the layout of the vertical style of balance sheet is that the figure for working capital is worked out automatically. This is shown as net working capital and can be seen clearly in the balance sheet in Table 3.17.

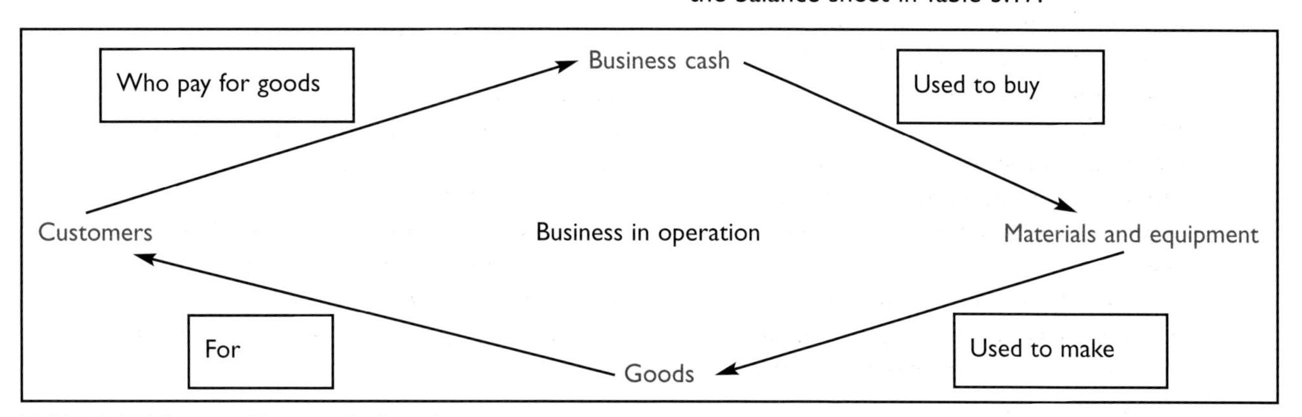

Table 3.18 The working capital cycle

Analysing the results from ratio analysis

A single result from a ratio calculation does not tell you very much about the business. The most important thing is to try to identify the trend over a period of time. This can only be done by carrying out the same calculation from sets of accounting data for different time periods. This information can then be presented in the form of a line graph to make it easier to identify the trend.

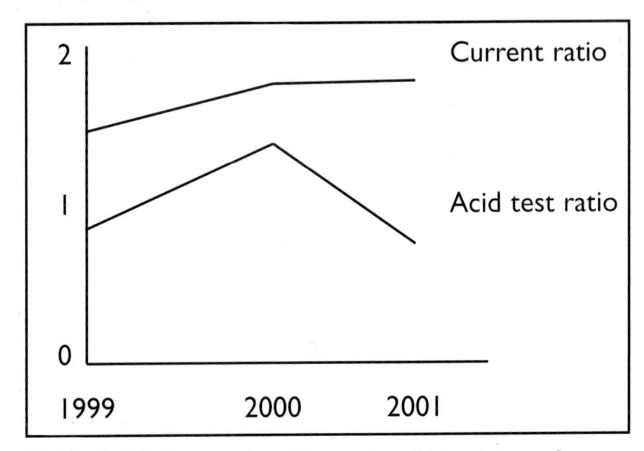

Table 3.19 Current ratio and acid test trend between 1999 and 2001

The current ratio is gradually improving while the acid test ratio has gradually got worse. What does this tell you about the business?

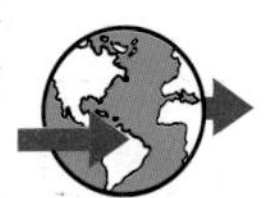

Return on capital employed (ROCE)

This is another important measure of how successful the business has been. By comparing the operating profit which the business has made with the capital employed, an assessment can be made of how well the business is performing. The formula for calculating ROCE is:

$$\frac{\text{Operating profit}}{\text{Capital employed}} \times 100$$

The data for this calculation cannot come from just the balance sheet. The figure for operating profit will be found in the trading, profit and loss account whilst the figure for capital employed can be found in the balance sheet.

$$\text{ROCE} = \frac{50\,000}{250\,000} \times 100 = 20\%$$

Liquidation

This is a process which happens when a business stops trading. It may happen because the business itself decides to stop trading perhaps because the owners wish to retire or because the liabilities of the business are greater than its assets.

In the case of an **incorporated** (Limited Liability Companies) organisation when its liabilities are greater than its assets, the business is said to be **insolvent**.

In the case of an **unincorporated** (Sole Traders and Partnerships) organisation, when its liabilities are greater than its assets, the business is said to be **bankrupt**.

People and organisations that are owed money (**creditors**) may appoint a **receiver**. The job of the receiver is to try to sell the company as a going concern so that the debts of the business may be paid. If no buyer for the business can be found, the assets of the business may then be sold off individually in order to raise money to pay off the debts of the business.

Daewoo calls in receivers

By Sophie Barker

DAEWOO Motor yesterday became the third Korean car company to go into receivership in three years, threatening 1,700 jobs at the company's British subsidiary.

However, a spokesman for the British division was quick to reassure customers and employees "it is business as usual".

He added: "Customers can be confident their warranties and service packages will be honoured. Daewoo Cars is a self-sufficient subsidiary that does not rely on funds from Korea."

The receivership means the Korean courts will either appoint an administrator to turn Daewoo around, or auction off its assets — something the company insisted "is not bankruptcy or receivership as we know it here in the UK".

Daewoo's $10 billion (£6·8 billion) debts have been frozen and the company has the Government's support to force through restructuring plans.

This comes despite opposition to the plan from the trade unions.

It was unclear whether the receivership threatened the potential sale of Daewoo to General Motors and Fiat.

Extract from a newspaper article reporting the collapse of a business.

Daily Telegraph

ACTIVITY 2

1. Complete the balance sheet below by calculating the missing figures.

	£	£	2001 £	£	£	2000 £
FIXED ASSETS						
Shop premises		60 000			50 000	
Fixtures and fittings		15 000			12 000	
Equipment		25 000			22 000	
Van		10 000			10 000	
			[ ]			[ ]
CURRENT ASSETS						
Stock	14 000			12 000		
Debtors	3 000			5 000		
Cash at bank	3 000			1 000		
		[ ]			[ ]	
CURRENT LIABILITIES						
Overdraft	0			8 000		
Creditors	10 000			4 000		
		[ ]			[ ]	
NET WORKING CAPITAL			[ ]			[ ]
NET ASSETS EMPLOYED			[ ]			[ ]
SHAREHOLDERS' FUNDS						
Share capital		50 000			50 000	
Reserves		15 000			10 000	
Retained profit		5 000				
			[ ]			[ ]
LONG-TERM LIABILITIES						
Long-term loans		38 000			40 000	
Medium-term loan		12 000				
			[ ]			[ ]
CAPITAL EMPLOYED			[ ]			[ ]

Balance sheet of Highfield Stores Ltd as at 30 June 2000 and 2001

2. Give two examples of fixed assets other than those in the balance sheet above.
3. Using the information in the completed balance sheet, calculate the following ratios for both years:
   - acid test
   - current ratio.
4. Assuming that the business made an operating profit of £24 000 in 2000 and £15 000 in 2001, calculate the return on capital employed.
5. Explain what the information in the balance sheet and the calculations you have done tell you about the business.

EXAM
Practice Questions

1. Below are extracts from Ditec Ltd's balance sheets. Study these carefully and answer the questions which follow.

	1998 £	1999 £	2000 £
CURRENT ASSETS			
Stock	220 000	595 000	700 000
Debtors	200 000	210 000	235 000
Cash in hand and at bank	55 000	19 000	5 000
CURRENT LIABILITIES			
Trade creditors	105 000	230 000	280 000
Overdraft	150 000	260 000	320 000
ACID TEST RATIO	1:1		

Ditec Ltd – Balance sheet extracts

(a) Calculate the acid test ratio for 2000. Show your working. (3 marks)
(b) From your calculation, and the figures in the table above, comment on any changes in the company's liquidity position. (6 marks)
(c) State and explain one way in which a company may improve its liquidity. (2 marks)

(Adapted from OCR Business Studies, Q1 Higher Tier Business and Change Option, June 1999.)

2. David Morris runs a market stall in Bowton, 'Jeans and Ts', selling jeans and T-shirts. The balance sheet that David drew up at the end of last year is shown below.
(a) Why does David need to make an allowance for depreciation on the balance sheet? (3 marks)

	£	£	£
Fixed assets			
At cost	22 000		
Less Depreciation		2 000	
			20 000
Current Assets			
Stock	18 000		
Bank	7 000		
Cash	3 000		
		28 000	
Less Current liabilities		6 000	
Net working capital			
NET ASSETS			42 000
Represented by:			
Capital at 1 January			40 000
Add Net profits for year			26 000
			66 000
Less Drawings			24 000
CAPITAL EMPLOYED			42 000

Jeans and Ts
Balance sheet as at 31 December 2000

(b) Calculate the value of the net working capital in the balance sheet above. (3 marks)
(c) Has David's business enough working capital? Give reasons for your answer. (3 marks)

(Adapted from OCR Business Studies, Q2 Higher Tier Common Core Paper, June 1999)

3. Nicole and Colin have been in partnership for three years. A summary of their financial information for 1999 and 2000 is given below.

	1999	2000
Sales turnover	£200 000	£300 000
Net profit	£60 000	£150 000
Net profit to sales	30%	50%
Capital employed	£100 000	£200 000

(a) Using the information above, calculate the return on capital employed for the year 2000. (3 marks)

(b) In 1999, the return on capital employed was 60%. Using this, and your result for the year 2000, explain what these results tell you about Nicole and Colin's business. (3 marks)

(c) Explain why the net profit to sales ratio is a better guide to Nicole and Colin's success than sales turnover. (2 marks)

(Adapted from OCR Business Studies, Q1 Higher Tier Business and Change paper, June 2000.)

ADVICE ON HOW TO ANSWER THE QUESTIONS

1. (a) Find the information you need to calculate the acid test ratio and write out the answer showing all the steps in your working out.
   (b) Compare your answer to part (a) above with the acid test ratio given in the data for 1998. Explain, in detail, the progress the business has made. Explain if it is likely to be in any difficulties or are things improving?
   (c) Think carefully about what the term 'liquidity' means. Consider how a business might obtain more liquid funds from its own resources.
2. (a) You will need to consider what depreciation is and how the 'cost' of depreciating an asset can be paid for.
   (b) Write down the formula for calculating working capital. Find the figures in the balance sheet which you can put into the formula and calculate the answer.
   (c) This question requires you to consider whether the business is likely to run out of working capital. You need to explain whether you think the business has enough working capital to pay for its day-to-day running costs.
3. (a) Find the information you need to calculate the return on capital employed and write out the answer, showing all the steps in your working out.
   (b) Compare your answer to part (a) to the information given and comment on the progress which the business has made between 1999 and 2000.
   (c) Explain what the net profit to sales ratio measures. Explain why it provides a more useful way of measuring the success of the business rather than just looking at how sales turnover has changed.

KEY TERMS

Balance sheet *A statement of what the business owns and owes on a given date.*

Liquidity *The ability of a business to pay off its debts at short notice.*

Fixed assets *Items which can be used more than once and which do not tend to change in value on a daily basis.*

Current assets *Items which are owned by the business which tend to change in value on a daily basis and which can be changed into cash fairly easily.*

Shareholders' funds *Money owed to the shareholders who own the business.*

Long-term liabilities *Money owed by the business which is not normally due for repayment within the next 12 months.*

Current liabilities *Debts which will usually have to be repaid within the next 12 months.*

Net working capital *The amount of money which a business has to manage and fund its day-to-day affairs.*

Net current assets *Current assets less current liabilities. This is the same as net working capital.*

Net assets employed *The total value of all the assets owned by the business.*

Capital employed *The total value of all the long-term finance provided to the business. Capital employed always equals net assets employed.*

Debenture *A long-term fixed interest loan.*

Depreciation *The process of reducing the value of a fixed asset.*

Insolvency *This happens to public limited and private limited companies when their liabilities are greater than their assets.*

Bankruptcy *This happens to sole traders and partnerships when their liabilities are greater than their assets.*

Creditors *People or organisations that are owed money.*

Debtor *People or organisations that owe money.*

Receiver *Person appointed by the creditors of a business when its liabilities are greater than its assets.*

EXAMINATION SUMMARY TIPS

- Assets owned by the business must always equal the liabilities or money owed by the business.
- The information in the balance sheet can be used to check on the progress which the business has made since the last balance sheet was produced.
- Liquidity ratios can be used to see how easily the business can pay off its debts.
- Other ratios can be used to identify a trend in the progress which the business has made.
- When interpreting the results of ratio calculations, make sure that you pass comment on the performance of the business. Do not simply restate the results of the calculations.
- A balance sheet is made up of a number of elements – examination questions may expect definitions and examples of the different elements.
- Make sure you can define and give examples of assets and liabilities.

Key Skills

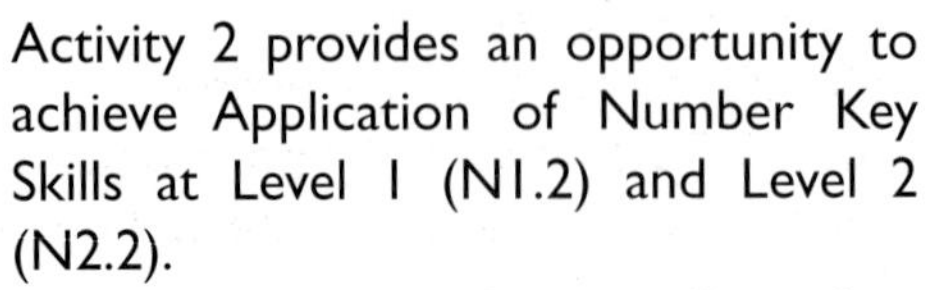

Activity 2 provides an opportunity to achieve Application of Number Key Skills at Level 1 (N1.2) and Level 2 (N2.2).

- To access Level 2, you will need to make sure that you answer part 4 of the Activity in detail by interpreting the information contained in the balance sheet and from your calculations.
- Show all your working. Do not miss out any steps of the calculation.
- Include in your Key Skills portfolio the source document (balance sheet) for the calculations you have done.

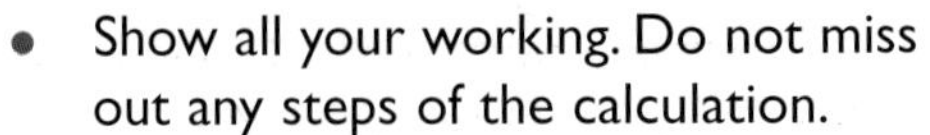

Production

Learning Objectives:
To develop knowledge and understanding of:

- the internal structure of organisations and how this contributes to the process of production
- business costs and revenues and the importance of controlling costs
- break-even charts, their construction, uses and limitations
- how the scale of production can be altered and how this can affect the costs and profitability of a business
- the importance of production, methods of production and how technology can be applied to the production process
- the importance of communications, kinds and methods of communication that are used in business, the use of Information and Communications Technology and how this may impact on the location and nature of work
- to develop the ability to analyse case study material related to production and communications, applying the knowledge and understanding gained
- to develop the ability to evaluate case study contexts in order to make reasoned judgements including recommendations.

Production is concerned with the making of goods and the provision of services. To make goods materials, people and equipment must be organised. Raw materials are processed and components assembled in some way. Cadbury's takes raw materials such as cocoa, milk and sugar and processes them to make chocolates. Rover assembles car components to make cars. The provision of services also requires the organisation of resources. British Airways must organises aircraft, airport access, air space, ground and flight crew, catering and entertainment in order to provide the service of air travel.

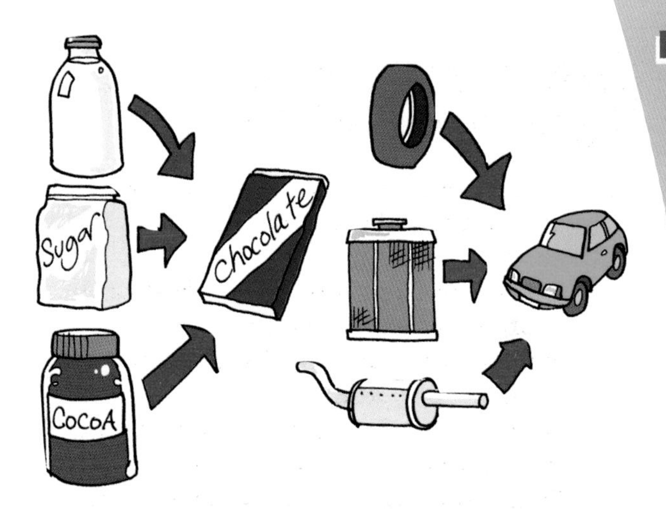

Production requires the organisation of resources.

SECTION 4

There are a number of decisions that firms need to make in connection with production:

- ***What to produce?*** Many firms are now market-oriented, meaning that they use market research to decide what to produce. There are still some firms that are product-oriented which means that they decide what they will produce first and then try to persuade people to buy the product.

Market research helps to decide what to produce.

- ***Where to produce?*** This is concerned with the location of the activity – in which part of the town, region, country or even part of the world it will make sense to locate the premises.

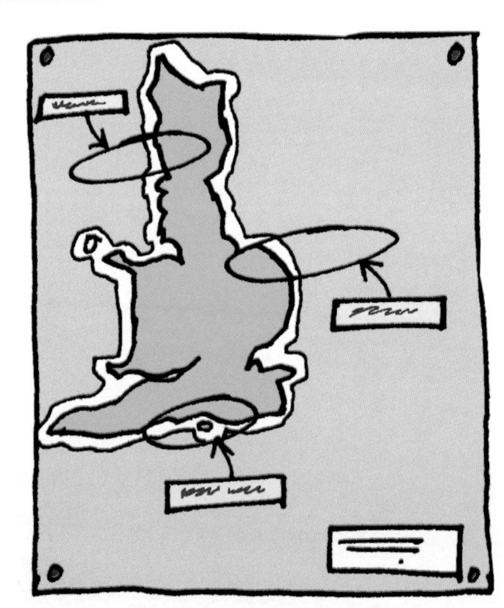

Choosing the right location is important.

- ***How to produce?*** This concerns the methods of production, what and how many people to employ, machines, vehicles, equipment, premises, materials, stock control methods, quality control and so on.

Firms can choose different methods of production.

- ***How to deal with legal and other external constraints?*** Health and safety is a legal constraint on a business. Environmental considerations and public relations will also influence production decisions.

Firms will be inspected for Health and Safety matters.

- ***How can technology help?*** Technology has changed the way in which many goods and services are produced. In particular, it can lead to savings in terms of costs. Sometimes the introduction of new technology leads to redundancies; sometimes it results in the creation of new jobs.

ACTIVITY

Prepare and carry out an interview with someone who works. A relative, neighbour or friend may be able to help. Alternatively, you might ask your supervisor during work experience. Record your answers. You will be able to use what you learn throughout the study of the Unit.

The purpose of the interview is to get a general picture of how production takes place in one particular business. The questions should deal with the following:

- What products or services does the business make?
- Where is the business located? What are the reasons for this location?
- What materials are used in production? Where do these come from? How are they ordered and stored?
- Which people are involved in production? What do they do?
- What machines, equipment, premises and vehicles are used?
- How does production take place? (A description of the process.)
- Where are the finished goods stored, how are they delivered to the customer?
- What changes have taken place in the last few years – to the goods and services produced, to the numbers and types of workers employed, the machinery and equipment used?
- What steps are taken to deal with health and safety risks – training, warning signs and so on?
- Is the business environmentally conscious?

Unit 4.1 Organisation charts

There are two ways in which we use the word 'production' in Business Studies. It is used in a narrow sense to mean only those activities that relate to the physical making of goods and the provision of services. Mixing dough to make bread would be an example of production in this narrow sense. It is also used in a broad sense to mean any activity that contributes to the process of production of goods and services. Activities such as personnel, marketing and accounting are a part of production process.

In this Unit, the focus is on production in its broad sense.

Specialisation

Many workers concentrate on one particular task. Examples of workers with one particular responsibility are personnel and finance managers, administrative assistants and accounts clerks, production operatives, lorry drivers and shop assistants. This is known as specialisation or the division of labour. The table below summarises the advantages and disadvantages of specialisation to a firm.

Advantages of specialisation

- Workers are more efficient because they practise one task, so improving their skills and talents.
- The organisation will increase its production.
- Costs may fall as the work is done more efficiently.
- Fewer tools are required since each worker needs only one particular kind.
- It is easier to automate the process of production when it has been broken down into a series of specific tasks.

Disadvantages of specialisation

- The work may be repetitive and boring for the workers and this can lead to a lack of interest and efficiency.
- Workers may only have one skill; they cannot switch to another task if there is not much work for them to do.
- Workers have more power to disrupt production by taking industrial action since other workers may be dependent on what they do.

Table 4.1 Advantages and disadvantages of specialisation

ACTIVITY 1

John Taylor runs a garage that maintains and services cars and fits car alarms. He employs a mechanic to do the maintenance and servicing of the cars and fits the alarms himself.

1. What are the advantages of this kind of specialisation to John's garage business?
2. What might be the disadvantages to the business of this specialisation?

Multi-skilling

Multi-skilling is when workers are trained to perform more than one type of task. For example, an electrician might also learn how to plaster walls. The advantage of multi-skilling is that it overcomes some of the disadvantages of specialisation. The

ACTIVITY 2

John Stubbs runs a garden centre. He employs five people. They share out the different tasks that need to be done – selling in the shop, driving the van to pick up materials and deliver produce, keeping the books and general office work, planting and tending to the plants and shrubs that they grow.

(a) What benefits will this method of working bring to the garden centre business?
(b) How else might John organise the workers? What benefits would this alternative way of working bring to his business?
(c) Do you think that there could be any disadvantages for the firm from this way of working?

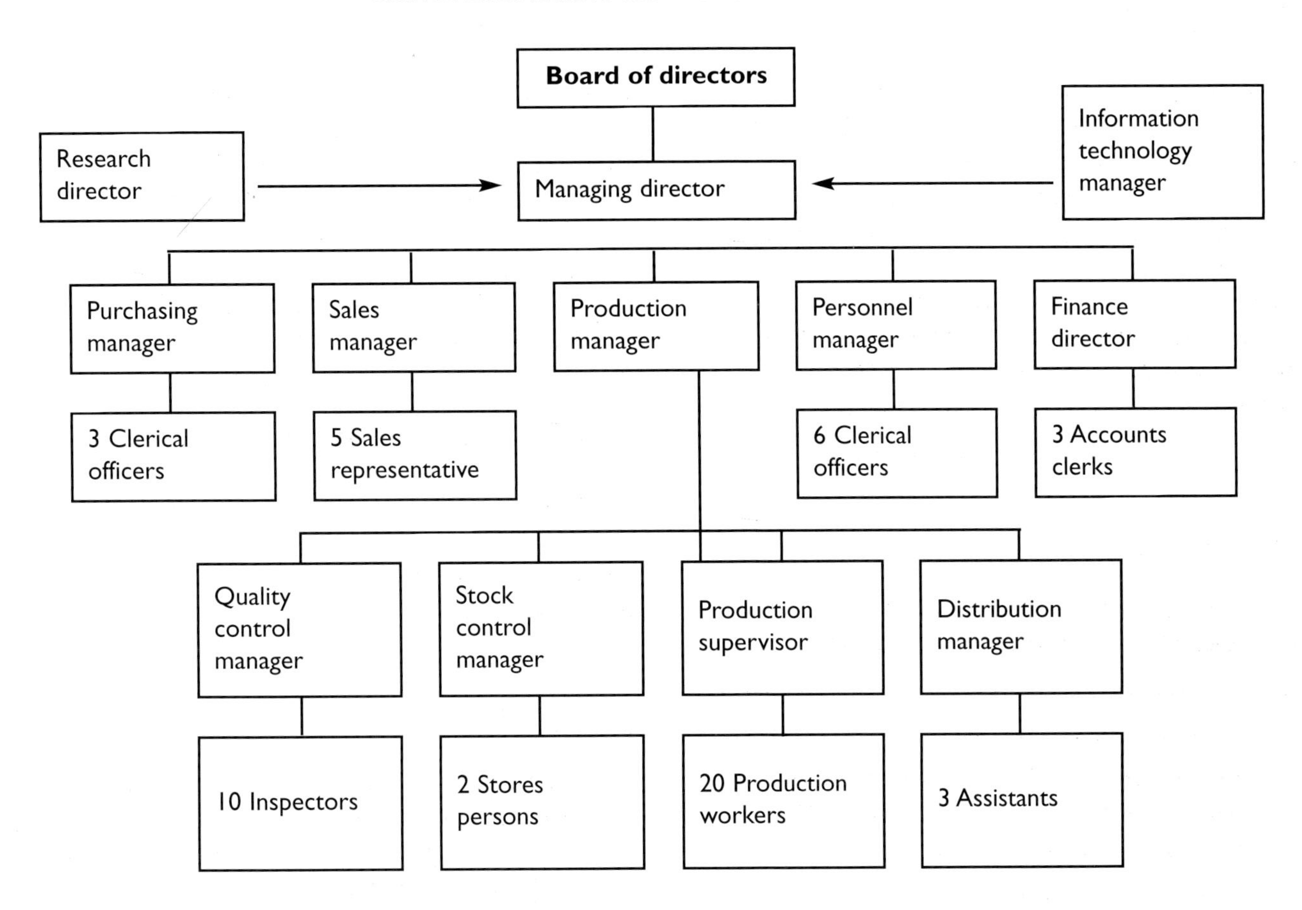

electrician would not need to send for a plasterer to complete a job once the electrical wiring had been put in place. This would save the firm time and money as well as providing the electrician with some variety in his or her work.

Organisation charts

Organisation charts can be used to examine how production is organised. They show how responsibilities in an organisation are divided up amongst different departments and people. An example of an organisation chart is shown above.

The jargon used in connection with organisation charts is very precise. In the explanation of organisation charts, important words have been highlighted.

Griffin Engineering Ltd makes components for motor cars. In this organisation, departments are organised by **function**. This means that each department has a specific job to do. For example, the purchasing department will be responsible for buying in the materials that are needed to make the components, the sales department will be responsible for finding customers to buy the components and the personnel department will carry out all the jobs connected with recruitment, training and relations with the workforce. The information technology and research departments have responsibility for helping all the other departments when they need it. They are known as **staff** departments. For example, the IT manager will give advice to other departments about the kind of hardware and software that the other departments should use.

ACTIVITY 3

Answer the following questions based on the organisation chart of Griffin Engineering Ltd.

1. Who is at the top of the hierarchy?
2. Who is the line manager of the sales representative?
3. Who are the subordinates of the finance director?
4. What is the span of control of the production manager?
5. Give one example of a staff manager.
6. How many layers are there in the organisation?
7. Who would the production manager delegate responsibility to for the stocks of raw materials?
8. Who would be involved in the line of communication between the managing director and the stock control manager?
9. Who would be accountable if the sales of the business did not reach the target set by the managing director?
10. The personnel manager delegates responsibility for advertising jobs and dealing with application forms to a subordinate. Write down which of the following might be benefits that result:
    - The subordinate may become more motivated because he or she feels that she has been given a specific area of responsibility.
    - The subordinate may feel that the personnel manager is taking advantage of him or her.
    - The personnel manager may feel that he or she is losing responsibility and may not be paid as much by the firm.
    - The personnel manager may have more time to oversee the work of all the members of the department rather than getting tied down by detailed work.
    - The subordinate may improve his or her management skills and this could lead to future promotion.
    - The work will be done by a specialist and so the quality of the work should improve.

The organisation is also a **hierarchy**. It has several **layers**. Those on the higher layers have more responsibility and **authority** than those on the layers below. Authority is the power to make decisions and the right to tell other workers what they have to do. **Accountability** goes with authority. If some thing goes wrong, the person at fault is the one with responsibility for that function. There is a **chain of command** with those at the top of the hierarchy being able to send instructions to those lower down. The managing director of Griffin Engineering Ltd has more authority than the production manager who is on a lower layer of the organisation. The managing director could send an order to the quality control manager through the production manager. This would represent the **line of communication** through which the order was made. The person that a worker is responsible to is their **line manager**. The workers that someone is responsible for are known as their **subordinates**. The number of subordinates that a manager is responsible for is known as their **span of control**. The sales manager has a span of control of five – he or she is the line manager for the five sales representatives who are his or her subordinates in the department. The line manager will have been **delegated** responsibility by his or her line manager. This means that he or she will have been given authority to make certain decisions and to carry out specific responsibilities. For example, the production manager may have delegated responsibility to the quality control manager for how the quality of production will be monitored. The information technology manager does not have a typical departmental responsibility. He or she is responsible for providing a service, technical support and advice, to all the other departments. Supporting departments across the hierarchy, the manager is a **staff manager**.

The benefits of organisation charts

These charts help organisations in the following ways:

- They show clearly who is responsible for which functions and tasks – what a person is accountable for. The work is delegated to specialists and so the quality of the work should be high.

- They show who a worker is responsible to, who they must take orders from.
- They help communication to take place within the organisation because they indicate the lines of communication that should be used.
- It shows how the different departments are linked together.

Formal and informal groups

The organisation shows only the formal groups, such as the departments, that exist in an organisation. They have specific jobs to do. Informal groups often come into existence in many organisations. These are not set up by the organisation. An informal group could consist of people from different departments who meet together every day to have lunch or who play together in the work's football or hockey team.

Sometimes informal groups are good for the organisation. Workers in one department may share ideas with workers in another department. Their discussion may lead to better ways of doing things. However, informal groups can have a bad effect if people in the groups have negative attitudes to the firm and to work and these de-motivate other workers.

Tall and flat organisations

The height of an organisation depends on how many layers there are in it.

Organisation A has a tall structure. It has five layers – many organisations have more layers than this. Organisation B has a flat structure. It has only two layers.

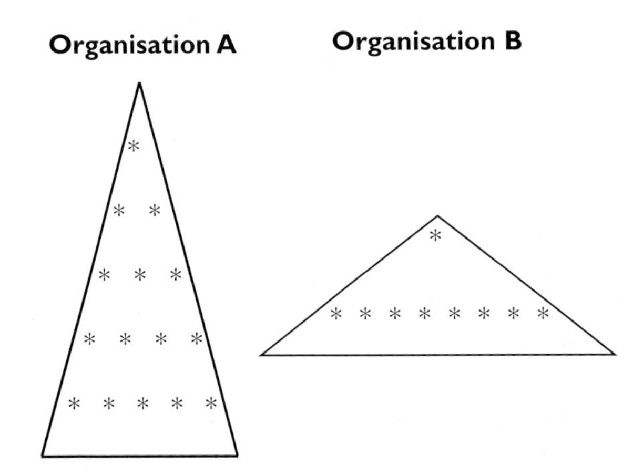

Advantages of tall structures	*Advantages of flat structures*
• The lines of communication and the responsibilities of the workers are clear. • The span of control of managers is likely to be narrower than in flat structures, meaning that he or she does not have too many people to look after. • There will be plenty of opportunities for workers to gain promotion which will motivate them.	• Communication from top to bottom will be quicker than in tall structures because there are not as many layers. • It is likely that fewer mistakes in communications will occur because messages do not have to be passed through so many layers. • People at the bottom may be encouraged to share ideas with those at the top because they will know who they are and what they are like. • The wider spans of control of managers will mean that they must delegate work. This will make the workers feel trusted and help to motivate them.

Table 4.2 Advantages and disadvantages of tall and flat organisations.

ACTIVITY 4

Midlothian Clothing Ltd is a company that imports fashion clothing made in South-East Asia.

Using the information provided below, write or word-process a short report about the proposal to de-layer. The report should contain a drawing of the organisation of the business and an explanation of the possible benefits and problems that would result from de-layering.

1. It has a board of directors, a managing director, national marketing, personnel, finance, purchasing and distribution managers. Below the marketing manager there are three regional sales managers each with a team of five sales representatives. The personnel and finance departments have three workers each. The purchasing department has four buyers. The distribution department employs 25 drivers.
2. It is planning to de-layer by laying off the three regional sales managers. The sales representatives would be given targets by the national manager. What benefits and what problems might this bring to Midlothian Clothing?

De-layering

This is when one or more of the layers of management are removed from the business.

In the Griffin Engineering Ltd organisation chart on page 103, an example of de-layering would be if the managers directly below the production manager were removed – the quality control manager, the stock control manager and the production supervisor. De-layering has the following advantages:

- It saves money since the organisation will no longer need to pay the salaries of the workers it has laid off.
- The responsibilities of those workers who were laid off would need to be delegated to the next layer of workers. If this happens, the workers are said to have been **empowered**. These workers may feel good about having extra responsibility and being trusted by senior managers to make decisions. However, some workers would not be happy to accept the responsibility.

EXAM Practice Questions

The following is the organisation chart for Carlton Press Ltd, a book publisher.

1. Describe the main features of the internal organisation of Carlton Press Ltd. (8 marks)
2. State and explain two advantages of having a formal organisation structure like this. (6 marks)
3. What are the benefits to Carlton Press Ltd of having a specialist sales manager? (2 marks)

(Adapted from the OCR 1998 Higher and Foundation Tier Core Papers.)

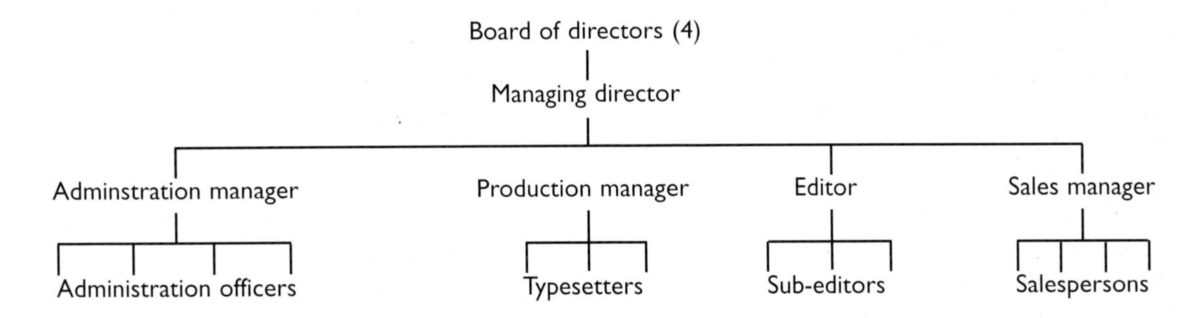

ADVICE ON HOW TO ANSWER THE QUESTIONS

1. The command word in Question 1 is 'describe'. You have to write down a description of how the business is organised. Business Studies, like many other subjects, has its own jargon. This question is a good example of where it is crucial to use the jargon of the subject. In the description you should use words like 'hierarchy', 'chain of command', 'span of control', 'line manager' and 'subordinate' and so on.
2. This question is designed to test your knowledge of the advantages of formal organisation structures and the benefits of this particular structure to the case study firm.
3. This question is designed to test your ability to apply your knowledge about the advantages of specialisation to the case study firm. Read over the list of advantages in the text and then work out how these will apply to the job that the sales manager must do.

Authority *The power that one person has to make decisions and to control what other workers do.*

Accountability *The responsibility that a person has for a job meaning that he or she will take the blame for what goes wrong as well as the credit for what goes well.*

Chain of command *The link in the levels of authority from those at the top with the most authority to those at the bottom with the least.*

Function *The specific job that a person or department must do.*

Hierarchy *This is when a business is organised from the top down, the people higher up the hierarchy having more power than those below them.*

Line of communication *The route that a message travels between the sender and the person that it is for.*

Line manager *This is a person who is directly responsible for other workers in the organisation.*

Staff manager *A person who supports other departments across the organisation.*

Organisation chart *A diagram that shows how the workers are organised in a business and who is in charge of whom.*

Subordinates *The workers that a line manager is responsible for.*

Span of control *The number of subordinates who report directly to the line manager.*

Specialisation *When workers concentrate on only one task or one responsibility.*

Layers *The number of levels of authority that there are in the chain of command.*

De-layering *When one or more levels of authority are removed from the hierarchy.*

Empowerment *Giving responsibility and authority to workers.*

Delegation *When a manager gives authority to a subordinate to make certain decisions which that manager is responsible for.*

Formal groups *Those groups set up by the organisation with the responsibility to carry out a function, for example the finance or personnel departments.*

Informal groups *Groups of people who meet but who have not been identified within the organisational chart.*

EXAMINATION SUMMARY TIPS

- Specialisation leads to many benefits for an organisation but it may also lead to some problems.
- Multi-skilling can overcome some of the problems of specialisation but it is not always possible or desirable.
- Organisation charts show who does what in an organisation. They help to show who has responsibility and for what. This helps communications to take place. A lot of jargon is used to describe organisation charts.
- Organisations may have tall or flat organisational structures. Different structures will meet the needs of different organisations.
- De-layering takes place when a layer of responsibility is taken away from an organisation. It can lead to benefits including the empowerment of workers who were previously supervised by the manager or managers who have been removed.

Key Skills

Activity 4 presents an opportunity to write a document (Communication C1.3 or 2.3). The document may be word-processed (IT1.3 or IT2.3).

Unit 4.2 Business costs and revenues

Sales revenue is the money that a business receives for selling the goods or services that it produces. Costs are the payments that a business makes in order to make goods and services. A business will make a profit if its revenue is more than its costs. It will make a loss if revenue is less than costs. When a firm makes a loss, it will need to borrow money or to use up its savings. These savings are known as reserves. If a business does not make profits, eventually it will not survive – lenders will stop providing loans or the reserves will be used up. For this reason, the management of revenues and costs is very important.

If revenue is greater than costs, a profit will be made.

Sales revenue

Another name for sales revenue is **sales turnover**. The money that a business makes in sales revenue depends on how much it sells and at what price. This can be summed up using a formula:

Sales revenue = Quantity sold × Selling price

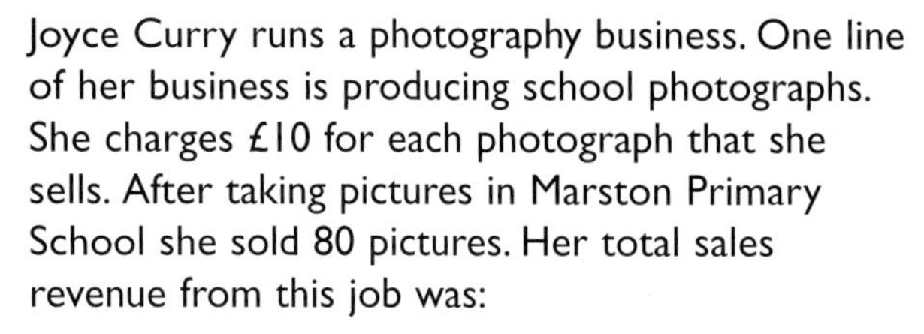

Joyce Curry runs a photography business. One line of her business is producing school photographs. She charges £10 for each photograph that she sells. After taking pictures in Marston Primary School she sold 80 pictures. Her total sales revenue from this job was:

Sales revenue = 80 × £10 = £800

Increasing sales revenue

A business may be able to increase its revenue by either:

- changing the price that it charges – either raising the price **or** reducing the price
- increasing the amount that it sells.

Raising the price

Raising the price may increase sales revenue, but not always. If the quantity sold did not change, when a firm raised its price it would increase its

ACTIVITY 1

The following questions are based on the photography business that Joyce Curry runs.

1. Calculate the total sales revenue if Joyce sells 120 photographs in a school at £10 each.
2. Calculate the total sales revenue if she sold 2 000 photographs per month for six months at £10 each.
3. In the previous six months the sales revenue she received from selling portraits was £10 000. She sold 200 portraits. Calculate the average price of the portraits that she sold.

sales revenue. Suppose that Joyce Curry had charged £11 for the pictures that she took at Marston Primary School and that she had still sold 80 pictures. Her total sales revenue would be:

Sales revenue = 80 × £11 = £880

However, some parents might have been put off by the higher price and decided not to buy a picture. The amount sold would fall. What happens to sales revenue would depend on how much the amount sold fell by. Suppose that when Joyce raised the price to £11 she had sold 75 pictures. Her sales revenue would now be:

Sales revenue = 75 × £11 = £825

Raising the price has increased the sales revenue in this case. However, suppose that when she raised the price to £11, the sales of pictures had fallen to 70. Her sales revenue would now be:

Sales revenue = 70 × £11 = £770

Raising the price has resulted in a decrease in her sales revenue. Thus, effect of the price change depends on what happens to the amount sold.

Reducing the price

Just as the effect of a rise in price on sales revenue depends on what happens to the amount sold, so too does the effect of a fall in price. What happens to the amount of a product that is bought when its price is changed is known as the price elasticity of **demand** of the product. See page 167.

Deciding when to raise or lower prices

When a business wants to raise or lower prices in order to increase its sales revenue, it needs to judge what will happen to the amount it sells. This will depend on a number of factors:

- *The number of competitors* – if there is no competition that customers can buy from, raising the price will not reduce the amount sold by very much.
- *What competitors do* – if competitors also raise prices, the amount is unlikely to fall very much.
- *Whether the product is a necessity or not* – if a good is a necessity, people will have to buy it even though it may be very expensive.

ACTIVITY 2

Joyce Curry decided to reduce the price of school photographs to £9.

1. Calculate her sales revenue if she still sold 80 pictures.
2. Calculate her sales revenue if the amount she sold rose to 100.
3. Calculate her sales revenue if the amount she sold rose to 85.

ACTIVITY 3

Suggest what would happen to sales revenue in each of the following situations. Give reasons for your answers.

1. A shopkeeper decided to raise the price of a box of matches from 10p to 12p.
2. The world price of oil rose. The Red Lion Service Station, like all other petrol stations, decided to raise its price to cover the costs.
3. A supermarket decided to reduce the price of its bread by 20%. Competitors left the price of their bread unchanged.
4. Malcolm Collier runs the only gents' hairdresser in Marston. The nearest competitor is in Mencaster, eight miles away. He raises his prices by 50p a haircut.
5. The Busy Bee Bus Company raises its prices by 15%. Its competitors raise their prices by 8% on average.

- *How much people spend on the good* – if the product is very cheap, people may not be put off buying the product by the higher price.

Increasing the amount sold

A business can increase its sales revenue if it can increase the amount it sells. Suppose that Joyce Curry was able to sell 90 pictures at Martson Primary School at the price of £10. The calculation of her sales revenue now would be:

$$\text{Sales revenue} = 90 \times £10 = £900$$

As well as reducing the price it charges, a business can increase its sales in a number of ways. Three possibilities are stated below:

- increase advertising
- sell in a greater number of outlets
- increase its product range.

All these are connected to the marketing of the product. You should read the section on Marketing to learn more about this.

Business costs

Wages, the cost of materials, rent, the telephone bill, interest on loans and transport costs are just some of the costs that businesses must pay. These costs can be classified under two headings:

Fixed costs

These are costs that do not change when the business changes the amount that it produces. Rent is an example of a fixed cost. Joyce Curry pays £1 000 per month rent for her shop and studio. This cost will not change in the immediate future even if she sells nothing.

Variable costs

These are costs that do change when the business changes the amount it makes. Joyce's variable costs will include buying paper and chemicals. The more she sells, the more she will spend on these. Variable costs may be calculated as follows:

$$\text{Total variable costs} = \text{Quantity sold} \times \text{variable cost per unit}$$

Joyce Curry pays £3 in variable costs for each picture that she produces. The total variable cost of producing 100 pictures would be:

$$\text{Total variable cost} = 100 \times £3 = £300$$

Total costs of production

The total costs of a business are found by adding together the total for all its fixed and variable costs. The total fixed costs that Joyce pays each month add up to £2 100. The total cost of producing 100 pictures would be:

$$\text{Total cost} = £2\ 100 + £300 = £2\ 400$$

Average costs of production

The average cost of production is the cost for each unit of a product that a business sells. It is calculated by:

$$\text{Average cost} = \frac{\text{Total cost}}{\text{Amount sold}}$$

The average cost for Joyce Curry to produce 100 pictures would be:

$$\text{Average costs} = \frac{£2\ 400}{100} = £24.00$$

It is important for a business to calculate average cost because it helps to decide what price to charge for the product. If the business wants to make a profit, it will need to set the price higher than the average cost of production. However, sometimes a firm will set the price lower than the average cost of production. It might do this because it wants to charge a low price so that it takes customers away from its competitors. Another reason would be to maintain production when the demand for its product was low. When a business does this it is known as **contribution pricing**. The price is set so that the business can pay the variable costs and some of its fixed costs. The business makes a loss in the short run, but when business picks up it will raise its price to make a profit.

ACTIVITY 4 

1. Draw a table with two columns. Head one table 'Fixed Costs' and the other 'Variable Costs.'
   (a) Some of the costs of that Joyce Curry must pay to run her photography business are stated below. Write them down on your table under the correct heading:
   - interest payments on a three-year loan
   - cost of photographic paper
   - cost of chemicals used to develop and print
   - the rent on her offices
   - bank charges
   - cost of her weekly advertisement in the local newspaper.

   (b) Think of four more costs that Joyce may have to pay. Add them to the correct column in the table.

2. Copy and complete the following table for the costs of Joyce Curry's photography business. She charges, on average, £10 for each picture. Her fixed costs are £2 100 and variable costs are £3 per picture.
   (a) Using the information in the table, compare the average cost of production when Joyce produces 100 units with the average cost at 1 000 units.
   (b) Predict the effect on profits of (i) a rise in variable costs to £5 per unit and (ii) a fall in variable costs to £2 per unit. You will need to draw two more tables to do this!
   (c) Recommend how Joyce could reduce her average costs of production.

3. Write a report about the production costs for the photography business of Joyce Curry and how profits might be affected by changes in them. Use the questions and the data to help you to plan what to write. If possible, word-process the report. Include the data about her production costs. If possible, use a spreadsheet to create this. If you know how to, enter the formula, where necessary, in each column. Otherwise, your teacher may provide you with a spreadsheet that contains the formula already. Use the spreadsheet to predict the effects of the rise in the variable costs from £3 per picture to £5 per picture and of the fall in variable costs to £2.

Pictures sold	Total sales revenue	Total fixed costs	Total variable costs	Total costs	Profit	Average cost
0	0	2 100	0	2 100		
100	1 000	2 100	300	2 400		
200						
300						
400						
500						
600						
700						
800						
900						
1 000						

Managing costs

Managers need to control costs.

It is important for firms to control costs. Lower costs may mean higher profits. Also, a firm that can lower its average costs can lower its prices and still make a profit. The firm may be able to attract customers away from its competitors because of its lower prices.

Some of the ways that firms can reduce average costs are:

- *Spreading fixed costs* – by increasing production, the average cost per unit falls. For example, if a firm has fixed costs of £100 000 and it produces 20 000 units of a product its average cost is £5. If the firm can raise production to 25 000 units the average cost would fall to £4. Spreading fixed costs is achieved by using fixed capital, like machinery, premises and vehicles, more fully.
- *Reducing the amount paid for resources* – this could be achieved, for example, by shopping around for a better price for raw materials, or reducing wage costs.
- *Increasing the efficiency of labour* – this may be achieved by improving their motivation (See Unit 6.2 Pay and motivation) or by changing the way in which they work, for example by switching from job to mass production (see Unit 4.5 Production and technology)
- *By achieving economies of large-scale production* – these cost savings are achieved in the long run as the business increases its scale of production, perhaps by moving into a larger factory. Economies of scale are dealt with in more detail in Unit 4.4 The scale of production.

Production costs and pie charts

Pie charts may be used to show the breakdown of production costs. The pie charts below show the breakdown of the selling costs of a pair of jeans that a market stallholder, David Morris, had to pay. The first chart shows his costs in 1988, the second his costs in 1998.

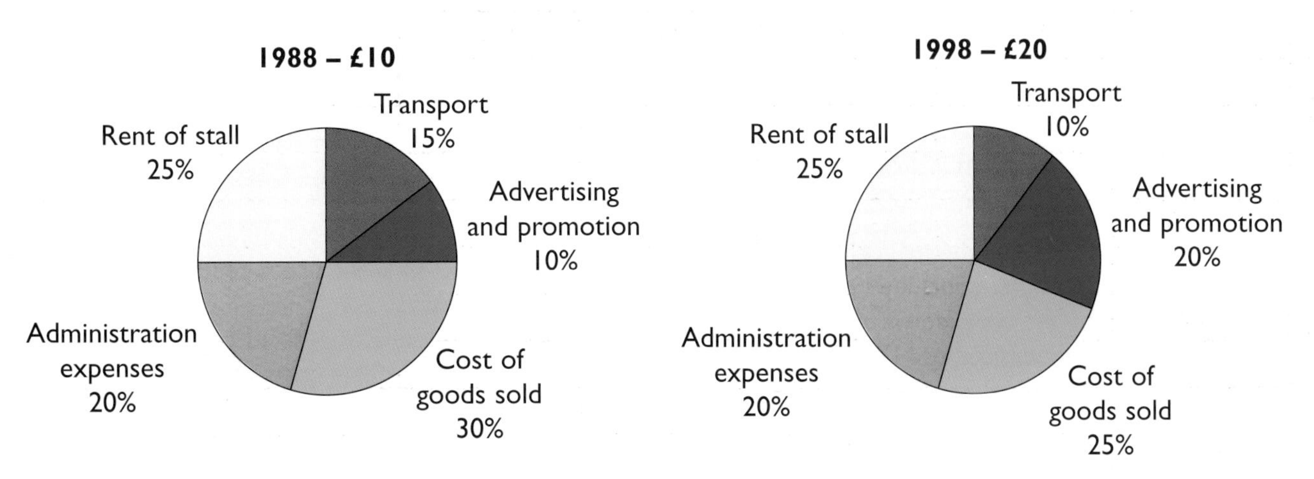

(Taken from OCR Business Studies GCSE Higher Tier Paper, 1999.)

Care must be taken when interpreting pie charts. The segments of each 'pie' show a percentage of the total. In the case of production cost pie charts, a segment shows the percentage of the total cost of production accounted for by one kind of cost. In the example, in 1988, 25% of the cost of selling a pair of jeans was paying the rent on the market stall. The total cost of selling a pair of jeans in 1988 was £10. This means that £2.50 was the amount that was paid in rent for each pair of jeans sold. The percentage paid in rent for the stall was still 25% in 1998. However, the total cost of a pair of jeans had risen to £20. This meant that the amount paid in rent for the stall for each pair of jeans sold was now £5.

Sometimes the percentage accounted for by one type of cost can decrease but the actual amount paid rises. This happens with transport costs in the above example. In 1988, transport costs were 15% of total costs. This means that £1.50 was the amount paid to transport each pair of jeans. In 1998, transport costs had fallen to 10% of total costs. The total cost of a pair of jeans had risen to £20 so the amount paid for each pair of jeans for transport was now £2.00.

ACTIVITY 5

Magdalen Engineering Ltd produces hydraulic equipment. The table below shows how the breakdown of costs has changed between 1995 and 2000.

	1995 Percentage of costs	**2000 Percentage of costs**
Rent for the factory premises	15	10
Cost of raw materials	15	20
Labour costs	20	20
Marketing costs	5	15
Administration costs	20	15
Other costs	25	20

The total cost of production in 1995 was £100 000. The total cost of production in 2000 was £200 000.

Write a report describing the main changes in the costs that have taken place. Include in your report pie charts showing the breakdown of costs for each of the years. If possible, use IT to help you to produce the report. Word-process the report. Use a spreadsheet package to produce a table of information and to create the pie charts.

EXAM Practice Question

Wanborough Park Hotel has 70 rooms. Thirty of these rooms and all the public facilities are in the main building. The other 40 rooms are in the annexe next door. The annexe is closed during the less busy periods of the year from November to April.

The following table shows cost and revenue figures for the hotel.

Fixed costs (Daily)	0–100 beds available	£2 000
	101–140 beds available	£2 100
Variable costs	Per occupant (May–October)	£20
	Per occupant (November–April)	£15
Revenue	Per occupant (May–October)	£50
	Per occupant (November–April)	£40

Wanborough Park Hotel – Cost and revenue figures.

(a) Explain the difference between fixed and variable costs. (4 marks)

(b) Give **two** examples of fixed costs and **two** examples of variable costs which might be appropriate for the hotel industry. (4 marks)

(c) Explain why, in this case, fixed costs are not the same regardless of the number of beds. (4 marks)

(d) During the period November to April, the hotel has an average of 80 occupants per night. Calculate the profit or loss that it will make each night on average during this period. Show your working. (2 marks)

(e) During the period May to October, the average occupancy rises to 110. Calculate the profit or loss that it will make each night on average during this period. Show your working. (2 marks)

(Adapted from OCR Modular Business Studies 1352, November 1999, Module 3 Test and Synoptic Assessment.)

ADVICE ON HOW TO ANSWER THE QUESTIONS

(a) The command word in this question is 'explain'. You are being tested on your knowledge of the meaning of the two terms. Learn the definitions of the terms and write them down accurately.

(b) The question is designed to test your ability to apply your knowledge. You need to think of costs that hotels are likely to have to pay and then, bearing in mind the definitions you have used in answer to part (a), decide whether they are fixed or variable costs.

(c) You need to read this question carefully. The question is really asking why fixed costs for the summer are more than those for the winter period. What additional fixed costs might the hotel have to pay in the summer when the annexe is open?

(d) and (e) The instruction, 'Show your working,' means that marks will be awarded for showing the correct method of calculation (even if you get the answer wrong). Often, there are more marks for the method than for the answer, so make sure you obey the command. Read the figures very carefully – it would be easy to confuse May to October figures with November to April figures. Write the method out neatly and fully – this will help you to avoid mistakes.

KEY TERMS

Sales revenue or sales turnover *The amount of money that a business receives from selling what it produces or provides.*

Fixed costs *Those costs that do not change as the business changes the amount it produces.*

Variable costs *Those costs that rise as the business increases production and fall when it reduces production.*

Total costs of production *The fixed and variable costs of a particular level of production added together.*

Average cost of production *The cost per unit made.*

Profit *The sales revenue minus the total costs of production.*

Contribution pricing *When the price of a product is set below the average total costs but above the average variable cost so that some of the fixed costs per unit are paid for.*

EXAMINATION SUMMARY TIPS

- Businesses earn sales revenues by selling goods and services.
- Businesses pay out costs in order to produce the goods and services they sell.
- The profit a business makes is the difference between its sales revenue and its costs.
- A business may be able to increase its revenues by raising or lowering the price it charges.
- There are different types of costs – fixed, variable, average and total.

Key Skills

Activity 4, Part 2 provides an opportunity for Application of Number work at Level 1. The calculations meet the requirements of calculating amounts (N1.2). Part 3 is an opportunity for both Communication and Information Technology. A written report would be evidence of your ability to write a document (C1.3). If you word-process the report you would working at Level 1 (IT1.3). If you know how to create a spreadsheet and enter formulae you can do this to predict the effects of the changes stated in the question. This would be evidence for IT2.2. If you can combine this data into your word-processed report, you will meet the requirements for IT2.3.

Activity 5 provides an opportunity for Application of Number work at Level 2 because you are required to perform calculations to make comparisons between two sets of data and present your results (N2.2 and N2.3). You have not chosen the data you need for the exercise and obtained it so the exercise cannot provide evidence for your portfolio but this is a good exercise for practising the skill.

The Activity, in the same way as Activity 4, provides an opportunity for Communication and Information Technology work.

Unit 4.3 Break-even

Businesses use information about revenues and costs to calculate their break-even level of output. A firm breaks even when its costs of production are equal to its sales revenue. This means that the firm does not make any profit, nor does it make a loss.

A firm breaks even when sales revenue equals costs.

Break-even analysis

Many firms use information about costs and sales revenues to predict whether they will make a profit, a loss or will break even. The information about costs and revenue may be estimated from what these have been in the past or what the firm thinks that they will be in the future. The information is presented in the form of tables and graphs.

David Adams plans to open a sandwich bar. The following table shows the costs and revenues that David expects for a range of sales from 0 to 1 200 sandwiches per week.

From the table, we can see that David will make a loss if he sells either 200, 400 or 600 sandwiches per week. If he sells 600 units, his loss is £100 per week. To avoid making a loss he must sell at least 800 units per week. This is the break-even output, when he does not make a loss but does not make any profit either. When he sells more than 800 units he will make a profit. If he sold 1 200 units he would make £200 profit for the week. The amount by which his actual sales are greater than the level of sales he needs to break even is known as the **margin of safety**. If David does sell 1 200 sandwiches in a week then his margin of safety is:

Margin of Safety = 1 200 − 800 = 400

Sandwiches sold	Sales revenue	Fixed costs	Variable costs	Total costs	Profit/Loss
0	0	400	0	400	−400
200	160	400	60	460	−300
400	320	400	120	520	−200
600	480	400	180	580	−100
800	640	400	240	640	0
1 000	800	400	300	700	100
1 200	960	400	360	760	200

Table 4.3 Sandwich Bar – Break-even analysis

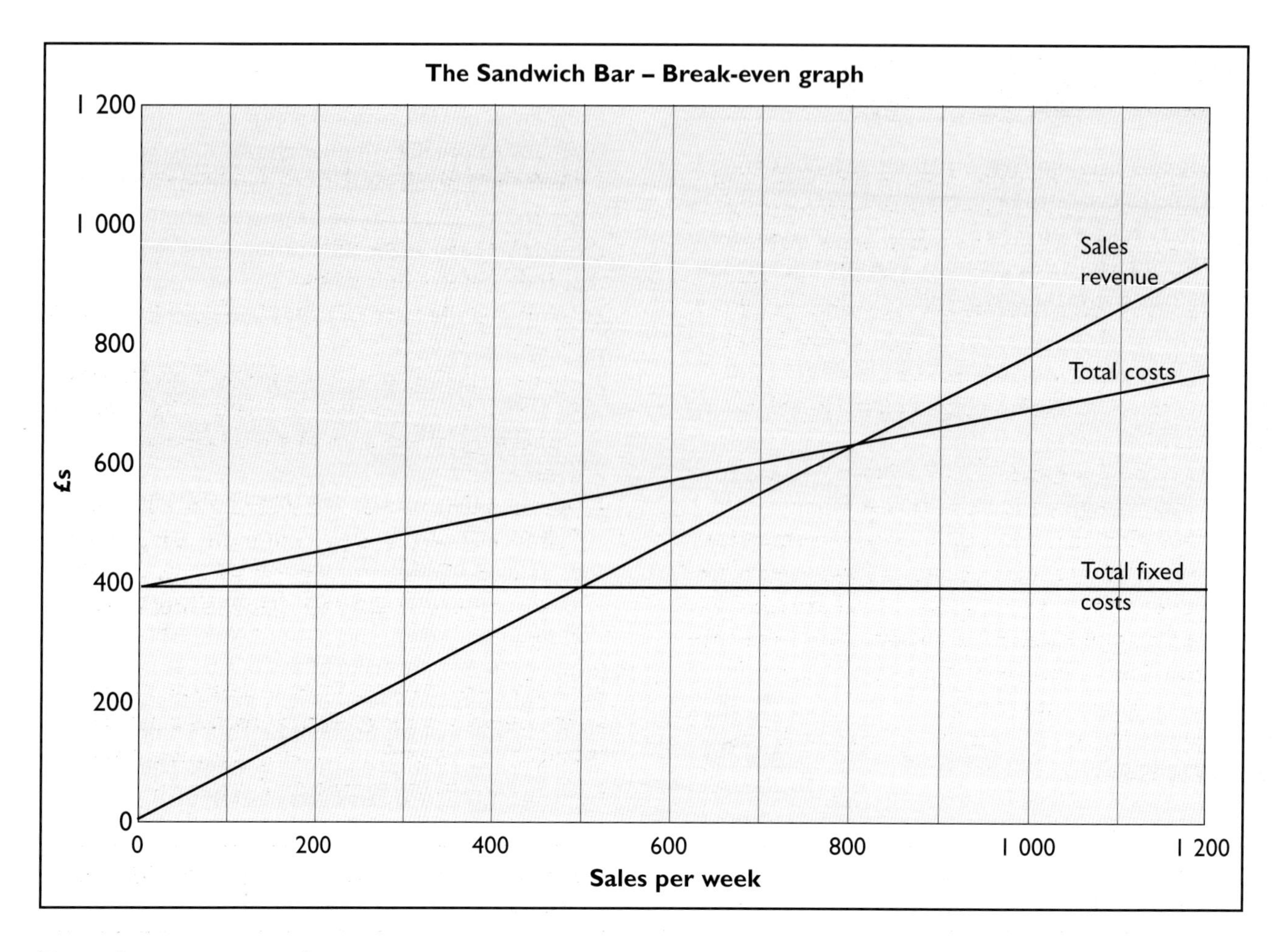

Break-even graphs

It is common for businesses to present break-even figures in the form of a line graph. The graph above shows the break-even analysis for David Adams' sandwich bar.

Uses of break-even analysis

People often use break-even figures when they are starting a business. These figures will help them to plan how much to sell in order to make a profit. If a person needs a loan from a bank, the bank manager will often ask to see a break-even graph as part of the business plan. Break-even information can be used to make judgements about prices and costs. The figures may show a need either to increase the price of the product to raise revenue or to reduce the costs. For example, David Adams may decide that a break-even figure of 800 is too high. He might be able to raise the price to increase the sales revenue. Alternatively, he may feel that this is not possible, perhaps because of the competition that he faces. If this were the case, he would have to see if he could cut the costs in any way. Perhaps he could use cheaper ingredients in the sandwiches to achieve this?

Limitations of break-even analysis

Break-even forecasts need to be treated with care. Businesses should remember that the figures are forecasts and that the future may turn out to be different from what they predict. The graph that shows the break-even forecast for the sandwich bar is based on estimates of what price David thinks he will be able to charge in the future, the amounts he will sell at that price and the costs of production connected with those sales. These may change for several reasons:

- The number of competitors in the market may change. If another sandwich bar opened in the

ACTIVITY 1

Paul Sherry runs a driving school. The fixed costs of running the school include the repayment of loans on the cars he owns and administration costs. He calculates these to be £500 per week. The variable costs are the costs of labour and petrol. He calculates these to be £20 per lesson. He charges £30 for each lesson.

1. Use this information to complete the table below.
2. Use the information in the table to draw a break-even graph for the driving school. Remember that you will need to measure sales revenue and costs in pounds on the vertical axis and lessons sold on the horizontal axis. You will need to plot three lines – fixed costs, total costs and sales revenue. It is important to label the axes and the lines clearly.
3. Draw a line on the graph to show the break-even point.
4. How much profit or loss would Paul make if he sold:
   (a) 70 lessons in a week?
   (b) 20 lessons in a week?
5. What would be his margin of safety if he sold 90 lessons in a week?
6. Suppose that he raised the price of his lessons to £35. Draw a new graph to show the effect of this change. What would be the break-even output?
7. Suppose that, at the original price of £30 per lesson, David was faced with costs rising to £25 per lesson. Draw a new graph to show the effect of this change. What would be the break-even output?

If possible, use a spreadsheet to provide answers to the questions above. Word-process a report, including the spreadsheet and graphs, about the break-even analysis for the driving school.

Lessons per week	Sales revenue	Fixed costs	Variable costs	Total costs	Profit/Loss
0					
10					
20					
30					
40					
50					
60					
70					
80					
90					
100					

same area, David may sell less or he may need to reduce the price that he charges to maintain his sales. David would find that he would have to sell more to break-even than he had forecast.

New competition may mean lower revenues.

ACTIVITY 2

Suppose that you plan to raise money for a charity in school by selling fairy cakes. The Food Technology teacher has said that you can cook in his room at lunchtime if you pay £2. This will be your fixed cost of production.

1. Plan how many cakes you will try to sell.
2. Work out the ingredients and materials that you will need to make these cakes.
3. Calculate the cost of ingredients for each cake. This will be your variable cost per cake.
4. Using your knowledge of break-even analysis, draw the appropriate table and graph.
5. Calculate
   (a) how many cakes you will need to break even and
   (b) how much profit you will make if you sell all the cakes.
6. Explain why you may not make as much profit as you predict.

(You may complete this exercise using a product other than cakes if this is appropriate).

- The cost of ingredients may change. If the cost falls, he will find that he does not have to sell as many to break even.

Calculating break-even

It is possible to calculate the break-even output without constructing a table or drawing a chart. To do this you need to use this formula:

$$\text{Break-even output} = \frac{\text{Total fixed costs}}{\text{Contribution per unit}}$$

The **contribution** per unit is calculated using this formula:

Contribution per unit =
Selling price of the product − Variable cost per unit.

Suppose that a picture framer has fixed costs of £10 000 per year. He charges £50 per picture that he frames. The variable cost of each picture he frames is £30. Using this information, the break-even output would be calculated by doing the following sums:

Contribution per unit =
£50 (selling price) − 30 (variable cost per unit) = £20

$$\text{Break-even output} = \frac{\text{£10 000 (Total fixed cost)}}{\text{£20}} = 500.$$

ACTIVITY 3

The figures below show costs and revenues for a toy manufacturer:

- total fixed costs of producing the toys are £50 000 per year
- variable costs per product sold are £2
- the selling price of the toys is £6 each.

Using the calculation method, work out how many toys the manufacturer must use to break even.

EXAM Practice Questions

Carlton Press Ltd publishes a Business Studies textbook. It forecasts the following revenues and costs for the book:

The variable costs are £2 per book

The book sells at £5

Sales of books	Total fixed costs (£)	Total variable costs (£)	Total costs (£)	Total revenue (£)
0	30 000	0	30 000	0
5 000	30 000	10 000	40 000	25 000
10 000	30 000	B	50 000	50 000
15 000	30 000	30 000	C	75 000
20 000	A	40 000	70 000	100 000

(i) Calculate the following:
A – The fixed cost of producing 20 000 books. (1 mark)
B – The total variable cost of producing 10 000. (1 mark)
C – The total cost of producing 15 000 books. (1 mark)

(ii) Calculate the profit or loss made if 5 000 books were sold. Show your working. (3 marks)

(iii) Use the information in the table to create a break-even graph. (6 marks)

(iv) Mark on the graph how many books Carlton Press Ltd have to sell to break even. (1 mark)

(v) Give **two** examples of fixed costs and **two** examples of variable costs that Carlton Press Ltd is likely to pay. (4 marks)

(vi) Explain why Carlton Press Ltd should take care when using a break-even forecast like this. (4 marks)

(Adapted from OCR Business Studies GCSE 1351, Foundation and Higher Tier Papers, 1998.)

ADVICE ON HOW TO ANSWER THE QUESTION

Parts (i) and (ii) require you to use your knowledge of the terms – fixed costs, variable costs, total costs and break-even – and apply them so that you perform the correct calculations.

Part (iii): Take care to draw the graph neatly and accurately. Marks will also be allocated for labelling the axes and the lines on the graph

Part (iv): Make sure that you read the graph at the point that the sales revenue and total costs lines cross and on the correct axis. You could check your answer by using the calculation method to work out the break-even output.

Part (v): You need to write a clear explanation of the problems of break-even forecasts, mentioning the changes that might occur after the forecasts have been made.

KEY TERMS

Break-even output *The output at which a firm neither makes a loss nor a profit.*

Break-even forecast *A prediction about the break-even output based on estimates of future sales revenues and costs.*

Margin of Safety *The amount by which a firm's actual output is greater than its break-even output.*

Contribution per unit *The amount by which the selling price of a product is greater than the variable cost. The amount is used to pay for the fixed costs of production.*

EXAMINATION SUMMARY TIPS

- Businesses use forecasts of sales revenues, fixed and total costs to analyse the break-even.
- The figures may be presented in a table or on a graph.
- The figures may be used to calculate the break-even output and the losses or profits that are made at different levels of output.
- The figures are only forecasts of revenues and costs – actual revenues and costs may differ.

Key Skills

Activity 1 requires the use of your Application of Number skills at Level 1 (N1.2 and N1.3).

If you use a computer to do this work you may be working at Level 1 or 2, depending on how much help you receive from the teacher to create the spreadsheets and the graphs. (IT1.2 or IT2.2). If you combine your spreadsheet data into a word-processed document containing the answers to the question, you may meet the requirements for IT2.3. You will need to make sure that you have used appropriate layouts, that the presentation suits your purpose and that the work is accurate, clear and saved appropriately.

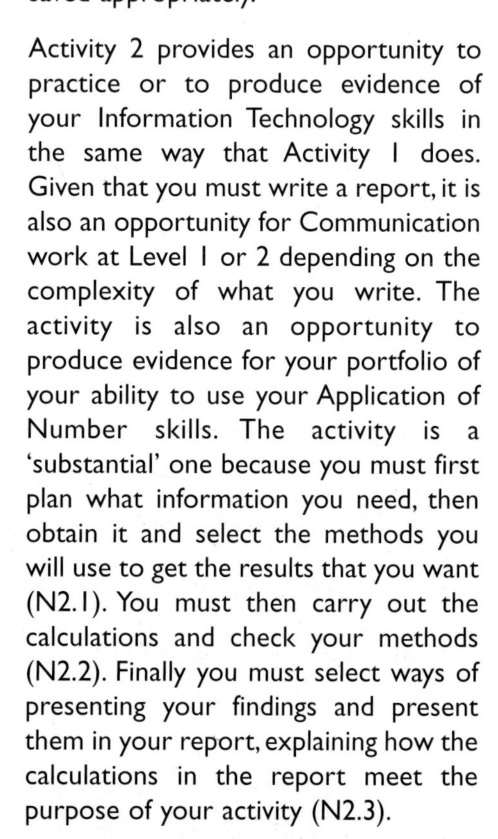

Activity 2 provides an opportunity to practice or to produce evidence of your Information Technology skills in the same way that Activity 1 does. Given that you must write a report, it is also an opportunity for Communication work at Level 1 or 2 depending on the complexity of what you write. The activity is also an opportunity to produce evidence for your portfolio of your ability to use your Application of Number skills. The activity is a 'substantial' one because you must first plan what information you need, then obtain it and select the methods you will use to get the results that you want (N2.1). You must then carry out the calculations and check your methods (N2.2). Finally you must select ways of presenting your findings and present them in your report, explaining how the calculations in the report meet the purpose of your activity (N2.3).

Activity 3 is an opportunity to practise your Application of Number skills at Level 1 (N1.2).

Unit 4.4 The scale of production

Every business has a **capacity** for its production. The capacity of a business is the amount that it is set up to produce with the resources that it has at present. Sometimes a business will produce more than its capacity. When this happens it is described as producing '**above capacity**.' Sometimes a business produces less than it is capable of producing. It is then said to be producing with '**excess capacity**.'

In 1998 Langdale Woollens operated from a small, converted barn in the Lake District. The barn, with the equipment in it, was designed to produce 30 knitted sweaters each week. 30 sweaters per week is the capacity of the business. In the winter, when sales are lower, the firm makes 20 sweaters. It has an excess capacity of 10. In the summer, production can be pushed to 35 sweaters per week. In these weeks it is producing above its capacity.

Economies of scale

A firm increases its scale of production when it increases its capacity. When the scale of production increases, it is likely that total production costs will also increase. Investment may be necessary to increase the premises and the equipment available to the business. The investment will raise costs. If a bank loan was used to finance the investment, interest charges will rise. As the scale of production alters, fixed costs may change. They will be different at each scale of output. The firm will spend more on variable costs as it uses more materials and power. However, the average costs of production may fall. When this happens the firm is said to gain **economies of large-scale production**.

In 1999 Langdale Woollens built an extension to its barn and installed some new knitting machines. It is now capable of producing 50 sweaters per week. The capacity of the firm has been increased. The total costs rose from £900 per week in 1998 to £1 000 per week. However, the average cost of production fell. The calculations show what happened:

1998

$$\text{Average cost per sweater} = \frac{\text{£900 (total cost)}}{\text{30 (number of sweaters made)}} = \text{£30}$$

1999

$$\text{Average cost per sweater} = \frac{\text{£1 000 (total cost)}}{\text{50 (number of sweaters made)}} = \text{£20}$$

The fall in the average cost of production for a sweater from £30 to £20 is an example of an economy of scale. Average costs fell as the firm's scale of production was changed.

Excess capacity – 20 sweaters produced

Capacity = 30 sweaters per week

Above capacity – 35 sweaters

ACTIVITY 1

Oxford Carpets Ltd produces high-quality carpets. The table below shows the costs of producing carpet using different scales of production. The scale of production is measured by the number of metres that the firm has the capacity to produce each week.

(a) Copy and complete the table above.

(b) What happens to the average cost of production as output rises from 1000 to 5000?

Scale of production (metres)	Fixed costs £	Variable costs £	Total costs £	Average cost £
1 000	10 000	20 000	30 000	30
2 000	18 000	30 000		
3 000	24 000	36 000		
4 000	28 000	40 000		
5 000	40 000	50 000		

Oxford Carpets Ltd – Costs of production for a range of outputs

Diseconomies of scale

Average costs do not always fall as the scale of production is increased. If they rise, a firm is said to experience diseconomies of scale. These usually occur because the firm becomes too big to be managed efficiently.

KINDS OF ECONOMIES OF SCALE

Purchasing economies
A firm is given a discount for buying in large quantities.

Managerial economies
A firm can employ specialist managers who improve efficiency.

Financial economies
A firm does not have to pay out as much money to raise finance.

Marketing economies
A firm saves on advertising and transport costs.

Risk-bearing economies
A firm produces a range of products, so is not dependent on one product.

Technical economies
A firm saves on production costs by using better methods and equipment.

ACTIVITY 2

What kind of economies of scale are the following?

(a) Busy Buses Ltd decides to replace its single-decker buses with double-decker buses.

(b) Jensen Fabrics Ltd is able to negotiate a lower rate of interest on bank loans than its smaller competitors.

(c) Marks & Spencer plc can afford to employ specialist buyers to negotiate deals with clothing suppliers.

(d) Holden's Supermarket chain decides to open a chain of petrol stations.

(e) Baldwin's Brewery Ltd starts to sell food through its public houses.

(f) Austin Engineering Ltd switches production of its hydraulic equipment to a larger factory using computer-controlled machinery.

(g) The growth of Home Soon Coaches leads to the employment of more office staff. The office manager decides that this is an opportunity for staff to specialise in specific areas of office work.

(h) Johnstone's Logistics has reorganised its structure. It now employs a specialist manager for each department rather than having managers responsible for several departments.

(i) When Munro Toys plc bought Talbot Toys Ltd its production doubled. The amount it spent on advertising rose by 50%.

The growth of firms

Firms grow in three main ways:

- Merging with other firms. A merger takes place when two or more firms agree to join together to become one larger firm.
- Taking over another firm. A take-over occurs when one firm buys control of another. This is achieved by buying enough shares in the firm to be able to outvote other shareholders.
- By internal expansion. This is when the business grows by increasing its production, perhaps by building new plant or new shops.

Types of integration

The diagram shows different ways in which a flour milling firm may grow:

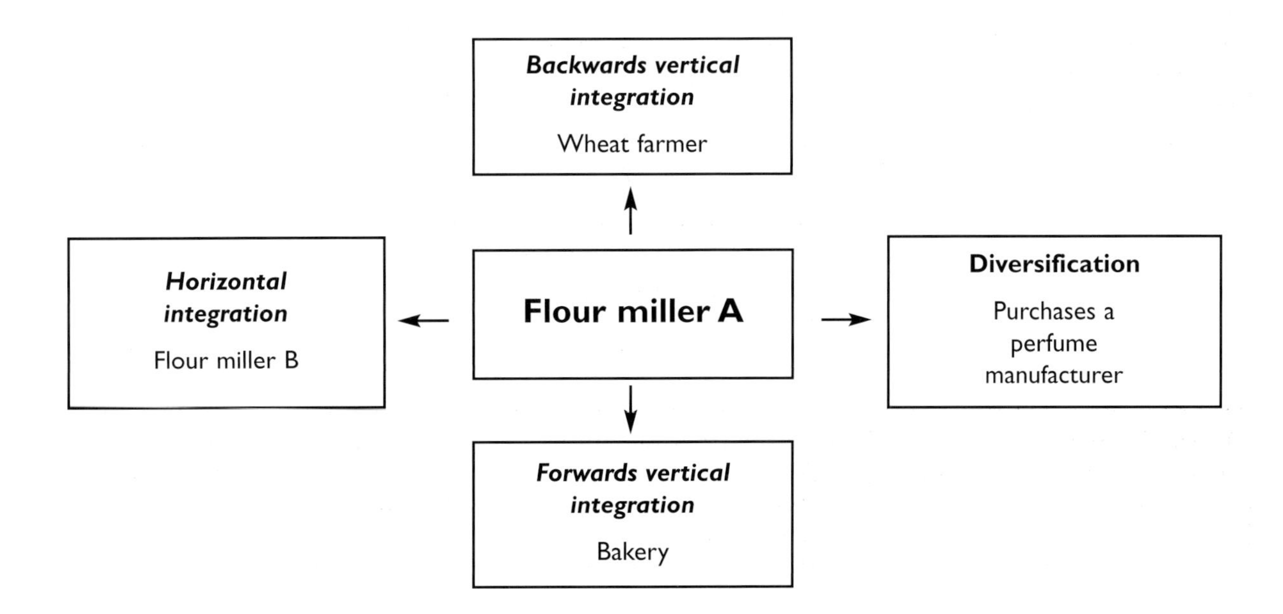

ACTIVITY 3

This activity is based on the example of the way in which Flour miller A in the diagram might grow his business. The advantages have not been written in the correct row. Redraw the table and write the advantages in the correct place next to the appropriate type of integration.

Type of integration	Advantage
(a) Backwards vertical integration	1. Flour miller A makes sure that he has a customer for the flour
(b) Forwards vertical integration	2. Flour miller A produces a different kind of product so that he spreads the risk.
(c) Horizontal integration	3. Flour miller A makes sure that he has a supply of his raw materials.
(d) Diversification	4. Production of flour can take place in a bigger flour mill, leading to economies of large-scale production.

The size of businesses

Measuring the size of a business

There are several ways in which the size of a business can be measured:

- *Sales turnover* – the value of the goods or services that a business sells in a year.
- *Market share* – the value of the sales of a firm is written as a percentage of the total value of sales in the market.
- *Number of employees* – often, the more employees a firm has, the greater its output.

ACTIVITY 4

The table gives information about businesses of different sizes for 1998.

1. What size of business is the most common in terms of numbers?
2. Which size of business provides the most employment in total?
3. Which size of business provides the least employment in total?
4. Which size of business accounts for the highest sales revenue in total?
5. Which size of business has
   (a) the highest sales revenue on average and
   (b) the lowest sales revenue on average?

	Small businesses 0–49 employees	Medium-sized businesses 50–249 employees	Large businesses 250 + employees
Number of businesses	3 626 620	24 610	6 660
Number of employees	9 652 000	2 508 000	9 434 000
Sales turnover	£732 985m	£265 701m	£928 302m

(Adapted from DTI website, DTI Small and Medium Enterprise Statistics for the UK, 1998.)

However, this is not always a good measure because some firms use a lot of equipment instead of labour.

- *The value of the assets of the business* – the value of the buildings, machinery and vehicles can indicate how big a business is.

ACTIVITY 5 

Use the internet to research statistics about how the size of enterprises has changed over time. Write a report, including the statistics, describing the changes.

Choosing the scale of production

There are a number of factors that will determine the size of business that a firm chooses to be:

- **The size of the market.**
  - *A large market* gives opportunities for firms to produce on a large scale and to gain economies of scale. This is true of food canning.
  - *A small market* is likely to be supplied by small firms. Small shops survive because they provide friendly, convenient service to people in a local community. Sometimes, like hardware stores, they may give advice to customers that larger competitors may not provide.
  - *A local market* may be supplied by local small firms. An example is the market for domestic building work – extensions, loft conversions and so on.
  - *The markets for services* that require personal attention, like hairdressing and made-to-measure tailoring, are often supplied by small firms.
  - Small firms often make *specialist goods*. An example is the manufacture of paint-spray booths.
- **The amount of capital needed.** Some businesses need a lot of capital. Generating nuclear power requires a massive investment in plant and equipment. Only large firms can operate in this type of business. Where only a small amount of capital is needed, small firms can set up. An accountant needs only an office and office equipment. There are many small accountancy firms, as well as some large ones.
- **Economies and diseconomies of scale.** When increasing the scale of production leads to lower costs, large firms are likely to exist. This is true of car manufacturing. When diseconomies result from increasing the scale of production, firms will prefer not to grow in size and small firms will exist.
- **The motives of the owners.** Many people enjoy running their own business. Growing bigger may mean taking on a partner or becoming a private or public limited company. This would lead to more people sharing control of the business. Many owners prefer to stay in charge and choose not to increase the size of their business.
- **Co-operation by firms.** Small firms sometimes work together to help them to compete against larger firms. An example of this is the voluntary chain, SPAR. Owners of small grocery stores all agree to buy their stock from certain wholesalers. The wholesalers are guaranteed large sales and so give bulk-purchasing discounts. In this way, the grocers can compete with the large supermarkets in terms of price.
- **Doing sub-contract work.** A large firm may prefer to contract out work to smaller firms so that it does not have to employ as many people. BG uses some smaller businesses to fit gas fires and central heating systems and to do maintenance work. One advantage is that the BG does not to pay wages to these gas fitters if there is no work for them.

ACTIVITY 6 

Use a local business directory or *Yellow Pages*. Find examples of businesses that are large, medium and small enterprises. Write an explanation of why there are businesses of different sizes operating in your area.

EXAM Practice Questions

Jenston Hypermarket plc operates a large chain of hypermarkets.

(a) In recent years large retailers like Jenston Hypermarket plc have increased their share of the market. What are the reasons for their success? (10 marks)

(b) Hypermarkets have many advantages for shoppers. Why, then, do so many small shops survive? (10 marks)

(OCR Business Studies, Question 2, Core Paper, 1993)

Welcome to Jenston Hypermarket PLC

JENSTON

We offer unbeatable prices on

- food
- drink
- clothing
- furniture
- electrical and household goods

Find us at the junction of the M93 and A94 near Borrington.

Capacity *The amount that a plant is designed to produce.*

Excess capacity *A business is said to have excess capacity when its level of production is less than its capacity.*

Above capacity *When a firm is producing more than its capacity.*

Economies of scale *The fall in the average cost of production that result from increasing the scale of production.*

Diseconomies of scale *When the average cost of production rises as the the scale of production is increased.*

Merger *Two or more firms join together to make one larger firm.*

Take-over *One firm buys control of another.*

This question is about the benefits that large businesses have (economies of scale) and the reasons why small firms still survive. Both parts of the question require that you apply your knowledge of economies of scale and the reasons for the need for small businesses to the case study business. In Part (a) you need to state the advantages that large hypermarkets offer and to explain why these exist. In Part (b) you need to discuss the market needs that small shops can meet. Remember that the stimulus material (the advertising leaflet in this case) is designed to help you!

EXAMINATION SUMMARY TIPS

- Firms may gain economies of scale when they increase the scale of their production.
- The scale of production refers to changes in the capacity of the firm to produce.
- Economies of scale are achieved when the average costs of production fall, even though total costs may rise.
- Diseconomies of scale exist when average costs rise as the scale of production is increased.
- There are several kinds of economies of scale.
- Firms can grow through mergers, take-overs or internal expansion.
- When firms join together it is called integration. There are several different kinds of integration.
- The size of a business may be measured in terms of output or employment.
- Small firms outnumber large firms.
- Large firms account for a large proportion of the total output of the country.
- The decision about whether to be a large- or small-scale producer is influenced by a number of factors.

Key Skills

Activity 1 provides an opportunity to practise your Application of Number key skill. The calculations required are examples of N1.2 calculations.

Activity 4 also provides an opportunity to practise your Application of Number skills. If you answer the questions set, you will provide evidence at Level 1 of your ability to interpret straightforward information (N1.1) and perform some calculations (N1.2).

Activity 5 is an opportunity to develop your IT skills and generate evidence for your portfolio at Level 2. You need to plan what information you will need and how to search for this – the DTI website may provide useful information. Your local council may also provide economic data about the local economy. You will need to select from the information you find information that you want to use (IT2.1). Once you have the information you need, enter it and bring it together in an appropriate form and explore and develop it – you might, for example, use a spreadsheet to create a pie chart of the share of output enjoyed by large-, medium- and small-sized firms (IT2.2). Finally, you must present the combined information in a consistent and suitable way in your report, making sure it is clear, accurate and saved (IT2.3).

Activity 6 is an opportunity to write a report (Communication C1.3 or C2.3).

Unit 4.5 Production and technology

Engels Stationery Ltd produces a variety of goods needed in offices. Its largest selling line is ring-pull files. It competes with a number of other firms that also produce files. To stay competitive, Engels Stationery Ltd must make correct decisions about the production of the files. It must consider:

- **The *costs* of production.** It is important to keep the costs of production as low as possible. The lower the cost, the lower the price that Engels can charge for the files. If its price is higher than prices charged by competitors, it will lose sales.
- **The *quality* of the files.** The files must be of good quality. If they are not, customers will not be satisfied with them. Customers may decide not to order any more files from Engels.
- **The *quantity* of files to produce.** Engels must make enough files to meet the demand for them. If it does not, it will have lost the opportunity to make a profit. Also, customers unable to buy what they want from Engels, may buy from competitors instead. These customers may continue to buy from the competitors in the future. It is also important for Engels not to produce too many files. If it produces more than it can sell, it will need to store the files and this will cost it money.
- **The files that customers *want*.** Engels must keep in touch with its customers so that it knows what kinds of files that they want. Firms that do this are 'market-oriented.'

Producing goods

Producing goods involves a series of activities. The first stage is to research what customers want and to develop and design products to meet their needs. Secondly, resources are used in the production process to create an output. Finally, the business may gain feedback from the customers. It may need to change the design of its product in some way, depending upon what customers say.

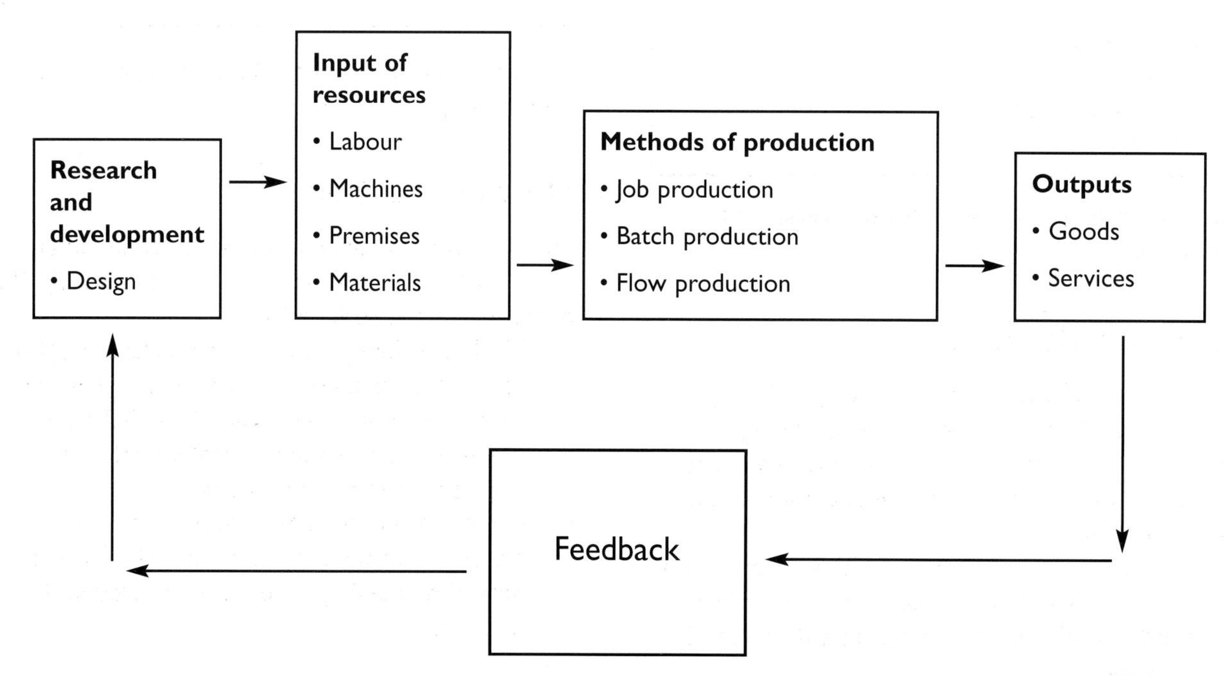

Producing goods

Methods of production

Job production

This method of production involves producing each product individually.

- Eunice Khan is a sculptress. She makes figures out of stone. She works on one sculpture at a time until it is finished.
- Marston Borough Council has paid for a new school to be built. The construction company that is building it will work on the project until it is finished.
- An architect completed the design drawings of the school.

Advantages of job production	Disadvantages of job production
• Products are usually high quality. • Products can be made to meet the needs of individual customers. • Workers often get more satisfaction from working on something until it is finished.	• Costs of production will be high. • Labour costs may be high because job production often requires skilled labour.

Table 4.4 Advantages and disadvantages of job production

Batch production

This method of production involves producing one type of a product for a while, then changing production to another type of product. The firm will switch back to the first product made when more are needed.

- Bakers use batch production. They may bake a batch of one kind of bread and then switch production to make a batch of a different kind of bread.
- Some clothing manufactures use batch production, switching production between different lines of garments.

Advantages of batch production	Disadvantages of batch production
• The needs of different customers can be met by making batches of different goods. • Batches are made to meet specific orders from customers and this may reduce costs because the goods may not need storing. • It may be possible to use specialist machines and to automate production so that costs are saved.	• It takes time to switch production from a batch of one product to a different batch. Machinery may need to be set up. This adds to the costs of production. • It may be necessary to keep stocks of materials and components to be able to switch production when required. Holding stocks costs money. • The tasks may be repetitive and boring for the workers.

Table 4.5 Advantages and disadvantages of batch production

Flow production

This method of production involves an assembly line. One kind of product is made continuously. The goods are mass-produced.

- Ford uses flow production to make cars. The cars are assembled on a production line. The cars move along a conveyor belt. Different workers and machines complete different tasks as the car moves along.
- Glass is made using flow production. The materials are heated and mixed. The glass is moved on flowing water to be cooled and polished.

Table 4.6 Advantages and disadvantages of flow production

Advantages of flow production	Disadvantages of flow production
• Large amounts can be made. • The costs of production for each unit made are low because the firm benefits from economies of large-scale production. • Machinery can be used, helping to keep costs low. • Improvements in technology mean that not all the products need to be the same; variations in design can be programmed into the computer-controlled machines.	• Goods are mass-produced and may not be of good quality. • It is very expensive to set up a production line. • Large stocks of materials may have to be kept to keep the production line supplied and this may be expensive. • If the production stops at any point on the assembly line (because of a mechanical breakdown or industrial action) there may be a complete shut down of production. • Jobs on an assembly line can be repetitive and boring.

ACTIVITY 1

For each of the production activities described below:

(a) Recommend the appropriate method or methods of production

(b) Give reasons for your recommendations.

(c) Explain the problems that the firm may face from using the method or methods of production that you recommend.

Production Activity 1

A small company produces three different models of caravan. Each model requires a different chassis. Some of the components the company makes are used in each of the caravans.

Production Activity 2

A specialist tailor makes made-to-measure suits.

Production Activity 3

A business produces millions of bottles of beer each day. The bottles need to be washed, filled, capped and labelled.

Technology and manufacturing

Labour is expensive to employ. Throughout history, firms have tried to replace labour with machines to save money.

- *Mechanisation.* This is when machinery is used but labour is still required in order to work the machine. A lot of farm work is now mechanised. A combine harvester reduces the number of labourers needed to reap and bale a harvest but still requires a driver.

- *Automation.* This is when machinery is used and a computer controls it. A lot of manufacturing production is now automated. Workers are still employed but only to programme and supervise the work that machines do.

Types of technology

CAD – Computer Aided Design involves the use of computers to design products. You may have used a CAD package in Technology. The package is used to draw the design of the product. Information about the product may be stored on computer. If design problems arise, the designer can ask the computer to suggest solutions.

CAM – Computer Aided Manufacture is when the machines used to make the product are controlled by computer.

CIM – Computer Integrated Manufacture is where a whole factory is controlled by computer.

The advantages of technology in production

- Large amounts can be made. This can lead to economies of scale, meaning that the unit costs of production fall.
- The productivity of workers improves. The output per worker increases and so labour costs fall for each product made.
- The quality of production can be improved because machines are less likely to make mistakes than workers are. This reduces wastage and so saves money. The improved quality may attract new customers.
- Production can be flexible. Machines can be programmed to produce a variety of products in order to meet the needs of individual customers.
- Repetitive or dangerous jobs may be done by machines rather than by people.

ACTIVITY 2

Kingston Carpets produces a range of high-quality carpets. The carpets are designed in a drawing office by a team of designers. Machinery is used to weave the carpets. The machines need to be re-set to change the designs of the carpets. The machines that are used are operated manually. The business is planning to introduce new technology.

(a) State two types of technology that Kingston Carpets could use to design and make the carpets.

(b) Explain the benefits that the automation of production would bring to Kingston Carpets.

(c) Explain the problems that Kingston Carpets might face when it introduces the new technology.

The problems of technology

- When a firm introduces new technology it may need to make workers redundant if the machines do the work instead of them. The costs of making the workers redundant may be high. There may be problems with the trade unions. They may take industrial action against the redundancies.

- The firm may need to recruit new employees with the skills to use the new technology. Often, these workers are in high demand and they may need to pay them big salaries.
- Some existing employees may need re-training to work with the new machines.
- Buying and installing the machines can be very expensive. A firm risks a lot of money when it introduces new technology.

Lean production

Another way to save costs is to use lean production. The most important feature of lean production is **JIT** or **Just-In-Time production**. The producer does not keep large stocks of components in a warehouse – this would be expensive. Stocks are ordered from the supplier as and when they are needed. When they are delivered, they are taken straight to the production line and used immediately. If there were faults with the stocks, production would come to a halt so it is very important that the seller can make sure that supplies are of good quality. Lean production also improves quality. Quality control is important at each stage in production. If the quality is not good, the production line will come to a halt because there would be nothing to use at the later stages of the line.

Quality control

Quality control is important for the following reasons:

- If goods are not of a good quality, they may not be able to be sold. The producer has wasted money.
- If poor-quality goods can be sold, it may be as seconds. The producer will have to reduce the price for these and so will lose sales revenue.
- The customer will not be happy if they receive poor-quality goods. They may decide to buy from another supplier in the future.
- Production may be disrupted if the quality of materials produced at an early stage in the process of production is not good enough for them to be used at a later stage.

Total Quality Management

Many businesses have introduced Total Quality Management to replace the traditional method of quality control. The traditional method involved the inspection of completed goods for faults – usually by quality control inspectors. Total Quality Management means that quality assurance takes place throughout the production process. Quality control is the responsibility of every worker.

ACTIVITY 3

Prepare a talk about your work experience. Your talk should deal with the following points:

- The name of the firm.
- What the firm produced.
- A description of how production took place. Discuss whether it involved job, batch or flow production.
- Describe the jobs that people did in the firm and what technology they used. Explain the benefits that the technology brought.
- Describe how quality was checked.

EXAM Practice Questions

Carlton Press Ltd prints books.

(a) Which method of production – job, batch or flow – do you think would be most suitable for printing books? Give reasons for your answers. (4 marks)

(b) How might Carlton Press Ltd benefit from the increased use of technology in the production process? (4 marks)

(c) What problems might Carlton Press Ltd experience if it introduces new technology? (4 marks)

(Adapted from OCR Business Studies GCSE, Question 5, Core Paper, Foundation Tier 1998)

ADVICE ON HOW TO ANSWER THE QUESTION

In your answer to Part (a) you need to relate your choice of method to the fact that Carlton Press will have to print a range of books and that it may need to re-print some books if they are very popular.

In Part (b) you will not be expected to know a lot of detail about the kinds of technology that are used in printing books. You need to explain the general points about the automation of the production process and the benefits that the firm would gain.

In Part (c) you need to suggest possible problems that the firm may have to deal with.

Key Skills

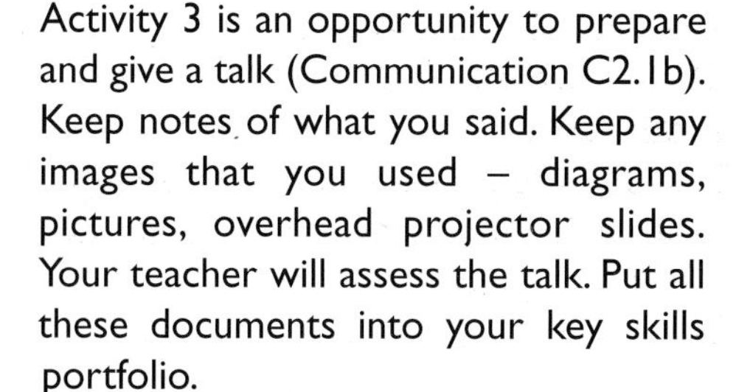

Activity 3 is an opportunity to prepare and give a talk (Communication C2.1b). Keep notes of what you said. Keep any images that you used – diagrams, pictures, overhead projector slides. Your teacher will assess the talk. Put all these documents into your key skills portfolio.

KEY TERMS

Job production *The method of production where products are made individually.*

Batch production *The method of production where one type of product is made and then production is switched to make a different product.*

Flow production *Production of one product takes place continuously using a production or assembly line.*

Mechanisation *Machines, controlled by workers, are introduced into the production process.*

Automation *Machines, controlled by computer, are introduced into the production process.*

Just-in-time *Stocks of materials and components are not stored but used immediately they arrive at the factory.*

Total Quality Management *The process where all workers are responsible for quality throughout the process of production.*

EXAMINATION SUMMARY TIPS

- Costs, quality, quantity and the wants of customers are important considerations in producing goods.
- There are three main methods of production – job, batch and flow production.
- Mechanisation and automation have been introduced into the process of production.
- Technology has changed production significantly and brought many advantages.
- Firms may experience problems when they introduce new technology.

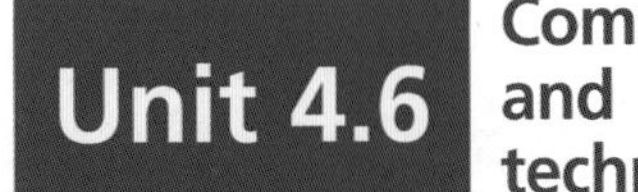

Unit 4.6 Communications and technology

What is communication?

Communication is the transmission of a message from a sender to a receiver. The diagrams show **one-way communication** and **two-way communication**.

Two-way communication takes place when messages are exchanged between sender and receiver.

Two-way communication is important for a number of reasons:

- Feedback from the receiver makes it clear that the message has been received and understood.
- It is good for generating ideas and coming up with solutions to problems.

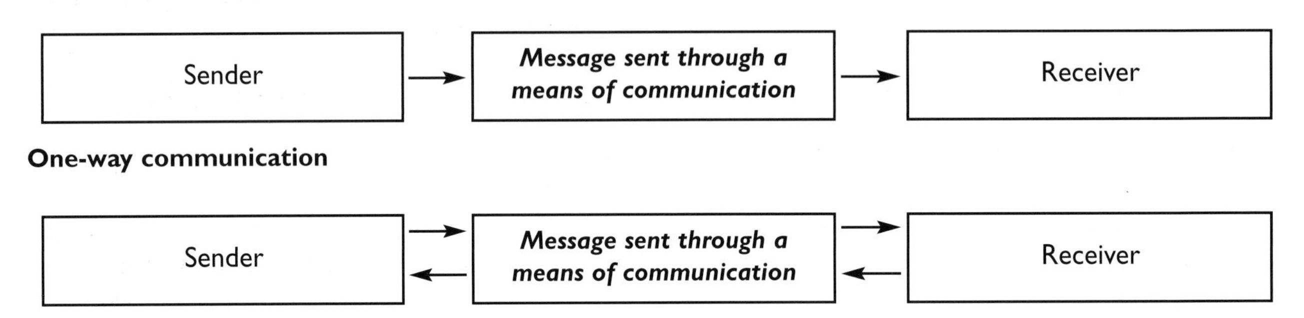

One-way communication

Two-way communication

Internal and external communications

Internal communications takes place between people who work in the same organisation. If a manager talks to workers (subordinates) it is an example of **downward vertical communication**. If a worker sends an e-mail to his or her boss this is **upward vertical communication**. **Horizontal communication** takes place when two people at the same level in the organisational structure communicate with each other.

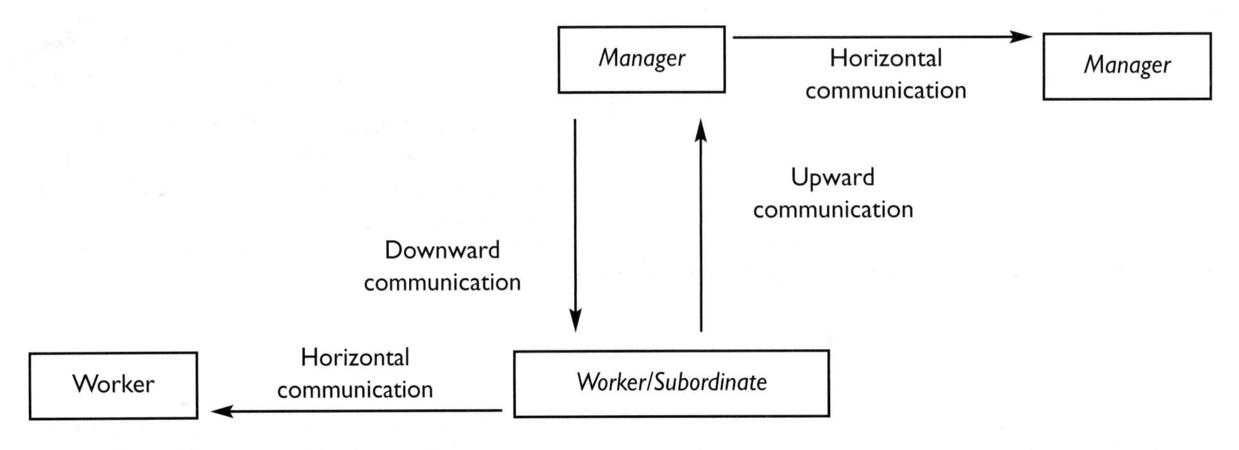

Horizontal and Vertical Communication

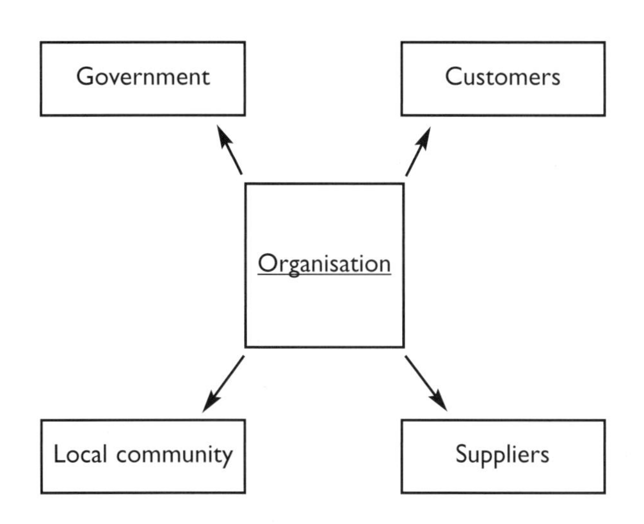

External communication

External communication takes place between one person in an organisation and someone outside that organisation.

Formal and informal communications

Formal communication takes place when the official means of communicating are used within an organisation. Examples of these are letters, memos, faxes, official meetings and reports.

Informal communication can be just as important, and sometimes more important than formal communication. An example of an informal communication is a conversation during a break or at a social event.

Methods of communication

Verbal communication

There are several ways in which people can speak to one another: face to face discussions (one-to-one or in group meetings), voice-mail, tannoy announcements, on the telephone, on the radio, through presentations or lectures or using video-conferencing.

Advantages of verbal communication	Disadvantages of verbal communication
• The person can check that the message has been understood by asking for feedback. • The person can emphasise points by their tone of voice or their body language.	• If there are a lot of people listening to a message it may not be clear that all have heard or understood it. • If the receiver of the message does not like what they hear, they may answer back and cause trouble. • There is no permanent record of the message (unless minutes of what was said are taken or a recording made). This may be important if a worker is being disciplined.

Table 4.7 Advantages and disadvantages of verbal communication

ACTIVITY 1

The table below shows some of the communications connected with Bolton Wanderers Football Club. Copy the table and then tick the boxes next to each item to say whether:

(a) it is an example of internal or external communication

(b) the communication is an example of formal or informal communication

(c) the communication is likely to be one-way or two-way.

Example of communication	*Internal*	*External*	*Formal*	*Informal*	*One-way*	*Two-way*
The team manager must talk with the directors about buying a new player.						
The ticket office must let the fans know that tickets for the cup final will be on sale from next Monday.						
Club officials talk to the police to agree security arrangements at games.						
The manager needs to discuss tactics with his coaching staff.						
The players complain about the manager's tactics as they change after training.						
The personnel officer needs to write for references for applicants for a job.						
The stadium announcer must tell away supporters that their coaches will meet them in Car Park A after the match.						
The chief groundsman must tell one of his staff to mark the lines more clearly on the pitch.						
The marketing manager discusses an idea with the personnel manager over lunch.						
The marketing department must negotiate prices of replica shirts with a supplier.						
The marketing department must tell customers about the special Christmas gifts on sale in the club shop.						
The ticket office manager must agree a rota with the office workers to make sure there is someone there during all opening hours.						

Written communication

There are many forms of written communications: letters, memos, reports, notices, faxes, e-mails, leaflets, books and so on.

Advantages of written communication
• There is a record of the message.
• The receiver can read and re-read the message to try to understand it.
• The message can be sent to more than one person at a time – for example, circular letters or advertising flyers.
• A written message can avoid confrontation.
Disadvantages of written communication
• It is not possible to check immediately that the receiver has understood the message properly.
• The success of the message depends on how clearly it has been written.

Table 4.8 Advantages and disadvantages of written communication

Communication using images

Pictures, posters, diagrams and charts and TV and films are ways of communicating using images.

Advantages of using images
• People often like looking at images.
• Images can have more impact – remember the saying 'a picture paints a thousand words!'
Disadvantages of using images
• As with written communication, it may not be possible to check immediately that the receiver has understood the message properly.

Table 4.9 Advantages and disadvantages of using images

ACTIVITY 2

1. Write a short description of each of the methods of communication listed below. Note the advantages and disadvantages of each to business:
   - telephone
   - business letter
   - facsimiles
   - posters
   - video.

2. For each of the cases (i)-(vii) below:

(a) You should say whether you would use verbal or written communications or use images. You may recommend more than one kind of communication.

(b) You should also should state what form the communication should take – for example, if you recommend written communication, state if a letter or memo or fax or other form of written communication should be used.
Give reasons for your recommendations.

(i) A school with 1500 pupils wishes to let them know that the school will not be open today because of problems with the central heating boiler.

(ii) A salesperson wishes to demonstrate the advantages of a new computer to a potential customer.

(iii) A holiday firm wishes to advertise its new brochure for next summer's holidays.

(iv) A project manager for a construction firm wishes to remind colleagues who work in several different departments located on different sites that there will be a meeting for all concerned later in the week.

(v) The social committee wants to advertise its summer barbecue to all workers.

(vi) A manager wishes to find out from workers in her department about an accusation made by a worker that he was racially abused by a colleague.

(vii) A firm wishes to advertise special offers for all its shareholders.

Barriers to communication

- ***Timing.*** The message may be sent at the wrong time. For example, a person who is in a rush to leave work for the day may not listen carefully to what his manager has to say to him.
- ***Clarity.*** The sender may not make the message clear to the receiver. This may be because the sender uses language that the receiver does not understand or assumes that the receiver knows more than he or she actually does.
- ***The attitudes of the sender or the receiver.*** The sender may 'talk down' to the receiver so that he or she does like what they hear. The receiver may not trust or respect the sender and so does not take notice of what is said.
- ***The wrong method of communication may be used.*** An e-mail giving an urgent message will not work if the receiver only checks for new e-mail at the beginning of each week.
- ***Feedback is not received or is not appropriate.*** The sender may not check with the receiver that they have understood the message. The sender might ask the receivers of a message to give feedback in writing. This would not be suitable if people do not want to put their feelings or ideas down on paper.
- ***There is a problem with the means of communication.*** E-mail may not be received if there is a problem with the receiver's computer.

ACTIVITY 3

For each of the cases below:

(a) Explain why the problem may have arisen.

(b) Recommend how you would deal with the following communications problems:

(i) Two workers have had an argument. A friend of one of the workers has said that the other worker has been saying bad things about him. As the manager of the office in which they both work, you do not want any 'bad blood' to affect how they work together.

(ii) A manager has sent a page of written instructions to a clerical assistant about how to layout a report but the assistant does not understand what is required.

(iii) Workers are not obeying a safety notice instructing them to wear hard hats at all times. Many of the workers have not seen the notice; others have seen it but have chosen to ignore it.

(iv) A school has sent a message home with a pupil asking her parents to get in touch about missing homework. The pupil has never passed the message on.

Information and communications technology

Work in offices has been revolutionised by information and communications technology. Sefton Education Business Partnership (SEBP) provides a service linking businesses and schools in the Borough of Sefton on Merseyside. The services that it provides include arranging work experience placements and mock interviews for all the pupils in Sefton schools, providing activities to develop personal skills, co-ordinating industry days and organising teacher placements. ICT is very important to the work of SEBP. Some of the uses that SEBP makes of ICT are described below:

- *Word-processing.* Letters, reports and teaching materials are all written using word processing software. The use of word-processing means that the work is done more quickly, the quality of the final copy is high, a record of all communications can be kept on the network and work can easily be edited and amended. Letters that are sent to contacts in several schools or businesses are easy to create. A database of contacts and their addresses is kept. When a general letter is sent out, the details of the contacts are mail-merged with the letter to produce individually addressed letters.
- *Graphics packages.* Images are created using these and are then inserted into word-processed documents to become teaching materials. Sefton EBP takes great care to make

sure that the teaching materials it produces are attractive to look at as well as having good content.

- *Spreadsheets.* The office administrator uses spreadsheets to keep all the financial records of the EBP. The spreadsheets are used to analyse the data to produce reports for the EBP board of directors. The administrator uses the spreadsheet to create graphs and inserts these and copies of spreadsheets into word-processed reports.
- *Databases.* Sefton EBP organises over 6 000 work experience placements each year. It maintains a database of all the employers that are willing to offer placements. It uses this to match against the requests of the pupils. A database of students is also kept. When placements have been arranged, the database is used to send the information to the schools and their pupils and to inform the employers about the pupils that have been placed with them.
- *Presentation software.* Each month, employers give reports to the board of directors about projects that have taken place and plans for the future. All the workers have found that using presentation packages, along with a computer projector to show the slides, improves the quality and impact of their presentations. Graphics, animations and sound can be included in the presentations to add to the impact.
- *E-mail.* This is now very important for both internal and external communications. The workers in the EBP receive agendas and minutes of meetings by internal e-mail as well as notification of social activities such as the Christmas dinner. Increasingly, communications with businesses and the schools use e-mail. Many faxes are sent using e-mail.
- *The Internet.* This is a really useful source of information for workers in the EBP. When they are writing teaching materials, the workers make use of web-sites for information. The Internet is also used to advertise the services that the EBP offers.
- *The Intranet.* All files are stored on an office server. Workers can save files to the shared area. This means that other workers can access the information on the files. Workers use this when the work may be useful to colleagues or if they want other workers to look at what they have done and to comment on it.

ACTIVITY 4

Write a report about the use of ICT in your school. Your report may deal with:

- the work of the administration (the school secretary and the bursar)
- the work of the examinations officer who is responsible for the entry of pupils for examinations
- the work of teachers – creating materials, teaching in class, keeping records, writing reports and so on.

In each case your report should cover:

(a) what ICT is used and what it is used for
(b) the advantages that the users have found from using ICT
(c) the problems that they have using ICT.

You should prepare questions to ask the people who use ICT. To save time and trouble, you may work in groups to prepare the questions. Arrange for one or two members of the group to carry out the interview with one of the workers. You might find it useful to post the answers that you get on the school intranet – other people in the class can have access to the information as well as pupils in future years.

Write your report. If it is practical, word-process your report.

The advantages of using ICT

- The productivity of workers is high. Workers are able to produce more than they could without using ICT and produce work more quickly.
- The quality of the presentation of the work is better.
- Information can be shared more easily.
- Large amounts of information can be processed very quickly.

- Communications, both internally and externally, may be improved and can be achieved more quickly.
- ICT makes the use of mail-shots of information to large numbers of customers possible at a reasonable cost.

Disadvantages of using ICT

- Workers need training to use the technology efficiently and this costs money.
- It is expensive to invest in computer technology. It also becomes obsolete (out of date) very quickly and needs replacing.
- Technical problems can occur with the computer. If the problem is on a server, all work may have to stop.
- Workers need to be aware of the health and safety issues related to using computers – they should use anti-glare screens and take regular breaks to prevent eyestrain. Some heavy users of keyboards have experienced repetitive strain injury (RSI) – problems with hand and wrist joints.

Government and ICT

Data protection law states that people are entitled to have access to data about them that is stored electronically.

Organisations that use ICT must comply with health and safety regulations.

The effect of technology on work

Where people work and the nature of the work that they do has changed significantly with developments in technology.

Working from home

Many workers are able to work from home. They may have an office in their home containing a computer, telephone and fax machine. They contact

ICT has changed where and how people work.

Advantages of working from home	Disadvantages of working from home
• The worker saves time by not having to travel to work. • The worker saves money by not having to travel to work. • The workers have more freedom about how much they work and what hours they work. • There may be fewer distractions at home than in a busy office environment.	• The worker may not be able to exchange ideas with fellow workers if he or she does not see them very often. • Some workers need the discipline of clocking on and off at work. • There may be a lack of space or facilities at home. • There may be distractions from family and friends. • The worker may miss the social side of working with other people.

Table 4.10 Advantages and disadvantages of working from home

clients by telephone or fax. Reports can be written on the computer and sent by e-mail to the client or to the employer. Meetings at the offices of the employer may not take place very often – perhaps only when problems arise that require face-to-face discussions to produce solutions.

Teleworking and call centres

A call centre.

There has been a growth in teleworking and call centres.

Peter Schonberg works in telesales for Martin Mulligan UK in St Helens. Mulligan's sells bar code equipment. Peter's job is to call firms to ask for their address and telephone number. He records these on a database. The sales team will ring these contacts to try to sell them the bar code equipment. The equipment is stored elsewhere. When a sale is made, the order is passed to the warehouse for the goods to be delivered and installed. The firm saves money because it does not need a lot of sales representatives with company cars who visit clients to arrange deals. Neither does it need expensive sales offices that people visit to view the equipment. In fact, the office is sited in low-rent, spare office space in a run-down part of the town.

John Didds works at Gifts for U call centre in Preston. He answers the telephone all day, recording orders for gifts chosen from the firm's Christmas catalogue. John has never seen any of the gifts that the firm sells, only pictures of them in the catalogue. Orders are entered onto the firm's computer system and will be processed at the warehouse on an industrial estate out of the town. Like Mulligan's, Gifts for U does not require expensive offices. Nor does it need shops on the High Street where rents are high and many shop assistants are required.

Electronic Data Interchange (EDI)

EDI is a network system linking different businesses. The network allows messages to be communicated electronically between the linked organisations. It is used for ordering stock and for making payments. Order forms, invoices and cheques are no longer needed for transactions to take place. This reduces the time and paperwork involved, reducing the number of employees needed, leading to cost savings. These systems are expensive to set up, though.

ACTIVITY 5

(a) What do you think are the main advantages of teleworking to businesses?
(b) Why might workers not like working in telesales or at call centres?
(c) Why might Electronic Data Interchange be unsuitable for a small business?

The importance of communications

Good communications are important to business. They are needed in every kind of business activity. Some examples are:

Kind of business activity	Example
Marketing	• Effective advertising that informs and/or persuades the customer to buy the product. • Market research that achieves good feedback from customers about their needs
Finance	• Clearly explaining a business plan to a bank manager to persuade him or her to give a loan. • Communications about income and expenditures so that accurate accounts are kept.
People in business	• Getting good information about applicants for a job so that a correct selection can be made. • Developing a good understanding of a job so that a person is trained properly.
Government and trade	• Businesses must understand the Government regulations that control business so that they know how to deal with them. • Businesses need to make applications for grants of money from Government.
Production	• Workers discuss quality so that wastage of materials is avoided. • Orders for stock are made so that production is not held up by a lack of stock.

Table 4.11 The importance of communications in business

ACTIVITY 6

For each kind of business activity listed in the table, write down one more example that shows why communication is important to business.

EXAM Practice Question

Robin Odell was made redundant from his job. He decided to spend his time working for himself, writing books. He will be using a computer, working from home.

(a) Discuss the advantages and disadvantages to Robin of working from home rather than renting an office. (8 marks)

(b) Explain how the Internet might help Robin in his book-writing business. (4 marks)

(c) Name three computer applications, other than the Internet, that Robin might use in his business, and explain how they will help him. (6 marks)

(Adapted from OCR Business Studies GCSE, Technology and Change Option Paper, Higher Tier, 2000.)

Part (a) of the question requires you to use your knowledge about the advantages and disadvantages of working from home and apply them to the case study – do not simply list them.

In Part (b) you need to discuss how the Internet might help with research for the books that Robin writes as well as helping communications.

In Part (c) you need to discuss the different kinds of software that Robin might use, what he would use them for and how they would benefit him.

Communications *The transmission of a message from a sender to a receiver through a means of communication.*

Feedback *The response made by the receiver of a communication that indicates that they have or have not understood the communication.*

Internal communications *Communications between people employed in the same organisation.*

External communications *Communications between people in an organisations and others outside that organisation.*

Vertical communications *Communications up or down the hierarchy within an organisation.*

Horizontal communications *Communications between people on the same level of the hierarchy in an organisation.*

Formal communications *Communications that use the official channels of communication within an organisation.*

Informal communications *Communications that are outside the official channels of communication within an organisation.*

ICT *The use of technology to facilitate communications.*

EXAMINATION SUMMARY TIPS

- Good communications are critical to business.
- There are many kinds and methods of communication.
- For communication to be effective it is important to choose the appropriate means of communication.
- There are many barriers to communication.
- Good communications deal with these barriers.
- Information technology has improved the speed and effectiveness of communications in business.
- Developments in technology have led to changes in the nature and location of work.

Key Skills

Activity 4 provides an opportunity for both Communication and Information Technology work as well as Working with Others.

For Working with Others you need to plan your research and draw up an action plan indicating who is responsible for what (WO1.1 or WO2.1). Carry out the tasks that have been allocated to you, seeking advice from others when you need. Keep a record or log of what you do (WO1.2 or WO2.2). Discuss your work with others as you do it, suggesting problems and how the work might be improved (WO1.3 or WO2.3). Make a record of these discussions

For Communication, you have the opportunity to take part in a group discussion planning and reviewing the work. Prepare what you want to say in these discussions and make a record of your contributions (C1.1 and C2.1a). If you carry out an interview one of your tasks, record the questions and answers (C1.1).

You will also produce a written report (C1.3 or C2.3).

Word-processing the report is an opportunity for presenting information (IT1.2). If you bring together information that others have produced for the report you may be able to work at Level 2 (IT2.3).

SECTION 5 MARKETING

Learning Objectives: To develop:

- an understanding of why marketing is important to businesses
- understanding of how businesses analyse and research the market for their products or services
- knowledge and understanding of the different elements that make up marketing
- the skills of applying marketing ideas to different business situations
- the skills of bringing together different parts of marketing in a single marketing strategy
- understanding of the impact of e-commerce on business activity
- understanding of the need for, and the methods of, protecting the consumer
- skills of analysis, selection and evaluation.

Introductory activity

The marketing of mobile phones

When a business wants to market a product, it must make sure that the product is something that people will want to buy. Mobile phones have become increasingly popular in recent years with four main businesses providing mobile phone services.

Your task: 

Imagine that **you** are in charge of marketing at one of the four main mobile phone providers. You have to think of a plan to market a new mobile phone service that will make your company profit and possibly take customers from your competitors.

When writing your plan you should think of the following:

- The price you will charge. Will it be less or more than the competition charges?
- Will you have any offers to tempt customers, such as free covers, cases, rent-free periods etc?
- How will you sell your phone service? Will you use mail order, or sell it through shops, or in a different way?
- The quality of your phone service. Will your service do something the competition hasn't thought of yet?

Your plan should be at **least** two sides of A4 paper, and you should give reasons why you think each of your ideas should be used to market the new mobile phone service. You need to design a suitable logo and invent a name for the new service. Use IT (if available) to present your plan.

Unit 5.1 Analysing the market

When a business wishes to sell a new product or service it must be sure that customers will want to buy it. Whether the business is selling to another business, or to consumers, there is little point in providing something that customers do not want.

Product and market orientation

In the past a number of businesses were product-oriented, which means they took little or no interest in what people wanted and made products that they hoped would sell. At a time when people had little choice of products, this system would work quite well. More recently, this has meant that products were developed which customers did not want and would result in losses for the business.

Most businesses are now market-oriented, which means they carefully find what people want before they develop a product. By doing this, a business would make sure that a product would be a success and hopefully make a large profit.

Market segments

Another way in which a business will analyse the possible market for its product is to consider the different market segments at which the product may be targeted. This involves looking at the different types of consumers that might buy the product.

Although each product will have its own market segments, common ways in which the customers for most products can be divided are as follows:

- Age – different age groups will buy different products.
- Gender – male and females will often (but not always) buy different products.

A watch is a product with many different market segments.

- Income – people with higher levels of income will want particular products.
- Region – consumers living in different parts of the country will have different tastes and needs.
- Interests – different people have different hobbies and interests. This will mean that a range of products is needed to satisfy all tastes.

ACTIVITY 1

1. Divide the following products into as many different market segments as you can. Use the information on market segments to help. You can illustrate the different segments if you wish.
   - tables
   - cars
   - magazines
   - hair shampoo.
2. Make a list of at least five different products that **both** gender groups of your age will buy. Explain why you think that both groups buy each product.

Socio-economic groups

An important way in which businesses analyse a market is to divide consumers into different groups. The groups are based on the occupation of the head of the household. The occupation a person has obviously affects the amount of money they earn, and will affect the way in which a business will target its products. Rolls-Royce will target their cars at one group and Skoda will target their cars at a very different group.

When a business wants to advertise a product aimed at a particular socio-economic group, it will need to be sure that the advertisement is being seen by that group. This will affect the choice of newspaper or magazine a business chooses to use for its adverts.

Socio-economic group	Examples of occupations
Class 1 Group A Professional	Doctors, judges, company directors
Class 2 Group B Intermediate	Teachers, department managers, solicitors
Class 3 Group C1 Skilled non-manual	Supervisory workers, secretaries, sales assistants
Class 3 Group C2 Skilled manual	Skilled manual workers, electricians, plumbers
Class 4 Group D Part skilled	Semi-skilled workers, assembly line workers, cleaners
Class 5 Group E Unskilled	Unemployed, casual workers, state pensioners

Table 5.1 Socio-economic groups

ACTIVITY 2

1. Draw a bar graph to show the percentage of each socio-economic group.
2. What socio-economic group would the following occupations be in: lawyer, bricklayer, refuse collector, pensioner, electrician, store manager at Next, window cleaner, car salesperson, managing director of a plc, barperson, headteacher, trainee hairdresser?

Disposable income

Another factor a business will consider in analysing the market is to look at the disposable income of consumers. Disposable income is the money a consumer has to spend after paying for essential bills such as mortgage, rent and electricity. Certain groups have more disposable income than others. A person with no bills to pay will often have a higher disposable income than a young person who has just got married, with a high mortgage and other important bills to pay. People retiring may see a fall in their income and have less to spend than they had in the past. A business may target certain products at these different groups of people.

Different products are aimed at different markets.

Mass, niche and test markets

When a business is looking at the market at which to aim a product, it needs to consider how many customers it is hoping to attract. A product or service aimed at lots of people is a **mass market product**. This will include things such as popular chocolates, family cars and household electrical goods such as videos.

Niche market products are aimed at much smaller groups of people, with products made being very specialised. This type of market would include hand-built cars, made-to-measure clothes and hand-crafted pottery. As very few products are made for a niche market they are usually more expensive than ones made for a mass market.

When a business is unsure about how a new product will sell, it may use a **test market**. This means that the product will be sold or tested in a particular area or with a certain group of people to test whether consumers like it. If the product sells well, the business may decide to sell it throughout the country. If consumers don't like the product, the business may decide to stop production or change the product and test it again later. By carrying out a test market a business is able to restrict the losses it would make if the product failed to sell. Cadbury used the North East of England as a test market for Wispa bars before selling the product throughout the country.

EXAM Practice Questions

Read the information below and answer the questions which follow.

MRW Electronics is a new business set up by three partners. The partners aim to take advantage of their computer skills and experience with other businesses to develop their own computer games. They are a market-oriented business and feel they need to analyse the market to see if their products are to be a success.

(a) Explain what is meant by 'market-oriented'. (2 marks)

(b) Give one reason why a business should be market-oriented. (1 mark)

(c) Explain which market segments the products of MRW Electronics are likely to be aimed at. (4 marks)

(d) Evaluate the benefits to MRW Electronics of test marketing its products. (4 marks)

ADVICE ON HOW TO ANSWER THE QUESTION

(a) The command word is 'explain'. This means that detail is needed in the answer. You must explain carefully what happens in a market-oriented business, possibly using MRW Electronics as an example.

(b) Here you are asked to 'give' a reason. This means you must say why the business should be market oriented. One reason only!

(c) Here you are asked to explain once again. The question asks you what market segments the products are likely to be aimed at. There may be many segments to write about, but don't forget to explain why a each segment will be suitable for MRW Electronics' products.

(d) In this question you are asked to evaluate. This means that you must fully explain the benefits of test marketing rather than the business doing nothing at all. Remember that the question refers to MRW Electronics, so your answer should evaluate the benefits to that business.

KEY TERMS

Product-oriented *Where a business makes a product and hopes to sell it without first analysing the market.*

Market-oriented *Where a business analyses the market and consumers' needs for a product before starting production.*

Market segments *How the market for a product or service is divided, for example by age or gender.*

Socio-economic groups *A method of dividing up the population based on the occupation of the head of the household.*

Disposable income *The amount of money a consumer has to spend after paying essential bills.*

Mass market *Making a product or providing a service aimed at a large number of customers.*

Niche market *A small market for a specialised product.*

Test market *Where a business tests its product in order to see whether consumers will buy it.*

EXAMINATION SUMMARY TIPS

- Most businesses are market- rather than product-oriented.
- Most products are targeted at a number of different market segments.
- Socio-economic groups are an important method by which businesses analyse a market.
- The amount of disposable income a consumer has is important to a business when targeting its products.
- Mass and niche markets are opposites. 'Mass' means large; 'niche' means small.
- Test markets are used by businesses to try their products before full production takes place.

Key Skills

The Introductory Activity provides an opportunity to evidence Communication Level 1 (C1.3) and IT Level 1 (IT1.2)

For Communication (C1.3), you must present the plan in a suitable form, making sure that it is clear and readable. Check for spelling, punctuation and grammar.

For IT1.2, you must use IT and choose a suitable layout for the plan, which clearly sets out what you are proposing. Design a suitable logo. Save the work so that it can be found easily.

Unit 5.2 Market Research

What is market research?

Market research is how businesses collect information on whether their products or services will be bought. It is important that a business carries out this research before it begins production, so that time, money and effort are not wasted on products that people don't want to buy.

What type of information should a business collect and why?

A business may need to collect information on the following:

- **Whether customers will buy the product.** This is a basic question as if there is no interest at all then the business should not continue with developing the product.
- **How often customers will buy the product.** Even if a lot of customers will buy the product it is important to find out if they will buy the product every week, every month etc. For example, a restaurant may find that enough customers will buy a meal, but only once every year. This might mean that the restaurant business is not really worthwhile.

- **The price that customers are willing to pay.** This is an important part of market research, as consumers may be very willing to buy a product that has a low price. The price must be high enough for the business to cover its costs and make a profit.

- **The type of customers interested in the product.** This information will help the business target its product at the correct market segment (see Unit 5.1).

- **Where the product should be sold.** It is important that a business knows where a product will sell. This might be in a certain part of the country or in a type of shop. For example, will teenagers buy expensive trainers in a supermarket or is it better to sell them in specialist sports shops?

Methods of market research

There are two types of market research a business will use. These are **primary research** and **secondary research**. Primary research is also known as field research and secondary research is sometimes called desk research.

Primary research

Primary research means collecting information first hand. This means that the business designs and collects the information itself, or perhaps pays a research organisation to collect the information for it.

Benefits of using primary research:

- The business asks the questions it wants in any research. This means it can find out exactly the information required.
- The information collected is up to date. Any research information must be as up to date as possible, as the opinions of consumers do change.
- The research can be designed in such a way that the information collected can be analysed easily.

Methods of collecting primary research information

Businesses will use one or more of the following methods when they use primary research:

- surveys
- consumer panels
- testing and observing.

Surveys

Surveys are the most common way of collecting primary information. They are usually in the form of questionnaires, which may be sent to consumers

There are many different types of surveys used in market research.

in the post, or put in with guarantee forms for products. Interviews are where consumers are asked questions and the person asking the questions (the interviewer) fills in the answers. Group interviews are sometimes used where a group of consumers are asked the same questions at the same time. Interviews can also take place over the telephone to collect information.

Advantages of using surveys

1. The questions can be exactly what the business requires, with detailed information being collected which can be analysed later.
2. When an interview technique is used, the person asking the question (the interviewer) can explain any questions that the person being asked (the interviewee) does not understand.
3. The correct amount of information can be collected when interviews are used. If a business requires the opinions of 1 000 consumers, then it can make sure that 1 000 interviews take place.

ACTIVITY 1

1. Design a questionnaire to collect information on a new soft drink called Wizzfizz, an exciting combination of exotic fruits with a new energy formula. You should have between eight and ten questions.
2. Briefly explain why you have decide to ask each of your questions.

Look at the questionnaire guidelines in the coursework section on page 278 for help in designing your work.

Disadvantages of using surveys

1. The questions being asked in a survey must be clear, otherwise customers will not understand, and later analysis will be incorrect. If a question asks consumers if they have seen an advertisement for a product, it does not mean they are about to buy it.
2. The interviewer must not ask questions in such a way that the interviewee is made to answer in a particular way, otherwise the information collected will not be accurate.

3. Collecting information by using surveys takes time and is expensive. Many smaller businesses will not be able to afford this type of research.
4. When postal surveys are used, many consumers may ignore the form and throw it away. To persuade consumers to return the completed questionnaire form, a prize is often offered as an incentive. Even with this system, a business cannot be certain how many survey forms will be returned.
5. Using the telephone to collect information may upset consumers, who dislike being disturbed at home, especially when they are just starting a meal when the telephone rings!

Consumer panels

Consumer panels are groups of consumers who are regularly questioned on test products and services. Because they are used to the idea of market research they are able to give clear and detailed information that a business can use. Questionnaires would be filled in correctly and the members of the panel would need little help. The people in the panel would be carefully selected for the product they are reporting on and are usually paid for the work they complete. Once again these are often expensive to set up and keep going, which means that only larger businesses, for example washing powder manufacturers, would use this type of primary research.

Testing and observing

This type of primary research involves consumers' reaction to products being recorded in some way. It may involve consumers being watched as they look at a new display in a shop, or consumers being invited to see if they can tell the difference between two similar products. This is sometimes done with the consumer being blindfolded and the scene used later in advertisements for television. Food products in a supermarket may be tested with consumers being invited to taste a small sample. Observers will then record the reaction to the product for later analysis.

This type of primary research is only suitable for certain products, with most services being unsuitable for testing and observing in this way.

Primary research – who to ask

When a business decides that it will conduct some primary research, it must carefully decide **who** it requires information from. This involves deciding what the **target market** for the product is likely to be. For example, if a business was thinking of introducing a new sports car, it would be of little use to question children under 15 years old. However if another business wanted to produce a new flavour of crisps, those under 15 would certainly be asked.

The use of guarantee forms for information is especially useful here as a business is collecting information from the very people who have bought their products.

Sampling

Sampling is an important part of primary research. If a business required information before developing a new product it would be impossible to question every possible customer. What is needed is a system for selecting a **number** of those consumers likely to buy the product who represent **all** the possible consumers. For example, if a school was thinking of changing its uniform and wanted the reaction of students, there would be no real point in asking **all** the students at the school. A few people from each year group could be questioned which would represent accurately the views of the other students.

Methods of sampling

- **Random:** This method means that each person has an equal chance of being selected for questioning. The selection of people may be done by computer, though the final results using random sampling may be of limited use to a business unless a high percentage of the correct target market is selected.
- **Quota:** This is a much more accurate method of sampling. It involves carefully selecting the consumers who are to be questioned. The

selection may be by gender, age, socio-economic group (see page 149) or any other feature a business requires. For example an interviewer may need to question 50% of females between 20 and 30, 25% of females between 31 and 50 and 25% of females aged between 51 and 75 if the business feels that this is the information it requires.

A business may further target the primary research at particular consumers, for example by asking football fans at a match their opinions on admission prices and the cost of the new home strip. For this type of information to be any use to the business, there would be little point in asking consumers who had no interest in football.

ACTIVITY 2

How would you collect primary research information on each of the following products? You need to cover the following in your answer:

- the method of primary research you would use and why
- who you would ask
- why you would ask those consumers
- how you would organise your sample.

The products:

1. washing-up liquid
2. televisions
3. denim jeans.

Secondary research

Secondary research, sometimes called **desk research**, is research that another organisation has already completed. Secondary research information can be found in a number of places, such as books, newspapers, magazines and Government publications through the Central Statistical Office.

Census data

This is also available through the Government offices. Every person living in Britain is questioned on how they live, what their income is etc. The information is extremely useful for businesses, and is collected every ten years. The last census was in April 2001. The next one will be in 2011.

Internet

There has recently been a huge increase in the information available on the Internet. Many companies now put information about themselves and their products on the Internet, all of which can be used by others as secondary research.

Internal data

Many businesses have their own secondary data. This is in the form of past sales figures, profits from departments as well as comments from customers. This is usually kept on computers and can be used by a business when it is making decisions for the future.

Advantages of secondary research

- As the research has already been completed by another organisation, secondary research is usually much cheaper to collect than primary research.
- A wide range of data is readily available, especially with the growth of the Internet.

Disadvantages of using secondary research

- The research information might not be **exactly** what a business wants. Remember that someone else has completed the research.
- The data may not be up to date. There are possible problems for a business which makes decisions based on outdated market research.
- The data might not be in a form that the business can analyse easily. Only by designing your **own** research (primary) can you be sure that it is in the form you require.

SWOT analysis

SWOT stands for:

Strengths

Weaknesses

Opportunities

Threats.

A business will carry out a SWOT analysis when it is looking at how it is performing compared to other businesses.

Strengths will examine what the business is good at doing. It may have a very good product, or it may have an office in every town in Britain so it can offer good service. A business may have extremely well trained staff who are well motivated. When looking at its own strengths, a business must be honest and not imagine strengths which are not there.

Weaknesses will look at the opposite of strengths, and examine what the business should improve. This might be difficult for business managers who may not wish to admit having weaknesses. Only when weaknesses have been identified can action be taken to improve performance.

Opportunities looks outside the business and identifies the possible opportunities there are that the business might take advantage of. This may be on a large scale with changes such as the opening of the Single European Market (see page 267), and on a small, scale such as the building of a new housing estate giving a window cleaner the opportunity to increase customer numbers.

Threats examines the problems that a business faces. This may be influenced by the Government, for example the changes in the duty free allowances for people travelling abroad meant that ferry companies and airlines were threatened by a loss of income. Other threats may come from the competition a business faces. Here a competitor may bring out a new and better product; for example in the computer games console market Sony was able to take market share from Nintendo and Sega with the introduction of the PlayStation. A business must not fall behind its competitors for long or it may find it difficult to make up lost ground. In other situations a competitor might cut its prices and so take some of your market share. A successful business will always identify the possible threats from other businesses and plan a solution.

ACTIVITY 3

Complete a SWOT analysis for your school or college. You will need to identify **strengths**, which might be new buildings, good ITC facilities etc. The **weaknesses** may be poor decoration, cramped facilities, lack of sixth form. **Opportunities** may include new courses, new housing developments nearby which will increase student numbers and the availability of grants to modernise the premises. **Threats** may include competitor schools or colleges who might be trying to increase their own student numbers.

Your SWOT analysis should be addressed to the headteacher and include all the different points you can think of that can **honestly** be applied to your school or college. You should aim to write at **least** one side of A4 paper. Take care with presentation, and use ITC if available.

USP analysis

USP stands for:

Unique

Selling

Point.

When a business looks at itself and how it might sell its products or services, it will often try to identify its unique selling point. This is the feature which makes the product or service different from the competition. It may have the lowest selling price, it may have the longest guarantee, it may be the most technically advanced. Whatever the unique selling point is, the business will usually use it in promotions (see page 183) to show consumers how good the product is, how much better it is than the competition, and why the consumer should buy it.

EXAM Practice Questions

Read the information below and answer the questions that follow.

Rave Ltd is a successful limited company which designs and makes up-market casual clothing aimed at females in the 18–30 age group. It is considering developing a range of clothing aimed at a similar male market. The marketing manager feels that the business should undertake some market research before full production takes place. The finance manager thinks that as the business is successful the money spent on research would be wasted.

(a) Explain why Rave Ltd should undertake market research for the male clothing range. (6 marks)

(b) State the socio-economic groups at which the clothing is likely to be aimed. (2 marks)

(c) Evaluate the benefits for Rave Ltd in using the following when researching the market for the new clothing range:
- consumer panels
- USP analysis. (6 marks)

ADVICE ON HOW TO ANSWER THE QUESTIONS

(a) You are being asked to 'explain' in this question. This means that you should write about the benefits **to Rave Ltd** when conducting market research. Remember, the information tells you that the business is successful. Why should such a business still spend money on market research? In this type of question try to think of as many reasons as possible, but always explain how each idea you have will benefit Rave Ltd

(b) This question asks you to 'state' your answer. There is **no** instruction to 'explain'. Simply write the socio-economic groups you think are appropriate. There is no need to explain what they mean.

(c) This is more difficult question which asks you to evaluate certain benefits to Rave Ltd. You should explain the benefits of using consumer panels and USP and how they can help Rave Ltd where other methods of research (such as other secondary research) do not. Remember to make sure your answer is about Rave Ltd and not just any business.

Market research *The collection of data on customer habits to help decision-making in marketing.*

Primary research *Data collected first-hand, often in the form of surveys. Sometimes referred to as field research.*

Surveys *Primary research data collected in the form of questionnaires and interviews.*

Consumer panels *Groups of consumers who are paid to comment on products and services. They are often kept by a business to act as a permanent method of testing their products.*

Target market *The group of customers to whom a business aims to sell its products. The target market may be other businesses as well as consumers.*

Sampling *The method of choosing a group of customers to represent the views of the target market for a product or service.*

Random sampling *Choosing a sample for market research where each customer has an equal chance of being asked. A true random sample is often difficult to achieve, and is not used as much as quota sampling.*

Quota sampling *A method of choosing a sample that represents the target market. If females buy 80% of a product, then there should be four females questioned to every male in a quota sample.*

Secondary research *The collection of data using research or information provided by others, such as magazines, journals and the Internet. Often called desk research.*

Census data *Data collected by the Government every ten years, questioning the entire population on their income, occupations etc.*

SWOT analysis *The process of a business looking at its performance against others, examining strengths, weaknesses, opportunities and threats.*

USP analysis *A business looks at its unique selling point to identify the feature that makes its product or service different. Often used to market the product.*

EXAMINATION SUMMARY TIPS

- Market research is important to the success of a market-oriented business.
- There are many reasons why market research should be undertaken. The most important is whether consumers will buy the product at the price the business requires.
- The two main types of research are primary (or field) and secondary (or desk).
- Primary research is often more use to a business as it can be designed for its exact needs and be up to date.
- Surveys, in the form of questionnaires and interviews, are the most common form of market research.
- Market research, especially primary, can be expensive.
- The Census is an important source of secondary data. The Internet is of growing importance, but remember that not all groups of people use the Internet.
- Market research should always be aimed at the target market for the product.
- Sampling means questioning a small sample of your market.
- Methods of sampling are random and quota. Quota is the more commonly used.
- SWOT analysis means looking at strengths, weaknesses, opportunities and threats.
- USP analysis looks at the unique selling point of a product, and identifies what makes the product different from those of competitors. May be used in advertising and other marketing activities.
- Not all businesses use all types of market research. Smaller businesses may use very little, if any!

Key Skills

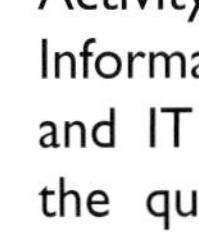
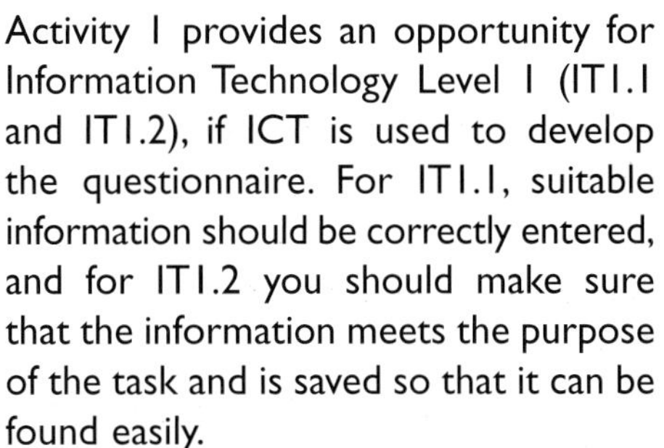

Activity 1 provides an opportunity for Information Technology Level 1 (IT1.1 and IT1.2), if ICT is used to develop the questionnaire. For IT1.1, suitable information should be correctly entered, and for IT1.2 you should make sure that the information meets the purpose of the task and is saved so that it can be found easily.

Activity 3 provides an opportunity to evidence Communication Level 1 (C1.2 and C1.3). For C1.2, you need to collect the necessary information, identifying the main points. For C1.3, the report needs to be presented in a form that meets the purpose of the exercise.

Unit 5.3 The market mix

An old rule for a successful business was that you must have the right product in the right place at the right time. Though this remains true today, there are other aspects to marketing that a business must consider.

The four Ps of the market mix

- Product
- Place
- Price
- Promotion.

Obviously a business must have a **product** which customers want to buy and it must be sold in a **place** which the target customers will use. In addition to this, the **price** of the product must be acceptable to the customer. If customers are to be attracted to the product, the business must undertake some **promotion.**

This way of looking at marketing is known as the **market mix,** and is made up of the **four Ps** of product, place, price and promotion. It is called a 'mix' because all of the four Ps must be 'mixed' in the correct way to make sure the product or service is marketed successfully.

The importance of a business having the correct mix cannot be over-emphasised. How the mix is made up will also change for businesses in different situations. For example, if a business is unknown it may have to put more into promotion (which includes advertising) than a business which has already built up a good reputation. A business that is in competition with many other businesses may have to be more careful about price than a business which has little or no competition.

The market mix is closely linked to market research (see Unit 5.2). From good market research, a business will have a clear idea of whether the product is something a customer wants to buy. Research will also have identified the price that customers are willing to pay, the places where they buy similar products and the types of promotion, such as advertising and offers, that interest them.

Success in marketing requires the correct mix.

Problems with an incorrect market mix

If the mix is wrong in any way, then the results can be disastrous.

In the 1980s Sir Clive Sinclair invented his C5 battery car. Sir Clive was well known, and attracted a lot of publicity for the new invention, a single-seater battery car. This meant that the early promotion of the product was good. The price, at £399, was thought to be reasonable, and it was available in many places. What **was** wrong was the product itself. Without detailed market research, the car was produced in the belief that consumers would want to own this new invention. Unfortunately for Sir Clive, consumers did **not** want to go along at a slow speed (15 miles per hour) at a height that meant that exhaust fumes from lorries and buses blew straight in their faces. The C5 was a famous flop, but shows very well that even a successful businessperson (Sir Clive had made his fortune making pocket calculators) can make costly mistakes if the market mix is not correct.

The C5 was never a successful product.

ACTIVITY 1 

Ask your parents about any products they can remember that were a failure. Try to find out **why** they were failures. Was the problem the product itself, such as the C5? Was the price too high, or was it because of some other reason? Can you think of more recent failures? Write up your findings in a report called Business Failures.

Other parts to a successful market mix

The four Ps are the main parts to the market mix for most businesses. There are, however, other considerations that businesses may have in the marketing of their products.

Packaging is sometimes called the fifth 'P'. For many products, such as electrical goods, packaging is there simply to protect goods being transported and plays no real part in the final sale of a product. When you see television sets for sale, they are not kept in their packaging. It would be strange to go shopping for a new CD player and simply see a pile of boxes from different companies. But for other products, such as children's toys, the packaging is vital and is often aimed at bringing the child's attention to the product. In these types of product, a great deal of care goes into the design of the packaging in order to make the product successful.

Packaging is not important for the final sale of certain products.

Customer services is becoming increasingly important in the marketing of products and services. In a business, customer services deal with enquiries and complaints from customers. As many businesses are seeing the value of keeping their customers happy, huge sums of money are being invested in systems which can keep customers returning to buy more products. Customer services in shops will deal with items which are being returned, often taking goods back which by law they have no need to do. The thinking is that customers will feel that the shop has treated them very well in a difficult situation and will return to spend more money in the future. Some businesses have opened large call centres around the country in order to answer customer questions and make 'courtesy' calls to make sure that customers are receiving good service. Call centres can be located in any area to service the whole country. Good customer services may be **the** reason why people return to certain businesses, in the knowledge that if something **does** go wrong, then they will be treated well.

EXAM Practice Questions

Alan Cropley is a sole trader selling musical instruments and accessories. He has just started in business and has been advised by his friend Richard that he should be careful with his marketing and pay attention to the four Ps of the market mix.

1. State the four Ps of the market mix. (4 marks)
2. Choose **one** of the four Ps and explain briefly why it is important in the marketing of a musical instrument. (4 marks)
3. Explain the importance of packaging in the marketing of the following products:
   - a piano
   - a violin
   - a CD. (4 marks)

ADVICE ON HOW TO ANSWER THE QUESTIONS

1. Here you are asked to 'state'. This means that no explanation is needed. A list of the 4 Ps is all that is required.
2. In this question it is important that you choose **one** of the Ps, possibly the one you feel you understand the most. There is no need for great detail in your answer as you are instructed to explain **briefly**. Remember to explain how your choice affects the **marketing** of a musical instrument, so your answer should be based on only that business.
3. This question asks you to explain the importance of packaging and **apply** the ideas you have to particular products. Exam question examples are usually chosen to bring out **differences.** This practice question is like that; you need to think of the different job packaging will do in the marketing of these products. You will lose marks in an exam if you simply explain how packaging can be used generally and fail to explain how it could be used for the products in the question.

Market mix The parts that make up the marketing for a product or service. Often limited to the four Ps but can also include packaging and customer services.

Four Ps Price, product, place and promotion.

Customer services The ways in which a business looks after the interests of its customers. Can include special departments in shops or the setting up of separate call centres.

EXAMINATION SUMMARY TIPS

- The four Ps should be remembered as the basis for the market mix, though packaging and customer services can also be included.
- You must be able to apply the market mix to different businesses in different situations. All parts of the mix are important, though in certain circumstances, one part may be more important than another.
- A successful business will link the results of its market research to how it uses the market mix.
- Call centres are a growing part of how a business looks after its customers. This process is all part of marketing.

Key Skills

Activity 1 provides an opportunity for Communication Level 1 (C1.1). For this you must take part in a discussion about the problems of marketing a product with a friend or relative. You must have evidence that you have collected useful information, and that you have listened to others and questioned what they say.

Unit 5.4 Price

The importance of price in marketing

Most consumers take notice of the price of a product when they buy it. Only a few very rich people can afford to buy products and services without bothering about the price. Because consumers are so concerned about price, businesses must make sure that the price they charge is at a level that consumers are prepared to pay. If a business sets a price too high, it will soon see its mistake when consumers simply refuse to buy. A business cannot set a price which is too low or it will not make the profits needed for investment and to reward those who have invested money in the business in the first place.

Setting the correct price for a product is a complicated process.

Factors that affect the price of products and services

There are many factors that affect the price a business might charge. A business may look at the price charged by competitors; it will have to consider its own costs and the level of profit it hopes to make. A new business may have to take into account the fact that consumers are not familiar with their name and may be reluctant to buy products unless the price is really low. These factors and others are covered in more detail on page 169.

Supply and demand

When businesses are considering the price of their products and services they will often look at supply and demand. **Supply** looks at the price-setting process from the point of view of the business. **Demand** looks at the same process from the point of view of the consumer.

Supply

Supply shows the quantity of a product a business is prepared to make and sell at a given price. Naturally, if a business can get a high price for its product, it will want to make and sell more, as there is greater opportunity to make profit. The opposite is also true. If the price of a product is low, a business will not want to make and sell many at all, as there will be little chance of profit.

Look at the following figures, which show the connection between supply and price.

Quantity supplied	Price
2	2
4	4
6	6
8	8
10	10

Table 5.2

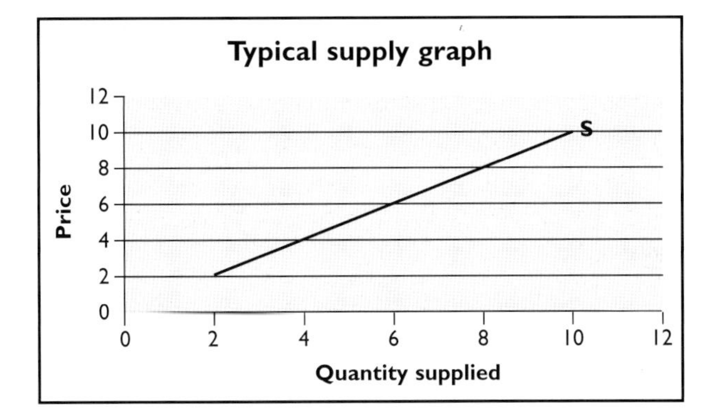

The graph shows that as price rises, the quantity a business is prepared to supply will also increase. Remember that with higher prices a business will see the chance of making higher profits. It will not want to supply many of the product at a lower price, as profits will be reduced. Obviously at a price of zero a business will not want to supply **any** products!

Demand

Demand shows how the consumer will react to changes in price. This is the **opposite** to how a business will react. Though there are exceptions, consumers will usually want to buy more of a product if the price is low. As the price increases, there are fewer consumers willing to buy.

Quantity demanded	Price
2	10
4	8
6	6
8	4
10	2

The following table of figures will show how this works.

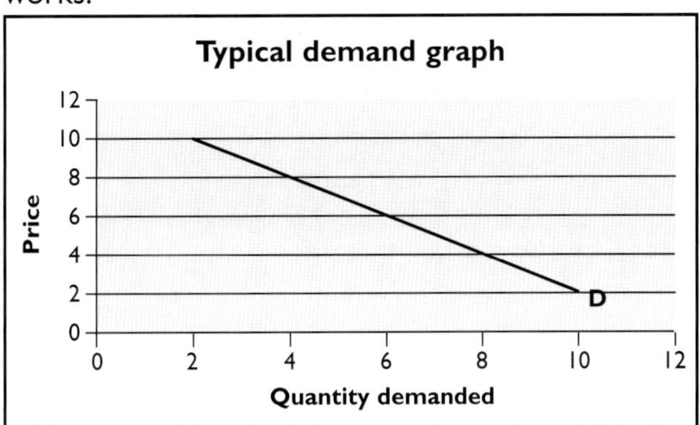

The figures and graph show that as the price of a product falls, the quantity demanded rises, as more consumers are willing to buy. Perhaps consumers see a bargain at the lower prices but feel they are either unable or unwilling to buy products at the higher prices.

Supply and demand: the equilibrium point

When the demand and supply lines are drawn together on the same graph the results are shown on the following graph.

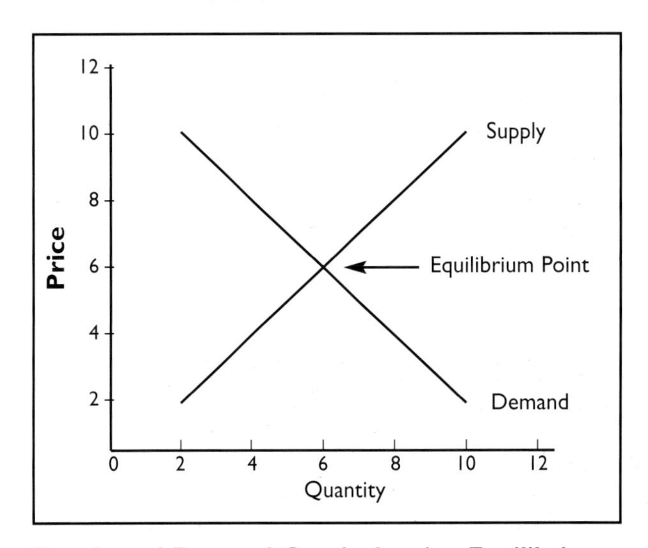

Supply and Demand Graph showing Equilibrium Point

As can be seen on the graph, the **equilibrium point** is where the supply and demand lines cross. It is at this point that the price for a product is set. Looking at the graph, we can see that the price is set at £6. At the equilibrium point, businesses are willing to supply six of the product at the equilibrium point price. Consumers, as shown by the demand line, are also willing to buy six of the product. In this way, the price for most products is set. Businesses cannot charge prices which consumers are unwilling to pay. In the same way, businesses will not supply goods at a really low price, even if the consumer will buy more. Naturally, businesses will often try to increase prices, but they must always take careful note of any change in the behaviour of consumers.

ACTIVITY 1

1. Draw a graph using the following figures for demand and supply. Remember to label the axis and the equilibrium point

Price	Quantity demanded	Quantity supplied
5	20	1
10	15	5
15	10	10
20	5	15
25	1	20

2. At what price will the product be sold?
3. What will normally happen to demand if the price (a) rises, (b) falls? Give reasons for your answers.

Changes in supply

A business may **increase** the supply of the product it makes in order to make more profit. This seems quite natural, a business wanting to sell more products and so make more profit. There are, however, problems for a business in this situation if the demand for the product doesn't increase. With more products to sell, and the same number of consumers willing to buy the product, a business will have to **lower** its price in order to persuade more consumers to buy. This can be shown in graph form.

Notice from the graph that as supply increases the line moves to the **right** and the equilibrium point falls to show the lower price. Looking at the graph, we can see that the price has fallen from £6 to £5.

If a business decides to supply **less** of a product, and demand stays the same, the line will move to the **left** and the price will rise. This is because the

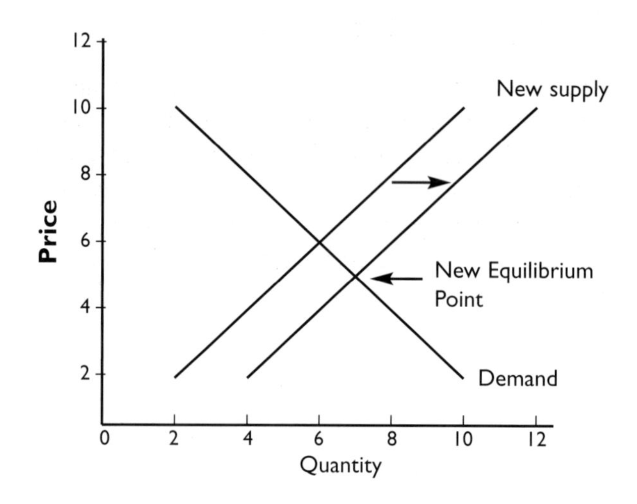

Graph to show an increase in supply

same numbers of consumers want to buy but there is not enough of the product for everyone. In this situation the price will rise. In severe winters the price of fresh vegetables in the shops will rise because they cannot be harvested, causing a fall in supply.

As can be seen in the graph, the reduction in supply has meant that the price has risen from £6 to £7.

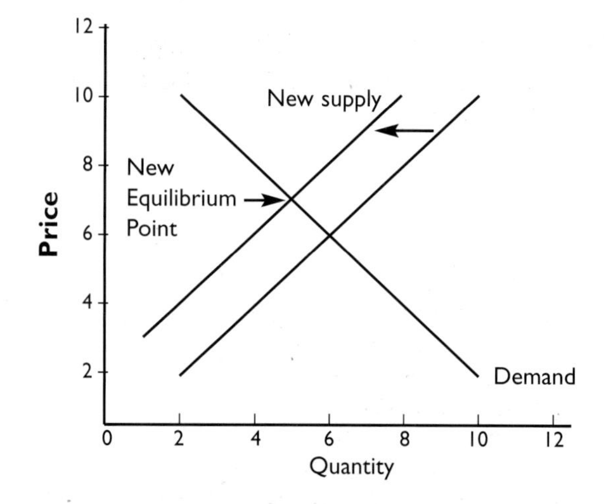

Graph to show a fall in supply

Changes in demand

When the demand for a product **increases** and supply remains the same, the price of the product will rise. This is because there are more consumers wanting to buy than there is supply of the products they want. A business can then charge more for the product until demand matches supply once again. This can be seen on the following graph.

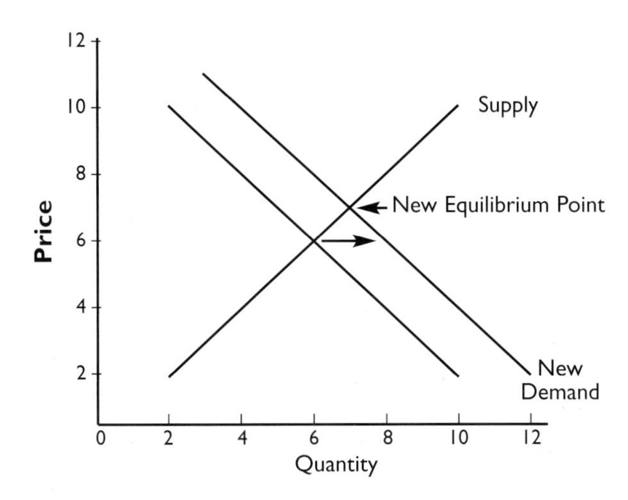

Graph to show an increase in demand

As you can see from the graph, the rise in demand moves the line to the right, showing the rise in price if supply remains the same. Looking at the graph, we can see that the price has **risen** from £6 to £7.

If the demand for a product falls, and supply remains the same, the price will fall. This can be seen in the following graph.

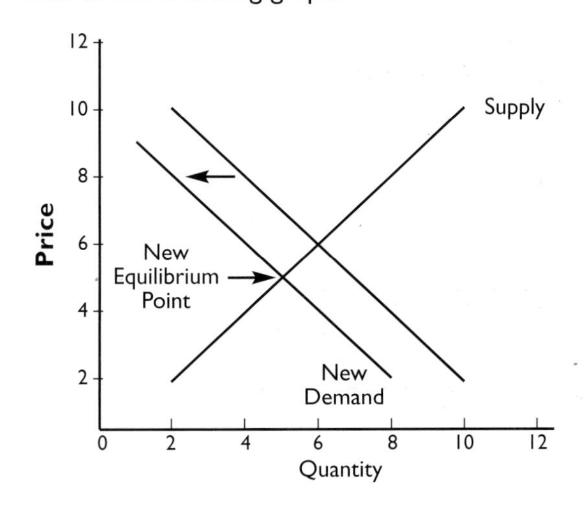

Graph to show a fall in demand

ACTIVITY 2

1. Use the ideas from supply and demand to explain the following:
   (a) the price of Christmas cards in January
   (b) the price of petrol in a fuel crisis.
2. Explain why a fall in demand causes price to fall.
3. Why does a fall in supply result in higher prices?
4. Explain why a business will be happy to see a rise in demand for its products.

This occurs because a business will be faced with unsold products due to the fall in demand. Looking at the graph, we can see that the fall in demand has caused a reduction in price from £6 to £5.

Price elasticity of demand

When a business is considering changing the price of its products, it is important for the business to know what will happen to demand. If the price is increased, will **fewer** customers buy the product? If the price were to fall, would **more** consumers buy the product? The understanding of how consumers react to changing prices will affect decision-making within businesses, as the level of future profits might well be affected. The measurement of how demand changes when prices change is called **price elasticity of demand**.

Price elasticity of demand is measured by the following formula:

$$\frac{\%\ \text{change in quantity demanded}}{\%\ \text{change in price}}$$

Notice that the changes are measured in percentages.

An example:

Imagine that the cost of petrol went up from 80p a litre to 88p per litre. This is an increase, or change, of 10%. After the increase in price, demand for petrol fell from 20 million litres a day to 19 million litres a day. This is a fall, or change, of 5%. If the formula is applied:

$$\frac{\text{\% change in quantity demanded 5\%}}{\text{\% change in price 10\%}}$$

This would give a result of 0.5.

A result of **less** than 1 shows that the demand for petrol will not change as much as the change in price. This we might expect. Petrol is a necessity for many people and if the price goes up, it has to be paid as **there is no alternative**.

Another example:

A restaurant owner thought that he could increase profits if prices were increased. Prices were increased from £5 to £6 per person, an increase or change of 20%. As a result of the price increase, demand fell from 50 customers a day to 25, a fall, or change, of 50%. Applying the formula:

$$\frac{\text{\% change in quantity demanded 50\%}}{\text{\% change in price 20\%}}$$

This gives a result of 2.5.

Some businesses have to carefully consider any price increases.

A result of **more** than 1 shows that demand will change more than price. In the case of the restaurant, the owner made a poor decision in putting up the price, as the demand has fallen much more than the higher price he is charging.

In both examples so far, there has been an increase in price. In the case of petrol, putting up the price should have little effect on demand, and so the businesses selling petrol may think little about any increase. In the case of the restaurant, the owner has to think very carefully about any price increase, as it will mean a large fall in demand. This is because consumers have alternative places to eat and will probably use other restaurants.

ACTIVITY 3

1. Using the formula for price elasticity of demand, calculate the price elasticity of demand for the following changes in price.
   (a) The price of petrol falls from 80p a litre to 72p per litre. Demand increases from 20 million litres per day to 21 million litres per day.
   (b) The restaurant owner reduces the price of a meal from £5 to £4. Demand rises from 50 to 75 customers per day.
2. What do the results of your calculations tell you about the effect on demand after reductions in prices for petrol and the restaurant?
3. What will the effect of a rise in price have on the demand for the following products? Give reasons for your answers.
   (a) cigarettes
   (b) CDs
   (c) butter
   (d) lager
   (e) *The Times* newspaper.

The Government and price elasticity of demand

When a Government needs to raise taxes to pay for hospitals, education and other public services, it too has to be careful where it puts the taxes. If it were to put taxes on goods that people can do without, then consumers will simply not buy the products that have gone up in price, and the Government will not get the taxes it needs. It is for this reason that the main targets for Government tax increases are goods and services where there is no alternative for consumers. Popular targets for tax increases are beer, tobacco and petrol, as no real alternative products are available.

The Chancellor of the Exchequer will think carefully about which products to tax.

Methods of pricing used by businesses

Businesses in different situations will use different pricing methods. The most commonly used methods are:

- competitor pricing
- 'cost plus' pricing
- penetration pricing
- skimming
- differential pricing
- promotional pricing
- psychological pricing.

Competitor pricing

This method simply looks at the price being charged by competitors to give a business an indication as to what price it should charge. If someone was hoping to set up a new window cleaning service, it would be sensible to see what prices any competitors were charging before the business opened. The new business may well charge slightly less than others, but the price will be based on the competition.

Cost plus pricing

It is vitally important for a business to look carefully at its costs before deciding on a price to charge its customers. If the costs of a business were greater than the price it charged, it would eventually close. Businesses will look at their total costs (fixed and variable) and add the profit they wish to make (the 'plus' part). Depending on factors such as supply and demand, a business adds the extra to costs it feels the customers will pay. Calculating profit in this way makes sure a business makes a profit, **providing** that it can sell the amount it needs.

Penetration pricing

When a business is unknown to the public it may have a problem persuading consumers to buy its products. Consumers are often reluctant to try new names, preferring to stay with the trusted brand names that they have always bought. To **penetrate** or break into this new market, a business may reduce its price to tempt consumers away from the established companies. Once it has established a name, and becomes accepted by the public, the 'new' business can put its prices up to the level of the competition. Penetration pricing should therefore only last for a short period of time, if it has been successful. As the price is lower than the business may want it would be impossible for the lower price to remain for long. It will not usually be used by a business that is well known but simply wants to bring out a new product.

Skimming

When a business introduces a new product that is clearly superior to its competitors', especially with technical products, the new product can often be sold at a higher price. This is because many consumers are prepared to pay more to have the latest products. The setting of price in this way is called skimming, or creaming. The computer games console market is typical of this pricing method. When a new console comes out, keen players are prepared to pay a very high price to be the first to use the product. After a while the product becomes 'ordinary' and consumers are no longer willing to pay the higher price. This results in a fall in demand, so companies reduce prices to encourage more consumers to buy. Like penetration pricing, skimming would normally be used for a short period of time only.

Differential pricing

This method of pricing is used when different businesses charge different prices for the same product when selling to different customers. It is common in the transport business where customers can often be charged a wide variety of prices for what seems to be the same product.

For example, on a train, there may be the following customers all paying different fares for the same journey, sitting in the same carriage:

- single ticket holders
- return ticket holders
- senior citizens
- children
- special day return
- ticket holders booked in advance.

A business will do this to attract different consumers. Whether a train is full or empty, it costs much the same to run, and so it is important to attract as many different groups of consumers as possible. A train may not be as busy after the morning rush hour, and so prices are lowered for the same journey to attract those people who don't mind travelling at that time. A similar style of pricing is used on buses.

Promotional pricing

Promotional pricing is a reduction in price used either to attract customers to an existing product or to sell off old products (as in a sale). Sales of a product may be falling a little and in need of a boost, or stock may need to be sold to make room for the next range of products. In both cases, promotional pricing can help the business. As with skimming and penetration pricing, it is only used for a short period of time, though sales in certain stores often seem to go on for most of the year!

Psychological pricing

This method of pricing is very common. As £9.99 **seems** to be **much** cheaper than £10, firms will price their goods in this way to attract consumers. Whether the price is £1.99 or £9 999.99, the intention is that consumers should feel they are getting a bargain and so help to increase sales.

Psychological pricing is designed to attract attention by seeming to be cheaper.

ACTIVITY 4

Which pricing strategy would you recommend for the following situations? Give reasons for your choice:

- a new chocolate bar, from a well-known manufacturer
- an established make of hair shampoo
- a new CD from a unknown 'boy band'
- a range of household dining furniture aimed at higher income groups
- a café introducing a new range of meals
- the latest model of car from Mercedes.

EXAM Practice Questions

JY Ltd is a new company wanting to break into the portable mini disc market. It knows it is competing against many established businesses, but feels that with a good product, at the right price, it will succeed.

1. Explain why JY Ltd should be concerned at being in competition with well-known companies. (4 marks)
2. Describe how JY Ltd might use 'cost plus' pricing. (3 marks)
3. Using the following list of pricing strategies, advise JY Ltd on the most appropriate methods to use in the marketing of the new mini disc player. Give reasons for your answer:
   (a) skimming
   (b) penetration
   (c) differential
   (d) psychological. (8 marks)

ADVICE ON HOW TO ANSWER THE QUESTIONS

1. Here you are asked to explain reasons for a business acting in a certain way. Remember to think of the situation JY Ltd is in as a new company. What advantages would a well-known competitor have over JY Ltd as the newcomer? What is the problem for a business in **not** having a well-known name?
2. In this question you must **apply** your knowledge and understanding of 'cost plus' pricing to the making of mini discs. You are **not** expected to have a detailed knowledge of the parts that make up a mini disc player. You **are** expected to know that 'cost plus' pricing is made up of various sections, which can be applied to JY Ltd.
3. This is an evaluation question where you are being asked to make a judgement, choosing between methods of pricing. Notice in the question the use of 'advise' and 'the most appropriate methods'. The 's' on methods is important, as it shows that **more than one** may be appropriate. Remember what you have been told about the business: it is new and is in competition with well-known companies. Make sure you give clear reasons for the methods you feel would be most appropriate.

KEY TERMS

Supply *The amount of a product or service a business is prepared to make and sell at a given price.*

Demand *The quantity consumers are prepared to buy at a given price.*

Equilibrium *The point at which supply equals demand. This sets the price and the quantity being bought and sold for a product.*

Price elasticity of demand *A measure in percentage terms of how demand changes when there is a change in price.*

Competitor pricing *Setting a price based on prices charged by competitor businesses for a similar product.*

Cost plus pricing *A pricing method which adds a percentage for profit to the total costs of making a product. This gives the selling price.*

Penetration pricing *Setting a price lower than the competitor businesses. Often used by new businesses to break into a market. Should only be seen as a short-term strategy.*

Skimming *Where a new product is more advanced than competitors, a price is set high as some consumers are willing to pay higher prices to own the newest technology. Sometimes called 'creaming'.*

Differential pricing *Charging different prices to certain customers for the same product or service. Often used in the transport industry.*

Promotional pricing *Reducing prices to give products a boost or to sell off old stock. Most commonly seen as sales in shops.*

Psychological pricing *Setting a price such as £9.99 instead of £10 to make the product seem much cheaper.*

EXAMINATION SUMMARY TIPS

- The setting of a suitable price is vital in the marketing of a product.
- There are many factors that affect the price of a product or service.
- Supply and demand graphs are drawn to show how businesses and consumers react when price changes.
- Equilibrium point is the meeting of supply and demand.
- Using and drawing supply and demand graphs is important to the understanding of price.
- When supply and demand change, the lines on the graph move.
- There are many pricing methods which businesses might use.
- Learn how important price elasticity of demand is to a business which is considering price changes.
- Different circumstances mean that different methods of pricing will be used by a business.

Key Skills

Activity 1 provides an opportunity to evidence Application of Number Level 1 (N1.1). To achieve this, you must identify and show the correct calculation in order to arrive at the answer. Information Technology Level 1 (IT1.1 and IT1.2) can be evidenced if ICT is used to draw the graphs. The correct layout must be chosen, with the work being saved where it can be found easily.

Activity 3 provides an opportunity for Application of Number Level 1 (N1.2). For this Activity you must show that you have worked accurately and you have checked your results.

Unit 5.5 Product

The importance of product in marketing

Businesses will always try to supply products that consumers will want to buy, at a price at which the business can make the profit it requires. This will often come as a result of analysing market research, where consumer needs are identified. A business can then make the product with more certainty that it will be a success.

Even with this 'preparation', there are still some considerations that a business will have to make when marketing the product.

Considerations for marketing a product

Price. As covered in Unit 5.4, a business will need to decide whether the product is to be targeted at the lower 'budget' part of price, or the higher 'up-market' section.

Design. Certain products, such as clothing and furniture, will be marketed on their design. A new design such as the Dyson cleaner gives the product a real advantage over competitors.

Image. How a consumer feels about owning a product may be used in marketing. It is more common in relation to exclusive products such as expensive sports cars, where consumers like to be seen to own certain goods.

Both image and design are used to market sports cars.

Research and development

Many businesses spend large sums of money on research and developing their products. Part of the research is investigating the needs of consumers, though research and development can also include testing whether an idea will work or not. In developing his bagless cleaner, James Dyson built many different versions before the ones we know today were ready to be sold. In the medical industry, new drugs are developed and tested over many years before they are allowed to be used on the general public. For a business to stay ahead of the competition, or even just to keep up with it, there may be large financial investment in research and development.

The product mix

Many businesses have more than one product or service they either make or sell. This is known as the product mix. If a business were to make only one product, that would be fine if consumers continued to buy the product. If, however, consumers stopped buying that one product, the business would certainly fail. By having a mixture of products, if one should prove unpopular, the firm could rely on others to provide sales revenue. By having a wide product mix a business recognises that not all consumers are the same and they have different needs. A car maker will sell different model cars that have different colours, different engine sizes, different numbers of doors and so on. The old idea of Henry Ford that a customer for his cars 'can have any colour . . . as long as it's black' would certainly **not** work in the 21st century!

Branding

Branding is the use of a well-known name that consumers connect with a product or service. Many consumers will only buy products where they know the name, making it difficult for unknown new businesses to be successful. In sports clothing, many teenagers will only buy products with a certain name or symbol, which is then used by manufacturers to market further products. A business with a brand name that is trusted by consumers will sometimes use that

ACTIVITY 1

Make a collection of different brand names and trade marks by looking in magazines, newspapers etc. Try not to use only one type of product but include shops, cars, toiletries, food, electrical goods and any others you can find. Cut out the information to make an A4-size collage (or bigger) of your collection. How many of your collection do **not** say the name of the business?

name to market products which are not part of their normal product mix. Boots is a business with a clear brand name, and has used that name to market holiday insurance, a product not usually thought of as something sold by Boots the Chemist.

The product life cycle

All products have a time span over which consumers will want them. This is called the product life cycle. No one would buy **exactly** the same product forever. Consumers' tastes change and products have to change to meet that changed demand. Sometimes products come back into fashion after a time when they wouldn't sell, clothes being a good example where different styles come and go. Other products have a longer life cycle; many food products have changed little over the years.

Some products remain much the same over a long period of time.

The life cycle of a product can be shown in graph form.

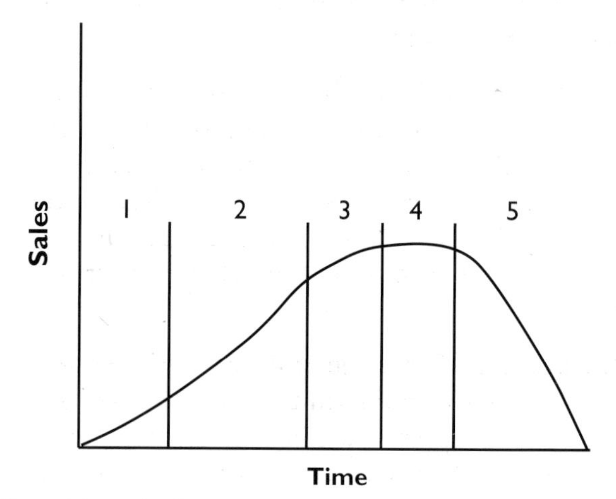

Stage 1 Introduction
Stage 2 Growth
Stage 3 Maturity
Stage 4 Saturation
Stage 5 Decline

The Product Life Cycle

As you can see, the graph is split into five sections, which are used to identify stages at which different marketing techniques need to be applied to the product to make it successful.

Introduction is where the product is launched or first put on sale. Before this a business may well have conducted some market research and invested money in developing the product. When the product is launched a business may advertise it in a number of ways in order to make sure that it gets off to a successful start remember, at this stage the product is unknown and consumers need to be told about it. Sales should rise steadily.

Growth is the second stage, where the sales show their most rapid growth. Advertising and other promotion support (see page 185) change slightly as the product will be generally known to consumers. The product is still 'new' and will be in great demand.

Maturity is the next stage, where sales are towards their highest, but most importantly the

rate of growth is slowing down. It may be necessary to support a product with further advertising and offers at this time to maintain sales against the competition.

Saturation. At this point the sales of the product are not growing at all, though clearly sales are still high. A business might be thinking about developing a replacement when saturation is reached, unless the life cycle itself can be extended. At saturation, a product may need some new offers to keep sales high.

Decline is the final stage in the life cycle. Here sales are falling and though the product may be given some support in the form of further promotional offers, consumers see the product as old and switch to those of competitors. It is at this stage that a successful business will have developed a new product to replace the one that is in decline.

Extending the product life cycle

As can be seen from the graph of the product life cycle, the highest level of sales is at the end of growth and into the maturity section. Businesses try to keep the sales of a product at this high level for as long as they can, as it will increase sales revenue and profit.

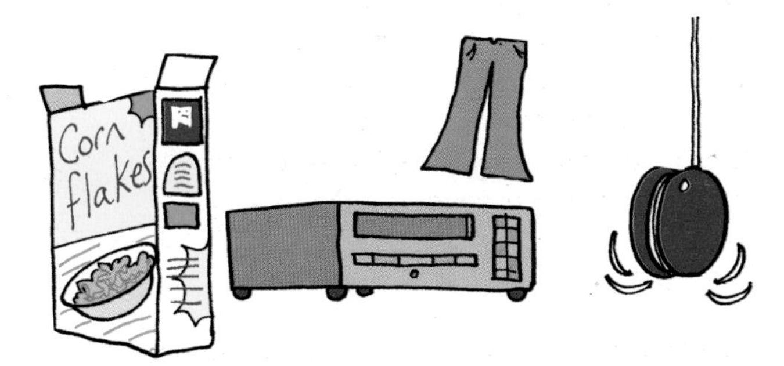

Different products have different life cycles.

A number of methods are used to try to **extend** the life cycle and keep the sales as high as possible for as long as possible.

ACTIVITY 2

1. Some products have lasted a long time, though others seem to last only weeks and months. Research the length of life cycles of different products in the following areas:
   - food products
   - electrical products
   - clothing
   - games.

Try to find at least five items in each section. Ask friends and family to help you find the age of products that had a very short or long life cycle. Use your research to complete the following chart. Two entries have been made to give you a start.

Name of product	Length of life cycle	Still on sale today?
Cadbury's Dairy Milk (food)	95 years	Yes
Sega Saturn (games console)	1–2 years	No

2. Which products had the shortest and longest life cycles? Why do you think these products had such different life cycles?

- **Advertising** the product more widely is often used to maintain sales.
- **Price reduction.** By reducing the price, the product will be more attractive to consumers, and so help maintain sales.
- **Added value** may be given to the product to prevent sales falling. Car manufacturers often use this method, where an older model is given 'free' extra items such as air conditioning, better audio equipment etc, to make it more attractive to consumers. A new model would not need such extras to sell it.
- **Other markets** may be developed. For example, if a business was at maturity level in

Britain with a product, it might export to countries where the product was only at the introduction stage, with plenty of future sales opportunities. In other cases, a business might simply try to sell its product to a different target market than the one first used.

- **Re-launching a product** as 'new' and 'improved', with possibly little real change, may persuade consumers to continue buying the product.

EXAM Practice Questions

1. Buzz Ltd is a small company that specialises in the designing and making of lighting for large rock concerts and other outdoor events. Products from Buzz Ltd have a life cycle of approximately three years.
   (a) Explain what is meant by a product life cycle. (2 marks)
   (b) State the five parts of a product life cycle. (5 marks)
   (c) Evaluate the benefits of advertising throughout the life cycle of a product. (8 marks)
2. Chris, the marketing manager of Buzz Ltd, is concerned that one of its main lighting systems is coming towards the end of its life cycle.
   (a) Advise Chris on how the life cycle of the lighting system might be extended. (4 marks)

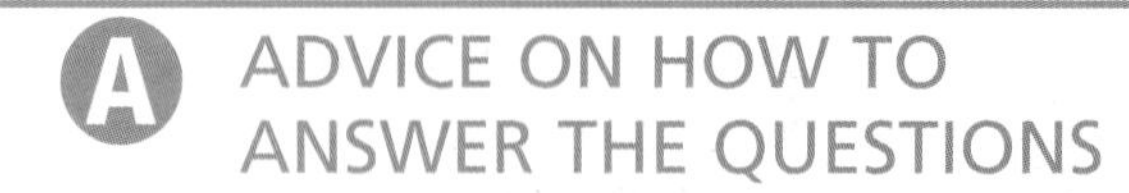

ADVICE ON HOW TO ANSWER THE QUESTIONS

1. (a) Here you need to give a definition of the product life cycle. Note that the question is worth 2 marks, so an extended answer is not necessary.
   (b) This is a knowledge question. The five stages should be stated with no explanation.
   (c) The command word in this question is 'evaluate', with a higher mark allocation (8). This means that you need to make a judgement of the benefits of using advertising throughout the life cycle of a product. Is advertising equally important at all stages? Are there other issues the business should be concerned with?
2. (a) Here you are being instructed to 'explain'. This means that you must show that you understand the methods used to extend the life cycle of a product, and apply them to the business in the question. You don't have to be an expert on lighting. There are methods of extending the life cycle of a product which can be applied to this situation as to many others.

KEY TERMS

Research and development (R&D) *is used to help introduce both new and existing products. The research may be testing products in a laboratory or conducting market research by interviewing consumers.*

Product mix *is the mixture of products or services a business markets. For example, Sony has a product mix which includes TVs, videos, camcorders, computer game consoles and hi-fi units.*

Branding *is the use of a name to market a product, eg Twix.*

Trade mark *is the use of a symbol or name to identify and market a product. It may be registered and be marked with 'TM' to make sure that other businesses cannot copy the trademark. Cadbury's is the registered trademark of Cadbury Limited.*

Product life cycle *is the life of a product, usually shown as a graph divided up into five stages: introduction, growth, maturity, saturation and decline.*

Added value *is the extra items that are added to a product to help sales. Often used to extend the life cycle of a product.*

Re-launching *occurs when an existing product is given a 'new' image to help boost sales and further extend the life cycle of the product.*

EXAMINATION SUMMARY TIPS

- Many businesses invest large sums of money on research and development in order to keep their products ahead of the competition.
- Having a varied product mix is helpful to a business when the sales of one or more products start to fall.
- Branding is becoming increasingly important in the marketing of a product.
- The different stages of the product life cycle require different marketing techniques.
- Remember that the length of the product life cycle is **not** the same for every product!
- Extending the product life cycle is important if a business is faced with large investments to develop a new product.
- Product is but one part of the market mix. A business cannot simply concentrate on developing a product and ignore the other parts of the mix.

Key Skills

Activity 2 provides an opportunity for Communication Level 1 (C1.1 and C1.3).

To evidence C1.1, you must show that you have taken part in a discussion with friends or relatives in order to complete the research. For C1.3, you need to present the information clearly in a form which is suitable, making sure that spelling, punctuation and grammar are accurate.

Unit 5.6 Placement

The importance of placement in marketing

It is often said that a successful business should have the right product in the right place at the right time. Though parts of price and promotion could be added to this phrase, it remains the case that a business has to have the product in the correct place for successful sales.

The **place** part of the four Ps is really in two parts:

1. where the product is to be sold
2. the method of distribution to be used to make sure the product gets to the consumer.

Where to sell the product

This is linked to the location of a business (see Unit 7.3, page 255), where a business may choose to sell its product or service in a town, an industrial estate, a village 'corner' shop, or in an out-of-town shopping mall. These decisions are important to a business that owns the shop itself. But what if you are a producer of a product without anywhere to sell it. What **type** of shop would be best for you? If you were making expensive furniture, would you try to sell it in a supermarket such as Tesco? Does that type of **place** suit the product? Consumers often have a fixed idea of what goods should be bought in certain places, and a business trying to sell 'different 'goods that a customer is not used to may not always work.

McDonald's has developed the place in which it operates.

Businesses will often extend the places in which they sell their products in order to maintain growth. McDonald's first developed its restaurants in town and city centres. It then moved 'out of town' to retail parks and leisure areas. Motorway service areas have recently been targeted for further expansion.

The methods of distribution

Distribution is all about getting the product to the consumer. It is of little use advertising something which customers want to buy and then failing to make sure the product is in the correct place.

There are different methods of distribution which are appropriate for different types of businesses.

Distribution method 1

Producer
|
Consumer

In this example the producer is distributing a product directly to the consumer. As the business will have to deal with each person who buys from it, this method is only possible with a small business. Imagine Heinz selling directly to everyone who wanted to buy their baked beans! The type of business where this method will be found is a small craft centre which will sell its products direct to its customers. Small bakeries will often do the same.

A business selling its products to another business will often use this method of distribution. This is because the number of customers will once again be small and can be managed easily. As soon as the number of different customers becomes too large, a business must consider another method of distribution.

Distribution method 2

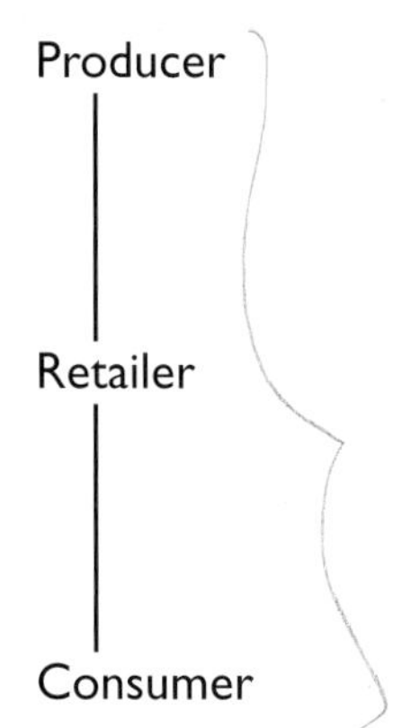

In this method of distribution, the producer sells to a retailer who then sells to the consumer. This method is common in electrical goods, with producers selling to shops such as Currys and Comet with consumers buying from these shops. Once again, it would be difficult for Sony to sell its products directly to each person who wanted a television. It is easier for Sony to sell a number of products to a retailer who then sells the products to the consumer.

Distribution method 3

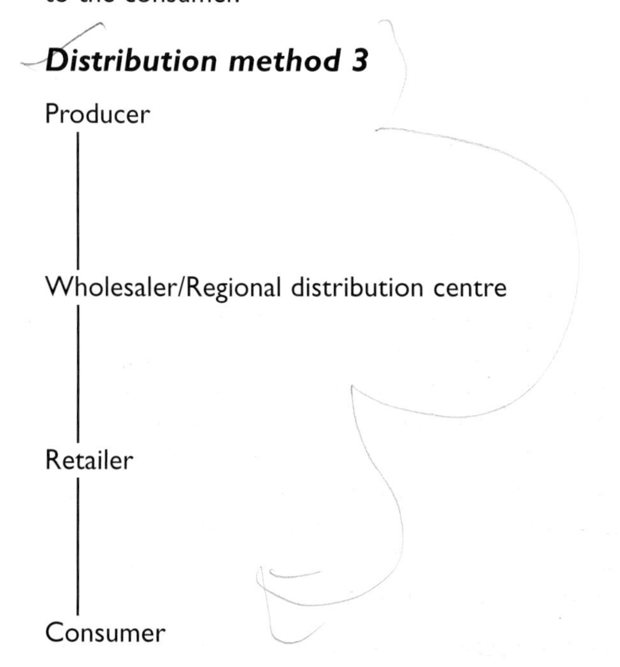

In this method of distribution, the producer sells to a wholesaler or sends goods to a regional distribution centre.

A wholesaler is a large storage centre able to take in deliveries direct from producers.

The role of a wholesaler is to break the bulk of goods sent by the producer. This means buying in large quantities from a manufacturer and then selling smaller amounts to a retailer. This is especially important in the distribution of food, where small shops are often not able to store large quantities and so need to buy their stock in amounts they can cope with. Take the example of soup. Large producers such as Heinz will be unable to deal directly with **every** shop that sells its products. It will distribute the cans of soup in large quantities to the wholesaler who will have a large warehouse to store the goods. Small retailers will then go to the wholesaler to buy, say, a tray of 24 tins of soup for sale in their shops.

Though the main role of the wholesaler is to break the bulk of goods between the producer and retailer, it does provide these other services:

- Credit can be given to the retailer, which enables the retailer to have the goods before paying for them. This trade credit means that a retailer can sell the goods, which provides the money to pay the wholesaler.
- The wholesaler may be able to deliver products to the retailer. This may be very helpful when the products are bulky and heavy, or if the products are frozen and require special transport.
- Where necessary, a retailer may need help with a product which the larger wholesaler will be able to provide.
- It should be remembered that the wholesaler provides a useful service to the producer, who would otherwise be unable to supply goods direct to the many consumers it might have.

The role of the regional distribution centre (RDC) is slightly different. The RDC is owned by the retailer and is used to store the products it will later sell in its shops. Marks & Spencer uses this system where producers send to the RDC which then distributes products to the shops as they are needed.

ACTIVITY 1

1. Explain why place is important in marketing.
2. Describe the role of a wholesaler in distribution.
3. Explain why a retailer should use a wholesaler.
4. Explain the difference between a wholesaler and a regional distribution centre.
5. For **each** of the following products, which method of distribution you would use? Give reasons for your choice:
   (a) a car
   (b) hand-made pottery
   (c) corn flakes.

Changing distribution of goods

The distribution of goods is now changing with the introduction of direct sales and **e-commerce.** E-commerce is dealt with in more detail in Section 5.8.

Direct sales is a method of selling goods directly to the consumer, often using the telephone, or sending catalogues to consumers for them to order direct. Well-known shops such as Next also have their own catalogue business for customers who prefer to shop at home and simply order by phone or using an order form. This saves the consumer both time and effort.

Catalogues are being used more as a direct selling technique.

Other direct marketing techniques include television sales through Teletext and direct offers as part of TV programmes on digital and cable channels.

ACTIVITY 2

For any 20 products you have at home (this can include food, clothes, furniture, electrical goods etc) find out whether they were bought:

- from a shop
- by mail order catalogue
- on the Internet
- direct from the maker.

Make sure you choose a variety of products. Display your results in chart and graph form.

EXAM Practice Questions

Artcraft Ltd is a limited company owned by two sisters, Amy and Chloe. They make high-quality jewellery to order. They are thinking of expanding to produce more jewellery to sell in shops, rather than direct to consumers.

1. Explain the advantages to Artcraft Ltd of selling jewellery direct to the consumer (4 marks)
2. Suggest two possible places where Artcraft could sell the jewellery should they expand. Give reasons for your choice. (4 marks)
3. Amy feels that the business should start selling jewellery through the local supermarket. Chloe thinks that selling through the main jewellery shop on the local High Street would be a better idea. Evaluate the benefits and problems of Amy's and Chloe's suggestions. (8 marks)

ADVICE ON HOW TO ANSWER THE QUESTIONS

1. Here you are asked to 'explain' advantages. What you must do is explain the advantages to Artcraft Ltd. You need to look carefully at the information given about the business and decide what are suitable reasons for Artcraft Ltd.
2. This question asks you to 'suggest'. This is the same as 'list' or 'state', and your ideas need no explanation.
3. The command word here is 'evaluate'. This means that you must look at the choices you have, think of any advantages and disadvantages of each choice and make a decision, giving reasons. Take care in this type of question with the **number** of advantages and disadvantages. It may be that you think of more advantages than disadvantages for one suggestion. This is where you need to judge whether the **smaller** number of disadvantages is more important than the **greater** number of advantages. Giving full reasons for any choice is essential. There are 8 marks available for this question, so a detailed, reasoned answer is required.

KEY TERMS

Placement *The part of the market mix that deals with distributing the product to the customer.*

Methods of distribution *The methods used to get the product to the consumer, for example: producer to retailer to consumer.*

Wholesaler *Part of the distribution that deals with breaking bulk between producer and retailer. A wholesaler buys large quantities from a producer and sells smaller quantities to retailers.*

Regional distribution centre (RDC) *Similar to a wholesaler but owned by the retailer. Used as a storage base to supply shops in a region.*

Direct sales *A method of selling by larger businesses direct to the customer by catalogues, TV etc. Though smaller businesses have often sold goods in this way, the term is usually used to include more recent distribution methods.*

EXAMINATION SUMMARY TIPS

- Placement includes both where a product is sold **and** the method of distribution used to get the product to the customer.
- Different products require different methods of distribution.
- More recent methods of distribution, such as direct sales and e-commerce, are becoming much more important for certain products.
- Smaller businesses usually have a more simple method of distribution; larger businesses tend to have a more complex system.
- Though the main role of the wholesaler is to break bulk, they do offer other services.

Key Skills

Activity 2 provides an opportunity for Communication Level 1 (C1.1 and C1.3) and IT (IT1.1 and IT1.2).

For Communication C1.1 you need to show that you have talked to others in order to investigate where products were bought. For C1.3 you need to present the results in a form which is suitable to the work you have been asked to complete. You must make sure that spelling, punctuation and grammar are accurate.

To evidence IT you must collect and use information which is useful for the question (IT1.1) and present the information using a computer (graph/ chart form), making sure that the data is saved so that it can be found easily (IT 1.2).

Unit 5.7 Promotion

The importance of promotion in marketing

Promotion is concerned with how a business is to market its product. A business must inform customers that it has a product to sell, and make customers feel that they need to buy the product. To do this, businesses will use a variety of methods, which need to be chosen carefully to have the greatest effect on customers. Without promotion, a business may have an excellent product which is a failure because consumers were not persuaded to buy it.

Promotion in the market mix

Promotion is linked closely to the other P's in the market mix.

Product

Clearly, a product needs to be brought to the attention of the consumer, which is normally achieved through advertising. A product coming towards the end of its life cycle will also need further promotion if the life cycle is to be extended. Another product with a short life cycle may need a lot of promotion to boost sales in order to repay the development costs of the product (and make some profit!) before the end of the life cycle.

Price

The price of a product should be set carefully in order to make it attractive to potential customers (see Unit 5.4). At certain times, the price may need to be changed to keep sales at the required level.

Place

A business may need to inform customers that it has a new shop or office opening which will

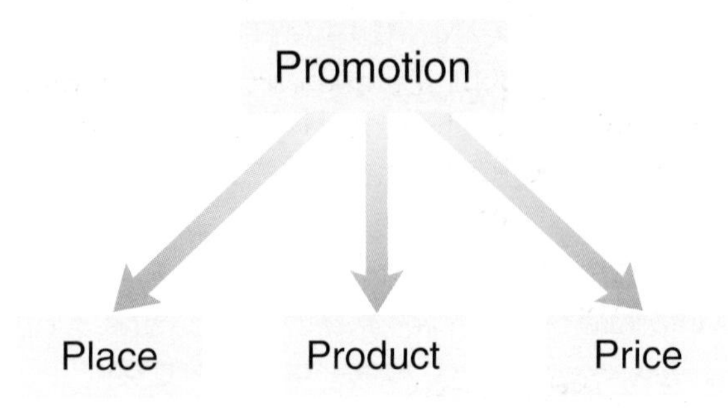

Promotion is closely linked to the other Ps in the marketing mix.

improve customer service. This will need suitable advertising. A business may feel that its strength is the excellent distribution system it has, delivering products the next day. This would need to be brought to the attention of customers in order to attract further sales.

The aims of promotion

Promotion has the following aims:

- to inform customers about a product (especially when new or changed)
- to keep a business ahead of its competitors.
- to create or change the image of a business
- to maintain or increase sales.

These aims will be used as necessary by a business, though they all try to keep sales at a level which is satisfactory for the business. As a business develops, the **emphasis** of promotion will change. When Sega first introduced its games consoles into Britain, its promotion was aimed at making people aware of the **name** 'Sega', which at that time was unknown. As the name began to be accepted, the emphasis of promotion switched to the **products** it was selling, such as Dreamcast.

It must be remembered that even the best-known companies and their products still need promotion. Nestlé continue to promote products such as Kit Kat even though they are market leaders. This is simply aimed at **maintaining** the product as a leading chocolate product.

Methods of promotion

There are many different methods of promotion a business might use. They include the following:

1. sales promotion
2. public relations
3. sponsorship
4. advertising

Sales promotion

Sales promotion itself can be divided into many different parts.

- **Price reductions** are often seen in shops in January in order to sell off all the old stock a shop no longer wants to keep. This will boost sales at a time when the products (such as Christmas cards) would not normally sell. Price reductions may also be used to sell off stock of an old model, in order to make space for the newer model. In this example, consumers who know an old model is to be replaced will not want to own it, unless of course there is a large price reduction!
- **Loss leaders** are another form of price reduction, often used by supermarkets. Here a business will lower the price of one or two items to such a point that there is little or no profit. The idea is that a consumer will be attracted to the supermarket by the price reductions, but while they are there they will also buy a number of other items (at normal prices) and so the supermarket makes the profit it needs.
- **Added value** is a sales promotion often used by the food industry. It involves giving 30% extra free and so on. As the cost of the product to the producer has not changed much by the offer it is a good way of drawing the attention of the consumer. A consumer may well be attracted to the product for the first time because of the added value, and then continue to buy it. Supermarkets will often offer goods at two for the price of one in the hope of consumers returning to the supermarket (saving money) and buying the product again.
- **Gifts** may be given with a product in order to increase sales. Garages sometimes give glasses after a customer has bought a certain amount of petrol. Crisp manufacturers often promote their products by putting gifts in the bag to increase sales.
- **Point of sale** is a method of sales promotion used at the place where the customer will buy the product. It can often be seen in large supermarkets where there may be a large display of a certain product (often at a key point such as the entrance) which attracts attention. This may also be linked to other offers, but frequently the display itself can increase sales. Within supermarkets, demonstrations or free tasting also attract consumers who may be persuaded to buy a product for the first time.
- **Competitions** can be used to boost sales, where customers are entered for a monthly prize draw, offering a variety of prizes. With higher-priced products, such as cars, the value of the prize is often very high, such as a continental holiday, or even the money you paid for the car being returned.
- **Free samples** are often used in cosmetics and other businesses to let the consumer try the product. Consumers may be reluctant to buy the full size of a product they do not know as they may not like it and so waste a lot of money. By providing a small sample, which may by simply posted through a letter box, or included in a magazine, consumers can try the sample and then buy the full size, knowing that they like it. Obviously this can only be used for certain products. A business such as Mercedes is unlikely to give away a free sample of one of its cars!
- **Merchandising** is becoming increasingly important in promoting certain products, especially films. When a new 'blockbuster' film is about to be released, a number of items are put on sale in some way connected to the film. These items can range from T-shirts to cuddly toys to key rings to posters. As with other methods of promotion, the intention is to bring the product to the attention of the consumer in order to increase sales. In the

Not all products will use free samples.

case of some merchandising, it may well make as much profit as the film!

- **After-sales service** can also be used as a sales promotion. In this case a business may offer a guarantee for a product, or extend an existing guarantee. Many businesses promise that if a customer sees a lower price in another shop they will refund the difference. This is meant to give the customer confidence when they buy a product, and so increases sales.

Public relations

The main difference between public relations (PR) and other methods of promotion is that PR is often free. Giving price reductions and free gifts can cost a big business many thousands of pounds, which has to be made up by increased sales. Public relations simply tries to bring the company and its products to the attention of the public at no cost. This is done by releasing stories to newspapers and other media about the company in the hope that the story will be printed. Where a famous personality is involved, the chance of such a story making the papers is increased. At a slight cost, a business may offer one of its products for a prize on a TV or radio show. In this way the business brings its product to the attention of the customer for little cost compared to paying for an advertisement.

ACTIVITY 1

For each of the following situations, explain what sales promotion method(s) you would use:

(a) A well-known jeans maker is ready to launch a new style of jeans, though it has a lot of old stock left.
(b) Smell It Cosmetics wants to promote its deodorant range which has not sold as many as expected.
(c) Eatdat Cheese wants to promote its new cheese that it is trying to sell in large supermarkets.
(d) Williams Cars feels that its new model is not selling as well as expected and it needs ideas on sales promotion.
(e) A famous baked bean manufacturer feels it is time to remind customers what a good product it makes, as sales have fallen slightly.

Sponsorship

Sponsorship is becoming increasingly important in bringing the name of a business to different customers. It is clearly seen in sports such as football, with teams from the Premier league to local pub teams having a sponsor. Though the sponsor may have a personal interest in the team (such as the pub team) there is a clear business aim in promoting the name of the business to as wide an audience as possible. With more sport, especially football, being shown on television, there is an increasing opportunity for a business to make its products known to a world-wide audience.

Sponsorship may also mean that an industry that is not allowed to advertise on television (such as tobacco) can still use television to bring its products to the attention of consumers.

ACTIVITY 2

1. Collect examples from newspapers and magazines showing sponsorship.
2. Make your own collage of your extracts.
3. Explain why businesses often spend millions of pounds on sponsorship.
4. Find the names of the sponsors for at least four English or other national teams in different sports. Try to find how much they paid in sponsorship.

Advertising

Advertising is one of the most important parts of promotion. We all see and hear advertisements for a huge range of products. On television they often seem to be more entertaining than the programmes!

The **type** of advertising to be used needs to be carefully chosen as do the **advertising media**, that is where the product is to be advertised. You would not normally expect to see the latest chart CDs and an industrial waste disposal machine being advertised in the same way in the same place.

For some products an **advertising campaign** is launched, which involves a series of advertisements in different forms over a period of time. In this way a producer can build up consumer knowledge of a product which will increase sales or get a new product off to a successful start.

Types of advertising

Informative advertisements simply give information without trying to persuade the customer to buy something by giving an opinion. For example an advertisement such as 'SALE STARTS MONDAY 9 AM' is telling readers that a sale will start on a certain day at a certain time. No comment is added as to how good the sale is to be or how much the customer should buy.

Persuasive advertisements try to persuade customers to buy the product. For example, an advertisement says: 'THE MOST FANTASTIC SALE EVER STARTS ON MONDAY AT 9 AM. BARGAINS FOR EVERYONE THAT NO ONE SHOULD MISS.' Here the advertisement goes beyond giving simple information, and tries to persuade the reader to go to the sale by claiming that there are bargains for everyone.

Other types of persuasion may be by the images and music that are used. This is all intended to attract the customers' attention and then influence them to such an extent that they buy the product.

Generic advertisements are not for a specific business, but an industry. For example, the milk delivery industry advertises the advantages of home delivery of milk without naming particular businesses.

ACTIVITY 3

1. Research advertisements in newspapers, magazines, television and radio. Use your research to complete the table started for you. You should aim for at least 20 different advertisements.

Product	Where advertised	Type of advertisement: Informative, persuasive or generic

2. Draw a suitable graph to show the number of advertisements you found to be informative, persuasive and generic.

Advertising media

A business must choose carefully where it is to advertise its products and services.

In making that choice, businesses will consider the following:

- The cost of advertising. A small business may not have much money to spend.

- The target market for the product. A business selling teenage fashions will advertise where teenagers will see those adverts.
- Whether the advertisement is part of a campaign, or a single advert.

Types of advertising media used by a business

A business has a wide choice of different media to use. The following chart summarises the advantages and disadvantages of each.

Advertising medium	Advantages	Disadvantages
Television	1. Reaches a large audience throughout the country. 2. Use of colour and moving images is very useful when the product itself moves, eg a car. 3. Can be targeted at particular consumers, eg advertising gardening products during that type of programme.	1. The cost. Advertisements at peak times, for example during popular soaps or films, can cost many thousands of pounds for a 30-second showing.
Radio	1. Much cheaper than television. 2. Good targeting of customers through different radio stations. Classic FM has a very different audience to local commercial stations. 3. A radio can be taken anywhere, unlike a television.	1. The product cannot be seen, which is important if you are marketing a visual item. 2. Not such a wide audience as television.
Cinema	1. The audience will often watch cinema adverts more closely as they have paid for the experience. 2. Adverts can be targeted at the audience watching. 3. Advertisements not allowed on television may be shown.	1. Although the number of people visiting cinemas is increasing, the audience remains small compared to television.
Newspapers	1. Good targeting of customer by using different newspapers. 2. Colour can add to visual effect of advert. 3. Choice of local, regional and national papers. 4. Different types of advertisement, display and classified	1. Not all socio-economic groups read newspapers. 2. Cost. A full-page advertisement in a national paper such as *The Sun* can cost many thousands of pounds.
Magazines	1. Possibly the best medium for targeting particular customer groups. All consumer interests are catered for, along with trade magazines aimed at the business buyer. This makes the advertisement very cost-effective. 2. High-quality colour gloss images can make products look attractive.	1. A magazine may only come out once a month. A business may need more regular adverts. 2. Some magazines have few readers and are not suitable for products aimed at a mass market.
Billboards and posters	1. Highly visual. Large images, often at side of roads 2. Can be targeted at particular areas of the country.	1. No real control of the people seeing the advertisement. 2. Limited message can be given, as it has to be read as people pass by.
Internet	1. One of the fastest growing advertising media. 2. Can target particular groups according to the site a customer is on. 3. Can use moving images as well as written information. 4. Can be saved by the consumer 5. Allows possible direct link to the producer.	1. Not used by all potential groups of customers. 2. Customers may see the adverts as 'in the way' of what they really need from an Internet site. 3. Can be expensive to set up.
Transport (eg buses)	1. Can be targeted at a certain area. 2. Cheaper than magazines and popular newspapers.	1. Space available for the advert is limited. 2. Only a simple message can be given.

ACTIVITY 4

1. Which advertising method, and media, would you use for the following products? Give reasons for your choice. Try to be as precise as possible in your answer.
   (a) A new CD from a top teenage band.
   (b) A famous washing powder.
   (c) The latest high specification computer.
   (d) A new-style chocolate bar from a well-known maker.
   (e) A special offer of furniture.

2. Julie owns the Cutting Room unisex hairdressers. She has recently moved to larger

premises and is wondering the best way to advertise the business. She is considering the following:

- local radio
- cinemas
- television
- local newspapers
- do nothing and rely on existing customers telling others.

Advise Julie on where she should advertise the Cutting Room, or whether she should do nothing. Give reasons for your choice.

The control of advertising

Advertisements are controlled in this country by the **Advertising Standards Authority** which checks on advertisements to make sure they are:

- ***Legal.*** You cannot advertise anything that will break the law, for example alcoholic drinks for ten-year-olds.
- ***Decent.*** Adverts must not cause offence, even though they may be legal.
- ***Honest.*** An advert must give a clear idea of a product. An advert may well be dishonest and yet not tell any lies.
- ***Truthful.*** All claims made in an advertisement must be true.

If a consumer feels that an advert breaks any of these rules they can complain to the Advertising Standards Authority who will investigate.

Why control of advertising is necessary

Consumers need protection against false and dishonest claims that may be made by business. Certain groups of consumers, especially children, are easily influencef by advertisements (children's adverts have even more rules). They should not be persuaded to buy something they don't want because of false claims in an advertisement.

The Government sees certain products as being harmful, for example tobacco. For this reason tobacco advertising is banned on television.

Direct marketing

This is another fast-growing method of promotion. It involves customers being sent details of a product directly to them, usually through the post. As the consumer might ignore much of the material sent to them, direct marketing is often called 'junk mail'.

Direct marketing relies on vast databases of information collected on a consumer. This may be from different sources, but usually from the different forms consumers fill in at different times. There is often a box at the bottom of a form, which asks the person whether they mind the information being used by others. This information is then used to target certain consumers with products that would seem to suit them.

EXAM Practice Questions

Sunlovers Ltd make a range of sun block lotions. They are bringing out a new range of products aimed at the teenage market. The products will not be cheap, though Sunlovers Ltd feel that, with the correct style of promotion, teenagers will want to buy them.

1. State and explain two methods of sales promotion that would be suitable for the new products. (4 marks)

The marketing manager of Sunlovers Ltd is wondering whether the company should use magazines or television for the main advertising of the new products.

2. Explain which two of the following media would be most suitable for the new products. Give reasons for your answer. (8 marks)
   - television
   - radio
   - teenage magazines
   - local newspapers.
3. State two reasons why Sunlovers Ltd must be careful about what they say in an advertisement about their products. (2 marks)

ADVICE ON HOW TO ANSWER THE QUESTIONS

1. In this question you are asked to explain, and to **apply** that explanation to Sunlovers Ltd. There are many different sales promotion methods so you must explain clearly why your choice would suit a business such as Sunlovers Ltd. In an examination, you would lose marks if you did not make a clear connection between your ideas and Sunlovers Ltd.
2. This question is again asking you to explain, though the difference here is that you are given a clear choice to make. You need to look fully at the advantages and disadvantages for each medium, and then evaluate which is the best, giving full reasons for your choice. You need to explain **why** one method, in your judgement, is better than the another. The question carries 8 marks and so a detailed, carefully reasoned answer is required.
3. This question asks you to state, and tests knowledge of the law relating to advertisements. No explanation is required.

KEY TERMS

Sales promotion *is the method by which a business tries, over a short period of time, to boost sales, eg reducing prices.*

Public relations *are the methods by which a business brings the product to the attention of consumers by articles in newspapers or other events. This is aimed at improving the image of the business.*

Sponsorship *is a way of advertising a business by providing money for an event or a particular team. Has grown in importance in football and other major sports.*

Loss leaders *are goods offered for sale with little or no profit for the business. They are intended to attract consumers who will buy other goods along with the loss leaders.*

Point of sale promotions *are used where the product is sold, eg displays.*

Merchandising *is the promotion of products by selling goods in some way connected with another product or event, eg the sale of figures of characters who appear in a major film.*

After-sales service *is the help given to customers after they have bought a product, eg a guarantee to repair the product in the first year.*

Advertising media *are the methods by which a business can advertise a product. Includes newspapers, TV and radio.*

Informative advertisement *is an advert that gives information only.*

Persuasive advertisement *tries to influence the way consumers think of a product, and so persuade them to buy it.*

Generic advertisements *are used by an industry rather than a particular business.*

Advertising Standards Authority *(ASA). Checks that adverts are legal, decent, honest and truthful. Does not cover TV and radio advertising.*

Direct marketing *involves contacting the consumer through offers sent directly, usually through the post. Sometimes referred to as 'junk mail'.*

EXAMINATION SUMMARY TIPS

- Promotion is a vital part of the market mix.
- Methods of promotion are varied and must be chosen carefully to fit a given business in a given situation.
- There is a range of places and methods for a business to advertise its products and services.
- Businesses must be inventive in trying to think of different ways to promote their products.
- Advertising can be expensive and must lead to increased sales which pay for the advertising that has been used.
- The Internet is a fast-growing method of advertising, but is not suitable for **all** products.
- The ASA is important in keeping a check on the advertisements businesses use.
- Any recommendation made for promoting a business must take into account the size of the market and the budget available for a product.
- Remember that advertising is expensive. Many smaller businesses may choose not to advertise at all, and simply rely on their present customers.

Key Skills

Activity 3 provides an opportunity for Communication Level 1 (C1.3).

For this you must present the information you have collected in a clear form which suits the question you are answering. You must make sure that spelling, punctuation and grammar are accurate.

If the Activity is completed using a computer, and suitable layouts are chosen for the chart and the graph, then this can be used as evidence to support Information Technology Level 1 (IT1.2). Make sure you save the data so that it can be found easily.

Unit 5.8 E-commerce

What is e-commerce?

E-commerce is a method of marketing, which brings buyers and sellers together electronically.

It has grown in importance through the latter part of the 1990s, and is now being used by more and more businesses, both large and small. Older methods of marketing are now being changed in order to introduce the new technology offered by the Internet. As more and more of the population use the Internet, it is likely that e-commerce will become a more important part of the marketing strategy of a business. It does have its problems, with some of the early attempts at e-commerce failing.

ACTIVITY 1

1. Research into new .com businesses, gathering information to complete the following chart. Aim for at least 15 different businesses. Use IT if available.

Business name	Activity	Date started

2. Draw a suitable graph to show the results of your survey. Use the following categories for each section:
   (a) retail
   (b) travel
   (c) financial
   (d) other.

Use IT if available.

amazon.com®

lastminute.com

Many new e-commerce businesses are now being established.

The pressure to change to e-commerce

There are a number of reasons why a business might feel that it **must** use e-commerce as part of its marketing activities.

Competition. When a business's competitors are offering an e-commerce service, it must seriously consider e-commerce itself if it doesn't want to lose customers. In this way, many businesses feel forced to change to e-commerce, even if they would prefer not to.

- **Productivity.** With e-commerce, businesses are more productive, that is they can produce more with fewer workers. This saves wage costs in the business.
- **Increased profit.** Because of the increase in productivity, profits are likely to increase. This is also helped by the opportunity in selling products to a larger market.

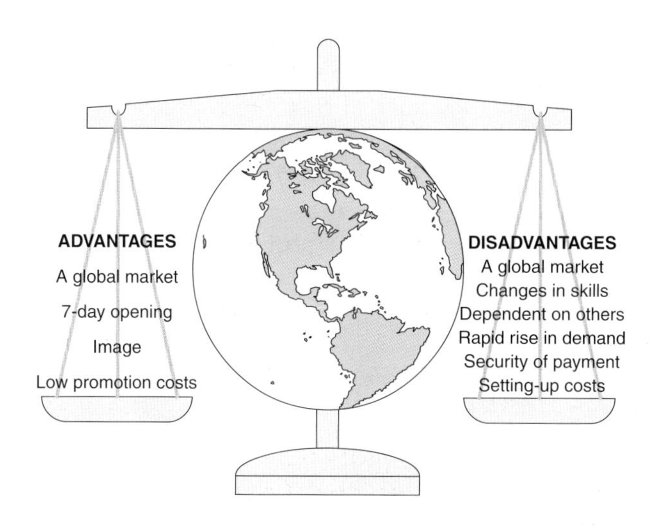

There are many advantages and disadvantages to a business when it uses e-commerce.

Advantages for a business when using e-commerce

- **A global market.** The potential market for a business using e-commerce is truly global. Even a small firm has the opportunity to sell to a world-wide market, even if it is only a sole trader operating from home. This brings a variety of linked advantages to a business:
  - (i) ***Economies of scale.*** Selling to a global market increases sales, which in turn will lead to increased production and the opportunity to take advantage of economies of scale.
  - (ii) ***New markets.*** Although a business might have reached saturation in its product life cycle (see page 174) in the home market, it can sell to different markets throughout the world where the product is new. This will help extend the product life cycle.
  - (iii) ***New products.*** When a business sells to different markets, it has the opportunity of developing different products, which will help provide a variety of sales income.
- **Seven-day opening.** E-commerce is open 24 hours a day, seven days a week, 365 days a year. This gives massive potential for sales. As many more customers shop from home at any time of the day or night, e-commerce is the ideal way of making sure a business takes advantage of changing ways in which consumers buy products.
- **Image.** Even the smallest business can present a professional and well established image through e-commerce. This means that customers will see a business that they are prepared to use, even though they may not have heard of it.
- **Low promotion costs.** When the global market that e-commerce can reach is taken into account, the promotion costs for a business are very low. This means that other methods of promoting may be dropped in favour of using e-commerce.

Disadvantages for a business when using e-commerce

- **A global market.** Although the global market can bring benefits to a business, it can also bring problems. Businesses are now in competition with firms throughout the world. Just as it is a benefit for British companies to sell to Australia through e-commerce, it is also easier for Australians (and the rest of the world!) to sell to Britain. The increased competition may force prices down with the possibility that profits may be reduced.
- **Changes in skills.** The skills needed to run an e-commerce business are different from those required for other businesses. This will mean:
  - (i) ***Training.*** Workers will need training on customer services by computer, distribution skills if in a warehouse etc. Training staff to use e-commerce will add costs to a business.
  - (ii) ***Recruitment.*** If there is to be an expansion of the business, new workers

might have to be found. In the short term, this will add more costs to the business when there is no guarantee that the new venture into e-commerce will work.

(iii) ***Website building and maintenance.*** E-commerce demands that the web site is maintained correctly. This may be beyond the skills of the workforce, resulting in specialist firms being employed, which adds further costs to the business.

- **Dependent on others.** A business using e-commerce is dependent on others for its success. The difficulty is that the e-commerce business has no day-to-day control of the businesses that it relies upon. For example, a business using e-commerce will depend on its Internet Service Provider (ISP) for the display of the business. If there is a product to be delivered, many e-commerce businesses will rely on other firms to deliver on time. Any delay may mean lost orders in the future. Compare this to the 'normal' operation of a shop selling direct to a customer.
- **Rapid rise in demand.** If a business is **too** successful in starting its e-commerce operations, it may be faced with so many orders that it has problems keeping to delivery promises it made. It is difficult to predict accurately the exact response e-commerce activity will bring. The reverse might also happen a business not achieving the expected sales increase, which will then mean possible staff redundancies and poor publicity for the business.
- **Security of payment.** Many potential e-commerce customers are worried at the security risk of using e-commerce. These worries are centred upon giving credit card details to buy goods on the Internet. To give customers confidence in buying goods online, secure web pages are used, often shown using a padlock-type symbol. To process credit card payments a business may need to pay another specialist business if it doesn't have its own arrangements with its bank. All these additional features of e-commerce add costs to a business.
- **Setting-up costs.** Although the promotion costs are small when compared to the potential number of customers, designing and setting up a website can be expensive. At best it is an **additional** cost that a business did not have, though this may be helped by reducing expenditure on other promotions.

There are many advantages for customers using e-commerce.

ACTIVITY 2

There are many different businesses that are developing e-commerce as a method of marketing their products. The following two examples show how businesses are developing e-commerce in different ways.

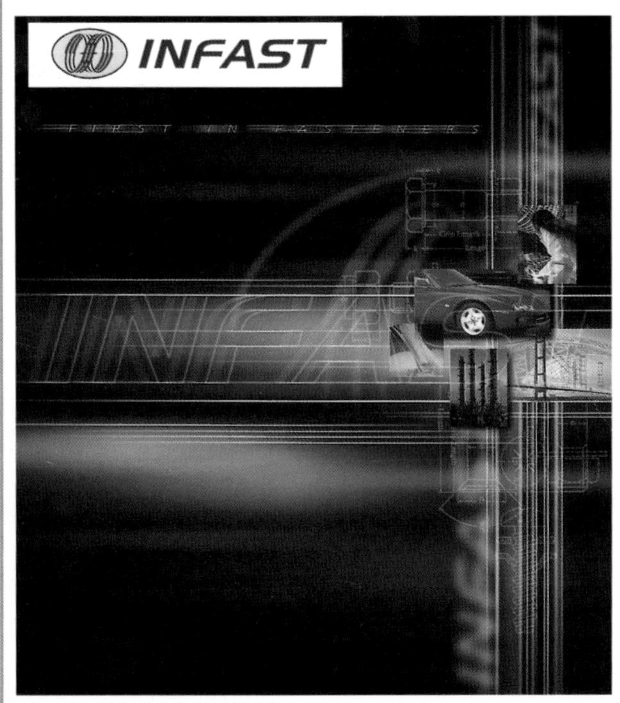

Courtesy: Infast Chesterfield

Infast Ltd is Europe's largest manufacturer and supplier of fasteners, with operations throughout the country. It supplies fasteners to such businesses as Ford, Jaguar, JCB and Honda. When dealing with larger customers such as Jaguar, there is no 'ordering' in the normal way from Jaguar. Infast itself keeps the Jaguar factory supplied with the fasteners it has agreed to buy. All Infast needs to know is how many cars are going to be made. E-commerce plays little part in this situation, though other ways of connecting businesses using e-commerce may be developed.

Infast is aware that other customers may wish to order fasteners using e-commerce. The business needs to make decisions for e-commerce in the following:
- web page design, cost and maintenance
- staff required for dealing with orders and other customer services, including technical support
- warehouse location for the distribution of orders.

As customers move to e-commerce, Infast feels it must do the same in order to maintain its high levels of customer service.

Clifton Court Hotel.

There is also the constant threat of competition and the need to stay one step ahead.
1. Explain why some parts of Infast's business are not suited to traditional e-commerce.
2. Why does Infast feel it must move more towards e-commerce?
3. Infast is a very large company. Why should it be concerned with the cost of developing e-commerce?

The **Clifton Court Hotel** in Blackpool is owned by Graham and Sue Kamp. Hotels such as the Clifton Court have previously relied on newspapers, magazines and past customers for their advertising, though when Graham and Sue took over the hotel six months ago, they thought they should use the Internet. This would enable them to:
- show photographs of the hotel facilities and prices
- advertise all over the world
- communicate much better with their customers.

The move to e-commerce has been a success, with 60% of bookings coming as a result of the web page. The owners feel that this figure will grow considerably in the future.

They now face a difficult decision. The charge they have to pay for the search engine where their hotel is registered has risen considerably, to £1 000. Graham and Sue are wondering whether they should pay the increase and stay with Internet marketing.
1. Why is a hotel a suitable business to use e-commerce, especially by advertising on the Internet?
2. Why do you think the owners of the hotel introduced e-commerce as a method of marketing?
3. Discuss whether the owners should stay with their web page advertising and pay the new amount of £1 000.

Advantages to customers of using e-commerce

For any product or service, customers can be other businesses as well as general consumers. The following advantages (and disadvantages) should be seen from the point of view of a business buying on e-commerce and a private consumer.

- **Price comparison.** When buying on e-commerce, prices can be compared easily, enabling the buyer to get the best possible deal and save money.
- **Seven-day availability.** Just as it is an advantage for a business to open on e-commerce seven days a week, the customer can also buy at whatever time they wish.
- **Wide range of products.** Because the Internet can provide world-wide access to goods, the customer has a much wider choice of products. The correct product, at the correct price, can be chosen more easily.

There are many possible problems for a customer when using e-commerce

Disadvantages to customers of using e-commerce

- **Lack of personal contact.** With e-commerce there is often no person to talk to directly. This may put some potential customers off using e-commerce as a means of buying goods. On the other hand, it may encourage others who prefer **not** to deal with people!
- **Problems returning goods.** If goods purchased on the Internet from a business in the UK are faulty, then consumers have the same rights as if the goods were bought from any other business. The protection is in the Sale of Goods Act 1994, which states that goods must be of 'satisfactory' quality and match the description given. Despite this protection, some customers might feel that it is easier buying from, say, a shop and being able to sort problems out much more easily.
- **Only image of goods seen.** When you buy something from a shop, you can see and touch the product, inspecting the quality. With e-commerce, only the image is available, which may not be suitable for some customers. If the customer knows the product well, such as a CD, there is less of a problem buying with just an image given on screen.
- **Security.** Security must be seen as a problem for the customer, as well as the business using e-commerce to sell goods and services. Credit card protection using encryption may be available, but this may still not be enough for some consumers.
- **Methods of payment.** Customers wishing to pay by cash will not be able to use e-commerce. Much of the payment is geared towards credit cards, which are not used by all consumers.
- **Technology.** To buy on e-commerce, a customer needs access to the Internet. Though the number of people having Internet access is increasing all the time, large groups, particularly the elderly, do not have the necessary access. A business wanting to sell using e-commerce must think carefully whether the target markets for the product are likely to be able to buy on the Internet.

The impact of e-commerce on business activity

The introduction of e-commerce is having a wide-ranging effect on business activity. It is also a fast-changing situation: you need to make sure that you have up-to-date information on new developments. What **must** be remembered is that some products and services are much more suitable than others to being sold by e-commerce. Industries that have adapted well to e-commerce so far include retail, travel and finance.

Already there have been changes in business activity in the following due to e-commerce:

- location
- new skill development
- levels of employment
- distribution
- customer services.
    - **Location.** The locations of some parts of business activity have become more footloose than before, thanks to e-commerce. A business will only need a telephone connection to take orders, which can be almost anywhere. This is often called the 'front end' of the business. A warehouse, storing goods to be sent to the customer when ordered, need not be in the same place as the office taking the order. In this case, a location near the motorway network may be more suitable. In this way, locating different functions of the business needs different considerations.
    - **New skill development.** A business launching e-commerce will need the workforce to have different skills. This may be connected to the maintenance of the website, replying by e-mail to customers or packing goods in a warehouse for delivery. All these jobs may not have been required before e-commerce. Extra training may well be required for all levels of staff. Workers may be recruited with the skills a business does not have itself. Some staff may feel threatened by the introduction of the new technology connected to e-commerce, especially if they are rather older and do not have ICT skills. Such staff need special care as they may well be vital to other parts of the business.
    - **Levels of employment.** The introduction of e-commerce may well increase and decrease the levels of employment. An existing business switching some of its operations to e-commerce may well find that it needs fewer staff due to the technology being used. The Abbey National Bank announced in October 2000 that it was to lose 1 500 jobs (20% of its total workforce) over the next three years because of e-commerce. Other businesses may use redundancy for staff without the necessary skills to change to e-commerce. However a new business starting with e-commerce will recruit new workers.
    - **Distribution.** This is changing with the introduction of e-commerce.

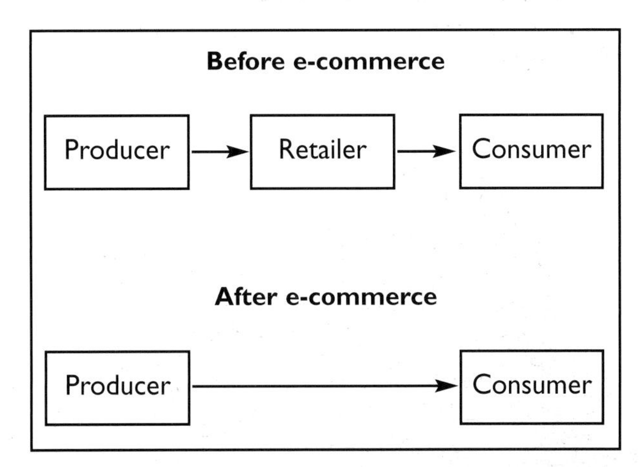

In this typical example the retailer does not have a role to play, since the goods or services are sent direct to the consumer from the producer. This may be through a warehouse, for goods such as books and CDs. It is often direct to the consumer when booking a holiday or opening an Internet bank account. The continuing importance of the older distribution system for such goods and services is in some doubt if e-commerce continues to grow.

Will shops close because of e-commerce?

- **Customer services.** Because of e-commerce, how a business looks after its customers is changing rapidly. Unlike traditional methods, there is no person-to-person contact if there is a problem. Staff in an e-commerce business need to deal with customers by email or possibly the phone. This may need additional training and new thinking on how to cope with difficult situations at a distance without ever meeting the customer. Speed of service is vital in this situation: a customer will not return if there is a long wait for goods to arrive, or if there are other unsolved problems.

ACTIVITY 3

1. Look in local and national newspapers for information on existing businesses that are changing because of e-commerce. Cut out the articles and arrange them on A4 or display paper.
2. Summarise the ways in which the businesses are changing to e-commerce, in particular the effect on staff, customers and location.

EXAM Practice Questions

1. PPM Ltd sells specialist travel books from a small shop in Barndon. It has used a mail order system for some years, though it feels that it could increase sales considerably if it used e-commerce.
   (a) Explain why e-commerce might benefit a business such as PPM Ltd when selling its books. (6 marks)
   (b) Explain how PPM Ltd might have to change its working practices if it used e-commerce. (6 marks)
2. Keith, one of the older workers at PPM Ltd, is worried about the possible introduction of e-commerce as he has few ICT skills.
   (a) Advise PPM Ltd on how it should deal with Keith in this situation. (4 marks)
   (b) Evaluate the advantages and disadvantages of a global e-commerce market for a business such as PPM Ltd. (8 marks)

ADVICE ON HOW TO ANSWER THE QUESTION

1. (a) The command word is 'explain'. You must make sure that your answer is not just a list of benefits. Notice that the question refers only to the **selling** of books. There will be advantages for PPM Ltd when it buys the books itself, but this is **not** required in your answer. Look for additional clues to help your answer. You are told that it is a **small** shop. This should be taken into account in your answer.
   (b) Once again the command word is 'explain', so make sure you don't just give a list! There are 6 marks available, so look for at least three separate, explained ideas to make sure you get full marks.
2. (a) Here you are asked to advise the business. There is no right or wrong answer for this type of question. What

you must do is look carefully at the situation you are given in the question and decide the best course of action. You may well give a variety of ideas, which the business can then consider. Avoid giving a list, and explain the ideas you put forward.

(b) In this question you are being asked to evaluate. This means you should make a judgement on whether the global market **for PPM Ltd** is a good idea or not. This type of question for 8 marks will be marked using a level of response mark scheme, where you are expected to put a balanced view of both sides of the argument and come to a reasoned conclusion. Remember that you need to write about PPM Ltd, not just any business.

E-commerce *The bringing together of buyers and sellers electronically.*

Productivity *The measure of levels of production in relation to the number of workers.*

Global market *A world-wide market provided by the Internet.*

EXAMINATION SUMMARY TIPS

- Remember that some businesses are not as suited to e-commerce as others.
- There are advantages for both businesses and customers when using e-commerce.
- E-commerce is changing how many businesses operate. Look carefully at how the work on e-commerce links with your other work on location, recruitment and training.
- You need to understand how e-commerce is used alongside other methods of marketing products and services.
- Because e-commerce is changing so rapidly, you must keep up to date with new developments.

Key Skills

Activity 1 provides an opportunity for Information Technology Level 1 (IT1.1 and IT1.2).

For IT1.1 you must find and select the correct information to go in your chart (this could include Internet use). This information needs to be brought accurately into the chart format. A suitable graph format should be chosen to evidence IT1.2, so that it meets the requirements of the question. All information must be saved so that it can be found easily.

Unit 5.9 Consumer protection and marketing

Why is consumer protection important in marketing?

When a consumer buys a product or service, they have a right to expect that the product is made correctly, that it has been advertised correctly, and that it will do the job it was bought for.

If there was no protection for the consumer, there may be less pressure on a business to make sure the product was made accurately, and that any advertising was within the law.

When marketing a product, therefore, a business must be fully aware of the laws and organisations which protect the consumer, in order that it can make any necessary adjustments in its marketing strategies.

How a business may be affected by consumer complaints

- Its advertising may be reported to the Advertising Standards Authority (see page 187) which might result in bad publicity for the business, and a loss of customers.
- If a lot of products are returned for being faulty, the business will have to pay for replacements and will also develop a poor reputation for quality.
- Consumers may raise ethical considerations if they feel that the business is involved in unfair and dishonest practices in its marketing.
- The overall image of a business will fall if consumers use laws and other organisations against it. Businesses in the 21st century are very keen to develop a good image amongst consumers, and so need to operate within the law and be seen to be operating fairly.

How the consumer is protected

The law

There are a number of Acts of Parliament that have been passed to help protect the consumer. It is felt that the consumer needs the law to help in any action against a large business organisation, which will be able to call on the help of specialist lawyers should there be any dispute. The laws below all affect how a business markets its products and services. Businesses cannot afford to be acting illegally.

The **Sale and Supply of Goods Act 1994** states that goods bought from a business must be 'of satisfactory quality'. This means that they must be made correctly and therefore fit to be sold. Consumers can ask for their money back if the goods are not. Goods must also match their description. For example, if a table is advertised as 'solid wood' it **must** be made of solid wood. Goods must be fit for the purpose for which they were bought. For example a pair of wellingtons must be waterproof!

The **Weights and Measures Acts 1963 and 1979** make businesses who sell products by weight state the weight on the packaging correctly. It is an offence if any underweight products are sold. Some products, such as alcohol, have to be sold in certain quantities.

The **Consumer Protection Acts 1978 and 1987** control, amongst other items, the advertising of prices for goods. A shop which advertises a reduction in price must have had those goods on sale at the previously higher price for a period of 28 days. The Acts also cover the labelling of certain dangerous items such as chemicals. If a consumer is harmed by any faulty goods they can claim damages from the business.

The **Unsolicited Goods and Services Act 1971** states that if goods are sent to you without being ordered, you can keep them without paying if they have not been collected within six months. If you tell the business to collect them, you can keep them after 30 days without paying.

A business must have sold the goods at the higher price for 28 days.

The **Food and Drugs Acts 1955 and 1984** make sure that the food we eat is fit for humans. They also control the labelling of food content. For example, a business selling fish pie must make sure it has the correct amount of fish. If there is less than the required amount of fish, the pie can still be sold, but it cannot be called fish pie.

The **Consumer Credit Act 1974** and the **Financial Services Act 1986** make businesses lending money state the Annual Percentage Rate (APR) for the cost of the loan. This enables the consumer to make a clear comparison between different businesses. Consumers must be given a copy of any credit agreement.

The **European Union** passes 'Directives' which give the consumer further protection. These cover issues such as doorstep selling, where a consumer is allowed a 'cooling off' period of seven days if they want to change their mind after being persuaded to buy something.

There are also Directives on food products, covering the use of additives and colouring.

ACTIVITY 1

For **each** of the situations below, explain what action the consumer could take. You should give the correct law, and explain why you think the consumer could take action.

1. John buys a pair of trainers labelled '100% leather'. When he tries them on at home he discovers they are plastic.
2. Tracey wakes up one morning to find a parcel has been delivered containing some cosmetics which she has not ordered. An invoice for £25 is enclosed.
3. Helen bought a new pair of jeans for £35, but when she tried them on before going out she noticed some stitching was coming away.
4. Adam bought a kilo of sausages from his local butcher. He thought there were not enough in the packet for a kilo. He checked them at home and they weighed only 800 grams.
5. Mary and her husband Ken were sold new double-gazed windows by a salesman who called at their house. They signed a form ordering the windows. After thinking it over the next day, they wanted to change their minds.

Organisations concerned with consumer protection

Trade organisations

These organisations are set up by the industry of which businesses form part. An example is the Association of British Travel Agents (ABTA) whose members are the travel agents that consumers will use to book their holidays. By seeing that a travel agent is a member of ABTA, a consumer will have extra safeguards (such as compensation) if anything goes wrong with their booking. By being a member of ABTA, a travel agent can market its products more successfully as a consumer will feel safer in making a booking with such a company. Similar organisations help the motor, house-building and other industries.

Independent organisations

The **Consumers Association** publishes *Which?* magazine, which gives the consumer independent advice on different products. This can help consumers make a better choice when buying goods. A poor report from *Which?* may affect how a business markets its products.

The **Citizens Advice Bureau** offers consumers independent advice on consumer matters and basic consumer law. The advice is free, and the bureaux are often found in local libraries.

The **British Standards Institute (BSI)** will test products to make sure they are safe and well made. Products that have the Kitemark symbol can be marketed more easily as they have passed an independent test, and will therefore be more attractive to the consumer.

The BSI Kitemark gives consumers the assurance of a product being safe and well made

Government-funded organisations protecting the consumer

'Watchdog' organisations such as OFTEL and OFWAT have been set up to protect the consumer against unfair practices (including the control of prices) by privatised industries. OFTEL watches the telephone industry and OFWAT watches the water industry. This has a clear effect on marketing as such businesses have an independent organisation watching over their activities. This means, for example, that they do not have the freedom to charge whatever prices they want. There are similar 'watchdogs' covering the electricity and railway industries.

The **Office of Fair Trading** makes sure the integration of differing businesses is not against the interests of the consumer. For example, by integrating, two businesses may control the market for a product, and so feel they could increase prices. If the Office of Fair Trading felt that this was against the interests of consumers, they could take action to prevent the integration.

ACTIVITY 2

1. How can the following organisations help the consumer?:
   (a) OFTEL
   (b) Citizens Advice Bureau
   (c) trade organisations such as the Association of British Travel Agents (ABTA).
2. Write an article suitable for *Which?* magazine, comparing three similar products. You can choose any products, for example three makes of trainers, three makes of toothpaste etc. Write a report that covers the following:
   (a) description of the products
   (b) how well they are made
   (c) how well they work
   (d) whether they are good value for money
   (e) your recommended best buy for the consumer, with reasons.

EXAM Practice Questions

1. Bird Enterprises Ltd is a business which makes light fittings for household use. It has developed a new range of table lamps made from steel and plastic. The marketing manager, Catherine, is concerned about how the new lamps should be described in any advertising campaign.
   Explain why the marketing manager should be careful about how the new lamps are described in any advertising campaign. (4 marks)
2. One of the lamps sold by Bird Enterprises Ltd caused injury to a customer when some wiring came loose. Explain what action the customer could take against Bird Enterprises Ltd. (3 marks)
3. Advise Bird Enterprises Ltd on why it must keep itself informed of changing consumer protection laws. (4 marks)

ADVICE ON HOW TO ANSWER THE QUESTIONS

1. Here you need to explain the importance of describing products correctly in advertising. You should give details of the correct law and explain the consequences for Bird Enterprises Ltd if it did not describe the lamps correctly.
2. This question tests your knowledge and application of consumer law. You need to give the name of the law that covers this situation and explain how the customer might benefit.
3. Here you have to 'advise' Bird Enterprises Ltd on why it should do something. You must explain the advantages to Bird Enterprises Ltd of keeping up to date with changing consumer laws, and also include the problems that would be created if it **didn't** keep up to date with changes.

KEY TERMS

Consumer protection *is the general term used to cover the laws and organisations that help consumers.*

The **Advertising Standards Authority** *ensures that advertising is legal, decent, honest and truthful but does not cover radio and TV advertising.*

Trade organisations *are set up by an industry to promote the industry by monitoring standards of care and service, eg the Association of British Travel Agents represents the travel industry.*

Government-funded organisations *which help protect the consumer include OFTEL and OFGAS. These 'watchdogs' regulate the industry and set standards for service and price levels.*

Independent organisations *which are involved in consumer protection include the Consumers Association (publishers of Which? magazine) and the BSI.*

The **Office of Fair Trading** *was set up in 1973 and gives general consumer advice as well as monitoring the development of new monopolies to ensure they do not act against the interests of the consumer.*

EXAMINATION SUMMARY TIPS

- Understand why consumers need protecting against some business marketing activity.
- There are a number of different laws that help the consumer. You should be aware of the main points of these Acts.
- A number of organisations help the consumer. You must be aware of the different roles they have.
- Remember that trade organisations help the businesses within an industry promote themselves as well as giving the consumer some safeguards.
- Understand why a business must be aware of the laws and organisations that help protect the consumer, and the possible consequences of ignoring the law.
- The Government helps support consumers through organisations such as the Office of Fair Trading and 'watchdog' organisations such as OFTEL.

Key Skills

Activity 2 provides an opportunity for Communication Level 1 (C1.3). You must present the information in a suitable report form that fits the purpose of the question. Make sure that your spelling, punctuation and grammar are accurate.

Learning Objectives:
To develop knowledge and understanding of:

- the needs of people as workers
- the needs of employers
- the stages in recruitment and selection
- the management and motivation of workers
- the types and benefits of training
- communications in business
- trade unions and the laws concerning workers.

You will be able to use this knowledge to analyse and evaluate business situations.

Introductory activity

The importance of people in business

John Toner runs Quality Windows and Conservatories. He employs 12 people in the firm. There are two sales representatives, one specialising in sales to commercial properties, the other dealing with domestic customers. Four people work in the factory manufacturing the UPVC window frames. There are three fitters and one bricklayer. There are also two full-time administrative assistants who act as receptionists, bookkeepers and clerical assistants. His opinion is:

'People are my most important asset. Along with myself, the sales representatives find new customers and give quotations. Accuracy is critical for the factory workers. Mistakes cost money in wasted time and materials. The fitters not only install the windows but they are the public image of the business as well. They must build good relations with the customers. Without this we would not get repeat business or word-of-mouth recommendations. The office workers are essential for keeping good records and for the general administrative work. Together we are a team, dependent on each other for the success of our jobs and the business.'

This view about the importance of people in business is common in all kinds of organisations. For many firms, appointing the right staff and getting them to work well is crucial to the success of the business. For this reason, firms often spend a lot of time, effort and expense to get the people-side of the business right.

Businesses need workers with many different skills.

ACTIVITY 1

- Explain why the workers in Quality Windows and Conservatories depend on each other.
- List the skills and personal qualities that the different kinds of workers employed by John Toner are likely to need in order to do their jobs well.

Getting the people-side of organisations right is not easy. The diagram below shows some of the things that organisations consider to ensure that the people who work for them are effective workers.

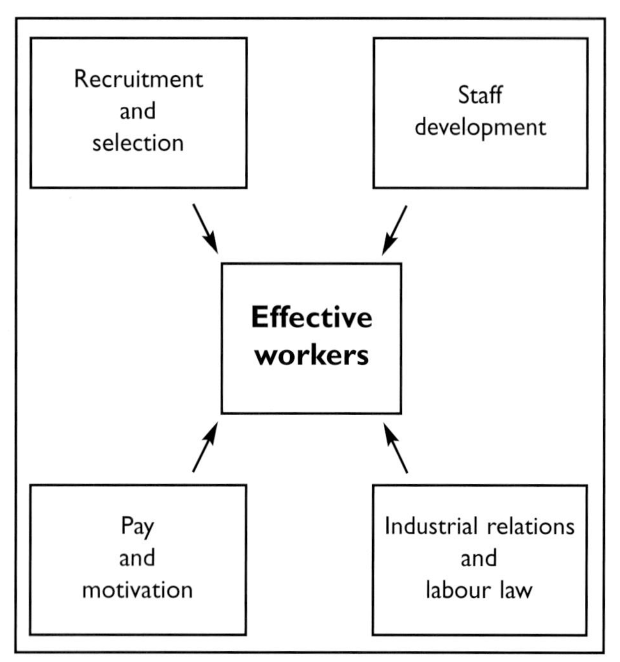

Effective workers

Recruitment and selection are about appointing the right kind of people to do the work. It is important to attract enough applicants so that the organisation has some choice. Information about the applications will help the organisation to decide which of the applicants will be most suitable. It can be very difficult to dismiss unwanted workers.

Motivation is about making workers work well, to produce good-quality products and services efficiently. Pay is one method of motivating workers but people do not work only for money. Organisations need to understand why people work so that they know what will motivate them to work well.

Staff development is about improving the skills that the workers have. Training is one method by which this can be achieved. Another method is appraisal. This involves reviewing the performance of the worker, identifying their strengths and weaknesses and producing an action plan to help them to improve.

Trade unions represent the interests of workers. They will try to improve the pay and conditions of the workers. They will also ensure that employers do not break the laws that are designed to protect workers and the rights of the individual. Poor industrial relations between managers and workers can have a very bad effect on the productivity of workers.

ACTIVITY 2

Write about an employee in a local business. Write this as an article to be included in the local newspaper. You may wish to include a picture of the employee or the premises of the organisation.

You will need to interview someone to get the information you need. The person you interview could be a relative, friend, neighbour or someone you work with during your work experience. It is important to prepare thoroughly for the interview – write down the questions that you will ask and decide how you will record the answers. You could write about: the organisation, the job the person does, the skills and qualifications they need for the job, what training they have had, who they are responsible to, who they are responsible for, how the person was recruited and selected, how they are paid, whether or not they are in a trade union, what they like and dislike about the job. The organisation may have a website that contains useful background information about what it does.

Key Skills

Activity 2 provides an opportunity for Communication work at Level 2 – writing a document (newspaper report) for a particular audience (readers of the local newspaper) (C2.3). The Activity also provides the opportunity to practise your IT skills or to develop evidence for your Key Skills Portfolio. Use the Internet to search for and find out information about the firm (IT2.2). Use a word-processing or desktop publishing package to develop the article (IT2.2), scanning a picture or inserting a digital photograph to combine information (IT2.3).

Unit 6.1 Recruitment and selection

There are several reasons why organisations may need to recruit workers:

- to replace workers who have left, perhaps because they have retired, gained promotion or been dismissed
- to add more workers to the workforce so that production can be increased
- to add workers with skills that the present employees do not have, perhaps, for example, computer skills.

Many organisations plan the recruitment and selection of workers very carefully. In larger organisations this is usually one of the jobs of the personnel or human resources department. There are three main stages to the process of recruiting and selecting workers. These are shown in the diagram below:

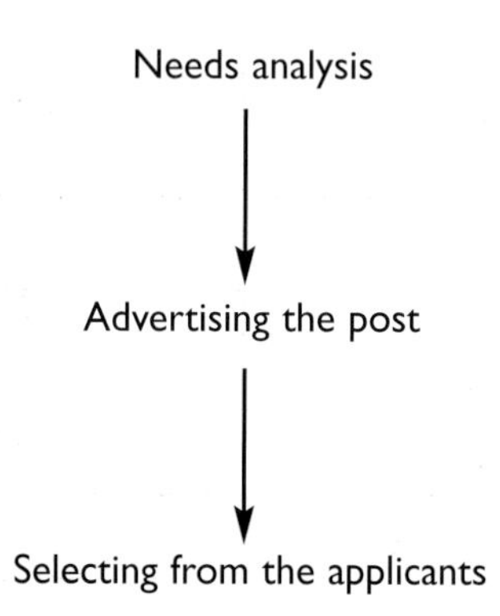

Needs analysis

There are several decisions that an organisation may need to make that are part of its needs analysis. These include:

- how many workers it will need to employ, how many will need to be full-time employees, how many part-time
- what kind of staff will be needed – what qualities and skills the workers will need
- when the workers will be needed – the times in the week when they must work, when their employment should start.

Once these decisions have been made, organisations often draw up **job descriptions** and **person specifications** for particular jobs. A job description details the duties and responsibilities that the worker must perform. A person specification states the knowledge, qualifications and experience and the personal qualities and skills that the worker will need to be able to do the job. These documents are useful. By putting the information down on paper, the organisation will have to have thought carefully about exactly what kind of employee it is looking for. The information will be used to plan and carry out the next stages of the process of recruiting and selecting workers. A job description and a person specification for an administrative officer are shown below and on page 207. This person specification shows how these documents can be used to help to plan the methods of assessment to use in the selection part of the process of appointing new workers.

Marston Education Department
Job Description

Post: Administrative Officer, Key Skills Project

Grade: Scale 4

Responsible to: Key Skills Project Co-ordinator

Job purpose: To manage the acounts of the project and to provide administrative support.

Main duties

1. To ensure that accounts are up to date and readily available.
2. To assist the Project Co-ordinator in the preparation and presentation of reports.
3. To provide flexible administrative support.
4. To establish good working relationships with Partners in the Project.
5. To carry out any other duties that it would be reasonable to ask of the assistant.

Sample job description

Marston Education Department Administrative Officer, Key Skills Project – Person Specification		
Personal attributes required	*Essential/Desirable*	*Method of assessment*
QUALIFICATIONS		
Educated to at least Level 3 of the National Framework of Qualifications (A level, or equivalent).	E	AF
EXPERIENCE		
Financial management experience of large budgets.	D	AF/I
Minute-taking.	D	AF/I
General administrative support for projects.	D	AF/I
KNOWLEDGE/SKILLS/ABILITIES		
Good interpersonal and communication skills, both spoken and written.	E	AF/R/I
Ability to work as part of a team.	E	R/I
Financial management and budgetary management skills.	E	AF/R/T
Computer literacy – setting up and using spreadsheets and databases and word processing.	E	AF/R/T
Knowledge of local authority financial procedures and regulations.	E	AF/R
SPECIAL REQUIREMENTS		
Current driving licence.	E	AF
Able to work unsociable hours.	D	I
Flexible and adaptable	E	R/I
Assessment methods: AF (Application form), R (Reference), I (Interview), T (Test).		

Sample person specification

ACTIVITY 1

Draw up a job description and a person specification for the following:

(i) A teacher of Business Studies.

or

(ii) A job that you have done – the work experience or part-time employment that you have done.

or

(iii) A job that a relative or friend does.

Advertising the post

Designing an advertisement for a job

Look at the advertisement below. What information is missing from this?

Ingham's Catering Ltd
Clerical Assistant Required
Start: As soon as possible
Contact: John Meeks

Job advertisement

This is not a very good advertisement. It does not give potential applicants for the job enough information. If people apply who do not have the necessary qualifications, skills and experience it will waste their time. It will also waste the time of workers at Ingham's who will have to read the applications and write back to these applicants to tell them that they have not got the job. It is important that a job advertisement contains information that will encourage people with appropriate skills and experience to apply. It must tell potential applicants how to apply. The design of the advertisement will also be important so that it will catch the attention of the reader.

Some of the information that might be included in a job advertisement is:

- duties
- qualifications needed
- experience needed
- salary details
- description of work
- hours
- place of work
- training opportunities
- future prospects.
- contact address
- details of how to apply for the job.

ACTIVITY 2 

Embassy Caravans makes folding trailer tents. It needs to recruit a production worker to work in the factory making the tents. All production workers need to be able to do some joinery, welding and sewing of materials. The basic pay will be between £12 000 and £16 000 per year, depending on experience. Overtime is available when the factory is busy. The business was set up in 1953. The address is Unit 10 Industrial Estate, Ormskirk L31 5XY. The telephone number is 01695 578899. Applicants will be expected to telephone for a discussion about the job and for an application form.

1. Draw up an advertisement for this post. You should use some or all of the information provided. The advertisement will go in the local newspaper which charges according to the number of words – so keep the number of words to the minimum necessary.
2. Why might the firm ask people to telephone for a discussion about the job before sending out an application form?

If possible, use a computer to create the advertisement.

Factors influencing the choice of media for the advertisement

The decision about where to advertise a post may be influenced by a number of factors:

- the type of worker required
- the number of workers needed
- the location of the work
- the size of the firm
- the amount of money the organisation has to spend on advertising for workers.

Internal or external recruitment

The first decision that may need to be made is whether to recruit internally or externally. Internal recruitment is when a job is filled by someone who already works in the organisation. Examples of ways that an organisation may use to advertise a job internally are on a notice-board, in a company (in-house) magazine for the workers or by e-mailing the details to all workers who might be interested in or able to do the job. The advantages of internal recruitment are:

- it is often cheaper to advertise internally rather than externally
- it may be quicker to recruit someone who is already employed within the organisation
- the person appointed will already know about the organisation, its aims and objectives and its ways of doing things
- the organisation can be confident, because the person appointed will be well known, that the person appointed will be suitable
- it can be good for the morale of the workforce to give opportunities for promotion.

However, internal recruitment may not always be appropriate. External recruitment is when the organisation fills a post with someone from outside the organisation. It will be appropriate when:

- there is no one in the organisation who would be able to do the job
- someone with new ideas is required
- it would cause unpleasantness between workers if the one of them was promoted.

Table 6.1 over the pages shows different media that may be used to advertise the post externally and illustrates when these may be employed.

ACTIVITY 3

For the cases below, state whether you would recommend the use of internal or external recruitment. Give reasons for your choice. What problems, if any, might the firm have to deal with as a result of your recommendation.

- The local council needs to appoint someone to cover for the office manager while she is on maternity leave. The office manager is expected to be on leave for six months.
- Computec Ltd assembles computers. Its production of computers has increased by 20% in the last year and is expected to rise by a further 15% in the coming year. It needs to employ one more technician to add to the eight technicians that it already employs to assemble computers.

Media used in external recruitment

Recruitment agencies

Mercuri Urval is a specialist recruitment agency. The use of recruitment agencies has increased significantly in the UK in recent years. These agencies will do a lot of the work involved in recruiting and selecting staff. For example, if a firm wants to appoint a new sales manager it may discuss its needs with a recruitment agency. The agency will draw up a job description and a person specification. It will then advertise the post and receive applications from interested people. From these applications, it may recommend a small number of people it thinks are most suitable for the job. The firm may then interview the people recommended before finally deciding which one to appoint. Using a recruitment agency saves time and money. The recruitment agency is a specialist organisation and will know best about how and where to advertise the post as well as what kind of information will be needed about the applicants to decide which to employ.

Selecting from the applicants

An organisation must decide whom it wants to employ from the people that apply for a job. To make this decision it needs information about the applicants. Table 6.2 on page 211 shows some of the ways in which organisations can get this information.

Media	Description	Job examples
Local newspaper	These usually contain a jobs section that local people would know to look in. It is not usually expensive to advertise in these.	Local newspapers are useful when an organisation knows that there will be people in the local community who will be able and available to do the work. Posts for hairdressers and clerical assistants are often advertised in this way.
National newspaper	These may have sections or even special supplements for advertising jobs. It is usually more expensive to advertise in national rather than local newspapers.	National newspapers are often used when recruiting skilled workers for whom there may be a shortage in the local community or for recruiting senior personnel. They will attract people from all over the country.
Specialist magazines, for example, *The Times Educational Supplement*, *The Lancet* (for doctors).	These will include specialist articles that interest particular types of workers.	Specialist magazines are often used for recruiting highly skilled specialists such as personnel officers, engineers and scientists.
Job Centres	These are centres run by the Government. They display advertisements as well as mentioning posts to unemployed people that they know would be suitable. It is free to advertise through these.	These are often used for semi-skilled and unskilled workers such as building-site labourers, supermarket shelf-stackers and cleaners.
The Internet	There are different kinds of websites that organisations can use, including sites that advertise a range of jobs or the organisation's own site. It is fairly cheap to use these sites.	Useful for attracting people with computer skills.
Word of mouth	This is when people in an organisation with a vacancy mention it to other people that they know.	Word of mouth is very commonly used. A friend may mention a vacancy; a consultant or adviser may alert someone they have worked with to an opportunity.

Table 6.1 Media used to advertise jobs.

Method	Description	Advantages
Letter of application	Letter written by applicant explaining why they believe that they are suitable for the post.	Shows a person's communication skills.
Application form	Applicants provide information in answer to questions on a form.	The firm can make sure that all applicants supply the same information so that it is easy to make comparisons.
CV (*Curriculum vitae*)	The applicant writes down personal details such as their address, qualifications, employment history and names of referees.	Shows the ability of the applicant to organise information. Easy to see essential details at a glance.
References	Someone who knows the applicant well describes the personal qualities of the applicant, what work they did and how well they did it, their attendance and punctuality record and any other information that may be relevant to the post.	References can be very honest assessments that can recommend whether someone should be appointed or not. Sometimes, though, firms give employees good references because they want them to leave.
Interviews	The applicant meets people from the firm for a discussion. Often the people making the appointment ask all the candidates for the job the same series of questions and then compare the answers that they give. Sometimes the candidates may be interviewed as a group.	The employee sees the candidates and can judge how well they present themselves and communicate and how well they are likely to get on with other workers. Group interviews are very useful for seeing how people might work in a team.
Psychometric tests	The applicant answers a series of questions, usually multiple choice, about themselves, what they like and dislike.	The test produces a profile or description of the personality of the applicant. Matched against the person specification, this can be very useful information.
Presentations	The applicant is asked to give a talk to the employer on a given subject.	This will show up the personal qualities of the applicant. It may also be an opportunity for the applicant to put forward their ideas about the job.
Tests	The applicant may be given a pencil and paper test or a practical test.	These tests give very specific information such as how good the applicant is at mathematics, typing or using equipment.

Table 6.2 Source of Information about job applicants

ACTIVITY 4

1. Collect job advertisements from your local and a national newspaper and from any specialist magazines that you are familiar with (you might find some in the school, college or public libraries). You may also collect advertisements using the Internet. Write a short report comparing the types of jobs that are advertised in each of the publications that you use.
2. Recommend appropriate media for advertising the jobs given below. In each case, give reasons for your recommendation. Note that there may be no single correct answer; you might want to recommend more than one medium.
   - Bowton Hospital wishes to appoint a doctor who is a cancer specialist.
   - A large, multi-national sports clothing firm needs to employ an experienced sales manager to head its European section.
   - The supermarket in Marston needs to appoint three part-time checkout staff.

ACTIVITY 5

For each of the situations described below, recommend how the organisation should get information about applicants for the jobs. You may recommend more than one source. Give the reasons for your recommendations. Each of the organisations expects to receive a large number of applications for the jobs.

- Homesafe Insurance plc requires experienced clerks able to use computer software to keep financial records.
- Bowton Borough Council requires five road sweepers for the summer period when the town is busy with visitors.
- Abbey Homes Ltd builds and sells houses in most regions of England. Sales have been poor for the past two years. The firm needs a marketing director with responsibility for sales throughout the country.

Choosing the method

Often organisations will use more than one method for getting information about applicants for a job. Sometimes one or more methods will be used to help the organisation to draw up a shortlist of applicants. This happens when there are too many applicants to see individually. The organisation may use letters of application, application forms, CVs and references to help them get a first impression of the applicants. Those applicants that it would like to know about are put on a shortlist. This means that they will be invited to the next stage in the process of selection. This might be an interview or a test of their ability.

EXAM Practice Question

Suzanne Hart runs 'Aunt Sue's Bakery Shop'. She needs to recruit three workers – two bakers and a sales assistant – to help her to run the shop. Draw up a plan for recruiting and selecting the workers that she needs. Give reasons for the recommendations that you make. (12 marks)

(Adapted from OCR Business Studies Q4, Higher Tier Core Paper, 1997.)

ADVICE ON HOW TO ANSWER THE QUESTION

This question requires you to apply your knowledge of all the different stages that are part of the process of recruiting and selecting staff. You need to use your judgement about the methods that should be used, for example, to advertise the jobs. There is no one correct answer to questions like this. To score high marks, you need to explain fully any recommendations that you make. The question will require quite a long answer. This type of question is ideal for testing the quality of written communication that you use.

Needs analysis *How an organisation decides how many and what type of workers it should employ.*

Selection *The process of choosing between applicants for a job.*

Job description *A document containing the title of the job, details of who the person is responsible to and the duties and responsibilities involved.*

Person specification *A document stating the qualifications, experience, knowledge, skills and qualities needed by a person to be able to do a job.*

Internal recruitment *When an organisation appoints someone it already employs to another job within the organisation.*

External recruitment *when an organisation appoints someone who is not employed by it.*

Recruitment agency *A specialist agency that carries out all the tasks involved in recruitment and selection of workers for an organisation.*

EXAMINATION SUMMARY TIPS

- People are a very important resource for organisations.
- The recruitment and selection process should be planned carefully.
- Job descriptions and person specifications are drawn up to help organisations to identify what kind of person they need.
- An organisation may recruit internally or externally.
- It is important to advertise jobs in media that potential applicants will use.
- Advertisements should be designed to attract applications from appropriately qualified people.
- The methods of selection used should provide the employer with the information to decide which of the applicants is suitable for the job.

Key Skills

Activities 2 and 4 provide opportunities to use your IT skills. If you combine information from different sources in the advertisement that you design, you may provide evidence for IT2.2 and IT 2.3. The report for Activity 4 may require you to use all three parts of the IT skill. Searching in the newspaper and/or on the Internet is evidence for IT2.1. If you word-process your report and enter information and bring it together with scanned images of newspaper advertisements or advertisements downloaded from the Internet, you will provide evidence for IT2.2. Producing a final version of the report that has consistent formatting of the combined information, suits the purpose and is accurate, clear and appropriately saved will provide evidence of IT2.3.

Reading the advertisements for Activity 4 requires you to use your Communication skills (C1.2). Writing the report is another example of using Communication (C1.3 or C2.3, depending on how complex the report is that you produce). Designing the advertisement for Activity 2 also uses the Communication skill of writing documents (C1.3).

Unit 6.2 Pay and motivation

Why people work

It seems obvious! People work to earn money. But is that the full story?

Neave Patel works as a shop assistant for Boots chemists in Marston. Her friend, Joseph Hardman, works as a sales assistant in the Oxfam shop next door. Neave is paid for the number of hours that she works. She is also given a discount on any goods that she buys from the shop. She has also been given some shares in the company. Neave's husband is very well paid. They live in a large house and have everything that they want. Neave says that she works because she likes to meet people, that she would be bored if she stayed at home all day. Joseph is a volunteer. He does not get any pay for the work that he does.

Joseph works, but not for money. His wife earns enough for them to live reasonably well. Joseph believes that it is important to make a contribution in life – he wants to do some good for other people. He is the manager of the shop and enjoys the respect he is given by people he works with and the customers who come into the shop.

These examples shows that there may be more to why people work than just money. The different reasons or motivations that people have for working are important – managers must be aware of these so that they know how to motivate workers.

Maslow's Hierarchy of Needs

Many writers have been interested in finding out why people work. Abraham Maslow said that people have a **hierarchy of needs**. The needs are explained below. Physiological needs are the basic needs; self-actualisation is the highest need.

- **Physiological needs** – these are the basic needs that all humans must satisfy to stay alive: – the need to eat and drink, the need for shelter and clothing.
- **Safety** – the need to feel safe from physical danger that might put you at risk of injury or death.
- **Social needs** – the need to be with other people, to get on with them, to have fun and to work in groups.
- **Self-esteem** – the need to feel that other people value what you are and what you do.
- **Self-actualisation** – the need to feel that you have been able to use the talents that you have to achieve your potential.

The pyramid on page 215 is one way of showing the different needs. It also gives examples of the different kinds of needs and how these might be satisfied at work.

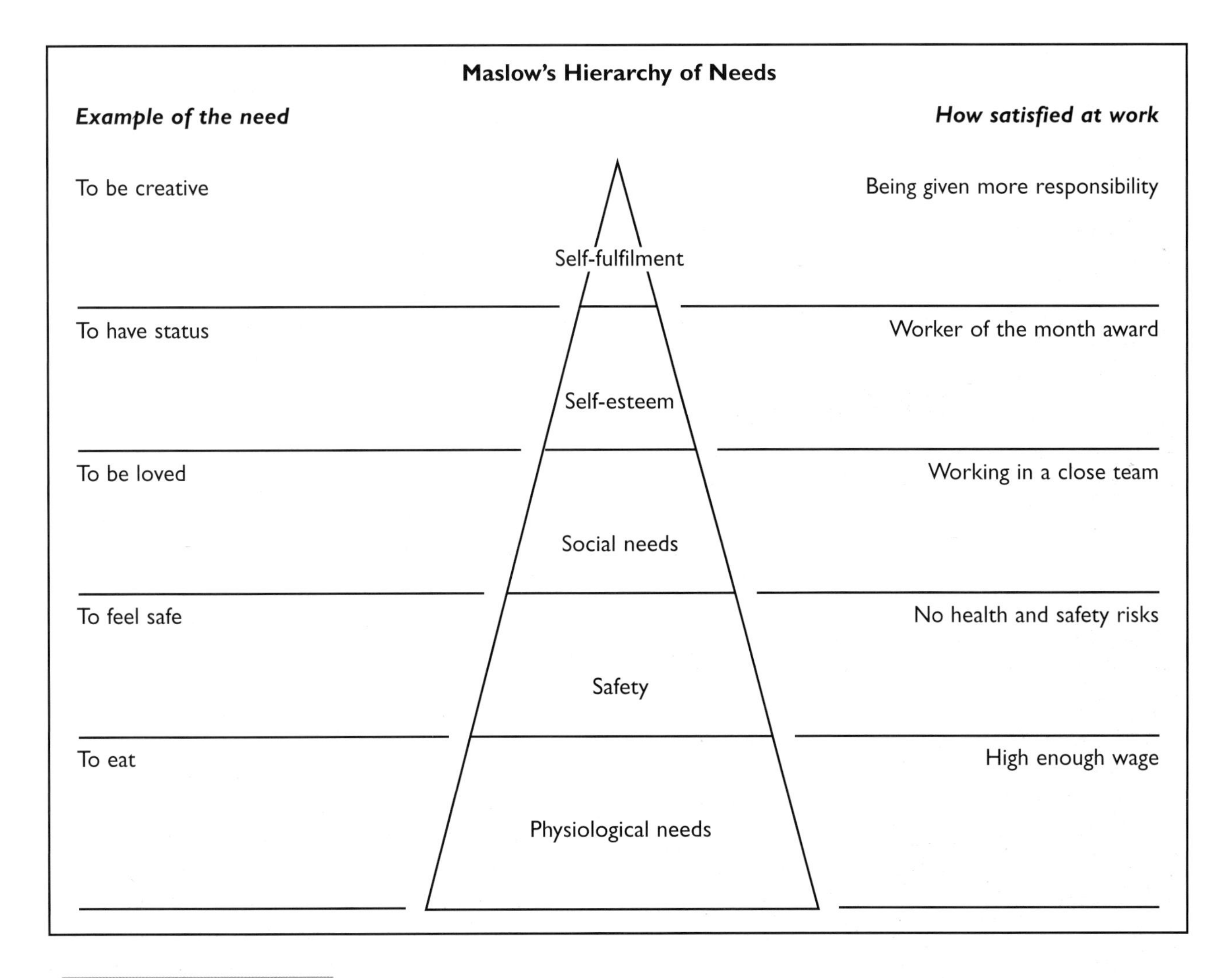

ACTIVITY 1

Copy out the diagram of Maslow's Hierarchy of Needs. Complete the left-hand side of the diagram by using the words typed in bold below to give more examples of each type of need.

- **Friendship** – the need to have other people to get on well with.
- **Recognition** – a desire to have other people acknowledge the work that we do, to pat us on the back.
- **Drink** – a means of satisfying the physical need for liquid.
- **Achievement** – the desire to do things, to reach goals.
- **Respect** – the need to be appreciated by others
- **Control** – the feeling of being in charge of what happens.
- **Fellowship** – the need to belong to a group.

ACTIVITY 2

(a) Prepare some questions to ask people why they work – relatives, neighbours or colleagues at work may be willing to help.
(b) You should try to interview three different types of workers. Write down their answers.
(c) Prepare for a discussion with other pupils in your class about why people work. Write down the main reasons that people have told you. Note any differences between the workers you have interviewed – the types of work they do, how much responsibility they have, what qualifications they needed to get the job. Try also to say which of the hierarchy of needs they say are important – remember work may satisfy more than one need.
(d) Take part in a group discussion in class about what motivates workers. As a group, try to list in order of importance the needs that work meets for workers.

The importance of motivating workers

Motivating workers is about encouraging workers to work hard and to work well. All organisations, whether in the private or the public sector, have objectives. If workers are working well then the organisation has a good chance of achieving its objectives. Workers who are working well are said to have high productivity. The importance of motivation and productivity is shown in the two examples below:

- Anselm's Pies introduced new measures to motivate workers five years ago. The result has been that the firm has increased the number of pies it makes and sells, increasing its profit. Also, the cost of producing pies has fallen. It has been able to reduce the price it charges for some of the pies that it sells and has still increased its profits. A local competitor closed down six months ago.
- Marston Council introduced new motivational schemes for all its office employees. The council found that the work was done more quickly and that fewer mistakes were made. The number of complaints that the council has to deal with has fallen.

Pay advice slips

A pay slip shows the amount of pay that a person receives and any deductions taken from that pay. A pay slip usually covers the period of a week or a month. **Gross pay** is the total income that a person receives before any deductions are made. **Net pay** is the amount that the person receives after **deductions** have been taken off. The main deductions are for **income tax**, **National Insurance** and **pension** (also known as superannuation). A pay slip will also show any **expenses** paid to the worker. For example, some workers use their own cars for their work and will usually be able to claim for the mileage they do.

Pay and motivation

The table below shows some of the methods of pay that are used.

Method	Description	Comments
Time rate	The worker is paid a set sum of money for each hour worked.	The worker may need to clock on and off to measure the hours worked. The system encourages workers to work a set number of hours but gives no reward for the quality of work done.
Overtime pay	The time rate may be increased to persuade the worker to work extra hours above the normal working day or week. Overtime may be paid at time and a quarter or time and a half.	It costs the firm more money but this may be covered by extra sales that the firm makes.
Salary	The firm agrees to pay the worker an amount of money for the year. This is divided by 12 and paid out monthly. The worker will not usually be paid for any extra hours that they work. However, they may receive extra money for reaching targets.	Salaries are often used to pay professional workers who have some kind of duty or responsibility for the people they serve and where it is difficult to measure what they produce – teachers and social workers, for example. However, there may be no incentive for the workers to work hard without some kind of additional reward.
Piece rate	This method of pay may be used where the work of individual workers can be measured. The worker is paid a sum of money for each item they complete. The more items the worker produces, the more pay they receive.	Piece rates motivate people to produce a lot. However, they may rush their work, making mistakes and wasting materials. Some kind of quality control is necessary.
Commission	This is paid to workers who sell goods or services. The amount to be paid is usually calculated as a percentage of the value of goods or services the worker sells.	This is a good motivator where the sales of workers can be measured. Sometimes sales people can become too pushy and can put off customers.
Bonus	This is an extra lump sum that may be paid to an individual or a group of workers when they reach a target level of production.	The target level of production needs to be realistic. If it is too high, workers may decide that it is not worth the effort to achieve.
Profit-sharing	The worker may be paid a share of any profits that the firm makes. It may be used to reward senior managers or where the individual contribution of workers cannot be measured.	The more successful that the business is in terms of profits, the more the worker receives. The problem may be that some workers may not deserve the payment if it is given to all workers in the business.
Fringe benefits or perks	The firm may give the worker non-money rewards. Examples of these include a company car, non-contributory pension scheme, luncheon vouchers and free health insurance.	These are sometimes cheaper methods of rewarding workers than giving them extra pay because tax may not be deducted. Workers often value these and will fear losing them if they lose their job. However, they are not directly related to performance.

Table 6.3 Methods of pay

ACTIVITY 3

For each of the following:
(a) state the method or methods of pay being used to reward each of the following worker and
(b) the amount of pay that they would receive.

1. Angus Deade receives £5 per hour and works a 35-hour week. In May, he worked four weeks. He also worked 12 hours overtime at time and a half.
2. Elsie MacIntosh receives £4 per hour and a commission of 10% of sales. Last week she worked 40 hours and sold £600 worth of goods.
3. Alastair Munro is the managing director of a firm. He receives £80 000 per year. He is also paid 2% of any profit that the company makes. In the last year the company made £2m in profit. He has a company car and is given free health insurance.
4. Wasim Ikram earns a basic salary of £30 000 per year. In October he received a bonus of £1 500 when the output of production department that he manages was 25% greater than the target level.
5. Morag MacTavish knits woollen jumpers. She receives £15 for each one produced. In April she knitted 20 jumpers.

Non-pay methods of motivation

It has been said that 'greed and fear' are the two main methods of motivating workers. The methods of pay described in the previous section are examples of motivating people by satisfying their greed. The threat of being made unemployed would be one way of motivating workers through fear. The 'greed and fear' argument may contain some truth. However, it may oversimplify what motivates workers.

Job rotation

This involves workers performing different jobs during the day, week or month. It stops them getting bored by doing the same work day after day. This is often done with workers who work on a production line. The jobs tend to be simple and do not require a lot of skill. This makes it easy to switch the workers around. However, it also means that they may move from one uninteresting job to another.

Job enlargement

This involves giving the worker some different tasks to do. A packer in a food factory may be asked to label boxes and move the stock to the warehouse. The worker does not have any extra responsibility but does have some variety in the work that they do.

Job enrichment

This involves giving the worker more responsibility. A production line worker may be given responsibility for checking the quality of the goods being made and writing a report to suggest improvements. Where job enrichment is involved, the worker is often given training to improve their skills so that they can deal with the extra responsibility.

Team-working and team-building

Workers may be put in teams according to the abilities that they have. Each person in a team has a particular task or type of work that they are responsible for. People often enjoy working in teams and do not want to be seen to let the group down by not performing well.

Sometimes groups of workers will be given responsibility for what they do. They will be free to choose how to make the product, when they will work, who will complete which tasks and so on. The workers may be more motivated because they feel in charge of what they do. When this happens the workers are said to have been **empowered**. Sometimes, but not always, the group may share a bonus for reaching targets. Empowerment is not only for groups of workers; individuals may be given freedom about how to complete a task.

One part of team building is deciding which workers to put together in a team so the team has the mix of skills and qualities necessary to make it work well. Another side is motivating people to get on well and feel a responsibility towards the group. This may be done in different ways:

- Some organisations have social events and activities. Many organisations have social clubs and works sports teams. These bring workers together outside work.
- An organisation may send workers on team-building courses. Outdoor pursuit activities are commonly used for this purpose. The workers are put in teams to take part in activities such as backpacking, rock-climbing and raft-building. While the activities are often fun, they also challenge people, both as individuals and as groups, to do things that may be dangerous or require initiative. Workers often see their colleagues in a different light and may appreciate their qualities more than they did.

Award schemes

An 'employee of the month' award is an example of an award scheme. The work of a worker is recognised in some way, perhaps by being given a certificate or having his or her name added to a list of employees of the month. These schemes can meet the need of the worker for self-esteem.

Promotion

Giving promotion to a worker is a way of giving recognition to their achievements and this may motivate them to continue to work hard. The possibility of gaining promotion also encourages workers.

Leadership

Leadership is about motivating others so that they perform well and contribute towards the objectives of the organisation. Some leaders motivate by inspiring people; others may bully and threaten. Leadership styles can be put under three headings:

- **Autocratic leadership.** This is when the leader makes all the decisions and expects the workers beneath him/her to carry out his/her orders. There will be little or no discussion with the workers about the work – workers are simply expected to obey workers.
- **Laissez-faire leadership.** The French term 'laissez-faire' means 'leave to do.' The leader will decide the main objectives of the organisation but the workers are given the responsibility for deciding how they are to achieve the objectives.
- **Democratic leadership.** This is when the workers are allowed to discuss plans with the leader and to influence decisions about what to do and how to do it.

ACTIVITY 4

State the method of motivation being used in each of the following cases:

1. Software designers have been asked to work together to identify the kind of software that schools are likely to need in five years' time and then to write it.
2. Marston Football Club are the bottom of the league. The players lack confidence and are dispirited by the poor performance. A new manager has been appointed. He has introduced extra training and has told the players that he will transfer anyone who fails to attend these sessions.
3. The workers at a chocolate factory have been asked to do different jobs on different days of the week. One day they may be involved in packing the chocolates, another day they may unpack and move the raw materials to the production line. All the work is considered to have the same level of responsibility.
4. John is a doorman at the Empire Theatre. He has been given the additional responsibility of meeting and greeting 'celebrity' visitors to the theatre and escorting them to the special hospitality facilities.
5. City High School has built a new English block to replace the mobile huts previously used. The building is light and airy. Teachers have started to play music in some lessons.

The style of leadership that is appropriate for a business will depend on what the organisation makes, how able and motivated the workers are, how well the business is performing at present, what problems the organisation faces and how urgently they must be solved. Different leadership styles may be used along with some of the other methods of motivating workers that have been discussed.

The environment

The conditions in which people work affect how well they perform. Conditions that are safe, warm, light and comfortable are more likely to motivate workers than dangerous, cold, dark and uncomfortable conditions. Open-plan offices, music and staff rest areas are other examples of changes to the environment that may help to motivate workers.

PAY ADVICE	GORMAN FURNITURE LTD		WEEK ENDING 4 JUNE
Employee	Employee number		
Ahmed Patel	34862		
Gross pay		Deductions	
Basic pay		Income tax	£42.00
Piece work		National Insurance	£19.60
		Superannuation	£14.40
Total gross pay		Total deductions	
NET PAY			

EXAM Practice Questions

1. Ahmed's job is to make legs for dining tables. He is paid as follows:
   - a basic rate of £5 per hour for a 40-hour working week
   - a piece rate of 50p per leg made above the minimum of target of 550 per week.

During the first week in June he worked 40 hours and produced 640 legs.

(a) Using this information, copy and complete the pay advice slip for Ahmed Patel above, indicating:
- basic pay
- piece work
- total gross pay
- deductions
- net pay. (5 marks)

(b) What benefits might the piece rate system of payment bring to Gorman Furniture Ltd? (6 marks)

(c) What are the possible disadvantages of the piece rate system of pay to Gorman Furniture Ltd? (6 marks)

(OCR Business Studies GCSE Q3, Higher Tier Core Paper, 1996.)

2. Colliers plc is concerned about the poor motivation of some of its workers. Giving reasons for your answer, recommend one method of improving the motivation of each of

the following workers:

- Shop assistants. These are low skilled and low paid. Many have second jobs.
- The ten clerical workers in the accounts department who do not get on well together. They are well paid compared to similar workers in other firms. They all have good skills.
- Asif Iqbal has worked for Colliers plc as a qualified maintenance mechanic since leaving college four years ago. He has shown a high level of competence in the past but now feels that the firm is taking him for granted.

(3 × 5 marks)

(OCR Business Studies GCSE, Q1 Higher Tier Core Paper, 2000.)

ADVICE ABOUT ANSWERING THE QUESTIONS

1. Part (a) tests your numeracy skills. You must read the information that you have been given carefully, especially that about the piece rate system that Ahmed is paid. You should do your working out in rough before putting the answer in the box.
   Parts (b) and (c) test your ability to apply your knowledge of the advantages and disadvantages of using a piece rate system of pay. Explain clearly what is meant by piece rates and how they are intended to motivate the workers making points that relate to the job that Ahmed does and Gorman Furniture Ltd. Do likewise when you discuss the disadvantages of piece rates.

2. The question requires you to use the skill of evaluation. There is more than one solution to each of the problems presented. You will gain marks for giving an appropriate solution but most of the marks are for justifying why your recommendation is relevant. You need to use the information about each of the types of workers to identify the problems of the workers and the needs that they have. This will help you to justify your recommendation.

KEY TERMS

Motivation *The encouragement given to workers to work hard and to work well.*

Productivity *The measure of performance of workers, usually in terms of the amount they produce or the average costs of production of what they make.*

Needs *The human wants and desires that work can help to satisfy.*

Pay *The money reward given to workers.*

Non-pay motivators *Methods of motivating workers that do not involve the payment of money as a reward. They meet needs in the hierarchy of needs other than basic or physiological needs.*

EXAMINATION SUMMARY TIPS

- There are many different reasons why people work.
- People have different kinds of needs that can be satisfied through work.
- Pay is an important motivator because it provides the money people need to buy the goods and services they need.
- Different methods of pay are used to motivate different kinds of workers.
- People can be motivated in many ways besides paying them money.
- The non-pay methods of motivation used should meet the needs of the people they are intended to motivate.

Key Skills

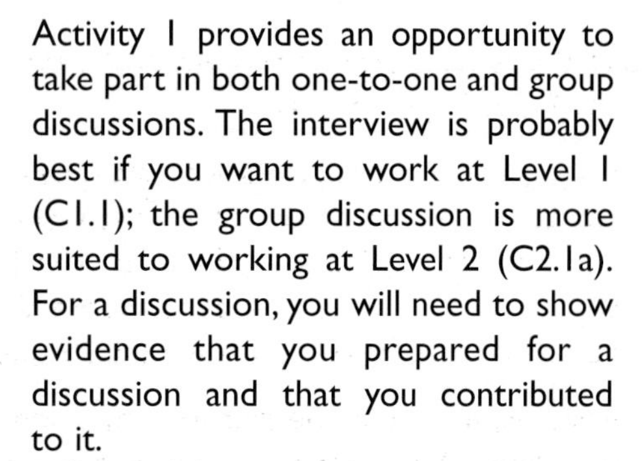

Activity 1 provides an opportunity to take part in both one-to-one and group discussions. The interview is probably best if you want to work at Level 1 (C1.1); the group discussion is more suited to working at Level 2 (C2.1a). For a discussion, you will need to show evidence that you prepared for a discussion and that you contributed to it.

The interview is an opportunity for a one-to-one discussion. The evidence of preparation will be your questions. The evidence that you took part in the discussion will be the record of the answers that your were given and a 'Witness statement' from the person you interviewed.

For the group discussion, the evidence of your preparation will be your notes on the motivation of workers as well as your interview questions and answers. After the discussion, you should record what you said in the discussions, examples showing when you listened to others in the group and responded to what they said and also what you said to move the discussion forward. Your assessor will need to sign a 'Witness statement' to confirm that you have met the requirements before you put all this evidence in your Key Skills Portfolio.

Unit 6.3 Training

- Training is important for the economy. To remain competitive in an international economy, the UK must have a supply of highly skilled workers who can help businesses to be efficient and to develop.
- Businesses in the United Kingdom are in competition with firms in the UK and from around the world. To compete, they must keep developing and improving what they sell and how they produce. Workers will need to develop new knowledge and skills. If their workers do not have the right skills, businesses will not be able to compete.
- For the individual, training is also important. It can help them to find a job, to do their job better, to gain promotion and to feel that they are improving themselves.

Training needs

Training is about developing the knowledge, skills and abilities of the workers. Different kinds of workers will need training for different reasons. Some of these are suggested below:

- **Technical skills** – workers may need to learn the skills needed to use a machine or to upgrade their skills to deal with new machines.
- **Personal skills** – workers may need to develop personal skills such as communication skills because these are needed in the work that they have to do.
- **Management skills** – a worker may have been given a promotion or may be seeking promotion. He or she will have to learn the skills needed to manage other people, controlling budgets, solving problems and so on.
- **New workers** – these will need induction training to introduce them to the organisation that they will work in.
- **Group working** – workers may need training about how to work together well, how to get the best out of each other.
- **Knowledge of new products** – workers may need to be told about new products that they have to sell so that they know what information customers will require.
- **Flexibility** – a firm may want to provide workers with a range of different skills so that they can do different jobs.
- **Re-training** – the job that a person did may no longer exist, perhaps because a machine does it instead. This person will need to develop new skills if he or she is to find employment.

ACTIVITY 1

State the type(s) of training need to be met in each of the following situations:

1. Annabel's, a hairdressing salon, has taken on a young trainee. He starts work next week. He needs to learn different skills, from washing and drying hair to cutting and perming. He also needs to learn how to deal with customers.
2. Annabel, who runs the hairdressing salon, wants to expand the business to offer a range of beauty treatments. She needs to develop her own skills before this can be done.
3. Tony Hart has been a machine operator at Lathom's Paints for 15 years. New machinery has been developed to do the work he did. The firm does not want to make him redundant. It has sent him on a training course to learn how to manage the warehouse.
4. Elegant Conservatories employs three window fitters. It is sending them on a basic electrician training course. They will be able to fit plugs and lights instead of having to call in a fully qualified electrician.
5. Marston Social Services Department needs to train three social workers to become bereavement counsellors.

On-the-job training The training is done in the place where the worker works. Either: • The trainee does a job and is given help by someone more experienced. *or* • The trainee will shadow another worker, learning the job by watching what they are doing and asking questions.	
Advantages	***Disadvantages***
• Trainee is given individual teaching. • Cheaper – no travel or accommodation costs. • Worker still produces whilst training. • Trained in the ways of the firm.	• Trainee may not produce as much as they would when working. • Trainer may need to leave his or her work to help the trainee. • The quality of the work may not be very good if a trainee does it. This could lead to wasted resources and/or a poor reputation for quality. • Not suitable for groups of workers.

Off-the-job training The worker will do the training away from where they work. Either: • The trainee will go to a different site, perhaps a college or special training centre. *or* • The trainee goes to another part of the site where they work, perhaps to a lecture room or resource centre.	
Advantages	***Disadvantages***
• Experts may provide training. • Trainee can use specially designed training equipment. • Workers often enjoy the change of environment.	• Usually more expensive because of fees, travel and accommodation costs.

Table 6.4 Types of training

Types of training

There are two main types of training – on-the-job and off-the-job.

More about off-the-job training

There are several different forms of off-the-job training:

- **Lectures.** These are good for telling people about things, for giving information. They are not good for developing skills.
- **Demonstrations.** The trainee watches someone show them how to do a job. These are good because you learn from an expert. It is often necessary to practise the work after the demonstration in order to develop the skills.
- **Role-play or simulation.** The worker experiences a situation as if it were a real work situation. The trainee practices the skills or practises how they would deal with the situation.
- **Team-building.** A group performs tasks together to develop. It helps them to learn how to work best in teams and to appreciate the different qualities that other people have.

Specialist training centres provide off the job training.

On the job training is done while the person is doing their job.

ACTIVITY 2

Recommend the method or methods of training that would be suitable for each of the situations below. State whether the training should be on-the-job or off-the-job and the type of training that should be given. Explain the reasons for your recommendations.

1. Direct Bank needs to employ ten new workers at its call centre. The workers need to be able answer calls correctly and use the computer software designed specifically for Direct Bank.
2. Braswell Insurance wishes to improve the typing skills of five clerical officers that it employs.
3. Plumbs Garden Centre wishes to train one of its drivers to be able to feed and prune plants when there is no other work for him to do.
4. Johnston Clothing Ltd wishes to train its supervisors to be able to deal with problems brought to them by staff. The problems may be minor or major issues. Some of the major issues that have occurred in the past have concerned bullying, racial discrimination and health and safety problems. There have been some heated arguments and unpleasant scenes.
5. Annabel's, a hairdresser, has taken on a young trainee. He needs to learn different skills, from washing and drying hair to cutting and perming.
6. Annabel, who runs the salon, wants to expand the business to offer a range of beauty treatments. She needs to develop her own skills before this can be done.

Life-long learning

Many older people that you know will have done the same job all their life. After school, they might have completed an apprenticeship or been to college and gained qualifications. From this they might have started in a job which they still do – perhaps for the same firm, perhaps for a different one. For you, it is more likely that you will need to change careers several times during your lifetime. This means that you will need to keep learning new skills or developing the skills that you already have. The Government has been encouraging workers to learn throughout their lives. At school, you may have been encouraged to keep a Record of Achievement or Progress File. It is a file to keep records of all your qualifications and achievements, and to keep plans for your future, writing down the job you want to do and the qualifications that you will need. The Government, and many employers, encourage workers to maintain this record throughout their working lives.

During recent years, the Government has introduced a national framework of qualifications. This framework includes different kinds of qualifications suited to different people. There are five 'levels' of qualifications; there are academic qualifications and vocational qualifications for different occupations. Training organisations that receive Government support must offer courses that lead to qualifications in the framework. There are three kinds of qualifications:

- **Academic qualifications** – such as GCSEs, AS and A levels and degrees.

- **General vocational qualifications** – vocational A levels, Intermediate and Foundation GNVQs (General National Vocational Qualifications) or vocational GCSEs – these qualifications show that a person has general knowledge and skills that are needed in an area of business. For example, a GNVQ in Leisure and Tourism will introduce the general skills needed in occupations in that line of business. Key Skills have become very important. These are general skills that are required by workers in many different kinds of employment. The Government has identified six key skills: Communication, Application of Number, Information Technology, Working with Others, Improving Own Learning and Performance and Problem Solving. Many businesses place great importance on these.
- **Vocational qualifications** – these qualifications show that a person is able to do tasks related to a particular occupation, for example, as a hairdresser, a plumber or as a clerical officer. Many of these qualifications are NVQs (National Vocational Qualifications).

ACTIVITY 3 

Investigate an occupation that you are interested in. Find out the qualifications that you will need to do the job – your careers library and the Internet will be good sources of information. Develop a plan to say how you will gain those qualifications. Write up your findings and your plan as a personal action plan. Note that you may need to gain both academic and vocational qualifications as part of the plan.

Staff appraisal

Many organisations have staff appraisal schemes. At least once each year, an employee (the appraisee) will meet with his or her boss (the appraiser). Together they will discuss the performance of the employee and ways of improving it. Many organisations set targets for their workers. For example, a salesperson might be set a sales target. If the worker reaches the target, he or she may be given extra money – performance-related pay. New targets will be set for the next year. Sometimes a programme of training and development is agreed. This programme may be designed to help the worker to improve their performance or to help them to get promotion.

ACTIVITY 4 

Appraise your own performance in Business Studies during the present term.

(a) Write down which part of the course has gone well. Why do you think that you were able to do this work well?

(b) Write down which part of the course you have found difficult. Try to explain why you have had problems.

(c) Now try to think of ways of improving your performance. Sometimes, this might simply be to concentrate more in class or to do all homework on time. Other targets might be to revise a certain topic by a certain date. You could do some past questions to test how well you have learned what you have revised. Your teacher will also be able to give you some suggestions.

Investors in People

The Investors in People award is a quality assurance scheme for organisations who provide structured opportunities for staff development. The organisation sets out its goals and targets in a plan. Staff training will be needed to achieve these. The whole programme must be properly evaluated. If the planning, implementation and evaluation of the programme meet the criteria, the organisation can be awarded IIP status. It can then display the IIP plaque in its premises and display the symbol on its letterheads.

EXAM Practice Questions

Denton Engineering Ltd produces low-bake spray ovens for spraying cars and drying the paint. The personnel department is responsible for training the workers at Denton Engineering Ltd. Some training is delivered on-the-job whilst some is off-the-job. The firm employs both production workers and office staff.

(i) Explain the difference between on-the-job and off-the-job training. (4 marks)
(ii) What are the advantages of on-the-job training for Denton Engineering plc? (4 marks)
(iii) Describe the problems on-the-job training may cause for Denton Engineering Ltd. (4 marks)
(iv) Explain the benefits that Denton Engineering Ltd may gain from staff appraisal programmes. (4 marks)

(Adapted from OCR Business Studies GCSE, Q5 Core Paper, 1995.)

ADVICE ABOUT ANSWERING THE QUESTIONS

Part (i) requires a short description of each type of training.
Part (ii) requires you to apply your knowledge of the advantages of on-the-job training to the production of the low-bake spray ovens.
Part (iii) requires you to apply your knowledge of the disadvantages of on-the-job training to the production of the low-bake spray ovens.
Part (iv): The command in this question is also to 'apply' your business studies knowledge to the case study firm. In this case, you need to state what the advantages of staff appraisal are and to argue how they might benefit this engineering firm – remember that some workers will be involved in production, others in marketing, others in administration and so on. Illustrate the points you want to make by writing about some of these different workers.

EXAMINATION SUMMARY TIPS

- Training is very important – for the economy, a business and the individual.
- Different organisations and different workers will have different training needs.
- Training may be done on-the-job or off-the-job.
- There are several different kinds of off-the-job training.
- Different types of training will be necessary for different kinds of business situations and different kinds of workers.
- People need to learn throughout their lives.

Key Skills

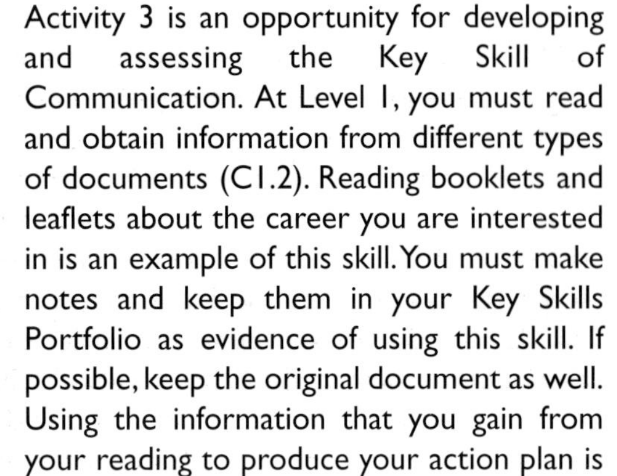

Activity 3 is an opportunity for developing and assessing the Key Skill of Communication. At Level 1, you must read and obtain information from different types of documents (C1.2). Reading booklets and leaflets about the career you are interested in is an example of this skill. You must make notes and keep them in your Key Skills Portfolio as evidence of using this skill. If possible, keep the original document as well. Using the information that you gain from your reading to produce your action plan is writing a document (C1.3). Keep the finished plan in your Key Skills Portfolio.

If the documents you use are extended documents, you may be working at Level 2 (C2.2). A detailed plan might also reach Level 2 (C2.3).

Activity 3 could also be an opportunity for using the Key Skill of IT. There is now a lot of information about careers available on the Internet or on CD-ROMs. You would need to plan what information you need and how to search for it. Once you have found the information you need, you would have to bring it together and develop your plan using IT. Finally, you would have to present the plan in a suitable way, ensuring that it is accurate and clear. You would have to show that you can save the work. You could work at either Level 1 or Level 2 on this task – it depends how complicated your piece of work is.

Activity 4 is an opportunity for developing or getting evidence of your competence in the key skill of Improving Own Learning and Performance. The Activity is asking you to complete a self-appraisal. You list your strengths and weaknesses. Then you write an action plan saying how you will improve. The best action plans use SMART targets. An example of a SMART target for this Unit might be: 'I will learn the definitions of the key terms connected with training by the end of the week.' The target is realistic; you can measure whether or not you have achieved it (by testing yourself) and it has to be achieved by a set date. It is also something that you are able to do.

Unit 6.4 Trade unions and labour law

The following is taken from an article in the *Guardian* newspaper (13 September 1999):

'The number of legal actions brought by employees has leapt by a third in the past 15 months. The annual report from the Advisory, Conciliation and Arbitration Service (ACAS) records 136,000 notifications of employment tribunal cases between July 1988 and June 1999 ... the figure represents a lot of grievances.'

An employment tribunal is a special court set up to deal with disputes between workers and employers. Its job is to decide if the employer or employee has broken the law. Sometimes, but not always, the worker will be supported by a trade union. Trade unions exist to protect the interests of workers. But why are so many people making complaints against their employees? Partly it is because laws have been created to protect workers. Partly it is because, in recent years, workers have become more aware of the rights that they have and they are more likely to seek compensation if they feel that they have been treated unfairly.

This unit deals with the laws designed to protect workers and with the work of trade unions.

Employment tribunals

These are courts of law. They deal with most of the laws relating to employment mentioned in the table on page 230 and some others including regulations dealing with disability discrimination, data protection and asbestos. If a worker sues an employer the tribunal will hear evidence for both sides. The tribunal then makes a decision. If the employer is found to be at fault, the firm can be made to pay compensation. If a worker has been dismissed unfairly, the tribunal may order that he or she be reinstated. The firm may also be fined for breaking the law. Another consequence is that the firm may receive some bad publicity if the problem is covered in the newspapers.

Health and safety issues may be dealt with in the civil courts. The Health and Safety Executive employs inspectors who visit places of work. They inspect the premises to check that they meet the health and safety regulations. Legal action can be taken against employers who breach the regulations. The court can order the employer to pay compensation and can impose fines. An individual worker can also bring civil actions against their employers.

An employer has the right to dismiss or sack an employee if they cannot do the job properly or if they behave badly in some way – known as misconduct. Very serious bad behaviour – for example theft or being drunk at work – is known as gross misconduct.

Employment laws

Table 6.5 summarises some of the main laws that exist to protect workers. The laws described in the table are designed to protect the worker from bad employers. However, employers do have rights as well.

Name of the law	Main points
Equal Pay Act 1970	This law was introduced to make sure that women are paid the same as men when they do similar work.
Race Relations Act 1976	This law was introduced to stop people of one race, colour, nationality or ethnic origin being treated differently than others. Direct discrimination is when one worker gets better treatment than another does – perhaps being given promotion when another employee is better qualified. There are some exceptions to the law – for example, if, for some reason, the job must be carried out by someone of a particular race such as a waiter in a Chinese restaurant.
Sex Discrimination Act 1975	This law was introduced to stop males or females being treated differently from members of the opposite sex. A job advertisement that says the job is for a woman would be against the law. There are some exceptions – for example, if, for some reason, the job must be carried out by someone of a particular sex (such as a female PE teacher who would need to deal with female pupils in the changing room).
Health and Safety at Work Act 1974	The law makes it the responsibility of the employer to protect the worker from dangers in the workplace. Responsibilities include providing safety equipment, washing facilities and toilets and adequate breaks.
Minimum Wage Legislation	This was introduced to stop workers being exploited by employers. It applies to people over the age of 18. For people in the age range 18–21 the minimum hourly wage rate is less than for those aged 22 years and over. In 2001, the rate was increased to £4.10 per hour. There are some exceptions to the legislation, including au pairs and members of the armed forces.
Employment Rights Act 1996	The firm does not need to give a worker a written contract of employment but it must give a statement of particulars within eight weeks of starting work. This states the job title, the hours the person must work, details of the job, the pay, when the worker will be paid, what deductions will be taken from pay, how much notice must be given to end the contract and any disciplinary rules that apply to the employee.

Table 6.5 Employment laws

Health and Safety at Work

There are a number of laws that deal with health and safety at work besides the 1974 Act mentioned in the table. These laws have helped to make firms more health and safety conscious. All organisations must now have a written health and safety policy. Employees must receive adequate health and safety training. Health and safety issues must be communicated to the workers through posters, on notice-boards, in training and so on.

ACTIVITY 2

In your school, there will be some health and safety issues that concern you – perhaps in the Technology rooms or in the Science Laboratories. Write an account of all the ways that these health and safety issues have been communicated to you.

ACTIVITY 1

Read the newspaper articles (a) – (f). These deal with cases that have been heard by an employment tribunal. In some cases, the tribunal had not made a decision for or against the person bringing the case. For each one, decide which of the labour laws has or may have been broken. Give reasons for your answer.

(a) 'A female coach who was denied an advanced training licence by the Football Association won £16 000 compensation … at an industrial tribunal yesterday.'
(*Guardian*, 29 June 1999)

(b) 'Among the cases of dismissal were a (an adult) sewing machinist working 60–70 hours a week for a wage of £1.60. Her employer had given false information on her pay slip saying she was on £3.60 an hour.'
(*Guardian*, 2 October 1999)

(c) 'A hospital consultant, Dr Feyi Awotona, was dismissed for gross misconduct from her post at South Tyneside District Hospital. Hospital staff said that she was "obstructive and confrontational" and had once left a labour ward without a consultant. Dr Awotona claimed that she had been dismissed unfairly. She said that a senior colleague had "astonished me by saying that because I was a woman and black there was a limit to what I could do at Tyneside".'
(*Telegraph*, 5 September 2000)

(d) 'On October 10,1996, two council workers died in an underground pumping chamber at Crymlyn Burrows sewage pumping station, near Swansea. Toxic fumes from a chemical discharge overcame Robert Preece and Robert Simpson. Preece had entered the chamber to carry out maintenance, a job he had routinely done, despite not having been given appropriate training or equipment by his employer.'
(*Guardian*, 24 March 1999)

(e) 'The tribunal said it was discriminatory for Eileen Halloran, 50, the former head of physical education at the City of London School for Girls, to be paid £7 000 less than her counterpart at the City of London School, a boys' school.'
(*Telegraph*, 27 March 1998).

f) 'The Croydon Tribunal ruled that Deborah Ugbechie, then a principal awards officer with Lambeth Council, had treated the two men as "token whites" and led a campaign in the department to ostracise them. At the hearing, the tribunal heard how Ms Ugbechie … humiliated the men and treated them as inferior to eight black women colleagues.'
(*Guardian*, 17 November 1999)

The statement of particulars

This must be given to the worker within two months of the worker starting employment.

The minimum wage debate

The minimum wage was introduced to stop businesses from exploiting workers by not paying them very much. For many businesses, the introduction of the minimum wage has had no effect – they already paid their workers above the minimum wage. For others, it has meant a fall in profits as their costs have risen. In some case, businesses have been forced to close down because they can no longer compete. Others have decided to cut costs by using machines rather than workers. Unemployment has been the result for some workers.

Redundancy

When a worker's employment is ended because the work they do is no longer needed by a firm it is called redundancy. The main reasons why a worker may not be needed are:

- the firm has started to use machines instead of labour
- the firm is producing less, so does not need as many workers
- the firm has gone out of business, so does not need any workers.

The law gives protection to workers who are made redundant. If they have worked for their employer for at least two years, the employer must pay them 'redundancy money' as compensation for losing their job. The law states the minimum that must be paid. Some employers pay more than the minimum. The firm may ask for voluntary redundancies. People may choose to be made redundant, perhaps because the redundancy money is good or because they are nearing retirement or because they want a change.

Trade unions

Examples of trade unions are the National Union of Teachers and Unison which represents workers in public sector organisations.

Trade unions set out to do two main jobs:

- **To act as a pressure group.** A pressure group is an organisation that seeks to influence government to make laws that are in the interests of its members. A trade union, asking government to limit working hours more strictly, would be acting as a pressure group.
- **To protect the interests of its members.** Unions help workers with all kinds of matters. These include:
  - working conditions
  - hours
  - redundancy
  - unfair dismissal
  - safety at work
  - race and sex discrimination
  - pay
  - holiday entitlement.

Benefits of union membership

Unions are able to help workers with these kinds of matters because:

- They have strength in numbers. The actions of a large group of workers will have more influence on employers than the actions of an individual.
- They can give expert advice and support. Unions employ specialists such as solicitors. These will be able to give workers expert advice about the rights the workers have and what to do in a dispute.
- They have the money to help to pay for expensive court cases.
- They will have trained negotiators who know how to deal with the employers.

Unions can also negotiate benefits for their members. Discounts in some shops and lower rates of interest on loans are examples of these benefits.

ACTIVITY 3

A friend has just started work as a teacher. She has written to say that some of the teachers she works with say that she should join a union. She is not sure what to do, especially as she will have to pay to be a member. Write to her to tell her about the benefits that she might get as a member of the union. Mention any disadvantages that there might be to joining a union.

Industrial action

This term refers to the actions that workers can take to try to achieve what they want in a dispute with the employer. Many disputes are settled before any industrial action takes place. The main forms of industrial action are:

- **Strike.** Nearly all workers have the right to withdraw their labour. Sometimes a strike can be by selected workers who have key jobs. If their work is not done, the whole of the production may have to stop. A strike involving all the workers is known as an 'all out strike'. It may be for one day or until the dispute is settled.
- **Overtime ban.** This is when the workers will only work the hours stated in their contract of employment. They will not work any overtime.
- **Work to rule.** This is when the workers will only do what the rules and regulation say that they should do.

Industrial action is designed to benefit the workers. However, it may also have costs for the worker. It will also harm the employer, the customers of the firm and the economy as a whole.

Costs to the workers

1. Lose wages.
2. May lose bonuses, commission, overtime pay etc.
3. If the firm suffers a loss of sales, workers may be laid off or made redundant.

Costs to customers

1. They are not able to buy the products they need.
2. If the products are raw materials or stock that they sell, they will not be able to produce or sell anything so they lose sales revenue.
3. They may lose their customers to competitors.
4. They may have to pay higher prices if they buy from another firm.

Costs of the firm

1. Cannot product or sell so loses income.
2. May make less profit.
3. Customers may take their business to competitors – sometimes permanently.

Costs to the economy

1. People and firms will have less money to spend – businesses will lose sales revenue.
2. The Government will lose tax revenue because people have less income and spend less.
3. Imports may rise if people buy from abroad rather than from British firms.
4. Unemployment may rise, increasing the cost of social security benefits.

Table 6.6 The costs of industrial action

Single union agreements

In some places of work, several different unions may represent different kinds of workers. Different **craft unions** may represent different kinds of skilled workers. **White-collar** unions represent office workers. A **general union** may represent some semi-skilled and unskilled workers. This can make industrial relations complicated. In some firms there are **single union agreements**. This means that all the workers agree to be a member of the same union. This can help the workers as well as the employers. The workers benefit because all the workers in the firm will speak with one voice and this may add to their strength. For the firm it is easier to negotiate with one union rather than several of them.

ACAS – Advisory, Conciliation and Arbitration Service

This organisation exists to try to settle disputes between workers and employers. First, it will give advice to both the employer and to the union. Second it will provide conciliation – it tries to find areas that both sides can agree upon to re-start negotiations when they have broken down. Third, it provides arbitration. When the two sides cannot reach an agreement, ACAS appoints an **arbitrator** who hears the arguments and makes a decision. This person will have to be acceptable to both sides. The union and the employer cannot disobey any decision the arbitrator makes unless they had agreed to non-binding arbitration.

ACTIVITY 4

The class should divide into three groups – one representing the employers at Practical Plastics Ltd, one the workers and the third ACAS. Each group should appoint two negotiators.

A dispute has developed between the workers and the management. The background to the dispute is given below:

Practical Plastics Ltd makes storage boxes for use in the home and in work. It has many competitors. Sales have been only just satisfactory for 18 months – enough for the firm to make a small profit. Workers are unhappy about conditions in the factory – some of the machinery is old and dangerous and the floor needs repairing in places. They are also unhappy about wages. Two years ago the wage rate was cut by 5% at a time when the firm was making a loss. The employers said that this was necessary to see the firm through a difficult period. Wages were increased by 2% last year. Inflation has run at 3% for the past three years. There are signs that the economy is improving – exports have risen in the last six months, as have incomes. The firm would like to buy some new machinery.

Each group should prepare its arguments. Also decide what actions you might take to help you to win the dispute.

Negotiations should take place between the negotiators of the two groups. One of the ACAS representatives should act as the chairperson. The negotiators may withdraw from the discussions on three occasions to discuss matters with the group they represent.

If it is not possible to reach an agreement, the ACAS group should decide what should happen.

ACTIVITY 5

Research an example of an industrial dispute. You might use the Internet or a local or national paper for this purpose. If you use the Internet, try a website for one of the national newspapers.

Write an account of the dispute including:

- why the dispute was taking place
- what actions both the management and the workers took?
- how the dispute was settled – if it was
- what costs there were – to the workers, the firm, the customers and the economy?

EXAM Practice Questions

(a) Suzanne Hart runs Aunt Sue's bakery shop.

(i) State **two** legal requirements she must meet when employing workers. (4 marks)

(ii) The workers that Suzanne employs are not in a trade union. What benefits can workers gain from being in trade union? (4 marks)

(b) Tastybread Bakeries Ltd is a large firm. A single union represents all the workers at Tastybread Bakeries Ltd. Explain the benefits of single union agreements to (i) the workers and (ii) the management. (2 × 2 marks)

(Adapted from OCR Business Studies GCSE Common Core, Higher Tier, 1997.)

ADVICE ABOUT ANSWERING THE QUESTION

These questions are testing your knowledge of labour law and trade union matters. Where knowledge is being tested it is particularly important to pay attention to the number of marks for the question – there will be one mark for each point made or for an explanation of a point.

Labour law *This term describes a number of laws that deal with relations between workers and their employers.*

Employment tribunal *A special court of law that deals with disputes between workers and employers.*

Contract of employment *A legal agreement between the worker and the employer.*

Redundancy *When employment is ended because the firm no longer needs the work that was done by an employee.*

Trade union *An organisation that represents the interests of workers.*

Pressure group *An organisation that tries to influence the Government and Parliament to pass laws in its favour.*

Industrial action *Actions taken by workers to put pressure on employers to give in to their demands.*

Industrial relations *The term for the dealings between unions and management.*

Single union agreement *The workers and the employers agree that all workers will be represented by only one union.*

EXAMINATION SUMMARY TIPS

- Labour laws deal with relations between workers and employers.
- Many laws are designed to protect the worker from employers who might treat them unfairly in some way.
- The worker can sue the employer if they think they have been unfairly treated.
- Disputes between workers and employers are heard at an employment tribunal. The tribunal can make a guilty employer pay a fine and pay compensation to the worker.
- Trade unions exist to help workers to deal with employers.
- Trade unions increase the power of workers because they represent the views of many people.
- Single union agreements exist in some firms. These simplify industrial relations between the workers and the employers.

Key Skills

Activity 3 is an opportunity for writing a document (C1.3 or C2.3). Make sure the letter contains relevant information. Organise the information in logical way. Use appropriate terms to explain what the benefits of unions are. Check your spelling, punctuation and grammar.

Activity 4 is an opportunity to take part in a discussion (C2.1a) either in the group or as a negotiator. Keep the notes you make in preparation for the discussion. Record the contributions you made and how you listened and responded to others and helped to move the discussion forward.

Activity 5 is an opportunity for practising or producing evidence for both IT and Communication Key Skills. A search of newspaper websites would be evidence for IT2.1. If this is then developed and presented in the form of a report it would be evidence for IT2.2 and IT2.3. The student would need to keep the materials downloaded from the Internet. They would also need to keep drafts showing how the report was developed.

The report would also be evidence of writing documents (C2.3).

Aiding and Controlling Business Activity

Learning Objectives:
To develop:

- knowledge and understanding of the ways in which business can be aided and controlled
- understanding of why business needs to be helped and controlled
- skills of selection, interpretation and analysis of information
- the ability of students to apply their understand of methods of aiding and controlling business activity
- the skill of making reasoned judgements as it applies to aiding and controlling business activity.

Introductory activity

Reclaiming and redeveloping derelict land – a case study

Pride Park in Derby is a site the size of approximately 240 football pitches located to the south-east of the city centre. It is the original site of Derby's railway vehicle and equipment manufacturing industry which no longer employs the vast numbers of people it once did. The land shown in the picture has also been used in the past for gas and coke works, landfill and gravel extraction. These activities have left behind a wide variety of contaminants including oils, tars, heavy metals and ammonia.

By the early 1990s, much of the land had become derelict. Road links to the area were poor. The owners of the land recognised the commercial potential of the land but were also aware of the development costs and were unwilling to take a risk in developing the site.

SECTION 7

Pride Park Derby.

Outstanding example of brownfield regeneration by the city of Derby

PRIDE PARK has been an outstanding regeneration success story for the city of Derby.

Conceived as part of the £37.5m City Challenge programme, Pride Park has brought a vast and largely inaccessible brownfield site into a thriving mixed use business and leisure park.

Earlier this year the "full" signs went up on the first phase of the development which has seen the creation of Pride Park Stadium, the arrival of major employers like Egg Financial Services, a hotel, restaurant, prestige car dealerships, David Lloyd Leisure, the new JJB Sports complex nearing completion, and a host of manufacturing and service sector businesses including the park's first occupant DIPT.

Local newspaper article commenting on the success of the development.

In 1993, Derby City Council secured £37.5m of funding from the Government's City Challenge scheme to develop this **brownfield** area. Working in partnership with the landowners and other agencies, the task of regenerating the area began. The intention was to create a modern business park which would meet many of the city's employment needs. It was estimated that the site was capable of generating in excess of 3 000 jobs by the end of the 20th century.

By the end of 2000, a large number of businesses had moved into the area. The Internet bank Egg has a call centre located at Pride Park, together with Derby County Football Club's new 35 000-seat stadium. Core Design, the company responsible for creating the computer game *Tomb Raider* and the character Lara Croft, has its office in Pride Park. Restaurants, pubs, car showrooms and many other business make up the business activity already attracted to the location.

Other well-known business activities located at Pride Park.

Pride Park is turning out to be a very good example of public and private sector co-operation.

There are many other areas in the country where former industrial land has been re-developed and put to alternative uses often with the help of money from both the private and public sectors of the economy.

Meadowhall Shopping Centre and the Millennium Dome.

- The Meadowhall Shopping Centre on the outskirts of Sheffield is located on the site of a former steel works.
- The Millennium Dome in Greenwich is located on the site of a former gas works.

Former dockland areas, coal mines and other industrial areas have been re-developed and turned into business parks or recreational activities. Some of these areas may be near to where you live.

Your task is to:

1. Find an area near to where you live or with which you are familiar which has undergone a similar change in use to the one described in the case study. If you cannot find a similar site, try to find one which has been developed from a **greenfield** site.
2. Draw a location map showing the nearest large towns and cities: main roads; railway lines etc.
3. List:
   (a) the use(s) to which the site was put before it was developed
   (b) the types of activities which the site is now being used for.
4. Explain the reasons for the changes in the use of the site.
5. Consider where the finance to develop the site might have come from. List the sources of finance you think will have been used.
6. Explain the benefits the development has brought to the local area.
7. Explain why the European Union, UK Government and local councils are keen to help with urban regeneration projects similar to the one in the case study.
8. List the most important factors which will affect the decision of a business to locate to a new area.

Unit 7.1 Government in the mixed economy

Economic systems

An economic system is the way in which decisions about what will be produced are made. There are three possible types of economic system.

The planned economy

In this type of economy, the Government decides everything. Officials, employed by the Government, plan production. The first stage in the plan is to decide what goods and services will be needed in the country in the next year, the next five years or even the next ten years. The second stage is to organise the factors of production – land, labour and capital – so that they produce the goods and services. Farms and factories are set targets for how much they must produce. They will be allocated resources so that they can achieve these targets. Usually the Government owns the businesses; there will be little or no private enterprise.

During the 20th century, several countries tried planned economies. Some of these were in Eastern Europe, including Russia, Hungary, Poland and East Germany. China also had a planned economy. By the end of the century, many countries had introduced market economies. North Korea and Cuba are countries that still have a planned economy.

The market economy

In this type of economy, private individuals make the majority of the decisions about what to produce. People are free to set up in business to produce what they wish. The people who set up in business are motivated, to an extent, by profits. They decide what to do by judging what will sell. Sometimes, market research is used to help them to make this judgement. Sometimes, business people rely on their 'business instinct.' Businesses also attempt to create a demand for their product through promotional activities. What is happening in a market will also be a signal about what people want to buy. If the price of a product is rising, it may be because the demand for that product is increasing.

The job of the Government in the market economy is very small. Its main responsibility will be to maintain law and order and to provide armed forces to protect against invasion by a foreign power. The Philippines is an example of a market economy.

Advantages of planned economies
The Government controls production to make sure that essential goods and services are produced.
The Government can control the distribution of the goods and service made so that everyone has a reasonable standard of living.
Disadvantages of planned economies
It is difficult for officials to decide what goods and services will be needed.
Production may be inefficient – managers and workers have little incentive because there is no profit motive.
Shortages of goods can occur and this leads to the development of a black market.
There may be no choice for the consumer.

Table 7.1 Advantages and disadvantages of planned economies

Advantages of market economies
What is produced is decided by the consumers and producers who buy the products.
The profit motive encourages enterprise and efficiency.
Competition exists between producers – this should lead to more choice and cheaper prices.
Disadvantages of market economies
Producers will only produce those goods that make them a profit – they may not produce some goods and services for poor people or that benefit society as a whole.
There may be great inequalities of income.
Firms, motivated by private profit, may ignore social costs of production.

Table 7.2 Advantages and disadvantages of market economies

ACTIVITY 1

Tellmart is an American national supermarket chain. It is said that America is an example of a market economy.

(a) Explain what is meant by the term 'market economy'.

(b) Explain **one** advantage and **one** disadvantage of a market economy to the consumer.

(Adapted from OCR Business Studies, Question 2, Business and Change Higher Tier Paper, 2000.)

The mixed economy

In this type of economy, private sector businesses will provide some goods and services while the Government will organise the provision of others through the public sector. Government provides public and merit goods. It also manages the economy. In practice, most countries are mixed economies. The UK and France are mixed economies. In theory, mixed economies bring the advantages of planned and mixed economies into the same economy.

ACTIVITY 2

Write an explanation of the advantages of having a mixed economy.

Government and the mixed economy

Public and merit goods

There are two types of goods and services that governments may provide:

- **Public goods** are those that cannot be divided up and provided only for people willing to pay for them – street lighting is an example.

ACTIVITY 3

There are state and private schools in the UK.

Read the article and answer the questions that follow.

'Most children in the United Kingdom are educated in state schools. These schools are usually run by the local council. Some children are educated in private schools. The parents pay a fee to have them educated. The fee varies depending on the whether the school is a boarding or day school and the reputation of the school.'

(a) Is education a public or a merit good? Give reasons for your answer.

(b) Why do you think that some parents are willing to pay for their children's education?

(c) Do you think that private schools should be allowed to exist as well as state schools? Prepare your arguments and then have a group discussion. Try to come to an agreement with the rest of the group.

- **Merit goods** are those that it is thought people should consume, both for their own good and for the benefit of society. Health care is a merit good. The economy needs a supply of healthy workers.

Public and merit goods are usually provided by public sector organisations. Local councils provide street lighting: the National Health Service provides many of the medical services. However, private firms will also sell goods and services to the Government so that it can provide public and merit goods. For example, private firms make and sell drugs to the health service.

Managing the economy

The Government has four main economic objectives:

Economic objective	Explanation – why it is a Government objective	Possible causes	Possible solutions
Reduce unemployment	• Unemployment costs money – the Government pays out welfare benefits to the unemployed. • Unemployment is also a problem for businesses – if people are out of work, they will have less money to spend on goods and services.	1. Demand for goods and services in the economy is low. 2. British firms are not competitive because of high prices, low quality or they are not producing products customers want.	1. Raise demand. 2. Encourage efficiency and innovation.
High economic growth – the rise in the amount produced in a country	• This means higher living standards for people, but: • Environmental problems may result – pollution, congestion etc.	1. High demand means that firms can increase production. 2. British firms are competitive internationally.	1. Raise demand. 2. Encourage efficiency and innovation.
Control of inflation – the rise in general prices	• Rising costs and higher prices make it difficult for British firms to compete. • People on fixed incomes become worse off.	1. Demand for goods in the economy is too high. 2. Production costs are rising – wages rising too fast, cost of imported materials increasing.	1. Reduce demand. 2. Reduce the power of the workers – weaken the unions, let unemployment rise.
Avoid balance of payments poblems – the record of spending on imports and income from exports	• If spending is greater than income, the country may go into debt.	1. Demand is too high, leading to high spending on exports. 2. British firms are not competitive.	1. Reduce demand. 2. Encourage efficiency and innovation. Protect British firms from foreign competition.

Table 7.3 The economic objectives of Government

ACTIVITY 4

Explain why the following statements may be true:
(a) Full employment is good for businesses.
(b) Economic growth is needed to help to reduce unemployment.
(c) Inflation can cause unemployment.
(d) If the balance of payments gets worse, unemployment may rise.

Explain the following:
(a) A rise in demand in an economy will help to reduce unemployment
(b) A rise in demand in an economy may cause inflation and a balance of payments problem.
(c) If British firms can become more competitive, unemployment will fall.
(d) If British firms can become more competitive, the balance of payments will improve.

Fiscal and interest rate policies

Fiscal policy

Fiscal policy is the Government's policy on spending and taxes. The Government spends money on services such as education, health and defence. There are two kinds of taxes:

Direct taxes. These are taxes on income and capital. Three important direct taxes are:

- *Income tax* – this is tax on income above a tax-free level of earnings. Most people pay income tax through the Pay As You Earn (PAYE) scheme. The employer calculates the tax to be paid and deducts it from the wage or salary of the worker to pass on to the Inland Revenue. Whilst this saves the individual time and effort calculating how much to pay, it costs the business to administer it.
- *Corporation tax* – the tax that companies pay on their profits.
- *Uniform Business Rate* – this tax is paid to the local council to pay for services.

Indirect taxes. These are taxes on spending. Two main indirect taxes in the UK are:

- *VAT (value added tax)* – this is paid by producers on the value they add to what they produce. Many businesses complain that calculating how much they must pay is time-consuming and expensive. The overall effect is to raise the cost of products – the final consumer often pays all the tax. This raises the price that is charged which can reduce demand.
- *Excise duties.* These are special taxes on goods like petrol, alcohol and cigarettes.

Interest rate policy

The Bank of England is now responsible for deciding the interest rate. It must raise interest rates if inflation is, or is likely to become, a problem. It will lower interest rates if there are no inflationary problems – this will then encourage economic growth and a fall in unemployment.

The Bank of England sets the interest rate.

Changing the level of demand in an economy

The Government may wish to raise or lower the level of demand in the economy. This will depend on the problem that it has to deal with. To encourage economic growth and reduce unemployment, the government will want to raise demand. To control inflation and avoid a balance of payments problem, the Government will need to reduce demand.

Raising demand	How it works
Fiscal policy	1. Reduce direct taxes – this leaves people and businesses with more money to spend from their income. Spending on consumer goods and spending by firms on investment should increase. 2. Reduce indirect taxes – this makes goods and services cheaper. 3. Increase government spending – the Government increases its own demand for goods and services such as education and health.
Interest rate policy	Reduce the interest rate. This increases spending because: 1. Lower interest rates mean it is cheaper for consumers and businesses to borrow money. 2. People and firms that already have loans such as mortgages will pay less in interest. They can use the money they save to buy other goods and services.

Table 7.4 Demand management – how it works

ACTIVITY 5

(a) To reduce demand, what should happen to (i) direct taxes (ii) indirect taxes and (iii) the interest rate? Explain your answer in each case.
(b) If the interest rate and taxes are reduced, why might this lead to inflation? What might happen to the balance of payments?

ACTIVITY 6

(a) Who will benefit most from cuts in taxes on income – the rich or the poor? Explain your answer.
(b) Who will suffer most from cuts in social security benefits – the rich or the poor? Explain your answer.
(c) If supply side policies are successful in helping British firms to compete and to expand how might this benefit the poorer people in the country?

Encouraging efficiency and innovation

Policies that are designed to encourage efficiency and innovation are known as **supply side** policies. The table shows some of the policies that governments can use:

Policy	How it can work
Cuts in direct taxes	1. For workers this means that their net or take-home pay increases. This may encourage them to work harder because they will keep more of the money that they earn. 2. Firms will keep more of the profits they earn. This encourages enterprise. They may re-invest the extra profits.
Reducing social security payments for the unemployed	1. This encourages people to work, because they will be less well off being unemployed.
Grants	1. Giving grants to firms will help them to pay for investments in new premises and equipment that will help them to produce more efficiently. 2. Grants can also encourage inward investment – foreign firms setting up in business in the United Kingdom.
Tax relief on new investment	1. This encourages firms to spend money on investment because they will pay less tax by doing so.
Education and training	1. These will provide firms with the skilled labour that they need in order to develop.
Improving the infrastructure	1. Building new roads and railways helps to make transport more efficient. 2. Building new factories and offering them at reasonable rents makes it easier for firms to start up or to expand.

Table 7.5 Supply side policies – how they work

EXAM Practice Questions

1. Jason Lee works for Colliers plc, which makes and sells chocolates in the town of Marston. His friend, Alison Stone, works for the Education Department of Marston Borough Council.
   (a) Using the evidence above, explain why Marston is an example of a mixed economy. (2 marks)
   (b) State **two** appropriate objectives for Colliers plc and **two** appropriate objectives for the Education Department.

(Adapted from OCR Business Studies, Question 1, Higher Tier Core Paper, June 2000.)

2. The pie charts below show the central and local government revenues collected from people and businesses in Marston in 1982 and 1990.
   (a) How has the value of revenue generated from income tax in 1990 changed in comparison with that generated in 1982? (4 marks)
   (b) From the taxes named in the pie charts, choose two which a sole trader business may have to pay. Explain how the payments might affect the business.

(Adapted from OCR Business Studies, Question 5, Higher Tier Core Paper, June 1996.)

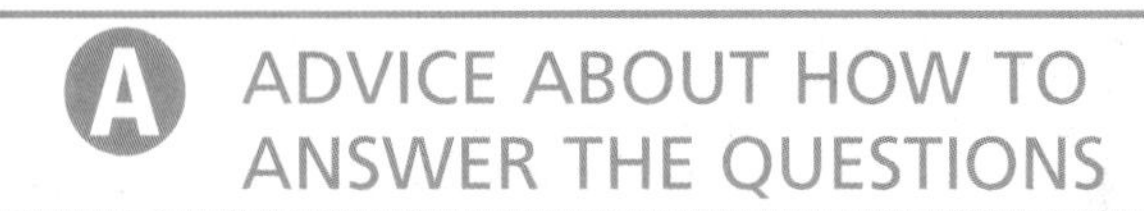

ADVICE ABOUT HOW TO ANSWER THE QUESTIONS

Question 1 requires you to use your knowledge of the definition of a mixed economy and then to draw on the evidence you are given in the stem to the question to say why Marston is an example of a mixed economy.

In Question 2 (a) you need to perform some calculations in order to compare how much was raised from income tax in each of the years. Note that the figures you are given on the pie charts are percentages of a total. Note also that the total amount of revenue from the different types of taxes changes from one year to the next.

Question 2 (b) requires you to use your knowledge of the taxes that business must pay. A sole trader will have to pay several of the taxes named, but not all of them. Choose two of these. You can write about the effect that the each tax might have on demand and on the costs and profits of the business. You could also write about how reductions in profits might reduce the amount of money for investment and expansion.

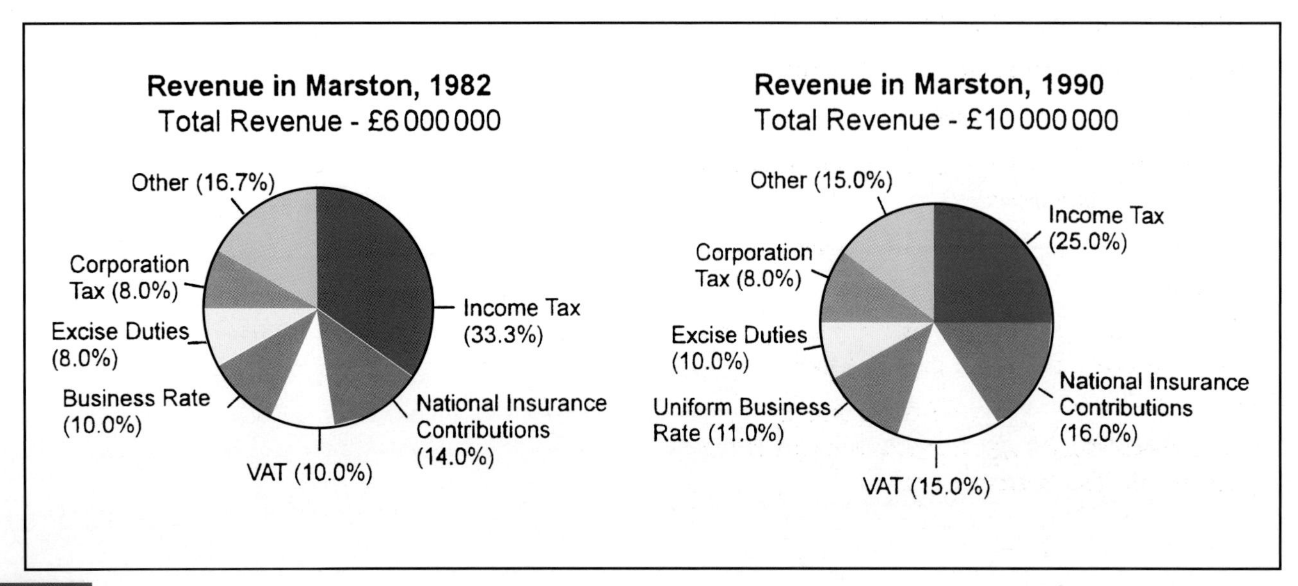

KEY TERMS

Economic system *The way in which a country decides what will be produced.*

Planned economy *An economic system in which the Government decides what will be produced.*

Market economy *An economic system in which producers and consumers are free to produce and consume as they wish. The market signals the demands of consumers and changes in demand.*

Mixed economy *An economic system in which there is both a private and a public sector. The Government also tries to manage the economy in the interests of the people.*

Public goods *Goods that are provided for the benefit of everyone in society. They cannot be provided for some people and not for others.*

Merit goods *Goods that benefit both the individual and society. It is desirable that everybody should consume these.*

Fiscal policy *The Government's policy about taxes and government spending.*

Interest rate policy *Now operated by the Bank of England. The interest rate may be raised or lowered.*

Supply Side Policies *Policies used by the government to increase the efficiency of businesses and increase the amount that they produce.*

Direct taxes *Taxes on income and on capital.*

Indirect taxes *Taxes on spending.*

Excise Duties *Additional taxes on some goods, eg petrol, tobacco and alcohol.*

Corporation Tax *The tax that companies pay on their profits.*

Uniform Business Rate *The tax that businesses pay to the local authority on their premises.*

Value Added Tax (VAT) *The tax that businesses add to goods and services. It is usually added to the price that the final customer pays.*

Unemployment *The number of people who claim welfare benefits because they are out of work.*

Inflation *The general rise in the prices of goods.*

Economic Growth *The increase in the amount of goods and services produced by all the firms in the economy.*

Balance of Payments *A record of the spending on imports and income from exports.*

Key Skills

Activity 3 provides an opportunity for a discussion (C2.1b) about private and public education. You should prepare for the discussion by writing down the points that you want to make. Try to guess what those with an opposing viewpoint will want to say so that you can argue back.

Unit 7.2 Types of market

Would you like to fly to the South of France for a weekend or a short break? A few years ago this was unthinkable for the vast majority of people. Nowadays a number of airlines are offering cheap flights to destinations in Europe, making short trips abroad affordable to many more people. One of the pioneers of cheap flight has been Stelios, the founder of EasyJet. Existing airlines, like British Airways, charged high prices for flights within Europe. None of the major airlines was prepared to reduce its prices. If they did, their competitors would reduce their prices also. All the airlines would reduce their profits because of the lower price. They preferred to compete with each other in terms of routes, quality of service and promotional activity, mainly advertising, rather than in terms of price.

Stelios believed that there would be a demand for cheaper flights. The secret was to make it profitable to provide these by reducing the costs as well as prices. This was achieved in several ways:

- People were encouraged to book directly, using the Internet. This saved money because travel agents were not involved, nor did EasyJet have to employ large numbers of staff to handle bookings.
- A 'no frills' service was offered. Passengers were not provided with a free meal during flights. Instead, they could buy snacks on the plane if they wanted to.
- EasyJet flew from airports that were not very busy and where landing fees were cheaper.
- Planes stayed only for a minimum period of time at an airport, leading to further savings on airport fees.

The rest, as they say, is history. EasyJet has grown. Other cut-price airlines have also done well. Some of the major airlines have introduced their own cut-price subsidiaries. The market for air travel has been changed. It has become more competitive. There are now more firms than before and price competition is now more important.

Stelios, the owner of EasyJet, helped to increase competition for air passengers.

Market forms

There are three main forms of markets – competition, oligopoly and monopoly. They differ in the number of firms that there are in the market and the kind of competition, if any, that takes place. Table 7.6 summarises features of each.

EasyJet and market forms

What EasyJet and the other cut-price airlines had done was to change the form of the market for air travel in Europe. Before they came into existence the market was an oligopoly. The main features were:

- There were a few large firms responsible for most of the sales.
- There was very little competition between airlines in terms of the price that they charged.
- The airlines used non-price competition – competing on routes, quality of service and promotions.

After the 'no frills' airlines entered the market, it became more competitive.

- There were more firms in the market.
- The airlines began to compete with each other on price.
- There was still competition using advertising.

FEATURE	COMPETITION	OLIGOPOLY	MONOPOLY
Number of firms	Many buyers (and many sellers).	A few firms are responsible for most of the sales in a market	One producer sells at least 25% of total market sales.
Products	All firms provide very similar products.	Different products in terms of design: – design – quality – after-sales service.	One main product available.
Forms of competition	• Price • Advertising	• Usually no price competition. • Non-price competition in the form of: – advertising – branding – different products – where the product is sold	No real competition – prices are often higher than they would be if there was competition.
Other features	Businesses are often small.	• Firms may make agreements with each about the price to charge. • Price leadership – one firm sets the price, others follow the lead.	Competition may be prevented by: – patents – economies of scale – high spending on marketing – high set-up and operating costs – restrictive practices.

Table 7.6 Features of different markets

ACTIVITY 1

Case study 1

Read the following case studies. Decide what kind of market each of the case studies is. Write down the features of each that help you decide what kind of market it is.

Motorway service station.

The *Daily Telegraph* carried an article describing the market for motorway services:

'The industry is dominated by Granada, which has a 39% share of the overall trade, operating 42 service stations. Welcome Break runs 22 service stations and enjoys more than 30% of the market. Road Chef, with about 17, is the third largest, while fewer than half a dozen stations are in independent ownership.

'An investigation by The Telegraph found that the cost of food and refreshments at the two main company's restaurants was often twice as much as at nearby independent cafes. In one example, in Yorkshire, the difference was even greater. The Heartshead Moor Welcome Break station on the M62 between Leeds and Halifax charges £6.99 for a full English breakfast. At the Sizzling Sausage Café in Leeds the same breakfast could be bought for £2.95.

'The food critic, Egon Ronay described motorway meals as typically "mass produced unspeakable rubbish."

The industry argues that part of the problem is the high operating costs and 24-hour opening.'

(*Telegraph*, 23 July 2000)

Case study 2

Fruit and vegetable wholesale market.

The Wholesale Fruit and Vegetable Market in Liverpool opens at around 4 am. The wholesalers bring their goods and set up stall. Grocers, mainly owners of small shops, come to the market to buy stock. The fruit and vegetables on offer vary little from stall to stall. Buyers go from stall to stall looking for the best prices.

Case study 3

The main petrol retailers in Britain are BP, Esso, Shell and Texaco. There are some independents but none of them match these firms for sales. Many of the garages that sell petrol for the large retailers are franchises. They are strictly controlled in terms of the price that they can charge for petrol. In practice, the price charged by one petrol station will be the same as that charged by others owned or controlled by the big companies. One of the main ways in which they compete with each other is in terms of sites. The best sites for petrol stations are on the main trunk roads. The retailers also compete with each other by offering loyalty cards – points collected on these can lead to money off a future purchase or to free goods.

Garage on a busy trunk road.

ACTIVITY 2

Draw a table with six columns like the one below.

Put the following statements under the correct heading. NB Some statements may appear under more than one heading.

- Consumers may benefit from lower prices because they can shop around to find the best deal.
- There is little or no choice of goods.
- Prices may be high – the seller knows that customers have no alternative.
- A wide range of goods with different features may be available.
- A firm may be able to get economies of scale and may be able to charge lower prices than if competition existed.
- Firms must be efficient to survive, meaning costs and prices must be low.
- A firm does not need to be efficient to survive – costs and prices may be high.
- Producers may collude with each other to fix a high price.
- Prices may be high to cover spending on advertising.

Different forms of market – advantages and disadvantages to the consumer

Advantages of competition	Disadvantages of competition	Advantages of oligopoly	Disadvantages of oligopoly	Advantages of monopoly	Disadvantages of monopoly

Market shares

Information is collected about the share of a market that businesses have. To calculate the share of a market that one business has, its sales are expressed as a percentage of the total market sales. Suppose that the total sales in the market for gloves are worth £50m per year. A producer of gloves, 'Handy Gloves', has total sales of £10m in that year. The calculation for its share of the market is:

$$\frac{\text{Sales of the business}}{\text{Total sales in the market}} \times \frac{100}{1} = \text{Market share}$$

$$\frac{£10\text{m}}{£50\text{m}} \times \frac{100}{1} = 20\%$$

This kind of information is often presented using a pie chart. The pie chart opposite shows the share of market that Handy Gloves has.

Market for gloves = Total sales = £50m

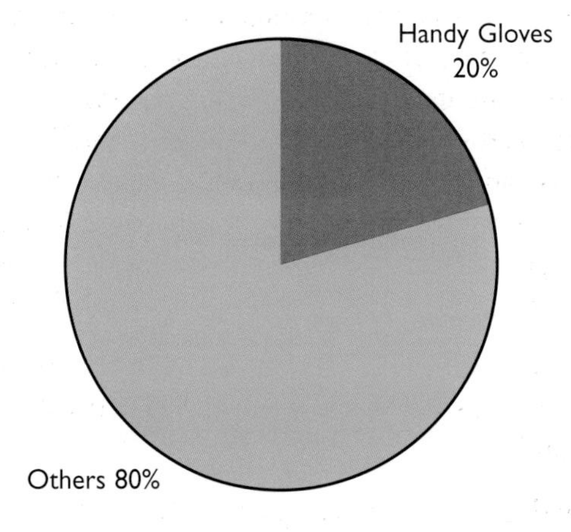

ACTIVITY 3 

Using the information provided, draw a pie chart to show the share of the market of each of the firms. This can be done on a computer by entering the data into a spreadsheet and then creating a chart from it.

Total market sales = £100

Firm A – £25m

Firm B – £10m

Firm C – £40m

Firm D – £15m

Others – £10m

Market shares and market forms

Information about market shares can be used to decide what kind of market exists.

Monopoly – A monopoly exists when a business has a market share of at least 25%. Any firm having 25% or more of the market is called a monopolist.

Oligopoly – An oligopoly exists when a few firms are responsible for a large percentage of total market share.

Competition – Competition exists when there are many firms all with a small share of the market.

Government and competition

Competition has advantages – prices are often lower and there may be more choice of goods for customers. Monopoly can have disadvantages. Prices may be high and there may not be much

ACTIVITY 4

The pie charts show market shares for two different markets.

Motorway services market – 2000

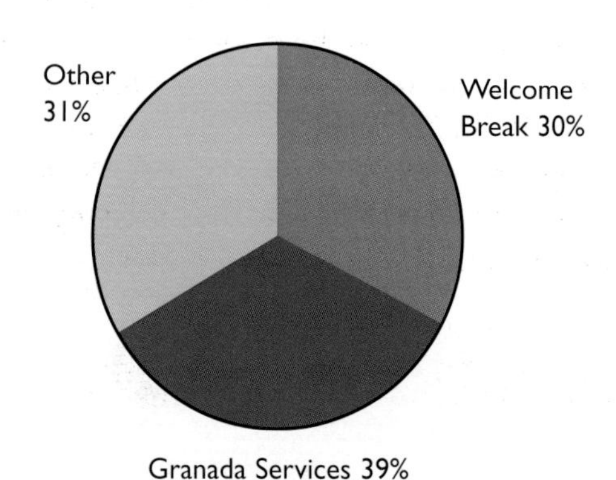

Source: Adapted from The Daily Telegraph, *23 July 2000*

UK car market – January to October 2000

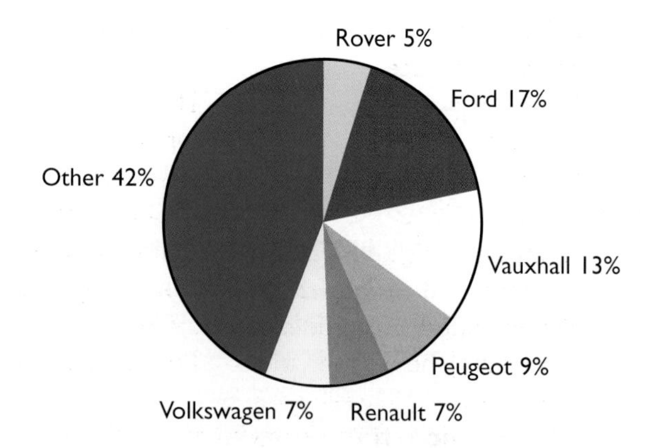

Source: Adapted from The Guardian, *October 2000*

(a) State which of the markets is a monopoly. Using your knowledge of the features of monopoly, what disadvantages might the consumer be faced with in this market?

(b) State which of the markets is an oligopoly. How would you expect the firms to compete with each other?

choice for customers. However, monopolies may not all be bad. Often they are large firms that benefit from economies of scale. The lower costs of production can mean that the monopolist is able to charge a lower price than would be charged if there were a lot of small firms in competition with each other.

In general, government in the UK has encouraged competition. However, governments have also taken the view that monopolies are not always bad. Monopolies are allowed to remain in existence if they are thought to be in the public interest.

To protect the consumer from businesses that prevent free competition, governments have passed laws. The following are examples of anti-competitive activities that it is illegal for businesses to do:

- firms agree to fix prices
- firms agree to limit the supply of goods so that the price is high
- firms agree which goods they will supply to particular businesses
- charging different prices to different customers without good reason
- cutting off supplies to a firm to force it out of business.

A number of organisations exist to deal with anti-competitive practices.

- **The Office of Fair Trading.** This is responsible for encouraging competition. If firms appear to be preventing competition, the Director-General of Fair Trading can order them to change what they do. If the Director is concerned about monopolies or mergers or the activities of the utilities (gas, water, electricity), he or she can ask the Competition Commission to investigate.
- **The Public Utility Regulators.** OFWAT (the Office of Water Services) and OFTEL (Office of Telecommunications Services) are examples of these. Their job is to make sure that the utilities charge fair prices.
- **The Competition Commission.** The Commission has two jobs. First, it investigates and reports on monopolies and mergers and the activities of the utilities. Second, it will hear appeals made by firms against decisions made by the Director-General of Fair Trading and the Public Utility Regulators.
- **The Secretary of State for Trade and Industry.** This will be a senior member of the Government. The Secretary of State can break up monopolies if he/she thinks they are against the public interest. He or she can also stop mergers taking place.
- **The European Union.** The EU also has laws on competition that businesses in member countries must obey.

Case study 1

In 2000, the Office of Fair Trading investigated complaints against Granada and Welcome Break about the prices they charge and the poor quality of their services. The Director-General was considering whether he should break up the two chains so that there is more competition.

Case study 2

The Government 'ordered electrical manufacturers to stop setting prices for their products and banned them from refusing to supply stores that offer discounts. The ruling also applies to video cassette recorders, hi-fi systems, camcorders, tumble driers, dishwashers and freezers. ... prices could fall by as much as a quarter'. (*Daily Telegraph*, 21 May 1998). The order was made after an investigation by the Monopolies and Mergers Commission (now replaced by the Competition Commission).

ACTIVITY 5

Use the Internet to research examples of anti-competitive practices and the work of the organisations that are responsible for competition in the UK. Useful websites are those for newspapers like the *Guardian* and the *Telegraph*, and organisations like the Department of Trade and Industry and the Office of Fair Trading.

Write a short report about the case that you have researched.

EXAM Practice Questions

1. Steptoe Ltd has a monopoly in the specialist footwear market.
   (a) What is meant by a monopoly? (2 marks)
   (b) Why should the Government control monopolies? (6 marks)

(Adapted from OCR Business Studies, Question 2, Business and Change Option Paper, Foundation Tier, June, 1998)

2. The ice-cream industry is an example of an oligopoly.
   (a) What does the term 'oligopoly' mean? (2 marks)
   (b) Why might competition between ice-cream manufacturers be good for customers? (2 marks)

(Adapted from OCR Business Studies, Question 2, Business and Change Option Paper, 1997.)

ADVICE ABOUT ANSWERING THE QUESTIONS

The first parts of both questions require clear definitions of terms. The answer to Part (b) of question 1 is that government should control monopolies to stop their disadvantages. You need to explain these possible disadvantages. In Part (b) of question 2, you need to apply the possible advantages of competition to the ice-cream market.

EXAMINATION SUMMARY TIPS

- Businesses operate in markets.
- There are three main forms of markets – competition, monopoly and oligopoly.
- The form of market influences the way that firms in the market behave.
- Different forms of market have different advantages and disadvantages.
- Government controls markets so that they work in the interest of the public.

KEY TERMS

Competition *A market in which there are a large number of sellers, none of which has a share of the market large enough to give them influence over the market.*

Oligopoly *A market dominated by a few firms.*

Monopoly *A market dominated by one seller.*

Monopolist *A firm that accounts for at least 25% of the sales in a market.*

Market share *The percentage of the total sales in a market accounted for by a firm.*

Product differentiation *Products are made to be different, or to appear to be different, in some way.*

Collusion *When firms make agreements to fix prices or restrict supply.*

Price leadership *When the dominant firm in a market sets a price and other firms set the same or similar price.*

Key Skills

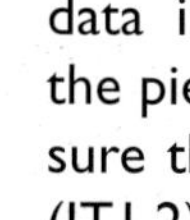

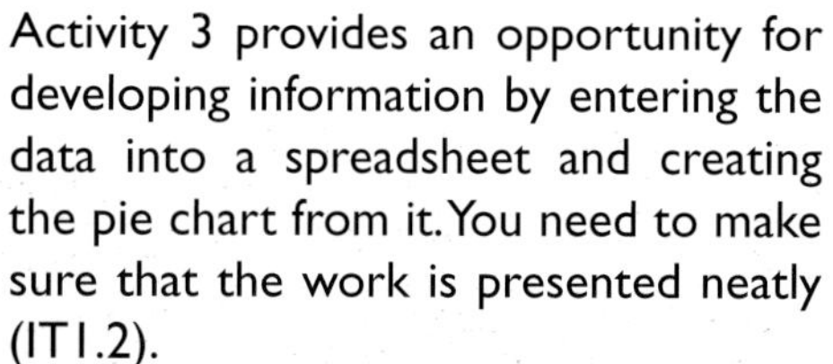

Activity 3 provides an opportunity for developing information by entering the data into a spreadsheet and creating the pie chart from it. You need to make sure that the work is presented neatly (IT1.2).

Activity 5 provides an opportunity to search for information using the Internet sites. You need to bring information that you find into a report. For Level 2, you need to combine different kinds of information, for example text and graphs, into your report. Make sure that the layout is consistent. Print off documents as you develop the report – for example, print off information you download from a website and include this in your portfolio. Your final report should also be included in the portfolio.

Unit 7.3 Location of business

Why is location important?

The decision where to locate a business is one of the most important decisions a business takes. Make the right decision, and the business may flourish and become very successful. Make the wrong decision, and the business may find it very difficult to succeed.

The wrong way to decide where to locate.

The right way to decide where to locate.

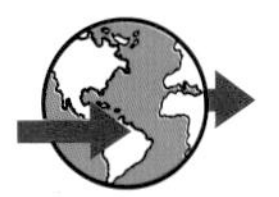

The factors affecting the location of business

There are a large number of factors which can have an influence on the location of business activity. It is rarely one factor which affects the decision to locate in a particular area but often a combination of factors.

Some of the location factors covered in this Unit will have little or no influence on the location decision which a particular business makes, whilst others will have a significant influence. Much will depend on the type of business activity. For instance, a bakery producing bread and cakes will usually need to be located near to the market it is serving. It can be difficult to transport fresh cream cakes long distances.

Fresh cream cakes do not travel well in warm weather.

On the other hand, a company producing clothing will probably need good access to the road network so that it can deliver its products to its customers who may be located all over the country.

Location factor	Explanation	Example
Availability of and access to raw materials	The costs of transporting some raw materials to a factory for processing can be very high. Businesses which depend on a particular raw material may choose to locate near to where it is available to help reduce transportation costs.	The United Kingdom imports large quantities of crude oil from the Middle East for processing in oil refineries. The crude oil is brought to the UK by super tanker. Oil refineries, like the one at Milford Haven in Wales, are located near to sea ports capable of handling very large ships because it is expensive to transport large quantities of oil inland.
The cost of the location	This is a very important consideration. The price of land and/or buildings can vary significantly in different areas of the United Kingdom. The amount of work needed to prepare the site will also be a factor. The cost of the location will have to be paid for through the prices charged for the goods or services supplied to the customer. An expensive location may result in high prices for finished goods or services.	Land in the south-east of England tends to be a much more expensive location than mid-Wales or the north of Scotland. One reason may be the fact that the south-east of England has a high-density population and land is in short supply. However, demand for locations in the south-east of England is much higher. The reason for this may be because of closeness to the Channel Tunnel.
Access to and nearness to markets	Some businesses like or need to be near to the markets which they serve. This mainly affects service industries as people are often not prepared to travel long distances to obtain the things they need.	Supermarkets are located near to the centres of population which they serve. How many of you live within three miles of a reasonably large supermarket?
Availability of labour	The level of unemployment can vary from region to region of the UK. In rural areas or where traditional industries such as coal mining, shipbuilding and textiles are in decline the availability of labour is usually good. In other areas, workers with particular skills might be in short supply. This has a significant effect on the decision where to locate as businesses will need to recruit labour locally.	Devon and Cornwall usually have a plentiful supply of labour during the winter. This is known as seasonal unemployment. In the summer, when the holiday season is in full swing, there can be shortages of labour as the demand for workers is high.

Table 7.7 The main factors affecting location of a business

Location factor	Explanation	Example
Climate and physical geography	Some areas of the country may be more suited to particular types of business activities than others. The location of agricultural activities is influenced by both climate and physical geography. Large manufacturing facilities like steel works need reasonably flat sites.	When did you see a banana plantation in the United Kingdom? Northern Scotland tends to be hilly and the land is not suited to growing cereals whereas East Anglia is much flatter and is suited to growing cereal crops.
Transport and infrastructure	Some areas of the country are better served by motorways, main roads and railways than other areas. The ease with which businesses can gain access to the transport system will have a significant influence on where to locate the business. This is particularly important if goods have to be moved great distances to the market. Some business may also depend on other local businesses to provide goods and services.	Areas with a low density of population, eg mid-Wales, are not well served by motorways and railways. Car manufacturing in the West Midlands is at the centre of the UK's motoring network. It has attracted many other businesses which make component parts for the car industry.
Tradition	Well-established businesses or industries are often located in particular areas of the country, for no obvious reason. Over time the business or industry may become one of the main employers in a particular area. Many of these traditional industries now no longer employ as many people as they once did.	Although shoes are manufactured at many places throughout the United Kingdom, Northampton was recognised as the centre of the UK's shoe industry. The nickname of the local football team – Northampton Town – is 'The Cobblers', reflecting the town's close association with the boot and shoe industry.
Type or nature of the product or service	Some products or services are very specialised and can only be undertaken in certain locations. Businesses providing these services may have relatively little choice over the choice of location.	Shipbuilding is always to be found in coastal or river locations because of the need to access the sea when launching the finished product.
Government policy	This is sometimes referred to as regional policy as it usually affects particular areas or regions of the country. The Government makes available a number of special incentives to encourage industry to locate and develop in areas which have high rates of unemployment. Further information is given below.	Traditional industries such as coal mining, steel, textiles and shipbuilding are in decline. These industries used to employ large numbers of workers. Areas of the country which once relied on these industries to provide employment now often have higher than average levels of unemployment.

Table 7.7 The main factors affecting location of a business continued

ACTIVITY 1

1. Draw a sketch map for an out-of-town retail park near to where you live or with which you are familiar. Mark on the map the main roads and nearby centres of population.
2. Explain the reasons why so many retail parks are being developed on the edge of towns and cities.
3. Explain the advantages and disadvantages of locating shops in a town or city centre.

Enterprise zones

These are small special areas which are centred on areas of particularly high unemployment or where a major industry such as coal mining or steel manufacture has gone into decline. Enterprise zones are set up to encourage investment which creates employment for the local workforce. This may be business parks or manufacturing facilities. Enterprise zones are to be found throughout the United Kingdom.

Each enterprise zone comprises a number of different sites in an area and is usually managed by a local council. Businesses locating to or developing in an enterprise zone may benefit from some of the following:

- simplified planning requirements
- tax allowances on capital expenditure
- exemption from paying **Uniform Business Rates**
- other assistance with finance or re-training of workers
- new or improved access roads.

The Government grants an area enterprise status for a period of ten years with the intention of encouraging private sector business activity to develop and provide employment opportunities in the hope of making the area more prosperous.

Assisted areas

Some areas of the country which are thought likely to benefit from encouraging new businesses to locate or develop there are designated assisted area status. These areas are much larger in size than enterprise zones.

Assisted area status is usually granted to:

- areas suffering from high rates of unemployment
- rural areas
- former coalfields.

Business locating to or expanding in an assisted area can qualify for grants which are used to improve employment opportunities by investing in new factories or equipment. Grants, however, are not payable for transferring jobs from one part of the country to another.

Regional Development Agencies

These have been established throughout England and have the responsibility of co-ordinating investment in a region in order to:

- improves people's skills
- promote economic development
- undertake social and physical regeneration
- advise on the availability of enterprise grants.

The Toyota car factory in the Midlands

Europe is the largest car market in the world. When the Toyota Car Company of Japan decided that it wanted to build a new factory somewhere in Europe it had in mind a number of requirements regarding the location of the factory. The main things which the company wanted from its new location were:

- a factory located close to the market it was supplying
- a flat greenfield site
- room to expand the factory in future years
- easy and quick access to main to roads and motorways
- a skilled local labour force which had experience of working in the engineering industry.

A site about the size of 750 football pitches, at Burnaston on the outskirts of Derby was eventually chosen because it met these requirements. By 2000, over 2 500 workers were employed at the site which is adjacent to two main roads, providing good communications with the markets which the company supplies. Since locating there, the company has subsequently extended the factory and put in a second production line and increased its investment to over £1 billion.

Over 80% of the cars produced at the factory are exported to mainland Europe and other markets.

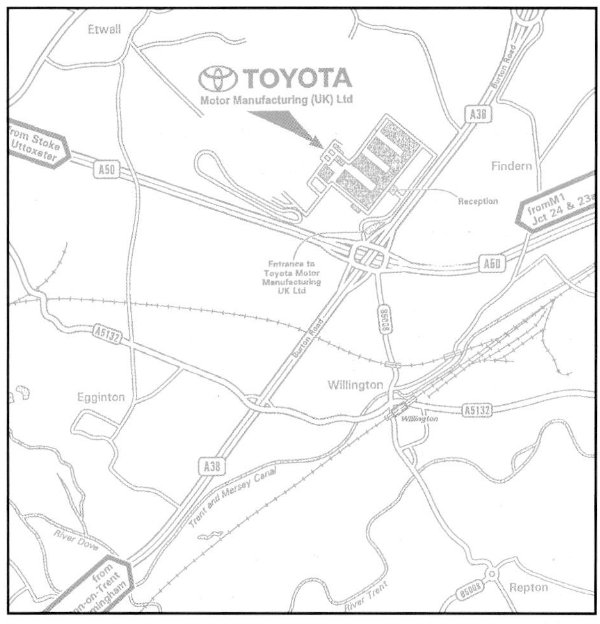

The location of the Toyota car factory in the Midlands, showing the good communication links.

ACTIVITY 2

This Activity is based on a question which appeared in an OCR examination paper. The Activity is designed to make you think about the factors which might affect the location of a garage business in the imaginary town of Marston.

Read the information in conjunction with the map of Marston and use your knowledge of the factors which affect the location of a business to answer the questions which follow.

1. State and explain two advantages of locating the garage business at Site A.
2. State and explain two disadvantages of locating the garage business at Site B.
3. Explain what other information John might need before making a final decision on the location of his garage business.
4. Explain how John's business might benefit if the town of Marston grows in size.
5. Recommend to John a location for the garage business.
6. Produce a leaflet for distribution to houses in Marston advertising the new garage. Do not forget to include a location map and information on some of the services which John's garage might provide. You may like to use your IT skills to help you do this.

John Taylor is thinking of opening a new garage business in Marston. He intends to sell petrol, provide car maintenance and fit car alarms. He is considering two possible sites for the location of the garage. They are marked A and B on the map below. Both sites have suitable premises for the business he is considering opening.

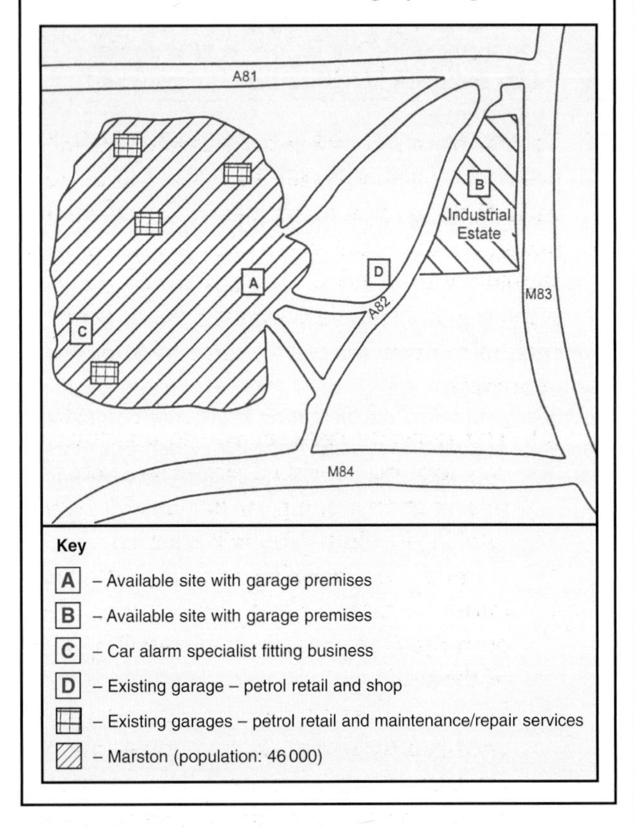

EXAM Practice Questions

1. Nicole and Colin decided to open their sandwich business by purchasing new premises.

   Below are two factors Nicole and Colin should take into consideration when deciding on their choice of location.

   COMPETITION WEALTH OF AREA

   Explain how each factor might affect their decision. (4 marks)

(Adapted from OCR Business Studies, Q1, Higher Tier Business & Change Option paper, June 2000.)

2. Dovetail, a medium-sized furniture manufacturer and retailer, has recently moved premises, locating to a number of large cities.
   (a) What benefit would locating near to large cities bring to Dovetail Ltd? (3 marks)

(b) Another factor which attracted the business to some locations is that they are in an enterprise zone. Explain one advantage and one disadvantage of locating in an enterprise zone. (4 marks)

(Adapted from OCR Business Studies, Q2, Higher Tier Business & Change Option paper, June 1998.)

ADVICE ON HOW TO ANSWER THE QUESTION

1. To answer this question successfully you will need to provide a detailed explanation of how each of the two factors listed in the question has an effect on the location of a business. You should try to develop your answer by providing an example which illustrates **why** each of the two factors affecting location is important.
2. (a) This question requires you to consider why locating near to a large city is of relevance to a company manufacturing and retailing furniture. You will need to consider whether there are any different locational factors which are likely to affect both the manufacturing and retailing sides of the business.

   (b) Before you can answer this question you will need to be certain that you know what an enterprise zone is. The question requires you to provide an advantage and a disadvantage for a company like Dovetail Ltd of locating business activity in an enterprise zone. The use of examples will help to improve your answer so that you gain all 4 marks.

KEY TERMS

Greenfield site *Industrial or commercial development in an area which has previously not been built on.*

Brownfield site *Industrial or commercial development which was previously derelict or occupied by another industrial activity.*

Enterprise zone *A relatively small area with high rates of unemployment which is given special help by the Government to attract new business activity.*

Assisted Area *A larger geographical area with above average unemployment to which the Government encourages business to locate by offering financial and other benefits.*

Uniform Business Rate *A type of tax paid by businesses to cover the cost of providing local services.*

Capital expenditure *Expenditure on fixed assets such as equipment or buildings.*

Infrastructure *The name given to basic services needed by business for it to operate effectively. Such things as roads, power supplies, telephones and water supplies would be included under this heading.*

Grants *Payment of money for a specific purpose which does not usually have to be paid back. Grants may be available from the EU, central government or local authorities to help businesses improve employment opportunities.*

Enterprise grants *Financial assistance to supplement loans from other sources. The enterprise grant is available to businesses in areas with higher than average unemployment, to help support business activities which might not take place without the support of the grant.*

EXAMINATION SUMMARY TIPS

- Learn the factors which affect the location of business and be prepared to give relevant examples to illustrate each factor.
- Make sure that you are able to apply the factors affecting location of business to a particular type of business given in an examination question.
- Remember that not all location factors will affect every type of business.
- Consider how the factors affecting location may change as the business changes and develops.

Key Skills

Activity 2 provides an opportunity to prepare a document about a straightforward subject which could include an image at Level 1 (C1.3) or Level 2 (C2.3).

Completion of an advertising leaflet using IT provides an opportunity to produce evidence at Level 1 (IT1.2) and possibly Level 2 (IT2.3).

- The last part of the Activity provides the opportunity to produce evidence which could be included in a Key Skills Portfolio.
- To satisfy the requirements of C1.3 you will need to produce a document which meets the requirements of the garage owner in terms of advertising his business. To access C2.3, a more detailed response will be required which will have greater structure.
- Using IT to produce the document should provide an opportunity to satisfy IT1.2, provided that the information is clearly presented. If possible you should include an image in your work. To satisfy the requirements of IT2.3 it will be necessary to combine information from different sources. This could involve incorporating a spreadsheet used to illustrate the prices the garage might charge for a range of services or scanning into the document promotional materials issued by car alarm companies.

Unit 7.4 The European Union

What is the European Union?

The European union is a collection of 15 countries in Europe, which aim to co-operate together on trade, social affairs and certain laws. In the coming years there are plans to expand the European Union further and bring the workings of the member countries closer together.

Year	Countries joining the European Union
1957	Belgium, France, Italy, Luxembourg, Netherlands, West Germany
1972	United Kingdom, Denmark, Eire
1980	Greece
1986	Portugal, Spain
1995	Austria, Finland, Sweden

Growth of the European Union

The European Union has grown since the original members started in 1957.

Many more countries, especially in Eastern Europe now want to join the European Union.

Map of Europe showing European Union members.

ACTIVITY 1 

Find out which countries want to join the European Union. Mark them on a map of Europe, and try to find any newspaper articles on **why** they might want to join.

The European Union – benefits to business

- **An enlarged market.** The population of countries in the European union is over 370 million. This makes it possible for a business in Britain to sell goods and services to a larger market, enabling the businesses to take advantage of economies of scale. The enlarged market may give business an opportunity to extend the life cycle of a product (see page 174) by exporting to new markets.
- **Common standards.** Throughout the European Union there are common standards on safety, quality and labelling of products. This means that a business no longer has to make different products for the different countries it trades with in Europe. This can save costs.
- **The Single Market.** The Single Market came into operation on January 1st 1993. The main features of the single market are:
  - (i) Free trade between member countries, without tariffs or quotas. This makes it easier for businesses to trade with other countries in the European Union.
  - (ii) Free movement of goods. There are no customs barriers to delay the movement of products.
  - (iii) Workers have the freedom to move and work between member countries, though the problems of language mean that such changes are sometimes slow.
  - (iv) There is freedom of movement of services. This has especially affected the banks and other financial services in Britain who can now sell their services throughout the member countries.
- **Grants and subsidies.** The European Union pays grants and subsidies to businesses in the poorer areas of Europe. This has greatly helped the coalfield and steel communities in Britain, which have seen great job losses and need assistance to help re-build businesses. Money has been spent on the building of new factories, improving transport systems and training workers in new skills. Farming areas have been given grants and subsidies to guarantee the price for certain crops, and to help create jobs away from their traditional farming roles.

The Single Market created opportunity for increased trade with Europe.

The European Union – problems for business

- **An enlarged market.** Although an enlarged market can bring benefits to business, it can also cause problems. Just as a business in Britain can export more easily to other member countries in Europe, all those other member countries can also export more easily to Britain. This means that if a business in Britain is not as efficient as competitors in Europe, it may well see sales and profits fall as consumers switch to imported goods from Europe.

- **The Social Charter.** This is a measure introduced by the European Union to help safeguard workers against unfair employment practices. Although it should not cause problems for businesses that treat their workers well, it has had an effect on a number of different businesses. The main items within the Social Charter are:
  (i) Full-time and part-time workers should have the same rights.
  (ii) A limit of 48 hours per week for workers. This has caused particular problems in the Health Service, where doctors have been working longer hours.
  (iii) The minimum wage. This has meant that some businesses have had to increase the amount they pay their workers, which in turn adds to costs, which may then mean that sales and profits fall. Some businesses have claimed that this might even force them out of business, with a resulting rise in unemployment. It must be understood that many British businesses were already paying **more** than the minimum wage, before the law was introduced. The introduction of the minimum wage is to help the estimated 1.9 million workers who are paid below the minimum.
- **Environmental standards.** The European Union has introduced new standards on water quality, waste recycling and pollution. Whilst these measures are set to improve the environment by providing cleaner beaches and less need for waste disposal, they do add costs to the businesses that are involved, and may cause some redundancies as firms try to reduce costs to pay for the improvements.
- **Common Agricultural Policy.** The common Agricultural Policy (CAP) has helped some farmers by guaranteeing minimum prices for crops, but in some cases the policy has worked against other farmers who, by being efficient, produce too much. This results in a surplus, which needs to be reduced. The dairy industry has had problems with the CAP, with many dairy farmers seeing profits reduced so much that their business is no longer worthwhile.

An enlarged European market will cause problems for inefficient businesses.

Age over 22	*Age 18-21*	**Age over 22 in training for first 6 months**	**Apprentices aged 22-25 on contract for less than 12 months**
Most workers will receive a minimum of £3.70 per hour	Workers will receive a minimum of £3.20 per hour	Workers will receive a minimum of £3.20 per hour (now being revised)	No minimum wage

Table 7.8 Minimum wage rates from October 2000

Source: Department of Trade and Industry

ACTIVITY 2

1. Design a leaflet explaining the business advantages of an enlarged market in Europe. Use IT for the design if available.
2. Look up the present minimum wage levels. You can find information on the Department of Trade and Industry website. Draw a bar graph to compare figures to show any changes to the 2000 figures on page 265.
3. How might membership of the EU affect the following businesses? Give details of any laws and regulations that apply to the situation.
   (a) A water treatment company that discharges water into the sea.
   (b) A farmer who relies on sales of milk.
   (c) A business that exports a range of electrical goods to Europe.
   (d) A cleaning business that pays all its workers £2.50 an hour.
   (e) A computer business that is very busy and expects all its workers to work 55 hours per week.
   (f) A business that wants to expand in a former coalfield area.
   (g) A security business that said its part-time workers should have fewer rights at work because they worked less than full-time workers.

The Single European Currency

A more recent feature of the European Union is the development of a Single European Currency, the Euro.

In January 1999 11 of the 15 European Union members chose to have the Euro as their currency. The UK, Greece, Denmark and Sweden decided not to join at the start, however Greece did join the single currency in January 2001. The countries in the single currency will start to use Euro notes and coins in 2002. They are said to be in the Euro Zone. A decision on whether the UK will join the single currency will be taken sometime in the future.

There has been a great deal of discussion as to whether joining the Euro will benefit British business or not.

Advantages and disadvantages for business in joining the Euro

Advantages	*Disadvantages*
Cost savings. When a business trades with another country, there has to be an exchange of currencies. This is costly, and can only put up the costs of goods and services. Having the same currency will help towards lower prices.	**Adds to costs.** All the business in Britain is in pounds, and so all the machinery, computers, tills etc. will have to be changed to Euros. This will cost businesses a lot of money to do. The change-over costs should only be seen as short-term.
Most trade is with Europe. As most of Britain's trade is with Europe, it makes sense to have the same currency.	**Loss of the pound.** A number of people will need to be educated on the use of the Euro. Any change-over might cause some confusion, especially amongst shoppers.
Stable exchange rate. As Britain's main trading countries will have the same currency, there won't be the changes in exchange rates that cause businesses so much concern. It is therefore better to join.	**A final decision.** Once any change has taken place, it will be difficult to change back. The decisions for the Euro in the future might not please some of the member countries, but they have to go along with it.

EXAM Practice Questions

1. Germany and the UK are both members of the EU.
   (a) What do the letters 'EU' stand for? (1 mark)
   (b) State **one** other country that is a member of the EU. (1 mark)

(Adapted from OCR Business Studies, Common Core Foundation Tier, June 1998.)

2. Explain how membership of the EU helps businesses in the UK to trade with businesses in other member countries. (6 marks)
3. Explain how the UK's membership of the EU might bring disadvantages to British firms. (4 marks)

(Adapted from OCR Business Studies, Q1, Common Core Higher Tier, June 1998.)

ADVICE ON HOW TO ANSWER THE QUESTIONS

1. (a) In this question simply write the two words which the two letters stand for. No further writing is needed.
   (b) Only one country is required. Writing any more will not add to your marks!
2. This is a longer, 6-mark question in which you are instructed to 'explain'. You should try to think of at least three separate features of membership of the EU which help businesses in the UK. Make sure you explain how the features you use will help business. Remember that question is about trade with other member states, not with any other part of the world.
3. In this question you need to think of the disadvantages of EU membership to British firms (not British people in general). The question is for 4 marks, which would indicate that two features, well explained, will enable you to achieve full marks. Once again, you must show how the features you use will cause problems for British firms.

KEY TERMS

European Union (EU) *The collection of 15 (as at 2000) countries in Europe which trade together and aim for closer co-operation.*

Single Market *The creation of a market without barriers within the EU from 1st January 1993.*

Social Charter *Measures to protect workers in the European Union from unfair working practices.*

Minimum wage *Part of the social charter, guarantees certain wage levels for workers.*

Common Agricultural Policy (CAP) *A policy, which controls price and production levels for farming in the EU.*

Single Currency *The use of one currency, the Euro, within the EU. As at 2000, 12 of the 15 members of the EU are committed to the Euro.*

Euro Zone *A name given to the countries in the EU which use the Euro.*

Key Skills

Activities 1 and 2 provide opportunities for Communication Key Skills at Level 1 (C1.2. and C1.3) to be achieved.

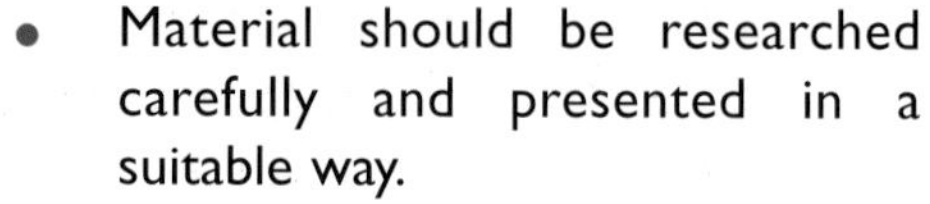

- Material should be researched carefully and presented in a suitable way.

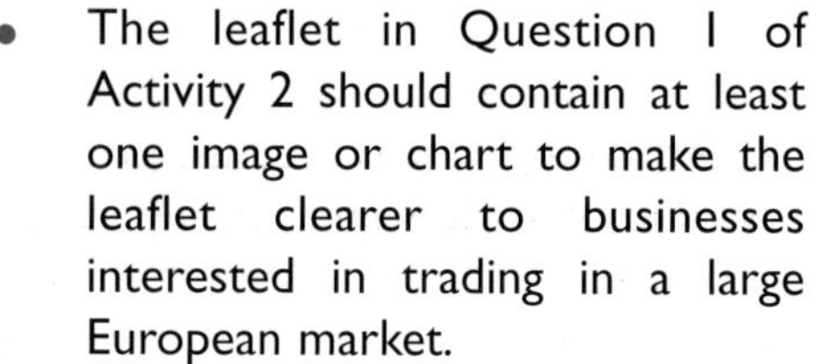

- The leaflet in Question 1 of Activity 2 should contain at least one image or chart to make the leaflet clearer to businesses interested in trading in a large European market.

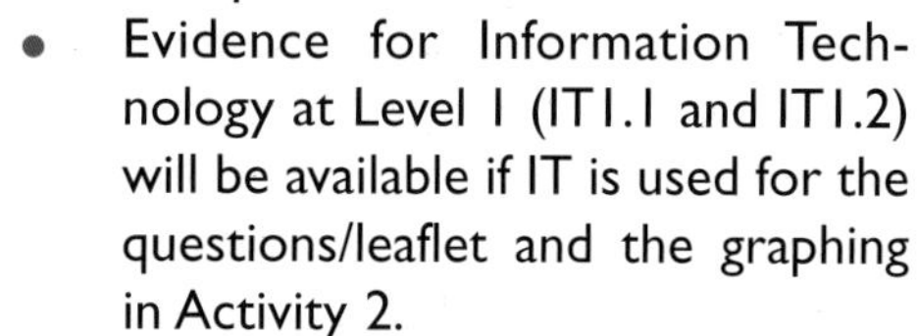

- Evidence for Information Technology at Level 1 (IT1.1 and IT1.2) will be available if IT is used for the questions/leaflet and the graphing in Activity 2.

EXAMINATION SUMMARY TIPS

- Make sure you understand the benefits to **businesses** of being part of the EU.
- Learn how the minimum wage might affect some businesses.
- The Single Currency is an issue for business, which has not yet been decided. Keep up to date with the arguments for and against.
- Remember that membership of the EU affects some businesses more than others. You must look carefully at the business situation you are given in an exam question and decide on the level of EU influence.
- This part of the specification can call for evaluation in an exam question; deciding which is the best course of action for a business to take. Be prepared to argue for or against a particular decision.

Unit 7.5 International trade

Why international trade takes place

International trade is the buying and selling of goods and services between different countries. There are a number of reasons why international trade takes place.

- **Cost saving.** It makes sense for a country to produce what it is good at and sell that product to another country. In this way all countries concentrate on producing goods at lowest cost, which benefits everyone.
- **Climatic and geographic reasons.** If a country such as Britain does not have the climate to grow certain products (such as bananas) it **has** to buy them from other countries. In a similar way, if a country does not have any natural resources of its own (such as oil), it has to buy it from other countries. In this way, international trade has to take place if countries want certain goods.
- **Political reasons.** A country might buy goods from another country simply because it is supporting that country. By buying goods in this way, jobs are created and the country prospers.
- **Consumer choice.** Even though many goods are produced by a country, international trade might still take place in some goods to give consumers more choice in what they buy. Many types of cars are made in Britain, but more makes and models are imported into Britain in order to give consumers more choice.

Benefits to business of international trade

- **A larger market.** By trading with other countries, businesses have a much larger market where they can sell their goods and services.
- **More profit.** By selling to a larger market, the sales of a business will increase and there is the possibility of greater profits.
- **Greater economies of scale.** As a business is selling to a larger market, it will need to increase production and so be able to take advantage of **economies of scale** (see page 123) and so produce cheaper goods. Producing cheaper goods will also help the business sell more goods in its home country.

Problems of international trade

Although international trade can bring many benefits to a country, there are problems that can arise.

- **Loss of jobs.** If a country makes goods very cheaply, and exports those goods to another country, workers in that other country might lose their jobs because consumers buy the cheap imports. In this way, consumers may benefit from cheaper products, but workers lose their jobs. This can lead to **structural change** taking place, where certain industries are greatly reduced because of goods coming from other countries. This has happened in Britain with the clothing and textile industry, where many products now come from overseas
- **Infant industries.** When an industry is new, it is called an **infant industry**. These industries are often at risk from foreign competition in their first few years. Competitors abroad may not wish to see the growth of new industries, and so lower prices in order to prevent them growing.
- **Greater competition.** Businesses have much more competition from all the other countries it trades with.
- **Less profit.** Because of the greater competition, a business may be forced to cut prices in order to continue selling its goods. This might result in lower profits.

ACTIVITY 1

1. Make a list of goods that Britain cannot provide for itself and has to import (eg diamonds).
2. Make a list of goods which are imported into Britain which are also made in Britain (e.g. cars).
3. Explain why international trade might create and lose jobs in some businesses.
4. Explain what is meant by 'infant industries'. How might infant industries be affected by international trade?

Practical difficulties for business of international trade

When businesses trade with other countries, there are a number of practical problems they face.

Problem	***Effect***
Language	This will affect all types of communication (written, phone etc). Can add to costs.
Risks	There are greater risks for a business when it deals with other countries. For example there may be a delay in payment or even no payment at all.
Currency	Currency needs to be changed when goods are paid for. There is the possibility that the **value** of the currency changes, which may cause further difficulty.
Transport	Distances for goods to be transported will increase. It may be necessary to invest in specialist lorries or other transport, which again adds to costs.
Measurements	Other countries may measure goods in a different way, have different operating systems etc. The alterations needed to goods will add to costs and make

Table 7.10 Barriers to internatonal trade.

There are many practical problems in international trade.

International trade: Protectionism

If businesses in Britain are not competitive with other countries, consumers in Britain will buy the goods from other countries and so force the closure of British business. The unemployment that would result would not be good for the Government and so **protectionism** may be introduced. Protectionism is designed to help protect the businesses in a country from foreign competition. There are three main measures that a Government might take to help protect business.

Measure	***Effect***
Tariffs	These are taxes on imports, and add to the **price** of imports. This will make the price of goods made in the home country seem cheaper and more attractive.
Quotas	These are restrictions on the **amount** of goods that can be imported. There is no control on costs, but when the limit (quota) is reached, then no more can be imported.
Technical	A Government might introduce technical specifications in order to limit imports. This might mean passing a law on how goods are made, in the knowledge that other countries may have difficulty in making goods in that way.

Table 7.11 Methods of Protection.

Problems of protectionism

- **Retaliation.** If Britain was to introduce tariffs and quotas against other countries, the other countries might retaliate and introduce tariffs and quotas against Britain. This would harm British businesses trying to export goods.
- **Price rises.** With tariffs causing an increase in price, consumers may resent seeing an increase in the price of their favourite products.
- **Legal problems.** It may be illegal for a country to introduce tariffs and quotas, even if it wanted to. As Britain is a member of the European Union, it cannot put any restrictions on trade between itself and other member countries.
- **Inefficient industry.** If a country protects its industries against foreign competition it may result in the industries becoming inefficient as they have no real need to keep up to date with new developments. In the long term this will benefit no one.

Protectionism is becoming less important in international trade.

ACTIVITY 2

1. Explain what is meant by: (a) tariffs (b) quotas.
2. When might Governments use tariffs and quotas?
3. Explain the problems that might be created when a Government uses protection measures such as tariffs and quotas.

Government support for international trade

The Government helps business wanting to export goods by offering advice through the Department of Trade and Industry (DTI) in the following areas:

- managing a website on European information, including the Euro
- contact lists for people to speak to about the Single Market (see Unit 7.4)
- information on product standards, which must be met because of laws passed in Europe.

Exchange rates

If you go abroad for your holidays you will know that you have to buy foreign currency if you want to buy goods in that country. If you are lucky enough to holiday abroad on a regular basis, you might have noticed that the **amount** of foreign currency you can buy changes from year to year. It is the **exchange rate** for the pound against other currencies, which determines how much holiday spending money you receive for each pound.

Businesses face similar problems if they deal in any way with goods from abroad. The exchange rate will fix the price they **pay** other countries for **imports**, or the amount they **receive** from other countries when they **export** goods. Businesses prefer a **stable exchange rate**, which means the exchange rate between different currencies stays much the same and a business can plan ahead, knowing what price it will pay or receive for goods from abroad. This is one of the aims of the **Single European Currency** (see page 266).

The results of changes in exchange rates

It is when changes take place in the exchange rates, that **problems** for businesses might arise. Businesses might also **benefit** from changes in the exchange rate, depending on whether the value of the pound rises or falls.

Example 1: A fall in the value of a currency

December 1999

Imagine that a business **exports** pottery to the USA. It will be very interested in how many dollars ($) it will receive for the pottery it sells. In December 1999 £1 is worth $1.5. The business has a teapot it sells for £4; it will require $6 (4 × 1.5) for the product. The Americans love the teapot and place a large order.

December 2000

It is now a year later. The pottery business is wondering whether the Americans want to place another order for some more teapots. The pottery business is pleased that it can still sell the teapot for £4. However, the exchange rate has changed from $1.5 to $1.4. This means that the price of the teapot to the Americans is now reduced to $5.6 (4 × 1.4). The Americans are delighted with the reduction in price and double the previous order. This in turn means that the pottery business has to take on more workers to make the extra teapots, and looks forward to higher profits.

This shows that a **fall** in the value of a currency **helps** businesses that **export**.

Another business **imports** computer software from America. It buys one item for $3. Using the same figures from above, in December 1999 it would pay £2 ($3 ÷ 1.5). In December 2000 it would pay £2.20 ($3 ÷ 1.4). This might mean that the business is no longer able to sell as many products due to the increase in price. This in turn would affect profits and levels of employment.

This shows that a **fall** in the value of a currency creates **problems** for businesses that **import**.

Example 2: A rise in the value of a currency

December 1999

A Sheffield-based business exports cutlery to Switzerland. It sells a knife and fork set for £20. The exchange rate is £1 = SF (Swiss francs) 2.3. The price for the set in Switzerland is SF46 (20 × 2.3). The Swiss like the cutlery and place an order.

December 2000

The pound has risen in value and the exchange rate is now £1 = SF2.5. The Swiss now see that the price of the knife and fork set has now gone up to SF50 (£20 × 2.5). They feel that they cannot sell the set at that price and refuse to place another order.

The business in Sheffield has to make workers redundant, as it does not have as many export orders as it used to, due to the increase in the value of the pound.

This shows that a **rise** in the value of a currency creates **problems** for businesses that **export**.

Another business imports watches from Switzerland. One particular watch is sold for SF100. Using the figures above, in December 1999 the watch costs £43.48 (SF100 ÷ 2.3). In December 2000 the watch costs £40 (SF100 ÷ 2.5). This means that the business will be able to sell more watches in Britain due to the lower price, and look forward to seeing the business expand and profits increasing.

This shows that a **rise** in the value of a currency **helps** businesses that **import**.

Changes in Exchange Rates Summary

Exchange rate falls	*Exchange rate rises*
Exporters benefit. More goods sold abroad, possibility of business expansion, increased sales, more employment and rising profits.	Exporters have problems with effect of price increase in other countries. Possibility of sales falling, redundancies and business closure if problem persists.
Importers have problems due to the increase in price of imported goods measured in pounds. As a result sales might fall, workers may be made redundant and the business might close if the problem persists.	Importers benefit. The cost of imports will fall as fewer pounds are needed to pay for them. This will mean that sales and profits might rise, more jobs may be created as the business expands.

Table 7.12 The effect of exchange rate changes.

ACTIVITY 3

1. Explain what is meant by 'exchange rates'.
2. The pound changes in value from £1 = $1.5 to £1 = $2. Explain how this change will affect:
   (i) a business importing motor cycles from America
   (ii) a company exporting cosmetics to America.
3. The pound changes in value from £1 = $2 to £1 = $1.8. Explain how this would affect:
   (i) a business importing machinery from America
   (ii) a business exporting knitwear to America.
4. Explain what is meant by a 'stable exchange rate'.
5. Why do businesses that trade with other countries prefer a stable exchange rate?

EXAM Practice Questions

1. Carlton Press Ltd publishes educational textbooks. It imports coloured ink from America.
   (a) Explain how a fall in the exchange rate from £1 = $1.5 to £1 = $1.2 might affect the price of the ink. (2 marks)
   (b) Advise Carlton Press Ltd on what it might do if the exchange rate fell. (2 marks)

(Adapted from OCR Business Studies, Question 1, Common Core Higher Tier Paper, June 1998.)

2. Carlton Press Ltd is concerned that cheaper books are being imported from developing countries where the labour costs are much lower. It feels that the Government should take action to reduce the number of cheap imports.
   (a) State two possible actions the Government could take to reduce the importing of the books. (2 marks)
   (b) Explain why the Government might not want to take action to reduce the imports. (4 marks)

ADVICE ON HOW TO ANSWER THE QUESTION

1. (a) You should show how the fall in the exchange rate will affect the price of the ink. Using simple figures and calculations will make your answer clearer.
   (b) Here you are asked to give advice. There are a number of possible options, though as the question is worth only 2 marks, there is need only for one explained idea. Remember that this situation, where a business finds that the cost of supplies from one firm go up, occurs many times, not always because of exchange rates.

2. (a) In this question you are asked to 'state'. This means that no explanation is necessary. 'State' is the same as 'list' or 'give'.
   (b) The command word is now 'explain'. Here you need to think **why** the Government might not want to take any action against other countries that are exporting goods to Britain. The question is for 4 marks, which means that at least two separate, explained ideas are needed in your answer.

KEY TERMS

Exports *The goods and services a country sells to other countries.*

Imports *The goods and services a country buys from other countries.*

Structural change *The large scale changes to industries over a period of time. Britain's industrial structure has changed from secondary to tertiary (manufacturing to service).*

Infant industries *Industries which are only just starting.*

Protectionism *The name given to methods used to protect business from the problems that international trade might cause.*

Tariffs *Taxes placed on imports, which will increase the price of the imported goods.*

Quotas *A limit placed on the amount of a product that can be imported.*

Exchange rates *The amount of one currency that another currency can buy.*

Stable exchange rate *An exchange rate that does not change over a period of time.*

EXAMINATION SUMMARY TIPS

- Understand why international trade takes place.
- Learn and understand the advantages and disadvantages of international trade.
- Though protectionism is not used as much as it was in the past, you still need to understand the measures that a Government can use to protect the businesses in its country.
- Exchange rates can be a problem to understand. Take time to learn the possible problems and benefits of changes in exchange rates. Remember that there wouldn't be such a problem if exchange rates didn't change!
- International trade and exchange rates affect some businesses more than others. Look carefully at any exam question in order to work out the possible effects.

Key Skills

Activity 3 provides an opportunity for Application of Number, Level 1 (N1.2) Key Skills to be achieved.

To satisfy the evidence requirements, you need to work accurately and explain how the results of your calculations are important to the businesses which are involved in international trade.

Coursework guidance

In the OCR Full and Short course specifications, coursework accounts for 25% of the total mark. However, coursework is **not** compulsory; your school or college may instead opt for an alternative case study examination based on material which you will see before the exam.

Why do coursework?

Coursework enables you to apply the ideas you have learned during the course to a real business situation. This will help you understand

- the use of business language and methods
- the methods of data collection and display used by business
- ways in which data can be analysed and evaluated
- how to justify ideas you are putting forward
- the choices that are open to a business when a decision has to be made.

In all of the above, your understanding of how business works will be increased, in preparation for the exams which will come at the end of the course.

The choices available when completing coursework

There are three choices available for coursework in the OCR full and short specifications

1. from the specification
2. your own choice
3. a title supported by the Principal Moderator.

From the specification

Within the specification there is a selection of titles for a coursework assignment. All of the titles are designed to help you to get the best out of the subject you investigate and enable you to achieve at your highest level.

Your own choice

You or your teacher may have an idea for a coursework assignment, which suits your interests and the material available in your area. This can work well, though the following need to be considered:

- Is there **enough** material to write an assignment? Investigating the marketing activity of the local corner shop may seem like a good idea, but there is unlikely to be sufficient marketing activity in such a business. If the investigation were to be on a larger business, such as a large public limited company, then there should be sufficient material.
- Is there **too much** material? A very general title which can use much of the work in Business Studies is of little use, and involves writing much more than the maximum word guideline.
- Will the title meet the assessment criteria? All assignments are marked using six assessment criteria (see below). You must check with your teacher that your idea will enable your work to meet these criteria. Your teacher must then contact the exam board in order to make sure there are no problems in using the title.
- The time taken to complete the work must be considered. It may be the case that you or your teacher has a good idea, but completing the work will simply take too long.

A title supported by the Principal Moderator

The Principal Coursework Moderator supports one additional title to the list in the specification. This approach involves joining a nation-wide investigation into a particular business situation, with schools and colleges gathering data using a common questionnaire. Individual candidates will then have use of data from a much wider area. Previous work has investigated BT plc and Pizza Hut. Your teacher will be able to obtain more information from OCR at the Birmingham office.

How an assignment is marked

It is important to know how an assignment is marked so that you can make sure that your work is correctly planned and researched. In this way you will ensure that you reach your best possible grade. Remember that coursework counts for 25% of the final mark!

Coursework in the OCR Full and Short course specifications is marked using six assessment criteria, each having its own mark. The following notes will help you understand how you can meet the requirements of each criterion.

1. Make the aim of your assignment clear, and explaining clearly how you are going to achieve the aim. (4 marks)
2. Collection of information must be thorough. You must collect sufficient data, primary and/or secondary, to complete the investigation you are undertaking. The information must be useful for the title of the assignment. There is no use in collecting information simply to make the assignment seem longer. Remember the guidance on the maximum length of the work. (11 marks)
3. The presentation of the assignment must be clear, effective and in a logical order. This might mean using graphs, diagrams, illustrations, photographs and maps, as well as writing. In some assignments, for instance involving location, a map is essential. In other investigations, such as marketing, maps may not be required. (7 marks)
4. You must use business language and techniques clearly and accurately in your assignment. In a marketing assignment you would be expected to use ideas from the market mix, including the different pricing techniques. You might even include price elasticity of demand! It is the use of business language and techniques in your work, which makes it clear that it is a Business Studies assignment. (11 marks)
5. The analysis of the data you have collected must be completed thoroughly. This does not mean simply repeating in words the information that is shown clearly in a graph. You need to recognise the importance of the results from your data analysis and how it might affect the business you are investigating. (12 marks)
6. You must evaluate the results from the assignment and make recommendations to the business. Any recommendations you make must be backed up by evidence from the data you have collected. There is no point in writing that 95% of people said that a business should do one thing but you knew better and it should do something else! This is an important section and is usually at the end of an assignment. Because it is the last part, don't rush to finish and let standards slip. (11 marks)

Quality of written communication

As well as the marks for six separate assessment criteria marks, you will also be given a mark for how clearly you express your ideas, along with your spelling, punctuation and grammar. (4 marks)

An example of how to plan a Business Studies assignment

The following section deals with one particular assignment. The suggestions and advice can, however, be adapted to help in all of the assignments.

Marketing is a very popular choice for a coursework assignment. It will enable you to:

- gather primary data
- analyse the results of that data
- use your knowledge and understanding of marketing
- make recommendations to a business if you think its marketing activities should change.

All of these activities will help you score high marks for the assessment criteria (see Activity on page 279) which are used to mark your work. It is important that you fully understand what you need to do for each of the criteria.

How to organise an assignment based on Marketing

1. General instructions

Check the general coursework instructions at the start of this unit.

2. The title

In your Business Studies specification there is a suggested title for coursework. The title is:

'Evaluate the marketing strategy of a familiar product or service, making recommendations on whether the market mix should be changed in any way.'

This means that you have to choose a familiar product or service, which you want to investigate. But how do you choose a suitable product? Use this checklist to help.

- Can you get information easily on the product or service? It is no use having an idea and then complaining that you are not able to find any information. Don't rely on businesses providing you with everything you want; they may be very busy and not have time to reply to your requests.
- Can you collect your own primary data using questionnaires or interviews on the product you choose? Don't investigate a product that only you know anything about! Everyone your age will have an opinion on popular drinks, clothes and fast food. There may be fewer people who have any opinion on the latest filing cabinet design.
- Remember that the assignment is on Marketing, so you will need to cover the four Ps of price, product, place and promotion. Will you be able to write about all these in detail with your choice of product?

3. Collecting the data

There are many ways to collect data for an assignment on Marketing. What you must remember is that the information you gather must fit the title. There is no point in collecting data on one type of car and then using information on another, even though it might be interesting to you.

You could gather data from the following:

- The maker of your product, though remember not to rely on this as a source of information.
- Questionnaires and interviews. Do remember to plan this part carefully to give you information on price, place, product and promotion. Look at the example of a questionnaire on page 279 which will give you more ideas.
- Newspapers, magazines and publicity material may provide lots of information, but be prepared to leave a lot of the material out of your work. It may **look** very nice, but does it help with the title of your assignment?
- Your own classwork (and this textbook!) will be important. You will need to use details on the four Ps in the investigation, together with all the **business** words and phrases you have learned on Marketing.

4. Analysing the data

This is an important part of the assignment. For higher grades in Business Studies you **must** remember the following:

- **Do not** repeat in words what a graph has already shown. You will simply be wasting your time!
- Try to explain **why** the results have worked out in a particular way.
- What is the importance of the results for the business you are studying?
- Be **exact** in your analysis. For instance, if 30 people had said they didn't like the advertising of the product, try to find out **who** those people were. Are they male? Are they female? What age are they? If you have this data from your questionnaire you could put your results on a computer database to help with the analysis. Your teacher could help you with this part of your work.
- Remember to cover **all** of the four Ps in your analysis. Valuable marks will be lost if you do any less.
- Always look for interesting results that may be unexpected. This will give you more opportunity to comment on your findings.

Analysis of data needs careful thought and attention.

5. Making recommendations

In a Business Studies assignment you should make recommendations which fit your title. In this Marketing title you should look at **all** of the four Ps once again and explain, with reasons, why any part of the marketing strategy should change. Remember that you may feel that the marketing strategy used cannot be improved. This is fine if you have evidence from your research to support your ideas. Use this checklist to help you.

- Look carefully at your results. What are the main things that you found? Was it something to do with price? Or promotion? Or place? Or product?
- What do the results tell you? Should the business keep its present marketing strategy or change?
- When making a recommendation **always** use evidence from your research to support your ideas.
- Figures should be used when writing about your results. Try to avoid using phrases such as 'a lot of people thought …' It is more accurate to write '40 people out of 50 thought …' It is even more accurate to write '80% of people questioned thought ...'
- Avoid making recommendations that don't fit the business. For example, if you have found that a small sole trader's advertising is not working, recommending that advertising on national television is **not** suitable. If the business you are investigating is a multinational plc then the recommendation may well be more appropriate.
- It is important that you use the results from the data you have collected. You must not ignore the results and simply write what your personal view of the business is.

Designing a questionnaire

The example questionnaire for XYZ Trainers on page 279 will give you some ideas on how to set out a questionnaire, and how the data being collected can be used at a later stage in your assignment. It is **not** intended to be a **full** questionnaire. There should be other questions you need to ask which will help in the investigation.

The questionnaire example can easily be adapted to an investigation that interests you.

ACTIVITY

Study the sample questionnaire above and use it to help answer the following questions:

1. Explain why it is important to have information on the age and gender of the interviewee.
2. Explain how information on price can be used in a Business Studies assignment.
3. Design two other questions which could be included in the XYZ Trainers questionnaire to attempt to find out:
   (a) what trainers are used for
   (b) which types and brands of trainers are bought at the moment.

   Explain how your questions will help you when completing an assignment.
4. If you were investigating a business making hair shampoo, how would you change the questions in the XYZ Trainers questionnaire? Set out your answers in the form of a questionnaire similar in style to the XYZ Trainers questionnaire.

A question on gender will help you analyse your data and make clearer recommendations in your assignment

You will need to know the age and gender of your interviewees. They may have different opinions on trainers. This will be useful information for the decisions you have to make!

A question on price is important in most questionnaires. It is useful because it tells you whether the business you are studying is charging the right price.

A 'how often' question will give you important information on how much money consumers are spending in a year. If you can show that a business has the right price and people are buying the product regularly then you can make suitable recommendations in your assignment.

A question on why consumers buy a product is important. This will help you write about the promotion of the product (another of the 4 Ps). The business you are studying may do a lot of advertising, is this what persuades most people to buy trainers?
Should the business change its promotion strategy? You can use information from this question in your recommendations.

Questionnaire on XYZ trainers

1) Gender of interviewee

Female ☐ Male ☐

2) Age of interviewee

11-12 ☐ 13-14 ☐ 15-16 ☐

3) How much do you spend on a pair of trainers?

Under £25 ☐ £25 – £40 ☐ £40 – £60 ☐ £60+ ☐

4) How often do you buy trainers?

6 months or less ☐ 6 – 12 months ☐ Over 12 months ☐

5) Where do you buy trainers?

Sports shop ☐ Supermarket ☐ Market ☐ Shoe shop ☐

6) What affects your choice of trainers?

Comfort ☐ Advertising ☐ Style ☐ Brand name ☐

Each question should have a choice of answers. This will help your counting of the replies easier. You should use no more than 5 possible answers for each question

A 'where' question on place will help you cover one of the 4 Ps in the market mix. You will find out if XYZ trainers are selling their products in the right place. If they are not, you can make recommendations, giving reasons from the data.

Designing a Questionnaire.

COURSEWORK SUMMARY TIPS

- Choose a title which interests you and which will provide enough data to research.
- Set the work out clearly and with imagination.
- Use only information which helps the investigation.
- Use business terms and techniques wherever required.
- Analyse the data fully, identifying the importance of results.
- Evaluate the evidence and make recommendations that are backed up by the analysis of your data.

Key Skills

A coursework assignment gives you an ideal opportunity to practise Key Skills and to collect evidence for your portfolio. You will have the opportunity in coursework to work mainly at Levels 1 and 2, but there is a possibility that some students may be able to reach Level 3.

The following are examples of how coursework can help with each Key Skill.

Key Skill	Example of application to coursework activities
Communication	Discussions and interviews could take place when collecting data. You may need to read and summarise information to provide background information for your work The completed assignment forms a report that may be used as evidence of writing one type of document.
Application of Number	In an assignment you will collect and interpret information from a variety of different sources. This data will be in various forms that will then need to be analysed. This will involve various calculations and the possible use of formulae. You must present the results of your research (usually in graph/chart/diagram form) and then interpret the results in order to draw conclusions and make recommendations.
Information Technology	You may wish to use IT for your assignment. This could be used to word process your assignment, search for information, analyse data using a database and present the data in graph or chart form.
Working with Others	You may complete research for an assignment with others, providing that any analysis and evaluation is undertaken on an individual basis.
Improving Own Learning and Performance	You may use an action plan to make sure you are on target with your work, and as a help to improve performance. You will have to show how much help was given by your teacher in developing any plan.
Problem Solving	Problems might arise during the writing of an assignment, such as how to find data, or if the business you were investigating closes down.